BIG STICK-UP AT BRINK'S!

Novels by Noel Behn

THE KREMLIN LETTER

THE SHADOW BOXER

BIG STICK-UP AT
BRINK'S!

BY

NOEL BEHN

G.P. PUTNAM'S SONS

NEW YORK

Library of Congress Catalogue Card Number 77-252

PRINTED IN THE UNITED STATES OF AMERICA

*It took six years and eleven men
to rob Brink's of $2,700,000.
It took another six years and $29,000,000
to catch them.*

"Whatcha gonna call it?"
"Call what?"
"The big stick-up."

*Tony Pino's final words to author
October 4, 1973*

PROLOGUE

A Tear in the Eye of a Smiling Corpse

Saturday, October 6, 1973:

Adolph "Jazz" Maffie, Thomas F. "Sandy" Richardson and the fellow from New York turned off River Street shortly beyond Cleary Square in the Hyde Park section of Boston, passed under a long stretch of faded canvas awning bearing the legend "Pannachio & Son Funeral Service," climbed three steps, strode across the creaky porch fronting a wood frame house, opened the rusty screen door and entered the ground-floor anteroom. They were met by Vincent James Costa. A few sober words were exchanged. Richardson moved off to shake hands with Michael Vincent Geagan, then joined Maffie and the New York man for the walk into the parlor. Maffie and Richardson genuflected and crossed themselves before the bier, stepped back to flank the fellow from New York and studied the deceased. Tony Pino's five-foot seven-inch body lay with its hands crossed in a white satin-upholstered coffin.

"Quietest I ever heard him," Richardson whispered.

"Yeah. It must be killing him," Maffie replied, intending no pun.

"It looks like he's smiling, don't it?" Richardson observed.

7

Maffie stared harder at the round, chubby face. "He's smiling okay. You think he's got the money right in there with him?"

I was the fellow from New York hearing this exchange. By then I knew Jazz Maffie's *sotto voce* question reflected speculations by many others at the wake and around Boston—including myself. In his lifetime Tony Pino may well have been responsible, directly or indirectly, for the theft of nearly $15,000,000.

Had there been a tear in the eye of the smiling corpse, then Tony Pino might well have passed on thinking about what is the focus of this book, the January 17, 1950, armed robbery of a Brink's Incorporated vault room in Boston. He considered the theft his masterwork. The FBI, which cited the holdup as both the "crime of the century" and the "perfect crime," considers the solving of the robbery among its highest achievements.

Though erroneously heralded by much of the media as the first million-dollar cash stickup in United States history, the 1950 heist in Boston was the largest ever perpetrated as of that date—an estimated $1,218,211.29 in currency and coin plus another $1,557,183.83 in checks, money orders and securities. The unique disguises worn by the looting gunmen helped prolong the most extensive and costly (an estimated $29,000,000) manhunt in an American nonpolitical criminal case. No such felony, before or since, has received the publicity afforded to the Brink's robbery.

In all, eleven men participated in the 1950 armed theft. Eleven days before the Massachusetts statute of limitations for the crime would have run out, one of the thieves confessed to the FBI, providing what continues to be the official chronicle of the robbery. By the time the trial began two other members of the gang had died. The remaining eight "stood mute" at their arraignment and allowed the judge to enter pleas of "not guilty"; subsequently they refused to take the stand in their own defense. Had they testified before the jury, an appreciably different version of events would have been heard—the account found on the pages to come.

In October, 1972, four of the six surviving gang members, Tony Pino, Sandy Richardson, Jazz Maffie and Vincent James Costa, sat down with this author to begin what may be one of the longest admissions of complicity ever offered—nearly 1,000 tape-recorded hours of it. All four, while volunteering to "confess," demanded money for their story. All four received that money. All four tended to talk in dialogue, as well as narrative, which led to the novelistic style of this book. All four were in their sixties and had very good memories when they chose to use them. At the onset the group let Tony Pino act as their spokesman, and that is one reason why what the author estimated would be an eight-month project took almost four and a half years.

Tony Pino, in his lifetime, was a monumental talker—and liar. He lied to this author for the better part of six months. Beyond the sheer joy he took in fibbing, Pino prevaricated in order to negate the testimony of the gang member who had turned prosecution witness; he also wanted to garner for himself every possible credit for the conceiving, organizing and directing of the robbery at Brink's. Only when the other three thieves, who sat in on most of the interviewing sessions, lost patience with the time-consuming lies and evasions and forced a confrontation did what the author considers to be the facts emerge. In later 1973 a fifth gang member, Michael Vincent Geagan, added his statement to corroborate the account of the crime. Like the other four robbers, he relived the experience as best he could. What follows then is the reconstructed history of the robbery at Brink's as revealed by five of its participants.

The Federal Bureau of Investigation has made data available from the 305 extant volumes of reports covering its six-year investigation of the robbery. The Suffolk County District Attorney's Office, the Boston Police Department, the Massachusetts State Police, the Superior Court of the Commonwealth of Massachusetts, the Boston *Globe* and Boston *Herald-American,* the Boston Public Library and Brink's Incorporated are among the organizations and institutions which have contributed to the 50,000 pages of documents collected for this project. Present and former FBI agents and Boston and Massachusetts policemen were among the 150 people interviewed. Also interviewed were the Suffolk County district attorney, Garrick Byrne; the late and honorable trial judge, Felix Forte; members of the jury; journalists who covered the case; the chief attorney for the defense; and the family and friends of the gang members. George W. Gunn at FBI headquarters in Washington, D.C., contributed yeoman service in searching for file material.

No reconstructed history is devoid of editorial judgment. One of the more persistent phenomena encountered by the author during interviews and researching official records and news accounts was the tendency for all parties to refer to the holdup as "The Great Brink's Robbery."

What makes a crime "great"? And why are so many people proud of the fact?

N. B.

New York City
November 30, 1976

You try to think logically and that's not the way to think because you don't know all the facts.

—ED POWERS
*Federal Bureau of
Investigation*

BOOK ONE

THE CLOUT

CHAPTER ONE

Return of a Thief

September 12, 1944:

"You've got to ax-centuate the positive," Johnny Mercer sang from the Philco cathedral radio.

"EE-liminate the negative," added Bing Crosby.

"And don't mess with Mr. In-Between," they both warned as five-foot six-inch, 170-pound Tony Pino let his gray jute trousers drop to the slat-wood floor, stepped out of them, bent to make recovery, momentarily forgot to breathe through his mouth and, by forgetting, sucked in a nostril full of "shit trench" stink which permeated the long, low, frigid second-floor supply room. He flashed a ticlike wince which always tautened his pudged-moon face into what appeared to be a mocking grin, resumed inhaling by mouth, grabbed up the trousers, tossed them onto a pile of already-discarded gray jute prison garb and stood sway-backed and potbellied and naked. Stab wounds ran along his thick neck and flabby left shoulder. There were bullet scars in the fleshy left buttock and thigh. He coughed to get the guard's attention. He coughed again. The belly heaved again.

The supply room guard hitched a thumb toward a high shelf, leaned forward and turned up the radio's volume. A 9 A.M. newscast began with word that Hitler's Fortress Germany had been invaded by General Patch's rampaging First Army.

Pino rose up on his tiptoes, brought down a newly postmarked carton. By the time General Patton's Third Army had penetrated the impenetrable Siegfried Line and British forces were dashing into the Lowlands he was dressed in a baggy, creased blue serge suit, white-on-white Arrow shirt, dotted tie and a pair of seven-year-old but never worn Florsheim shoes.

The guard summoned a runner, filled out a yard pass and as an afterthought said, "Good luck."

Pino flashed his ticlike grin, plucked the pass from the guard's finger and grabbed up three comic books and a copy of *Popular Mechanics.* He led the way down the steps and out into a vast and hazy prison enclosure dominated by looming, hand-hewn granite block structures grown mawkish red-black with age and coal smoke drifting in from railway yards beyond the twenty-foot-high turreted and guard-mounted walls. He continued breathing through his mouth as he waved an expansive good-bye to the contingent of Crap Brigade cons hosing out the thousand-odd cell-numbered toilet buckets near an open latrine trench.

His pass was presented at the rotunda building. A screw opened the gate in the wire mesh barrier, and Pino stepped past, leaving the runner behind; he climbed the circular staircase, waited while another wire mesh barrier was opened, strode up a corridor and entered the guardroom without knocking. He ignored two burly civilians seated on a far bench, went to a door, knocked and in his raspy, slightly high-pitched voice announced, "Pino, Anthony."

A clerk guard emerged munching a sandwich, dropped a sheath of papers onto the desk and said "Sign at the Xs."

Pino signed without reading, opened an envelope, removed and counted $600, the rebate from his commissary account, argued he was entitled to an additional $10 he knew damn well was awarded only to convicts with no known source of income, finally abandoned his demand, pocketed the money, stood waiting.

The clerk countersigned several of the forms, tore off parole board copies, held them out.

After having served six years, eight months and six days of two consecutive three- to four-year sentences for the crime of breaking and entering in daytime with intent to commit a felony, as well as possession of burglary tools, Antonio Pino, alias Anthony Pino, Tony Pino, Anthony Pirro and John Gurno, had paid his debt to the Commonwealth of Massachusetts and was therefore officially rehabilitated—on parole for two more years, but a free man.

He stepped across the room to where the two burly men were standing and held out his wrists.

"Sorry, Tony," the larger of the federal marshals said while the smaller man jerked Pino's arms around and up behind his back and clamped on a pair of handcuffs.

"What the hell, you're only doing your job," Tony replied.

"Don't worry," the larger federal officer whispered, holding open the rear door of a car parked at the base of the rotunda building, "I hear they'll have you out before the day is over."

Threat of reincarceration seemed to have little effect on Pino as he rode away from Massachusetts State Prison, better known as Charlestown since it stood in the Boston district of that name. He had spent better than a fourth of his thirty-eight years in state penal institutions, as the result of three separate convictions. Two of the terms he had served exceeded one year in duration, thereby warranting his present federal arrest for an infraction committed when he was less than a year old.

Anthony Pino was born on May 10, 1907, near the tiny vineyard village of Divieto, Province of Messina, Sicily. His father was away in America. The delivery was performed by a midwife and occurred in a dirt-floor shanty his family had occupied for generations, but to which they never held title. A local priest registered the birth.

Had Tony remained on the *padrone*-owned soil of his forebears, he might not in all his years have traveled more than twenty miles from Divieto. Like his father and grandfathers and great-grandfathers, Tony unquestionably would have become a tenant farmer and tended the *padrone's* grapes from dusk to dawn. More likely than not, he would have been denied an education since that was the way it was with the eldest child of a peasant family—the eldest worked so the younger might have free hours in which to receive rudimentary schooling. Tony's father, Francesco, was an eldest child and was illiterate. His mother, Katerina Arena Pino, was also an eldest child and illiterate.

Had he remained, Tony Pino probably would have married and at an early age reared a family where and how he had been reared. Compared to millions of others throughout Europe, it wouldn't have been all that bad an existence. Granted, he would never have earned much money, cash-in-hand money—less than $80 in the best of years. On the other hand, he and his family would seldom have gone unfed. A two-room clay-walled shack would always have been at his disposal, plus a quarter of an acre on which to grow whatever food he needed, plus a share of the crop for the *padrone.*

The incentive that prompted Katerina's semiliterate younger brother, Pietro Arena, to scrape, scrimp and finally muster the $40 fare to the New World was a steamship company placard posted on a wall in Divieto: It promised that anyone, absolutely anyone, regardless of birth, could own land in America.

There was no particular reason for Pietro to select Boston, other than its being the destination on the ticket issued him. He was, by apprenticeship and a half year's actual practice, a barber. And there was need for barbers in the poorer sections of the Massachusetts port city. Pietro easily found employment. He saved and in 1906 leased the cheapest one-man shop he could find—on D Street in South Boston, a volatile Irish immigrant enclave called Southy by the locals. He sent a letter back to Sicily urging his newly acquired brother-in-law to come to Boston as soon as possible, not to wait until the baby was born, to emigrate at once while employment opportunities remained good.

Francesco and his pregnant twenty-one-year-old bride began another cycle of scrimping and borrowing and finally sold their single wedding present—a brand-new pick and shovel—and in late 1906 "Frank" joined "Peter" in Southy, shared the one-room apartment above the barbershop and found a job three blocks away, driving the horse-drawn wagon of a used-paper dealer fourteen hours a day, six days a week, for $6. He found extra work on Sunday. He held his eating down to a meal a day, if that, and after fourteen months sent a ticket back to Sicily.

On a long-forgotten date in 1908, eight-month-old Tony Pino was in his mother's arms being carried down the gangplank from a four-stack coal-burning "Guinea clipper" named *Columbia* whose holds had been converted into bedless dormitories and which made the advertised two-week Atlantic crossing in twenty-one days.

"Katherine," like Frank and Peter before her, arrived at Boston Harbor without official paper (WOP), save for a letter from the village priest attesting that she was of good character and properly married and mother of a male child.

Ten months later the young Pino family was ensconced at noisy Andrew Square in Southy's Lower End—an animated wasteland of high hopes and despair and joyless three- and four-story wood-frame, often brick-façaded apartment buildings—where they would remain another fourteen years.

Frank worked long hours trying to meet the bills and rent and save enough to bring over more of the relatives. And relatives were arriving—Uncle Joe and Aunt Elizabeth—among others. Katherine always seemed to be pregnant and spending her days and nights taking one of the babies down to the toilet in the basement or fetching water from the hallway tap or washing or shopping or cleaning or sewing or preparing meals—all this in a tiny three-room third-floor apartment that reverberated day and night from the trolley, horse wagon, horse carriage, auto and truck traffic below the windows. The flat was freezing in winter, suffocatingly hot in summer; always smelled of cooking.

Throughout, the Pino's spirit was generally high. They were a tightly knit and loving clan. Frank spent every Sunday with the family, managed to maintain a degree of patriarchal rule, attempted to see that his brood grew up adoring God and respecting the law of the land and taking full advantage of their opportunities.

Tony attended the Catholic church and, when old enough, first parochial, then public grammar school. He was always home promptly for meals. Sunday dinner with the whole family in attendance was his favorite. Aside from household chores he was out of doors, as he would have been in Divieto—as most of the neighborhood children would have been back in Ireland.

But the streets of Southy were a far cry from a rural lane or pastoral glen. It was a tough place in a tough time and even tougher for the hyperactive, competitive, hot-tempered, plump little Italian boy whose non-English-speaking parents had settled amid the nearly destitute, generally uneducated, often intolerant Irish.

"Mother of God, if you didn't stand your ground against them Irish from the day you was born, you're a goner," Pino recalled. "They don't trust a living soul, including themselves. And that goes for the teachers and nuns and priests and cops. Everything was Irish then. So you gotta prove your point fast, see what I mean? Prove you can hold your own."

And from the earliest of ages, this proving—not coping—this showing other boys, Irish boys, that he was as good as they were was of great importance to him. He learned to fight with his fists, but never well, and therefore learned to sustain one devil of a beating. He wielded a club or knife with moderate efficiency, but tiny "dago" Tony wasn't really going to scare anyone with brute ability. How could he? His funny round face, his sugar-bowl haircut, his bulging tummy and short, stubby legs and ill-fitting clothes were enough to make you laugh. When he became angry, red-faced and out of control, as often was the case, he went into one of his tantrums and began jumping up and down and cursing and threatening. And that could make you laugh all the more. Young Tony Pino grew aware of this reaction other boys had to him, and he began using it to his own advantage and acceptance; incorporating his inherent Arena sense of robust humor and Pino gift of nonstop gab to the fullest, he became the madcap kid of the block, the neighborhood jester—the clown.

Tony couldn't win many running races or pass a football very far, but his short, thick fingers were facile and strong. He was adept at building things and fixing things, which didn't account for very much in the world of the young.

There were other areas where he more than held his own, often winning the esteem of his particular crowd of urchins. He could climb a tree or shinny up a drainpipe with the best of them. Tony was also one of the most accomplished liars Andrew Square ever produced. There was often no particular reason for lying. It was merely something he did naturally, which seemed to be as much a characteristic or congenital talent as his humor. Often he employed the fibbing to con his teachers or the priest or the nuns. Some thought he was the most well-behaved, clean-cut, delightful little boy in the neighborhood—and he usually was, at school or at church or at home.

In an age when finding or stealing coal to feed the ever-hungry potbellied kitchen stove was considered a routine duty for the children of the financially strapped, chubby six-year-old Tony Pino excelled at the latter. He appropriated his baby sister's perambulator almost every night of the week, boldly rolled up the block, across the street and into a railroad coalyard and returned with a full load of the precious black fuel. His parents believed the perpetual explanation that he had picked the lumps up one at a time along the tracks, never suspecting that their eldest was peddling off the overage at three cents a pound.

Membership in a neighborhood youth gang dedicated to the five Bs—baseball, boosting (shoplifting), boozing, burglary and brawling—when he was seven soon allowed Tony to display his superiority in boosting and burglary. He was fearless, inventive, insatiable.

Tony Pino's first arrest came at the age of eight for stealing a ride on a streetcar. The following year he was apprehended trying to swipe candy from a vendor's stand, dragged into court on two charges of breaking and entering and larceny, reprimanded by the judge, released and subsequently thrashed by his father, two teachers and one nun.

The youngster promised his parents he'd go straight, swore the same with his hand on a Bible to the priest, took the first in a long series of legitimate jobs he would hold for the rest of his life, gave his earnings to his parents as he would more or less try to do the rest of his life, helped out his junk-collecting Uncle Joe Pino, thereby learning the skill of furniture rebuilding and refinishing—and went right on stealing. He passed a good portion of his ill-gotten gains on to his parents under the guise of salary bonuses or lottery winnings.

By the time he was shot in the buttock and thigh atop a fence, while trying to escape a police raid prompted by the theft of some cakes and milk the gang had stolen and were consuming, fifteen-year-old Tony's record boasted eight arrests, three probations and one seven-month stint in a reformatory for a $20 theft—$20 in cash taken from his junk peddler Uncle Joe's basement-apartment storeroom.

When thirty-one-year-old Tony Pino was taken across the Charles River from Boston to Charlestown and incarcerated at Massachusetts State Prison on January 6, 1938, his recorded arrests totaled twenty—another two and one-half years had been spent in a reformatory. And he was by no means a big-time hood. The feds had never heard of him. Until recently not even the news-sharking crime-beat reporters of the Boston dailies were aware of his name.

Pino's reputation among the cons who had known him on the outside was diverse. Inmates who had worked with him before, Jimma Faherty, Mike Geagan, Sandy Richardson and Henry Baker, ranked Tony a master safecracker, a top-rate case man and ingenious organizer-operator of well-drilled robbery teams. And Tony, according to his supporters, wasn't lacking in muscle with politicians and the cops. For God's sakes, said they, hadn't Tony been caught dead to rights up in Manchester, New Hampshire? Hadn't an eyewitness identified him as the guy who walked in with a pistol and stuck up the joint? And hadn't three local cops—three of the biggest Boston cops including Jim Crowley—all said they saw Pino sitting in a Boston restaurant when the heist was coming off in Manchester? You don't get Detective Jim Crowley going to bat for you unless you got plenty of muscle, believe you me, fella.

Tony Pino's con enemies were numerous, vocal, hardly charitable and usually Irish. They called Tony the Pig, claimed he was the messiest, cheapest son of a bitch that ever lived, a loudmouth blowhard given to constant exaggeration and flat-out invention instead of concrete criminal achievement. After all, how could a chronic shoplifter like Pino organize and run anything big, of major illicit merit? To begin with, he was Italian and this was Boston—Irish Boston. Times were changing. But not enough for good, solid Irish crooks to let an Italian booster tell them what to do. Consider Tony's so-called crew. Everyone knew that the Irishmen working with him were falling-down drunks. Nice fellows, but drunks. And there was a Jew on it, too. A nice guy and clever thief, but a Jew. And what had they ever scored that was worth crowing about? Had they ever pulled off a major haul? No. Had they ever risked breaking a federal statute? No. They were small beans—nickel-and-dime operators. And Tony the Pig was a goddamn lousy stoolie, a rat. An informer. A Jim Crowley informer. Jim Crowley owned him and used him and got him off the hook up in New Hampshire so Pino could go right on informing on fellow crooks.

Most of these assessments were shared by a majority of officers at the Boston Police Department—an almost totally Irish cadre.

Two allegations which bothered Pino the most were contradictory: that he was a rapist and that the shooting incident which almost took his life when he was fifteen had left him impotent and sterile.

Once inside Charlestown (Massachusetts State), Pino fashioned a new image. He energetically became a merchant, one of the lowest forms of prisoner species—a con who makes a profit from other cons. Pino sold any bit of prison property he could lay his hands on. To facilitate the pilferage, he remodeled his prison coat and trousers with trick or hidden pockets. A half shoulder of beef could be slipped into the baggy pants and smuggled out of the kitchen freezer. This access to prison foodstuffs eventually resulted in Pino's opening a private kitchen—right in the foundry where he was assigned. He and fellow prisoners and several screws would stand roasting meat and potatoes over the molten sewer lids.

The indefatigable merchant-prisoner gave a great deal of time to mixing powders and poultices which he quietly marketed as surefire cures for crab lice, diarrhea, constipation and other institutional maladies. Pino's alchemy led to a near disaster when one of his concoctions blew up.

After World War II broke out and American civilians faced shortages of many staples, convict Pino of Charlestown Prison was often blessed with a surplus. Cigarettes and liquor and candy bars were smuggled in with regularity. Screws solved their transportation problems by visiting inmate Pino and receiving either bona fide gasoline ration stamps or the address of two local stations that would fill car tanks on presentation of a written note bearing his signature.

The secret to this wartime profiteering lay in Pino's propensity for entering into partnerships. An assistant cook conspired with him to steal rationed beef in bulk from the prison cold-storage locker. Rationed canned goods and sugar by the case were obtained by another partner—a storeroom screw. Yet another business merger was effected with a guard who drove a prison supply truck, who delivered the precious cargo beyond the wall to two more partners—each of whom ran a filling station and paid for the contraband with a combination of cash and items to be smuggled back into Charlestown.

Not every successful undertaking was profitable. His three guard partners in the rationed food theft ring beat him out of the money, never depositing a cent in his outside account, as per agreement.

Not every undertaken venture was successful. Tony's attempts to establish a private laundry inside Charlestown by cutting off buttons and in other ways mutilating inmates' uniforms that were sent to the regular and free prison laundry ended when a group of indignant cons worked him over in a lavatory late one evening.

That Pino harbored any regret as he rode away from Charlestown Prison in the custody of federal marshals the morning of September 12, 1944, was due to oversight and a bit of bad luck. He had never bothered to apply for United States citizenship. A 1942 Board of Immigration Appeals ruling, citing Pino for having twice served prison terms of one year or more in duration, deemed him an "undesirable alien" and ordered his deportation to Italy.

"I had them citizen's papers all filled in and ready to mail two or three times and don't know why I didn't," stated Pino. "But let me ask you, if I became undesirable, where did I learn it, huh? I got here when I was eight months old, so you can't blame Italy for me turning crook. I'm not ashamed of being a crook, because that's what I could do best. When you're a little kid, you do what you can do best; then all the other little kids pay attention to you.

"Now, if you wanna see luck coming up bad, you take them two pinches that sent me to the can [March 29, 1928, to October 29, 1930, at Massachusetts Reformatory for abuse of a female child and January 6, 1938, to September 12, 1944, at Charlestown], them two arrests the immigration people used against me.

"That abuse thing was worse than a frame. It was stupidity, see what I mean? I'm only twenty at the time and going straight, and there's nothing more stupid than that. A green punk. I got this honest job bootlegging, making maybe a hundred bucks a night and buying them fancy suits. The shiny kind. It was Prohibition time, and this one night me and another bootlegger let go at one another [with knives]. Slash at one another over who sells them dollar pints on what corner. That's where the scars come from on my stomach. So the ambulance comes, and they go and patch us up at the hospital and take us to the police station. Well, we ain't gonna prefer no charges against each other, so they let us go. I start walking out, and some young girl they're bringing in starts pointing at me and yelling, "He's one, he's one. He was there, too. He did it to me, too."

" 'Mother of God,' I thought, 'what's she yelling about? What is this thing anyway?'

"Now, what I find out later is the cops raided a friend of mine's apartment. The bootlegger I work for. Raided a party at his apartment and find a couple of girls, only one ain't up to age. She's escaped from a girls' reformatory, too. I know who she is but never talked to her. So she says I was at the party raping her along with the others. I can't go and confess I been in a knife fight or they'll book me for assault. And I'm too young and dumb to plead guilty and take a lower sentence like they're offering. I think being innocent is enough. Anyway, she was crazy, and I did thirty months.

"That's when I got bitter and started listening—started learning about peeling and other things [during incarceration for abusing a female child]—and that's when I became a real crook, too. A guy from Illinois—I'll never forget him—started teaching me about petes [safes]. When I got out, he sent me to old Jake. Old Jake had been the best pete man ever born, and he liked helping out young, promising fellas. Right away, the first night almost, he took me with him on a score. I learned the way you should, by doing. Pretty soon I was teaching him a thing or two—the student teaching the teacher, see what I mean? So maybe if that crazy girl hadn't fingered me, I'd be an honest man. I don't think so, but maybe.

"Now the guy that was really crazy was the Minister. He's

this common house thief who's running around cleaning out apartments and running straight to the telephone and telling the cops, 'Hello, this is the Minister speaking to ya, and I just committed another breaking and entering.' This Minister's rifling and calling day and night and driving everyone cuckoo. Got everyone peeking under beds and pokin' up chimneys. Only I don't know nothing, understand? Never heard of him.

"Okay, it's Thanksgiving [1937]. I been doing pretty good taking petes. Got together a lot of reliable fellas, a good crew, and I'd say we was doing two or three pieces of work a week. This was Depression time, so we put in extra effort.

"So we all eat our own turkey dinners at our own homes and tell our families we're going out for a walk, and we meet up. We drive to Rhodes Brothers Market on Massachusetts Avenue. It's bad times, like I said, Depression, and this pete in there must have sixteen-thousand dollars inside her—all them receipts for Thanksgiving food. I looked the place over pretty good, know it inside and out, only someone screws me up. Someone pulled down the outside metal door in back, and that's the way I was planning to go in. So I tell the fellas to wait a couple minutes and come round to the front door. I pick the lock to the side door so nobody knows it's been picked and come on through and open the front door—let the fellas in the front way, see what I mean?

"So what I don't know is this is the Minister's favorite neighborhood. And it's Thanksgiving, too, and a man has just finished eatin' his turkey and reaches over to the windowsill where he had his pipe. What he seen through the window is my fellas going in the front door of the joint. This man with the pipe thinks he's seeing a whole platoon of ministers.

"Okay, I'm inside moving the pete out. I've got a man holding the leg 'cause they're heavy, and I'm moving it out so I can start peeling. I hear a siren, and somebody said, 'Jesus, you hear a siren?'

"I said, 'Don't pay no attention. That's probably an ambulance going by.'

"I take out the tools, and all of a sudden there's banging on the door, and I let out a holler, 'Don't nobody move. Stay below the counter and lie on your bellies.'

"It works. The cops look in the window and don't see nothing and start going away. The fella I told to lay near the window to be lookout decides they're already gone and starts sliding toward us. Only the last cop is just passing the window and sees this fella sliding along like a snake. This cop lets out a holler, 'Did you see the man in there? He's in there. He's in there.'

"He thinks he's seen the fucking Minister, and all of Boston comes running. Every cop on the force is trying to bust in. I gotta couple a fellas along who ain't from Boston, so I tell 'em they better not run or they'll get killed. Boston cops do lotsa killing when they get excited. So we grab the tools and run to the cellar and hide the tools and then hide ourselves in the candle room where all the chicken eggs are, where they look inside the eggs with a candle to see if the eggs is rotten. We hear the cops break in upstairs and go running and shouting all around and come on downstairs. And don't do nothing 'cept whisper to one another when they get down to the basement. I know we're cooked, see, so I don't wanna take no chances. Get shot unnecessarily. I yell out, 'Lookit, we have no pistols.' We're not armed and ready to give ourselves up.

"And they said, 'Come out, come on out.'

"They bring us upstairs and out into the lot where no one can see, know what I mean? None of the reporters or the couple of dozen innocent people who is watching can see. So now maybe we're surrounded by maybe a hundred cops, and they're all panicked and start jostling me.

" 'Whatcha getting mad about?' I ask 'em. 'You grabbed us, ain't that enough?'

" 'The nitro,' they say to me. 'Whatcha do with the nitro?'

"They're scared to death of nitro, and we don't have none along, but I don't tell 'em that.

" 'Stick your nose up my ass and you'll find it,' I tell 'em.

"I guess that's what caused all the trouble. Maybe I did push one of 'em—gentle like—but first thing you know one of 'em hits me over the head with his rifle. And all the rest of 'em start hitting me with fists for no good reason, can you imagine?"

For the first time, Tony Pino's name made the front page of local newspapers. According to the headline account in Boston's

Daily Globe, 1,500 bystanders witnessed the capture by thirty police officers in which the thieves made a "frantic" bid to escape.

Kicking wildly, swinging with both arms, the five men went down under the rush of policemen after one of the alleged robbers, Anthony Peno, 30, of Kennebec St., Dorchester, tried to snatch the revolver of a patrolman, whose arms previously had been jammed in the door.

The September 12, 1944, trip from Charlestown Prison across the river to Back Bay Boston took approximately fifteen minutes.

"So the two feds drop me off at Charles Street [Suffolk County Jail]," Pino explains. "I'm sitting in there waiting for Jimmy [Tony's brother-in-law, Vincent James Costa]. He's the one who's supposed to go post the bail. The son of a bitch is two hours late, and some fairy con is trying to get me to take a shower with him, so when he [Costa] gets there, I let him have it.

"Where the goddamn hell you been all this time?" I tell him.

" 'I got caught in traffic,' he tells me.

"That got me. 'What the hell traffic can there be in five goddamn blocks? It's only five goddamn blocks from the bailman to here!'

"Well, it makes no sense arguing with ignorance. So I walk outta Charles Street. I'm a free man. Mary's waiting in the car—she's my fiancée. Aunt Elizabeth and Uncle Joe are in the car, too. So is my sister Nancy. Nancy's married to Jimmy [Costa]. Everybody hugs and kisses me, and we all drive out to my father and mother's house in Mattapan. My father, me and my brother and some cousins built the house with our very own hands—I think back in 1923 or 1924. We got a helluva buy on the land, too, 'cause it's right next door to Calvary Cemetery. Look out their back window and there's the stiffs.

"Oh, that was some party we had. All the aunts and uncles and cousins. I musta put on twenty pounds eating that delicious food. Some of the older aunts and uncles was at the party they had back in Italy when I was born, and they start talking about the old days—how everybody was scrimping and saving to get over to Boston and went on scrimping and saving when they got here so they could bring the next one over. They were proud of that, and so was I. I always liked hearing about it.

"My father wants me to stay out at the house in Mattapan with them, but I tell them I can't. I have to stay at Aunt Elizabeth's apartment house in Dorchester. Dorchester is closer into town than Mattapan, and Jimmy's already moved my stuff there.

"So everybody was happy and dancing and enjoying themselves. Nobody mentions where you been for six years. They never do. They're honest, law-abiding people. I'm the only rotten apple, but I never admitted it. They never admitted it, too. They gotta believe everything I tell 'em or else they'd go nuts. But when I promised them I'm rehabilitated for good, I really meant it. I know you always mean it when you first come out, but this time I meant it for real. It was the least you can do for the people that love you."

CHAPTER TWO

Whip Cream

Tony Pino began serving his parole with a minimum of expenses. He occupied, rent free, the second-floor flat of Aunt Elizabeth's three-story apartment building at 3 Fuller Street, Dorchester, Boston's southernmost section. Owing to wartime priorities, he had no telephone; he made the majority of his calls from the top-floor apartment of his aunt or the ground-level apartment of Nancy and Jimmy Costa. Certain phone conversations, those relating to his legal predicament, were placed up the block at the home of his attorney. For more private telecommunications he walked the three blocks to his fiancée Mary Fryer's apartment. The most confidential calls cost him a coin in the outdoor phone booth down the block from Fuller Street at the rapid transit station.

He had no suit other than one sent him at Charlestown just before his release, only three pairs of underwear and two of socks and three or four shirts. Everything else had been mistaken as old clothes by Aunt Elizabeth and destroyed a week before.

Because the Commonwealth of Massachusetts had long ago revoked his driver's license and because insurance companies, as in the case of many professional criminals, had refused to issue him an auto policy, he owned no car; he had sold the one registered under a cousin's name back in 1938. For the better part of two weeks Mary Fryer took mornings off from her nursing assignment at a nearby hospital to drive him around Boston, reacquainting him with the post-Depression city, more than anything, trying to consummate their nine-year engagement by finding a large apartment for them to share. Mary paid for lunch. Afternoon chauffeuring was delegated to Jimmy Costa, who always found some way of sneaking off from his job as presser in a clothing factory. Costa paid for late snacks and drinks. Every evening either Mary or Costa drove Tony out to her parents' house for dinner.

He had no job and didn't particularly want one, but he needed one to meet parole board stipulations. Boston's ports and industry were booming as a result of the war and offered a wide variety of employment opportunities even to ex-cons, so, like it or not, he couldn't hold out for long. He didn't like it. Almost every opening required manual labor. Tony hadn't exerted himself all that much in stir.

He had no money other than the $600 he had earned at Charlestown, and by his second week of freedom it became obvious he would need much more than that. The lawyer required $1,000 to begin the fight against deportation. Tony borrowed $500, laid out $500 of his own and was left with approximately $75.

His first boosting, which had more to do with practice than gain, had occurred the second week Mary was driving him around Boston. Both had gone into a five-and-dime so Mary could buy some thread. When her back was turned, Tony swiped an emory board.

Not long after, he was reunited with Big Steve, a former partner in the boost. Their first week's shoplifting take was a disappointing $180 per man.

The lawyer intimated to Pino that bribing several high state officials was the expedient way to fight deportation. Once paid off, these officials could get the governor officially to grant Tony a full and complete pardon on his 1938 conviction for the Rhodes Brothers' robbery. Such a pardon would technically strike the offense from the books and leave him with a record of only one for which he had served a year or more in prison. Since the minimum federal requirement for deportation was the serving of two jail terms of no less than one year for two different convictions, the United States Immigration Board would have no action against him and would have to drop the case.

The estimated cost of securing such a pardon was $5,000, and $1,500 would have to be paid almost immediately. The balance would be due in the coming months.

Had Pino wanted to go back into safe theft, as he now contemplated, there were many obstacles. His prize collection of thieves' costumes, which Costa had transferred from the storage shed behind the Mattapan house to the basement of 3 Fuller Street, wouldn't fit in the overcrowded and locked closet, had been discovered and mistaken for old clothes, along with Tony's regular clothes, and burned in the furnace by Aunt Elizabeth the week before he was paroled from Charlestown. The battered leather valise containing burglar's tools was safely in the cellar under lock and key, but many of the implements had become outmoded even before Tony went away. The use of wartime-developed miracle metals—ultrahard metals—in the construction of new safes rendered even more of the tools obsolete.

He had considered reactivating his prewar robbery crew, but there were even greater difficulties. Jimma Faherty was still in prison, along with Henry Baker. Mike Geagan was out, but off in the Merchant Marine sailing the North Atlantic, the provision on which he had received an early parole.

The one remaining bright spot was Pino's old-time pal and former robbery crew associate, as well as fellow con, Sandy Richardson.

"With all the others gone, that leaves us only three hands," Pino had stated in their first meeting in late September.

"Two hands, Anthony," Sandy had answered.

"Three," Pino had insisted. "I'm thinking of bringing in Sam."

"Sam's on the same boat with Mike."

"Mother of God."

"Anthony, I think you ought to know—"

"The Kid," Pino interjected, "we'll bring in the Kid!"

"Gus?"

"Sure, why not? I promised him up at Charlestown he could come along anytime."

"Anthony, Gus came right out of the joint in May and went right into the Army."

"Why are you telling me all these horrible things?"

Sandy parked in a lot beside a waterfront bar without answering.

"Where's the plant?" Pino asked as they left the car.

"There isn't óne."

"Whaddaya mean, there isn't one?" Tony demanded. "How can you do business if you don't have no plant?"

"We don't have a plant because I didn't rent one. I didn't rent one because I don't need one. Try to understand, Anthony. There's a lot of strong feelings about the war. What I'm trying to tell you, I guess, is I haven't been on the grab since I got out!"

Pino seized Sandy's arms. "Are you standing there more or less saying you're laying off because of the war?"

"That's what I'm saying more or less. Our men are getting killed fighting!"

"And nobody's making a buck off the whole thing? No general or supply sergeant or congressman or nobody isn't robbing the country blind while them boys is getting blasted?"

"That's their business, not mine!"

"Okay, okay," Pino said quickly. "Now what about after the war? You thinking about getting off your ass after?"

"Once we've won, why not?"

"We're winning already. Every place you look it says we're winning."

"*After*—not *before,* Anthony. Save any of the malarkey about *future* planning. After!"

"Okay, after. Okay."

Pino followed Richardson to the wharf railing and stood absently staring at a large white ship with a red cross which was docking.

"Can you gimme some goddamn help at least?" Tony finally muttered. "Nothing overwhelming, only some steers?"

"I know you and know myself. If I start giving steers, the next thing I know I'll be back on the bend."

"Mother of Christ, Sandy, I just come out of the can. I'm gonna need hands, and I don't know who the hell's around. All I'm asking is, who the hell's around?"

Richardson considered the request for a moment, then responded, "None of our guys."

"Not even extras?"

Defense production had drastically curtailed production of civilian automobiles, creating a simultaneous scarcity and boom in its used-car market, so Pino would have to come up with more money than anticipated to buy the mobility he now needed. Arranging for a counterfeit driver's license until he could get a bona fide one would also cost. A cousin's wife would soon be giving birth, and Pino never could bring himself to boosting presents for a baby—he would have to buy them. An uncle was having trouble with a mortgage payment. Mary had found at least six apartments and was already pricing furniture. Costa was demanding payment for some gasoline consumed while chauffeuring Tony around.

And time was running out. Prime crooking time. Night time. Tony would soon have to take a job to meet parole board regulations. The only one he had lined up was at night.

Big Steve reached out, scooped three shirts off a pile and stuffed them through the trick door in the side of what appeared to be a large gift-wrapped box. He turned, pushed through the noon-hour crowd clogging the department store main floor, set the box down on the counter and began inspecting argyle socks.

"Can I help you?" asked a department store clerk.

"Browsing," Big Steve answered.

The clerk smiled, gave a curt nod. Big Steve smiled, gave a curt nod back and continued fondling the socks. The clerk stood watching him, then moved away to wait on a customer. The customer was Jimmy Costa, who pointed at an item in the display case behind the counter. The clerk turned to fetch it. Big Steve slipped a pile of socks into the trick box, then started examining sweaters. The clerk's back was still turned. Two sweaters were halfway in the box. A large, powerful hand clamped onto Big Steve's wrist. A second large, powerful hand seized his neck and forced the shoplifter's head forward.

"Good work, good work," Pino called, hurrying up to the

burly salesman holding Big Steve down over the counter. "God-damn good work. We've been trying to catch this lousy thief for months. What's your name, fella?"

"Alwin," the salesman replied as Pino grabbed Big Steve by the back of the collar and brusquely pulled him up.

"Alwin, I'm giving you full credit for this pinch. I'm personally telling the president what ya done. Now go back to work, go back to work. Don't wanna terrify the honest customers, do we? Go back. I'll handle this lowlife like he oughta be handled."

Pino jerked Big Steve around, picked up the trick box and hurriedly led his boosting partner out of the store by the scruff of the neck.

Twenty minutes later they were in a store three blocks away—and back on the boost.

There was trouble, big trouble, Pino explained when he rendezvoused with Richardson late in the evening on a deserted street running along Fort Point Channel in South Boston. And when Sandy asked what kind of trouble, Tony complained that he still didn't have a phone in his apartment and that his parole officer was demanding that he take a job within a week and that he couldn't find a used car to buy at a reasonable price and that he hadn't liked any of the apartments Mary had found and that she had warned he'd better like one quickly—but all that wasn't the real trouble.

Deportation was the real trouble. Tony had visited his lawyer earlier in the day. The price for buying off the state official had jumped to $30,000. And $10,000 would have to be paid almost immediately. The balance would be due in the coming months.

And when Richardson asked, Pino said no, no, he didn't have anywhere close to ten grand. And when Sandy said he could lend Tony five grand right away and probably muster up another five grand in a week, Tony said, "I ain't asking for charity! I'm asking for loyalty!"

"NO!" Sandy categorically said.

"Whacha saying no for before I spoke what's on my mind?"

"I've had dealings with that mind, so I'll tell you no right now. No, I'm not going on the bend with you."

"Where the hell am I going to raise that kinda substantial money unless I do some work, and how can I do the kinda work that pays substantially unless I got you along?"

Sandy had no immediate answers.

"I sure as hell ain't gonna raise it going on the penny boost with the Polack. I told you already what happened with him. We almost got grabbed."

They were walking now, and Sandy still had nothing to say.

"You wanna come visit me in Salerno, is that it?"

"You're from Sicily, Anthony, not Salerno."

"That shows you what an atrocity it is to deport me," Pino responded. "I don't know one Eyetalian city from another."

"I can get you the first ten grand, and maybe I can get you more. You can pay me back when—"

"Sandy, the score I got in mind ain't strategic, see? It's got nothing to do with war production. It's underwear, Sandy. Goddamn unimportant underwear and not soldiers'. It's ladies' drawers."

"How did you come across something like that?"

"I had nothing to do with it. Jimmy found it."

"A pete job?"

"Yeah—and a real sweet chunk of chocolate cake, too."

"What the hell does Jimmy know about spotting a pete?"

"He don't know nothing, only he used to work at the joint. Wanna take a look?"

"No!"

"Okay—I'll knock it over with the Polack."*

"Stop being idiotic."

"That's all I got left to me is the Polack or Italy."

"Anthony, I doubt that President Roosevelt will call a truce just so he can convince Mussolini to take you back."

"But the war's gonna be over any day, you said so yourself. If I don't get the deportation settled now, I'm cooked. I got no choice but to go with that dumb Polack."

"Mike mentioned a person the last time he was here. A new person called Jazz. Jazz Maffie."

"Jazz?" Pino reported. "What kinda name's Jazz?"

*AKA, Big Steve.

"The person's name."

"Where's he from?"

"Here in Boston. From around Roxbury. He runs a book."

"Bookies is nothin'."

"Mike says this Jazz is the exception, that he only uses the book for storefront. No one knows he's out for work except Mike and another guy."

"You saying Mike's been on the grab with him?"

"That's the impression I got."

"Light or heavy?"

"With Mike it has to be both."

Pino considered. "Unh-unh. I don't like the idea of working side by side with no bookies. They gimme the jitters."

"It's your trip to Italy, not mine," Sandy said, walking away.

Pino changed into the white baggy work clothes he had boosted that morning, packed three salami and cheese sandwiches, two peaches, an apple, a container of sweet pickles, four candy bars, two comic books and a thermos of milk into the lunch bucket he had been forced to pay for in cash, left his Dorchester apartment, walked two blocks to the Fuller Street stop of the rapid transit system, and caught the 6 P.M. train for Boston.

He walked the ten blocks from South Terminal to the D Street warehouse of Stop and Shop, one of the area's leading retail chain grocers. A union steward explained that until full membership in Local 22 was granted, Pino would work as an assistant order filler, cart pusher and truck loader at $80 per week. Once a union card was issued, base pay would rise to almost $100, plus overtime. The work by and large, he was told, should be a breeze.

Pino time-clocked in at 7 P.M. He punched out at 5 A.M. in a state of near collapse. Attempts to find a taxi failed. He somnambulistically managed the ten blocks back to South Station only to learn the train service to Dorchester didn't begin until 6 A.M. He dropped onto a bench, fell asleep sitting upright, awoke in time to catch the 10:30 A.M. local.

Pino phoned Big Steve from the Dorchester Street station, postponed their scheduled boosting expedition for another day, dragged himself to his 3 Fuller Street apartment, plunged onto the bed and ended his first full day of rehabilitated labor sleeping facedown, spread-eagled and fully clothed.

The second night of work proved more exhausting than the first. The third was even worse. The fourth he hardly remembered until there was a pounding on the door.

Under ordinary circumstances Mary Fryer stood a good two inches taller than Tony Pino. When she wanted something, the inches multiplied to feet, and now, as she marched into his second-floor flat, she not only was in want, but was serving an ultimatum. Tony was told to get dressed, come with her, make a final decision on which of two apartments they should take or go on living right where he was—alone. He got dressed.

The second premises they reinspected that afternoon, the four-room layout at 1955 Columbus Avenue, Roxbury, provided Pino with pause. Tony had grown up at Andrew Square, knew what it was to live at a noisy intersection, and the Roxbury building was at the corner of Washington Street and Columbus—smack-dab on busy Egleston Square. If this wasn't enough to keep you up nights, there was always the elevated which ran over Washington Street. Tony couldn't see the need for two bedrooms. Mary could; she had a married daughter and a grandson. More likely than not the grandson would be staying with them a great deal of the time. Tony pointed out that the flat didn't have a dining room and was emphatic about not liking to take his meals in the living room. Mary was equally emphatic. She'd be doing the cooking, and he'd eat where she served the food—kitchen or living room. The rent bothered Tony. He felt that $25 a month was "unethical highway thievery." Mary let it be known that living with a man didn't mean she was dependent on the man, proclaimed she and she alone would be signing the lease and she and she alone would be paying the rent from her salary if she continued working or her savings if she retired— and she and she alone would determine what was or wasn't a fair price. She thought $25 was fair.

The location did offer certain advantages. An ample number of shops were in walking distance. If Tony wanted to entertain a business associate in the immediate neighborhood, there was always the J.A. Club one block down. Right up Columbus Avenue, on the same block as the apartment, stood a late-hour eatery called the Egleston Square Diner—just the type of place where a man whose wife was often away at work at dinnertime or who himself was often up in the wee hours of the morning might stop for a bite or cup of coffee or, if he feared his phone was being tapped, to make a call or two. Pino occasionally liked to take the steam, and around the corner was a steam bath—or, as he called it, a spa. Public transportation was readily available, and should he get a car, he could both park and service it directly across the avenue at a Socony gas station operated by his old friend Tony Gaeta—the same Tony Gaeta many suspected had supplied the gasoline ration stamps which Pino had bartered with inside Charlestown Prison.

The premises afforded one minor but strategic plus to an indefatigable crook who was used to being surveilled or to beating fast retreats even from his own home. The apartment was on the first floor. The hallway outside led both to a front and back door. Hurrying from the flat and through the rear door and down a short alley, Pino could be on Atherton Street behind the building in less than half a minute.

No details of the intended living arrangements were revealed at the traditional Sunday afternoon dinner of the Pino clan other than a statement by Tony that he had signed a lease on the Columbus Avenue apartment and Mary would be furnishing it prior to his taking occupancy in a few weeks. That night he drove back to Stop and Shop with his cousin.* He began loading promptly at 7 P.M., and the going was easier. He didn't manage to stay awake while waiting at South Station, but at least he didn't miss the 6 A.M. train back to Dorchester. He was up before 2 P.M. on Monday afternoon and out on the boost with Big Steve and Jimmy Costa. The two-hour expedition was disappointing; it netted only four sweaters and two business suits, both of which happened to be Tony's size. Big Steve suggested they lay off a few days, opined that Pino was too tired to work the boost effectively. Tony flew into a rage and blamed Big Steve's conservatism for the poor take.

*Pino's cousin, a truck driver for Stop and Shop, had arranged for Tony's job.

Late Monday afternoon Costa drove Pino to a foundry. Hot haggling over prices erupted before an order for a three-section wedge, essential to Tony's type of safe peeling, was placed.

He finished loading his last Stop and Shop truck about 4 A.M. on Wednesday, hung around joking with warehousemen until checkout time at 5, then walked up D Street, turned left and followed Summer Street on across the bridge to South Station. Pino plunked himself down on a waiting bench and tried to nod off. He wasn't tired. He went outside into the predawn darkness and meandered farther down Summer Street. A camera store caught his attention. He gazed through the glass, noting both the wide selection of merchandise and the location of the cashier's office.

Pino took a different route back to South Station, a route that passed an open Western Union office. His pace slowed as he studied the night clerk standing behind the message counter. The uniformed man was almost as pudgy as Pino, but slightly shorter. A second clerk emerged from the door behind the counter, putting on a company jacket.

Thursday morning after work Pino reversed his spotting of the previous day. He first walked past the Western Union office. The pudgy clerk was again behind the counter. Tony walked on to the camera store, entered the adjacent alley and checked the rear door. The lock could easily be picked. He returned to Summer Street, thought of going back to South Station to wait for the six o'clock train, checked his wristwatch, found he had a full thirty minutes to kill and decided to forage northward.

A block farther up he veered right onto Federal Street, a narrow thoroughfare leading into Boston's canyonesque financial district. All remained dark and motionless until Pino approached the Chamber of Commerce building at 80 Federal. Light shimmered dimly from an alleyway to his right. He turned in. The glare was brightest behind a brick fence near the opposite end, near Congress Street. Pino moved on and peered around the barrier's corner. An unlit parking lot lay ahead. To the left loomed the rear of the Chamber of Commerce building. Light spilled from a row of glass doors fronting a marble main-floor corridor. To the left of the doors and leaning back against the building wall was a uniformed guard holding a long wide-barreled weapon—possibly a shotgun. Backed up and parked odd-angled to the left of the guard was an armored truck.

Pino ducked into the shadows on the opposite side of the alley, inching along to achieve a better vantage point.

Two more uniformed guards pushed a large metal box on wheels out through the glass doors.

Pino hurried from the alley, and glanced back over his shoulder as he crossed Congress Street. The metal box was being steered toward the shimmeringly outlined truck. He skirted around a block-wide construction site between Congress and Pearl streets. The three uniformed guards were standing and chatting in a dim refraction of lobby light. The metal box rested—unattended—a few feet away.

Tony sauntered up Pearl Street, keeping his eyes focused across the construction site, Congress Street and the parking lot. The gun-toting guard stepped to the truck and pulled open a door. The other two guards hoisted the metal box and rolled it inside. One of them climbed in after it. The gun toter locked the door, then followed the other guard around the truck's cab. The doors were unlocked. Both men climbed in.

The engine kicked over. Headlights burned on. The armored vehicle pulled away from the building, accelerated across the unlit parking lot, slowed, turned right onto Congress Street, gained speed. Not until the truck passed under a streetlight was Pino able to discern that it was painted white. The lettering on the armored vehicle's side read "Brink's."

Pino kept walking. His gaze shifted from the illuminated marble corridor and rose to the towering façade above. Every window was dark except for a line of three on what he determined to be the fourth floor. A man in shirt sleeves was seen passing behind one.

A rumble became apparent. Pino glanced up Congress Street to see headlights approaching. Only after they passed under the streetlamp could he see that the vehicle was a second armored truck. It cut sharply, bumped the curb, swerved into the parking lot, stopped about ten yards from the Chamber of Commerce building. A uniformed driver jumped out, locked the cab door and headed for the building. As he did so, a third armored truck roared past without turning in, continued two blocks farther down Congress Street and took a hard right.

Pino found a pitch-black recessed alcove on Pearl Street to stand in. It offered a head-on view up the marble corridor. At the opposite end was a second row of glass doors that he assumed opened onto Federal Street. Two more armored trucks pulled into the lot.

Pino stepped from the doorway, tucked his lunch pail tight under his arm, walked up Pearl Street, turned left and followed Milk Street across Congress Street and onto the intersection of Federal Street. One armored truck stood before the Chamber of Commerce building. Another was parking.

"Mother of God, I couldn't believe what I was seeing!" Pino asserted. "There was all them money trucks standing there, and once they started loading up, I knew they was mine. I damn near shouted, 'Hey, you fellas, go easy with that merchandise. It belongs to me.'

"I don't know how I ever got home, but I musta been jumping up and down on the train seat all the way. And when I got home, I was all perspired thinking about it. I had maybe four belts of whiskey and a hot bath trying to stop thinking about it, but I was beyond help. I was electrified.

"Now I was rehabilitated, too, understand? I wasn't going to steal a cent more than I needed for my deportation and moderate living. But when a man walks right up to you and says, 'Here, take all my money,' it would be bad manners to turn your back on him.

"The terrible thing was I had nobody to tell it to 'cause I didn't have a phone, and if I did, it wasn't any good. Here Mr. Brink's was going to make me a millionaire, and the whole goddamn world was fast asleep."

CHAPTER THREE

Sandy

It was dawn and nineteen degrees above zero. Five-foot seven-and-one-half-inches, 145-pound Sandy Richardson tightened the parka hood around his scarf-protected face until only his blue eyes could be seen. He turned into the whiplash wind and, driving the metal hook hard into a huge burlap bale, squatted, tensed, lurched backwards, strained and tugged and gathered momentum, and dragged his 800-pound load across the ice-splattered wood pier and into the Army Terminal warehouse at Castle Island.

He watched the final sled lowered from the ship's hold be unloaded, then, with his longshoremen cronies, made straight for Melodie's Saloon.

Sandy sat drinking in the saloon until 8 A.M., then, shoulders lowered, pushed through a gathering gale to the large seamen's hall just within the Army Terminal gates and neighboring the paymaster's shack. A crap game begun the previous night was noisily under way in one corner; another was starting to form not far off. Neither game was small or restricted to longshoremen. Military personnel and a few well-known Boston area high rollers were already trying their luck. Others were expected as the day progressed.

The "shoots" could hardly be termed impromptu. Ex-convict

Richardson and two partners were founding fathers, as well as proprietors of the enterprise.

Sandy hadn't planned on staying long, but the presence of two detectives in the larger game altered his strategy. He removed his parka and galoshes, stripped down to one layer of work clothes, washed his sharp-featured, ruddy-complexioned face in a cold-water sink, Vitalised and combed his sandy hair and took over supervision of the second game. The phone call came soon after.

"Hi," he said into the receiver.

"Oh, God, Sandy, you won't believe it," Pino announced breathlessly from the other end of the wire. "There's never been anything like it in the history of the world, understand? Since Christopher Columbus first came—"

"Slow down," Richardson demanded. "Slow down and tell me what you're talking about."

"Oh, Sandy, Sandy, I seen something like nobody ever seen before."

"I gather that, but what the hell was it?"

"I seen something delicious, Sandy. Delicious with *whip cream*! Whip cream like you never thought could be, and it's all ours. It belongs to us. A fella's insisting we take it. He's standing there, holding it out and begging us to come take it off his hands. Chasing us up the street with bags of candy and shouting and pleading for us."

"All right, all right, I get the idea," Richardson interjected. "When do I get a look?"

"Oh, Sandy, Sandy, it's a miracle. A goddamn living miracle. You'll have to pinch yourself twice to remember you're not dreaming. It's a sight like—"

"When do I look?"

"Come pick me up after work—and bring a pail, know what I mean?"

Had it been a year to the day earlier, Thomas Francis Richardson, AKA James Garely, Thomas Kendricks, Patrick T. Nash, Thomas Richards, Sandy Richardson, would have been running a risk driving off at 4 A.M. the next morning. Parole regulations expressly forbade meeting with other known criminals. His parole, however, had ended on September 25, 1943, with a bill of excellent conduct.

Several local detectives were less optimistic concerning Richardson's postprison deportment. In their opinion he was a graduate of the old South Boston Gustin Gang and a seasoned gunman. One police sergeant remained convinced that Richardson and Pino had been partners since childhood days in an assortment of skulduggeries that eventually germinated into the safecracking and stickup ring operation which ended when Tony was sent to Charlestown Prison. In fact, Richardson didn't meet Pino until both were in their late teens, even though they were reared only ten city blocks apart and much of their upbringing was similar.

Thomas Francis Richardson's maternal and paternal grandparents had fled Ireland during the potato famine and settled in Newfoundland, where his mother and father met, married, then moved on to America and South Boston. Sandy was the young couple's only child, born on March 22, 1907, in their groundfloor $9-a-month apartment at D and Bolton streets.

The elder Richardson, like Tony Pino's father, earned a borderline subsistence living by driving a horse and wagon long hours six days a week. Sandy's mother worked as a housekeeper when times were good, taking whatever jobs she could find on darker days. Their joint income might have sufficed for a family of three had not Richardson's father been a drunk. Gin was often purchased before food, and a gin binge almost certainly meant a thrashing for young Sandy. Beatings were hardly an exclusive parental privilege. The nuns and priests at St. Vincent's Catholic Church were not loath to mete out Old Testament retribution when the obstreperous Tom Richardson acted up at Sunday school or mass. The teachers at Hawes Hall School, where Sandy went through first and third grades, were also fast with ruler raps across the knuckles or backsides. When Richardson matriculated to the Bigelow School, he seemed to calm down, at least in the classroom. Sandy took a shine to studies, particularly English. When he graduated the ninth grade, there was even some talk of going on to high school; the necessity of earning money dashed such illusions.

Sandy's first illegal activity, like that of Pino, was stealing coal from railroad yards. By the time he was six Richardson belonged to a local street gang whose activities included baseball, drinking, clubbing rats to death in waterfront pier buildings, fighting, boosting and burglary.

"The stealing wasn't as much an amusement as a necessity," Sandy recalls. "We were all dirt poor, and often the only way we could get something, including the shirt on our back, was to steal it. I'm not excusing the theft as justifiable by any means. Many of the boys who were in as bad a way as our crowd never stole a thing. And most of my gang gave it up sooner or later. But I never saw anything wrong with taking what I needed, even after I was old enough to have jobs. I always had a job (long-shoreman), and I always stole. Perhaps my logic was that I had to take full advantage of what few opportunities existed then. You were hungry for anything that would get you out of the rut of the moment. For example, gin was plentiful and cheap. When I was six, you could say I was a hopeless gin drunk. When I was thirteen or fourteen, I won a pistol in a crap game and started sticking people up."

Sandy's first two arrests occurred in 1922, when he was fifteen. Both were for drunkenness. He worked with various partners-for-crime over the next few years, gained the reputation of a petty thief, in general, and small-time holdup artist in particular, became a full-fledged stevedore, purchased a car and began dressing in the sharp suits popular among hoods of the day, as well as frequenting the better-known gangster saloons, restaurants and gambling dens in the Greater Boston Area.

Richardson first ran across Tony Pino in 1926. Prohibition was in full bloom, and both nineteen-year-olds, each in his own territory, were peddling dollar pints of booze. At the time of these early and generally social encounters, Sandy had been drinking heavily, so heavily that his thievery was adversely affected. Pino couldn't abide drinking and had more or less abdicated robbery for what he considered to be the legitimate trade of bootlegging. But the chubby little Italian couldn't stop thinking about crime; what's more, he couldn't stop talking about it. The thin, wiry Irishman was a listener. Pino possessed the type of imagination Richardson respected. Sandy had the type of logic and caution Tony sorely needed.

The two young hoodlums worked a score or so together and found they complemented each other in several more ways. Pino was a natural spotter, a case man; Richardson showed an aptitude for rechecking a potential job, finding weaknesses Tony's fast eye often missed. Pino was a mass of impatience; Sandy stoically the opposite. Tony was compulsively enthusiastic; Richardson inveterately reserved. Pino was a blazing extrovert, an egocentric who mistook attention for acceptance; Richardson was introverted, preferred avoiding the limelight, was supportive of Tony's self-professed but untested leadership ability. Pino had the type of large, warm, closely knit family Sandy had always found appealing. They pulled more jobs together—usually small burglaries and stickups. Disagreements arose and were usually settled with ease. There was one minor point at which they were always at odds: Pino fancied himself a master chef; Sandy, on his hungriest days, could not digest one spoonful of Tony's food.

On July 3, 1927, Richardson got married. On March 29, 1928, Pino was sent to the Massachusetts Reformatory for abuse of a female child. The Depression struck, Sandy had his first child, employment opportunities for longshoremen all but vanished, and in 1930 Tony, who had learned the rudiments of safecracking behind bars, was paroled.

The pair of twenty-three-year-olds resumed their illicit partnership, rented an "office" in Dorchester—around the corner from a candy shop owned by Tony's Aunt Elizabeth—where they stored bootlegged booze, guns, tools and contraband. Richardson brought in a young thief and part-time longshoreman he had met in 1929—Jimma Faherty—and the three began concentrating in the area where Pino was rapidly excelling—safecracking. Before long, additional manpower was required. The takes weren't all that big, averaging perhaps $2,500 per cracked pete, but when four or five a week, and sometimes two a day, were knocked over, profits mounted. All participants shared equally in the loot. No one, including Richardson and Pino, was exclusively committed to the gang's activities. Tony established his own outside partnership for boosting and petty burglary. Sandy limited his noncrew arrangements to stickups.

In 1932 Richardson received his first jail sentence, a year at the House of Correction for carrying a weapon. His record at this time totaled nine offenses, including three drunkenness charges, one robbery while armed, one larceny of auto and one breaking and entering at night.

On the morning of October 2, 1934, Miss Alma Salvi, twenty-one, had finished collecting rents for a series of buildings in West Somerville and was starting for her car when two men approached. One poked a gun in her ribs while the other snatched away a brown folder containing $1,633 in cash and $426 worth of checks. The pair dashed off with Salvi in screaming pursuit. Another woman shoutingly joined the chase. The pair of robbers jumped into a sedan, and a third man at the wheel gunned away from the curb. As the car sped off, rent checks and $71 in cash were thrown from its windows.

Less than an hour later a patrol car sighted a tan sedan traveling at breakneck speed, gave chase and managed to force it to a stop. Apprehended were thirty-year-old Thomas F. Richardson and twenty-six-year-old James Ignatius Faherty. No money or guns were found. Sandy and Jimma were arraigned in Somerville Court. Both pleaded not guilty. Each was granted a two-week postponement and released on $1,000 bail. Both jumped bail and disappeared. Faherty was seized in New York during the spring of 1936. Richardson was apprehended five months later. Faherty pleaded guilty and took the stand to say that Richardson was innocent. Sandy pleaded not guilty. On September 26, 1936, Richardson, accompanied by Faherty, entered Massachusetts State Prison to serve five to seven years on one count of armed robbery. On January 6, 1938, Tony Pino joined them.

It was a ritual they had performed before, a language they had spoken or hadn't spoken from the earliest of days, something they had done and would always do without realizing they did it. Richardson drove in the early Friday morning darkness, asking for a final destination. Pino rode beside him, steadfastly, if not coyly, refusing to reveal the whereabouts of the "whip cream," giving directions block by block while they were mobile, remaining mute as he led the way on foot.

"Anthony, enough of your games," Sandy declared once they were seated in the recessed Pearl Street doorway Pino had used the morning before.

"Just open your bucket and eat an apple, Mr. Richardson," was the counterdemand.

"I'm doing nothing until I know what we have."

"I'm telling nothing so you can see things happen like I seen things happen."

Sandy flipped open the top of his lunch pail and, in fact, took out and bit hard into an apple.

"Is your apple tasty, Mr. Richardson?"

"Go screw yourself."

"Well, if you'd like a little cream to sweeten the flavor, just raise your eyes and tell me whacha see."

"A hole in the ground," Richardson snapped, referring to the construction site where the new telephone company edifice would be erected.

"And on the other side of that hole?"

"For the love of God, Tony."

"Whacha got on the other side?" Pino persisted, grinning down into his lunch pail.

"The Chamber of Goddamn Commerce building."

"Well, don't let it get away from you, 'cause that's where the whip cream factory is."

Sandy surveyed the looming structure. Lights glared in the ground-floor marble corridor. Scattered windows were lit on floors above.

"How far in did you get?" he asked Pino.

"I been no further than right here."

"Then how do you know it's a score?"

"Eat your apple."

Richardson cocked a finger at Pino, was about to let loose, sighed, shrugged, tore the wrapping away from his sandwich. A rumble arose off to the right. A set of bouncing headlights dotted the blackness up Congress Street, grew in size and intensity and passed under the streetlamp. Sandy discerned the silhouette of a square high-carriaged truck. The vehicle turned into the unlit parking lot, circled wide, stopped, resonantly reversed gears, backed up and came to rest several yards short of the Chamber of Commerce building. A shadowy figure jumped down, appeared to be locking the cab door, then strolled forward and crossed into the outer perimeter of light splash. The man was wearing a uniform of gray, sharply creased trousers, a flared jacket and a chauffeur's cap. Cinching the jacket was a gun belt and holster. The man pushed through one of the glass doors, strode up the marble corridor, stopped and picked up a wall phone, almost immediately replaced the receiver, continued up the corridor, slanted right and stepped from view.

"What is your candid idea of the wonders we're beholding, Mr. Richardson?"

"On the positive side, Anthony, definitely on the positive."

"Why's that?"

"Unless my tired eyes deceive me, I would say that the individual we are peeking drives what a crook would call a money wagon. In addition and forthwith, he is presently engaged with a twofold intention. He is either going to deliver a load of whip cream or take some out."

"Dollars to doughnuts it's take out, Mr. R. Give you seven to ten he's taking it right out from the dollar factory."

"Whose factory?"

"It's printed plain on the side of the truck."

"I can't see a thing the way it's parked, and before I get mad and walk out of here, I suggest you tell me."

"Pickle, Mr. R?" Pino held out a jar.

Some minutes later a uniformed guard carrying a long weapon emerged in the marble corridor, sauntered forward through the glass doors and took up casual sentinel in the shadows near the back of the truck.

"Is that a rifle or shotgun he's holding?" Sandy asked, peering hard across the construction site.

"A gas gun."

"I've seen as many gas guns as you've ever seen gas guns, and I've never seen one that looks like that."

"And I've never seen a rifle or shotgun that looks like that."

"Which doesn't make it a goddamn gas gun."

The spectacle of a portable cloth hamper being wheeled down the marble corridor by the driver and another uniformed guard ended debate. The hamper was pushed past the glass doors and up to the rear of the truck. The sentinel guard moved forward, pulled open a door in the vehicle's rear, then, lowering his weapon, stepped back. The third guard climbed up inside the truck. The driver began lifting small sacks out of the hamper and passing them into the open door.

"What would you say them lovely items are, Mr. Richardson?"

"Pouches, Anthony. Pouches not unsimilar to those used for the safe and rapid delivery of payrolls."

The driver stood to the side. The sentinel guard came forward, closed the door in the back of the truck with the third guard apparently still inside and leaned down as if he were fitting a key into a lock.

"How many pouches would you say were loaded, Mr. Richardson?"

"Sixteen, Anthony. Exactly sixteen."

"How do you account for the fact I counted seventeen?"

"That's because you always exaggerate. There were sixteen. Three had a lot of smash (coins) inside. The two biggest were the lightest, which means, hopefully, all cash."

The sentinel guard climbed into the cab just as the truck's starter began to whine. Not until the third try did the engine kick over.

"Unbelievable," Sandy muttered.

"How unbelievable?"

"Conservatively, I'd say a boy of five with a water pistol coulda grabbed her off."

"That easy, huh?"

"Those guards were rather elderly gents."

"I couldn't see their faces from here."

"Neither could I, but they weren't moving like any twenty- or thirty-year-old. I'd say they were well up in their forties and maybe beyond."

"Keep a peek when she passes the lamp and maybe you'll see who it belongs to." Pino indicated the streetlight across the construction site on the near side of Congress. The truck drove under. Unlike the vehicles of the previous morning, the side of the white armored vehicle bore no name.

"All right, Anthony, which company is it?"

"Don't feel there's nothing unpatriotic about taking them?"

"I am merely a neutral and curious bystander—and anyway,

money carriers are insured to high heaven. The sloppy way this outfit behaves, they deserve to be knocked off. It's a disgrace.''

"Kinda appetizing disgrace, don't you think?''

"Which one?''

"Tell you over dinner.'' Pino rose.

"We're having dinner?''

"I need something hot.'' Pino started off up the street. "Meet you around at Bickford's.''

Richardson made off down the street, cut back, reached the restaurant to find Pino at an isolated table devouring a house special of liver, mashed potatoes, string beans, deep-dish apple pie, bread, oleomargarine and a side order of baked beans—but not particularly in that order.

"Who?'' Sandy said sitting down.

"The biggest?''

"Brink's?''

"You won yourself an apple pie,'' Pino said, sliding the deep dish across the table.

"You've got to be crazier than I thought.''

"Don't getcha.''

"No one loots that company. No one's ever gotten five cents from them as long as anyone remembers. For the love of Jesus, Tony, those—''

"Tony?'' Pino muttered with his mouth full. "What became of Anthony?''

"That outfit has the best precautions ever put together. They spend millions on it.''

"I thought you told me a five-year-old little kid could score her.''

"Well, they probably got something on those trucks we don't know about.''

"They got it, I'll beat it. Don't you like your pie, Mr. R?''

"Not the pie or the whip cream.''

"I ain't gonna press the matter no more, Mr. R. Let your conscience be your guide.''

It was a reversal of roles they had played before. During the balance of the meal and while Richardson drove him to Dorchester, Tony was uncharacteristically quiet; when he talked, he never mentioned thievery of any type. Sandy, as he rarely did, kept bringing up crime, made a reference or two to Brink's.

"I can't say that I wasn't intrigued with the idea of grabbing Brink's—what dishonest man wouldn't be?" Richardson asks. "What honest man wouldn't be? I didn't think Anthony had come up with the score just to sucker me in. He knew what I knew. I was suckered enough already by that truck, the sloppy guards—weak soul that I am.

"I knew that when I went back on the bend, it would be for good. I wanted that to be my choice, not Anthony's. Anthony played me just right. The less he had to say about Brink's, the more my curiosity got the better of me.

"Around the time I got to Dorchester I said, 'I realize your predicament (*i.e.*, with deportation), Anthony. If it's any help, I'll look the joint over again and give my opinion—but it's not a commitment!'

"Anthony said, 'Sure thing, Mr. R. What say we make it next Thursday, so you can see it like I saw it the first time?' "

At approximately 5:30 A.M. the metal box rolled into view in the marble corridor and was pushed forward and out through the glass doors by two Brink's guards and on up to the rear of the parked armored truck, where another guard—his rifle or gas gun leaning against the wall—stood. One of the guards who had rolled the metal box disappeared up into the back of the armored vehicle. The other guard and rifleless uniformed man squatted, seized the metal container at the base, called out something to each other, lifted with all their might, struggled to lift higher and just barely managed to hoist it onto the truck.

"See anyone around?" Pino asked from the darkness of the doorway on Pearl Street.

"Not within a hundred miles," Sandy replied.

"Thinks she's a touch?" Pino began peeling an orange as the rifleless guard took up his weapon and headed for the cab of the truck with a second guard.

"Perhaps on some far future date a group of desperadoes might have themselves quite a time."

"Stick her up with guns, huh?"

"You've been seeing what I've been seeing?"

"You was right the first time, Mr. R. It's too goddamn dangerous going in with guns. They probably got something secret and nasty on that truck that'll get us pinched just thinking about her."

"Anthony, what are you angling after?"

"I was just thinking why risk our ass on one punky load when we can walk away with the whole kaboodle. See up along there?" Pino asked, pointing.

Richardson stared up at the line of lighted windows in the Chamber of Commerce building.

"Lay you fifty to two that's where their vault is, Mr. R., and if it is, that's where we're going. And we ain't waiting for no war to end neither. We're walking right in and cleaning them out thorough and complete. Not leave 'em one lousy dime to even buy coffee with."

"Anthony, you're definitely a menace to yourself."

"Menaceful and cooking. Honest to Christ, Sandy, I ain't felt this good since before Rhodes Brothers."

"Let's take a walk."

It was a dialogue they had before, a debate on the merits of armed robbery as opposed to safe theft. Richardson, as they strolled across Post Office Square at dawn, championed holdups. He maintained, as he had usually maintained, it was a fast and efficient method of operation, didn't require a plant or burglar tools or the long and perilous time inside the premises.

Pino, as he usually did, voiced opposition to the use of guns. Being caught on the street with burglar's tools was bad enough, but should a weapon also be found on your person, the resultant penalty could be all the harsher. Being apprehended on premises was a simple matter of breaking and entering; being seized on premises carrying burglar's tools was breaking and entering with intent to commit robbery plus possession of burglar's tools; being arrested while in the process of cracking a pete was burglary and/or safe theft. But, again, should firearms be detected in any of these instances, the subsequent penalty might well be longer. Should you be trapped and use your pistol, attempted homicide or even murder might be the verdict. And Massachusetts was a

bad state for weapons to begin with. Being found in possession
of a machine gun was a mandatory life sentence.

A stickup required no more or less casing than safecracking—
to Pino's way of thinking—but it did involve more planning and
split-second timing in its perpetration: arriving on the dot, scoring on the dot, making your getaway.

Tony Pino preferred the leisure of a safe theft, breaking in at a
time of your own choosing and, if need be, spending all night
peeling or cracking open the pete, casually slipping away with
loot.

"And no one knows what the hell's gone on till the next morning, see what I mean?" Tony said. "They come into their office
the next morning and open their door and find they been wiped
out. You're at home sleeping and they're shouting into an empty
pete.

"So anyway, I got Sandy arguing about which one is better.
I'm being psychological, see? The madder I make Sandy, the
more hooked he gets. I been doing it all my life with him. He's
the fella that calms me down when I go cuckoo. Sometimes I go
cuckoo 'cause I can't help it. My ideas run away with me. So
now I go cuckoo on purpose. Sandy thinks I ain't up to no big
piece of work. And I know better than him I ain't, only he don't
know I think that. He kinda suspects it, but he don't know for
sure.

"So I know Sandy's drooling inside over Brink's—who ain't?
I gotta convince him I'm going right in and screw it all up. I tell
him crazy things about freezing their pete with liquid oxygen and
using them secret gases to put the whole building to sleep—wild
stuff. I do my cuckoo act for him—make my eyes get big and
wide and slobber on my chin.

"Sandy takes the bait and says, 'Anthony, don't you think we
oughta find out where the goddamn pete is to begin with?'

"Well, I knew that all along, but I made him think I forgot. So I
says, 'I'd rather hold the guy out the window and make him tell us.'

"So Sandy gets madder at me, and the first thing you know,
we go right into the lobby of the Chamber of Commerce building. It's morning rush hour, and Mother of God, armored trucks
from two or three companies is lined up and down on Federal
[Street]. We're holding our buckets, and he takes downstairs,

and I take upstairs; I work the lobby, and he works the arcade down below.

"Let me give you the layout, okay? You come in from Federal, go through the glass doors so you're facing down at the doors on the Congress Street side.* Now right as you come in there's a marble staircase to your right and one to your left. The one to your left goes downstairs to the arcade. The other goes upstairs. Then on each side of the lobby is the elevators. Maybe four or five of them on each side of the lobby, facing one another. Then you come to more marble staircases—one going up and one going down.

"So when we come in off of Federal, I don't concentrate on the staircase going downstairs to my left. Sandy goes down it, and I keep walking past. I keep looking to the elevators to my left 'cause that's where we saw the Brink's guards head for and come from. I go over to the bulletin board. I look at all the companies that live in the building, and I find Brink's. Brink's has got a couple of floors, so you figure their safe's gotta be on one of them. But it could be in the basement, too. Over near that bulletin board I see a wall phone—the phone we seen a Brink's guard call on.

"So now Sandy comes up in the lobby and I go down into the arcade. The arcade is full of them little shops where they gyp hell out of you. I come up, and I spot Sandy down at the other end of the lobby. I give him the signal saying I ain't found where the pete is, and he gives me the same thing back. Then I give him the signal saying let's get outta this joint. Too many detectives live around this place for a couple of desperate characters like us to be hanging around too long. Sandy's over near Federal, so he goes right out them doors. I come up in the lobby to follow. Now I'm about ten feet from the glass door and whodaya think I see coming off the street and right at me? A Brink's guard pushing a cart. A handcart. I bend right down and tie my shoelaces. Keep tying and untying. And the cart passes right under my nose, and so does what's in it—long, thin brown packages. Well, I ain't been a thief all my life for nothing. I know those packages are

*Main entrance is on Federal Street, back entrance on the Congress Street parking lot.

straight from the Federal Reserve Bank down the block and full of brand-new money. I spent a lotta time, before I went away, looking over the Federal Reserve.

"So I'm tying and untying and watching the cart kinda upside down. It rolls right up to the first elevator (on the left—nearest the Federal Street doors on the northern side of the lobby). And it stands there waiting. I'm bent over, getting desperate. You can only spend so much time with a shoelace. But I get lucky. The elevator door opens, and the elevator inside is empty. The guard pushes the cart on, and some secretary tries getting on, too. The guard stops her and makes her take a different elevator. That means this can only be Mr. Brink's private elevator. That's good to know, too—in case we wanna stick him up someday. I beat it t'hell outta there and over to Bickford's."

Richardson at Bickford's didn't deny that Brink's was potentially right for scoring, even implied he might be willing to go along on safe theft—when the time was ripe. In his opinion, and he told this to Pino, the time wasn't ripe.

"We didn't have the equipment to take on a score one-tenth the size of Brink's," Sandy relates. "We had nothing, and as a matter of principle I wasn't going to help in obtaining these things. Anthony said not to worry, he'd get all that on his own. I still wouldn't answer him whether I wanted in or not. I was on the brink—Jesus, that's a slip for you—"

Richardson, at Bickford's, recounted a reason for even delaying further casing of Brink's.

"You're not in shape, Anthony. I watched you in the lobby. You were running around like a schoolboy."

"I got carried away," Pino replied between mouthfuls and without looking up from his plate.

"Anthony, you wouldn't expect a doctor to lay off six years and a half and then come into a hospital and do a difficult brain operation, would you? He has to work up to it. You have to work up to it. You need practice."

"That's what I been telling you all along. Let's score on that ladies' underwear factory Jimmy found."

"That's my whole point. You're not even thinking like you used to. One joint doesn't get you back in shape."

"Two weeks from now we'll make a dozen scores—and all old petes. The kind my gear can open."

"How the hell are you goin' to find scores loading up trucks all night at Stop and Shop?"

"Didn't I tell you? Starting next week I got a promotion. I'm unloading 'em. I'll be on the truck helping the driver make his deliveries. And you know where we unload, Sandy? Up dark alleys in the dead of night all over town. Ain't it wonderful? So what say we get busy with the two joints I lined up already?"

"Two? A minute ago you only had one."

"I just come across a second."

"Where?"

Pino shoveled in another mouthful. "Pick up your menu."

"I told you I'm not hungry."

"Pick it up, Mr. R., and read her real good."

Richardson raised the menu.

"What you see?" Pino asked.

"Gravy stains."

"What else?"

"A list of unappetizing dishes."

"Look at the price column, Mr. R., and add it up and divide it in your mind. Everything averages out to ninety cents. Now just look around you and then count the people. It's six o'clock in the morning, and they're already thirty customers. From here on it gets three times as busy and stays busy. Then, if you look behind me, you can see where the cashier sits. And right behind her, you can see where there's a door. Figuring from where this place is built, that door goes to an alley—see what I mean?"

Early Sunday evening Pino led Richardson into and through the South Boston premises of a women's underwear manufacturer. The safe was old and large and perfect for peeling, right for the tools Pino had on hand.

No cashier's ledger could be found.

"How much did Jimmy say she was worth?" Sandy asked, looking down the rear steps from the office.

"Eight to ten grand most evenings of the week. Friday's payday. They got up to fourteen in her Thursday night."

"It's a three-man job."

"Then you're coming along?" Pino all but shouted.

"If you find a third man."

"We'll bring Jimmy."

"That's worse than Big Steve. I want a third man with experience."

"Jesus, Sandy, I been promising Jimmy some action for ten years."

"I don't go inside unless everyone's had experience."

Costa was waiting impatiently in his apartment when Pino knocked on the door.

"Well?" he asked.

"Well, what?" Pino replied, handing over the car keys.

"You got Sandy or don't you?"

"Of course I got him. Only I changed my mind about you."

"What's that supposed to mean?"

"It means you're too goddamn green and inexperienced, and I ain't taking you inside."

"It's my goddamn score. I found it."

"And it's my goddamn crew and I'm boss and I'm deciding you ain't ready yet. You get your share for finding it, and maybe if I feel like it, I'll give you a break and let you drive."

"Break? I've driven you and Sandy a hundred times."

CHAPTER FOUR

Jimmy

Vincent James Costa was born on February 18, 1914, in a second-floor Hanover Street apartment in Boston's North End, a picturesque and historic Casbah that had been appropriated from poor immigrant Irish by even poorer immigrant Italians, thus becoming known as Little Italy.

Though his Sicilian mother and father, like most of the area's parents, were stern, law-abiding and religious people, the narrow prerevolutionary streets on which Paul Revere and William Dawes had once strode offered other examples.

"When I was a kid, we all knew what a big-time crook was, and most of us looked up to them," Costa recalls. "I was always working to make money from the time I could walk. You wanted money because the parents were so poor. And I had all kinds of legitimate jobs, but they didn't pay nothing. But these racket guys would drive up in those big touring cars filled with pretty girls and all the money they wanted. I remember one of them giving us kids five bucks each just to stand and watch his car while he and the girls went to eat at a restaurant. Jesus, five bucks was almost as much as my father made in a week."

Costa's earliest idol was on the threadbare side.

"I adored my uncle. My uncle used to shoot crap on street corners. He was the best crap shooter in North End. I used to come and watch him shoot crap on Sunday right after I finished church. He used to let me shoot, too. That's what I called Sunday school—my uncle letting me shoot.''

Dice were not all that was being shot around the neighborhood. On two occasions young Costa, like everyone else, had to dive for cover as a pair of rival gangs, the Italian North End crowd and Irish Gustin's from Southy, roared through in open touring cars, shooting at one another. Years later when the Sicilian dons invited the Gustin leaders to a friendly meet over a Hanover Street restaurant—ostensibly to work out a peace treaty and allocate bootlegging territory—and gunned down the Irishmen, Costa had run over in time to see the cops lifting the bloody corpses from the sidewalk.

Jimmy was also tardy when somebody pumped twenty-eight slugs into a mobster named Griffith. Griffith lived and, three days after he was released from the hospital, went into Joe the Barber's only to be shot again in the barber chair. Six-year-old Costa and his pals arrived as Griffith walked out into the street, kept walking and after several blocks crumpled and died.

Then there was a racket guy named Scarzi. Scarzi was fooling around with another mobster's wife and, as a result, got his throat slit from ear to ear. He staggered down the street, shouting for help and pressing a blood-soaked handkerchief to the "squirting" wound—with Jimmy and associates following at a safe distance—was refused refuge by a novelty store operator, reached the corner of Hanover and Battery and dropped dead on the sidewalk outside the apartment building where his mother lived. The kids were all Italian and talked it over and had to admit that Griffith, an Irishman, held the record for the "walking dead"—he had traveled a helluva lot farther than Scarzi and didn't cry or scream any—and was the toughest guy they'd ever seen. When seven-year-old Jimmy Costa was playing hide-and-seek and ducked into a warehouse and found his thirty-year-old cousin lying dead and decapitated, he didn't register much shock and didn't tell anyone what he had seen.

"There was a lot of crime then," Costa explains. "Oh, yeah, a lot of deaths. A lot of killings. The cousin was a bad apple to begin with. A minor mob guy. I guess he crossed somebody he shouldn't. But none of us were surprised.''

Costa saw nothing unique with his childhood, felt North End was no different from other places on earth.

"If you're honest and good, you're honest and good. If you're a son of a bitch, that's what you are. You're born the way you are. I was a nasty son of a bitch. I loved my sister, but that didn't stop anything. I used to rob all her money. Everything she saved—her money. I used to con her for money and never pay her back. You don't learn that, you are that. You don't even think you're doing nothing bad, not when you're a kid. And punishing don't do any good.

"I was the apple of my mother's eye," Costa relates, "but when I was bad—oh, my God Almighty. She used to kill me with bites. She used to bite me all over when I did something bad. She had a temper, my mother, God rest her.

"And my father used to strap hell out of me with the razor strap, whale away at me with the strap so hard I nearly didn't feel it. Except when I went on the bed. I never understood that. But it didn't stop me from robbing my sister or being bad. Oh, Jesus, I was nasty back then."

At the age of six, Vincent James Costa and several friends burned a waterfront warehouse to the ground after the owner refused the children access to their favorite swimming pier. His first recorded arrest came two years later, on September 7, 1923: a larceny charge for swiping baseballs, bats and footballs from a delivery car. He was fined $3.

In 1928 fourteen-year-old Costa lied about his age and began driving a taxi. He also attempted to start a lottery, only to be warned off by local toughs. The operation shifted to real estate ventures, but few North End Italian immigrants were interested in buying summer homes in New Jersey. When the Depression came, Jimmy lost the taxi driving job and turned to neighborhood bootlegging. Even in good days an Italian community that made its own wine was hardly a bull market for cheap rotgut. By 1930 Costa had found better prospects in downtown Boston, where he and another young bootlegger tried their hand at counterfeiting, auto theft and a few minor burglaries. The following year Jimmy took on the affectations of the fashionable hoodlums of the day—double-breasted suits, spats, camel's hair overcoats, soft hats—and, most important, hung around the speak-

easies and restaurants along Massachusetts Avenue and Boylston Street, often called Gangster's Row. It was here that he first
met Tony Pino.

"I had him figured for a seventeen-year-old flimflam man,"
Pino, who was twenty-four at the time, revealed. "He always
had unethical deals going, and some of them was legitimate. The
first thing he ever tried selling me was a kennel in Newton. A
kennel full of them red chow dogs. Sandy, me and Jimma [Fa-
herty] had the crew going good, so what the hell did I need with a
kennel? So I buy a couple of the chow dogs. I beat him way
down on price. Now I can't shake the kid. Every time I turn
around there he is with another unethical deal. It's not that he
figures me for a bite; it's he idolizes me. I don't know what to do
with the kid. I introduce him to my sister Nancy, and he goes
and marries her. Now I got a goddamn chow dog salesman in the
family, a brother-in-law who thinks he's a crook but ain't ever
been pinched for anything respectable."

On July 15, 1931, Costa was apprehended on a pair of traffic
violations: not slowing down and speeding. Shortly after his
marriage to Nancy Pino in 1932, he received another traffic violation. His fourth and fifth arrests occurred in 1934 for assault
and battery on wife and non-support of family. The charges
were dropped after Pino interceded and effected a reconcilia-
tion.

"Tony was the best goddamn thief I ever met," states Costa.
"The best. And he was the world's biggest liar, too, as far as I
was concerned. He kept promising to take me on the heavy, and
all he kept doing was taking me on the boost with him and Steve.
For chrissakes, I'd been boosting since I could walk, and there
wasn't any money in it. The money was in the big stuff—in taking petes.

"So after Tony got sent away [in 1938 for the attempted robbery of Rhodes Brothers], I said, 'What the hell.' I went out and
tried the heavy on my own. I tried sticking up some guy, and oh,
my God, was I rotten at it. All I got was a dollar seventy-five and
four months in Norfolk.

"After I came out of Norfolk, I tried enlisting in the Army,
but they weren't desperate enough to take me. I was dead broke
and took any job I could—legitimate job. I end up working at

Kalis Clothing. Kalis made those Eisenhower jackets for the Army, and I get paid piecework, paid for each one I press. I'm a presser there.

"I kept visiting Tony in Charlestown [Prison], too. He started in again about how I'd be on the crew once he got out. Like a dumbbell, I fell for it all over again. And when he gets out, he starts acting like he owns me. Bossing me around in front of people, for chrissakes."

Jimmy Costa's public acceptance of the tyranny was, in part, deceptive. Once alone, the two brothers-in-law argued incessantly, with Jimmy usually in the right and often shouting down Tony. Nor did the so-called "messenger boy" hesitate to change a Pino dictate should he feel it advisable. But of course, only Costa knew this. Usually undetected by friends and associates was Tony's reliance on Jimmy in both a practical and cathartic sense.

Five-foot-six-inch sad-faced Jimmy Costa had become the captive and sole confidant of the inveterately distrustful Pino, was privy to almost every detail of Tony's life, illicit or otherwise. In terms of work relationships, Pino couldn't have chosen a better person. Jimmy had, among other attributes, an exceedingly retentive memory and could recall details Tony often forgot or got jumbled.

Vinnie, as some friends and relatives called Vincent James Costa, had faithfully and for six and a half years, acted as official liaison between imprisoned Tony and outside contacts. He had also "held" most of Pino's stolen money and during this same period watched the account diminish to nothing as he paid off obligations, per instructions. It had been Jimmy who conferred with lawyers over the deportation actions and finally used the last of his brother-in-law's funds to obtain the bail bond which effected Pino's release from the Charles Street Jail. It was Jimmy Costa who arranged that Tony stay at Aunt Elizabeth's apartment, just as it was Jimmy Costa who transported Pino's possessions to the basement of that building.

It was Jimmy Costa who was still fighting with the phone company to get an instrument installed in Tony's flat. It was Jimmy Costa who was still visiting used-car lots and talking to friends trying to locate an auto Tony could buy or use. It was Jimmy

Costa who had just procured a forged driver's license Pino refused to use.

Now, in mid-October, 1944, as Pino prepared to reestablish his thievery crew, it was Jimmy Costa who was delegated a good deal of work.

"It was like going into any small service business," Costa relates. "You need an office, in our case a plant, and personnel and equipment and transportation.

"The only difference is, no one can know what you're doing. Our big difference was Tony didn't want to spend a goddamn dime. Even when he had it, he never spent it. Tony's motto was: You have to steal to steal. And you know what the first thing he told me to go out and get was? Guns. Guns is definitely a cash outlay, and we don't need guns anyway. The last thing we want is guns. He was going in on the light [breaking and entering and safe theft], not the heavy [armed robbery]."

"So I tell Tony the hell with guns and the hell with laying out any money for you. I'm not even part of the crew, so why should I do any of those things for him? Tony says he'll give me half of his share on Brink's. I know he's never going to keep his word on that, so I tell him I want to be partners on the score I found him and want to be partners on the other scores like that— the pete score. The only way you make money is when you're a full partner. I'm a full partner with Tony and Zig [AKA Big Steve] on the boost. And I want the same thing with some pete work.

"Tony says he can't guarantee he'll get me on the old crew if he ever gets them back together. He's right about that. Each guy's got a vote on who comes in. And a couple of 'em don't like me. He says he just about has Sandy ready to go back to work. He promises me I can drive for him and Sandy on their first job, and after that, he'll try to work out a partnership between the three of us—Sandy, me and Tony.

"So I say, okay, I'll help him getting the gear. But it still doesn't make any sense. Even if we get the stuff, there's no place to take it. We don't have a plant. I got a perfect truck all lined up, but there's no place to put that either. The first thing I remember grabbing were license plates. I took a set off a truck in Newton and took another set off a car in Wellesley."

* * *

Pino kicked the last of the cartons into the rear hallway of the local Stop and Shop grocery store, locked the door, told the waiting truck driver he had to take a leak, strode up the alley and relieved himself, examining the rear wall of a well-known fabric manufacturing concern. Immediately after work, he walked to the Chamber of Commerce and examined the building along Pearl Street. He particularly liked a tall, narrow edifice and tried its locked door. Twenty minutes after that he walked past the telegraph office; he saw only the thin, lanky clerk on duty. A half hour later he was in downtown Boston, where he entered an all-night novelty print shop whose placard announced twenty-four-hour service.

"You print up them business cards?" Pino asked the proprietor.

"Sure do."

"How much?"

"Two ninety a hundred in one color. Three fifteen in two."

"Can't get it in twenty-fives?"

"Nope. No twenty-fives or fifties or seventy-fives—only hundreds."

"Tell you what, gimme hundred of the two nineties."

"Reading how?" the proprietor asked, taking out an order form.

"Greater Boston Construction Company."

"Address and phone number?"

"No address. No phone number." Pino dropped the money on the counter. "Pick 'em up tomorrow, okay?"

Richardson wandered through the promenade of the Chamber of Commerce building. No door to the subbasement could be found.

Big Steve examined the ersatz mohair overcoat in the mirror, took it off and tossed it on a table, tried on and examined a tweed single-breaster, then several more coats, discarding them all on the table. Shaking his head at the nearby salesman, he tried on another. The salesman walked off. Big Steve tossed a stack of overcoats out the open window, glanced down to make sure

Costa was there, hung the garment he was wearing back on a rack, walked from the men's section of the Boston department store. Pino saw him leave, swept a pile of earmuffs off the counter and into his trick bag and left.

The strip of celluloid slipped down between the frame and door edge, caught the tongue of the lock and pressed it in. Pino pushed open the door, stepped inside the unlit front hallway of the tall, narrow office building on Pearl Street, waiting for his eyes to adjust to the darkness. He studied the sharply rising staircase, unbuttoned his oversized ersatz mohair overcoat, took out a flashlight, beamed it up the staircase and hurried back out onto Pearl Street.

"Hey, fella, you got a can in here?" he asked, stepping through the door of the telegraph office.

"Gee, friend, we're not suppose to let—"

"All the cans over at the station is busted, and I'm damn near dying."

"In the back," the tall clerk said with a head toss.

"I'll never forget you."

Once in the rear, he flushed the toilet, stepped out of the lavatory, removed a company uniform from a hanger and stuffed it under his oversized coat.

Tony Pino had his first costume.

Sandy studied the large iron safe with his flashlight, carefully checked the front hall leading into the factory section of the women's underwear company, crossed the office, examined the steps leading down to the alley, concluded to himself that it might be a two-man job after all. But a risky two-man job.

Jimmy and Tony sat on the cellar floor at 3 Fuller Street sorting through the burglar's tools. The hydraulic jacks just weren't working properly, and the sectional wedge still didn't fit together properly. Almost everything else, though dated, was usable. The binoculars were in excellent shape.

Big Steve boosted a stack of empty envelopes from a telegraph office in Providence, Rhode Island.

* * *

Tony and Jimmy excused themselves from Sunday dinner at the elder Pinos, drove northward and retraced the route of the Stop and Shop delivery truck on which Tony worked. Costa made a mental note of the half dozen potential scores Tony had spotted during the previous workweek.

Big Steve boosted a large paddle lock in Marblehead.

"Hey, buddy, what's your name?"

"I ain't nobody's buddy," Pino said, signing out at the Stop and Shop warehouse.

"What's your name?"

"Take it on the arches," Pino snapped back as he walked out.

The elderly Winchester matron poured out a cup of tea, handed it to Costa, explained the "For Sale" sign in her front yard was intended for only reliable customers—and that Jimmy certainly did look that. It wasn't merely a car being sold, she wanted him to know, but something that had served her faithfully for five years. Part of the family. Costa promised he would treat it well. In that case, she told him, the price was $250.

Each flight of wooden steps creaked in the darkness; so did the upper floor landing. Pino stopped to get his breath. A blast of light caught him full in the face. He all but fell back down the steps. He inched back up on his hands and knees. Peeking into the hall, he saw the beams coming through a rear window and deduced they were emanating from a nearby building. He crept forward up the hall. Once in darkness he rose and cautiously moved on to the two doors at the end of the passageway. He selected the one to the left, tripped the lock with his celluloid strip, slipped inside, stood assessing the layout, then went to the pair of facing desks in front of the window—peered out the window and over at Congress Street.

Oh, gracious, no, she couldn't speak of the matter over the telephone, the matron told Costa over the telephone. If he wished to discuss business, he could drive out to Winchester. By the way, the car was still available—at $250.

The receptionist at the textile firm office explained that it was Saturday and she was the only one in and didn't have the vaguest idea where to look to find out if any of the firm's 200 employees was the one to whom the wire was addressed. Pino, wearing the telegraph company uniform, told her the envelope he carried contained a money order, asked if there wasn't someone else who might know where to find the addresses. The young woman suggested he go down the hall, past the cashier's office and out into the plant and talk to the maintenance man.

Big Steve boosted a roll of masking tape.

"Great Boston Construction Company?" the Dorchester real estate agent read aloud from the business card devoid of address or telephone number.

"We're in cement," a large, balding, red-haired man, sporting a red handlebar mustache, answered with a slightly Irish accent. He wore no overcoat or hat, was nattily attired in an expensive sharkskin suit and red bow tie. "A couple of us returning veterans feel there'll be a postwar need for cement."

The real estate agent pushed away his morning mail and opened a loose-leaf notebook. "I might have fifteen thousand feet available at Walnut and Washington, Mr. . . . Mr.—"

"Ferguson's the name. Walter Ferguson. We were wondering about that space of yours over near the water?"

"At Savin Hill?"

"The same."

"Those are only garages. Two-car garages."

"We're only a small and growing company. How much are they?"

"Just one's available. Thirty dollars a month. Two month's rent in advance."

"Make it twenty, and you have yourself a tenant."

Walter Ferguson left the office, drove into central Boston, parked his car in an alleyway off Massachusetts Avenue, entered a rear door, hung his jacket in the closet, snapped red garters on each of his shirt sleeves, tied an apron around his waist, pushed another door and resumed his duties as a bartender.

Twenty minutes later he was serving Jimmy Costa.

"How much did it come to?" Ferguson was asked.

The bartender flashed two fingers, then five. "Two months up front. No lease, just a receipt." He laid the receipt and several bills on the counter along with a key.

Costa paid for his drink, left a $10 tip and exited.

"Two hundred and fifty dollars and not a cent less," Costa was told on the Winchester front porch by the matron. "And if there's any more haggling, young man, the price will go up."

"Offer her a bill and a half," Pino said when Jimmy joined Tony and Big Steve on the afternoon boost.

"For chrissakes, Tony, she just told us, she'd jack it up if we do that."

"Okay, one seventy-five and that's the limit!"

They put the masking tape and paddle lock Big Steve had boosted for them on consignment into the borrowed station wagon of a friend, bade their shoplifting partner good-bye, drove to 3 Fuller Street, loaded on a battered bureau they carried up from the cellar, stopped at a neighborhood hardware store, where Tony swiped two cans of whitewash while Jimmy boosted two brushes and the morning paper. By 4 P.M. they had masked the windows with newspaper and were busily painting the brick walls of the Savin Hill garage. Costa drove Pino to work at 5:30, drove on to a Charlestown foundry, paid for and picked up the remodeled three-section pry, went to the 3 Fuller Street cellar, toted out a box of lock tumblers and the leather satchel containing burglar's tools, brought all the gear back to the Savin Hill garage and neatly placed it in the bureau and continued whitewashing the walls. When Costa left at 11 P.M., the paddle lock Big Steve had boosted was clamped on the door.

The nonexistent crew had a plant.

The late Saturday night tour began at the new Savin Hill plant, moved on to the office in the tall, narrow building on Pearl Street, past seven or eight business establishments Pino had cased—only to find they required more than three men for robbing and that his current tools weren't adequate for cracking their safes—and nearly a dozen more locations which had not as yet been entered and looked over and assessed for potential scoring.

Richardson was impressed with the progress.

The tour ended up in the cashier's office at the textile firm. Again Sandy was impressed, was particularly pleased to find a payroll which indicated the 200 employees received the weekly salary in cash on Thursday—that, therefore, on Wednesday night the safe must have more than $20,000 in currency. The safe was an old-fashioned model, the type Tony's present burglar's tools could peel with ease. What Sandy didn't like had to do with positioning and carpets. The door between the cashier's office and an abutting hall was wire mesh. The safe was against the rear wall, in a location which offered a partial view of the wire door and hall beyond. While they cracked the safe, their backs would be to this door. The hall itself was covered by carpeting, which meant the pair of safecrackers wouldn't hear anyone coming until whoever it was was at the door and looking in.

Pino suggested they move the safe completely out of the door's sight line. Richardson suggested he try it. Pino took up the challenge, couldn't budge the mammoth iron box. Sandy and Tony together couldn't move it.

"Guess we're gonna need a third man," Pino said sadly, "someone to keep the peek on the hall."

"Guess so."

"What about Jimmy?"

"Emphatically no."

"But there isn't anyone else. You gonna let twenty grand go to waste just 'cause you're picky?"

"Better picky than pinched."

"When you're right, you're right, Mr. R. Guess that only leaves women's drawers."

"That's a three-man job, too."

"No, it ain't. I been in there again. The two of us can handle her."

"I've been in there again, too. What if a hack comes out of the back?"

"There ain't no hack. I looked the whole joint over nose and toes."

"I'm pretty sure I heard a noise in back."

"That's rat country. Big dock rats in all them old buildings. It's a two-man job, and unless you and me get busy on something soon, we're gonna rot with age and start thinking mosquitoes is airplanes."

"Mosquitoes *are* airplanes."

"Huh?"

"Never mind. What about those other joints you've been looking over?"

"I told you, my tools won't open 'em. I gotta buy new tools and can't do that unless I got what's inside here." Pino slapped his hand on the safe. "Jesus, I hate to see this go to waste."

"Why don't you call Mike's friend?"

"Who's that?"

"Jazz Maffie."

"Not that goddamn bookie again?"

"Yes, the bookie."

"You married to that guy or something?"

Sandy had a chat with Costa, said he had nothing against a three-way partnership between the two of them and Tony regarding small scores, but insisted Jimmy not go inside on pete jobs until he gained some practical experience. Jimmy wanted to know how you gain practical experience unless you do go inside.

"When the conditions are right is when you gain it," Sandy explained.

Pino boosted a milk bottle—an empty milk bottle. He was sitting in Elizabeth Di Minico's kitchen having breakfast, and when his aunt turned her back, he reached out, grabbed an empty milk bottle off the counter, stuffed it in his shirt, got up, feigning a sudden stomach cramp, hurried on down to his apartment and hid the empty glass bottle under some clothes in a bureau drawer.

Costa crept forward, trying to avoid a litter of discarded cartons and wrapping paper, quietly opened the cab door, got inside, turned the key that had been left in the ignition and drove the green-paneled flower delivery truck out into the night. Once it was safely stashed in the Savin Hill plant, he and Pino began painting the vehicle with the white enamel Mary had rejected for her apartment.

Richardson held the satchel while Tony tripped the lock in the side door of the South Boston lingerie factory building. They slipped inside, stole up the steps and made their way forward through the unlit offices.

Thirty minutes later the safe door was peeled open. Sandy began taking out the bills and coins as Pino packed away his tools. Footsteps were heard. The two thieves fell to the floor. The dark outline of a night watchman was seen at the opaque glass door. The silhouette stood for a moment, then moved on.

"Where t'Christ did he come from?" Pino demanded after, as they sped away in the flower truck with Costa at the wheel.

"Maybe from the basement. Maybe from upstairs. Maybe from any of the places we couldn't watch because there was only *two* of us! Here's your share."

Pino took the small linen bag of money and coins Richardson had prepared. "How much?"

"Eleven hundred."

"You saying there was only thirty-three hundred in here?"

"I took out everything there was—and that's all there was."

"You goddamn lying son of a bitch," Pino snarled, grabbing Costa by the neck, "you said there was five or six in there."

"There was—when I worked there five years ago."

"And was there a hack there, too, you didn't tell us about?"

"There wasn't any hack. Hey, Tony, let go, will ya? I gotta drive."

"I'll drive ya. Off a deep pier. I shouldn't even give you your share."

"For chrissakes, Tony, is it my fault you didn't spot good enough to see a hack?" Costa said, then added, quietly, "And I told you from the beginning—you needed three men inside."

Pino slumped back in the seat. "I can't understand where the hack came from." He finally looked around at Richardson. "What was his name?"

"Whose name?"

"That goddamn bookie you been pestering me with."

"Jazz Maffie."

"Okay, tell him he can come and see me."

"According to Mike, if you want a meet, you have to go to see him!"

CHAPTER FIVE

Jazz

Jazz Maffie clenched an unlit cigar between his teeth and handed his black mohair overcoat, white silk scarf, gray kid gloves and soft black fedora to the hatcheck girl at Jimmy O'Keefe's, a popular and bustling restaurant on Boylston Street in Boston. The thirty-three-year-old Maffie genially gave instructions to have his wife shown into the dining room when she arrived, swept the hair back from his roughly handsome Neapolitan face, fluffed up the handkerchief in the breast pocket of his smartly tailored suit jacket, straightened to his full six-foot one-inch height and strode into the men's bar. He pushed through the crowd, draped his bare arms around a pair of detectives seated on stools, paid off the bet one of the officers had won on a football parlay and ordered drinks.

By the time Jazz joined his wife and three family friends in the dining room of Jimmy O'Keefe's he had settled his gambling accounts for the day and bought drinks for all the winning bettors, as well as one or two losers. Maffie was in the process of ordering when the hatcheck girl signaled that he was wanted on the phone.

The caller was a "mutual friend," who told him "Tony wants to make a meet."

"How soon?"

"Tomorrow morning. His place in Dorchester."

"Tomorrow noon. At my apartment in Quincy. You bring him over."

Jazz hung up before the caller could reply.

"Oh, I'd heard all about Tony Pino from Mike Geagan," Maffie recalls. "And I expected Superman. One of them rogues you see in the movie pictures. One of those James Cagney guys.

"I opened the door at eight o'clock the next morning, and there was this mutual friend with a little fat guy.

"I couldn't believe it. I'm looking at Tony Pino, and I didn't know whether he was a nut. I thought he was laughing and he had one of those pumpkin faces and squat hats that made him look funnier than he was. I didn't know he did that all the time, that it wasn't a smile or laughing, just twitching.

"So Tony Pino said, 'We were riding by and thought we'd drop in to see you and say hello.'

" 'Oh, well, just don't stand there. Come on in and have something to drink.'

" 'I don't drink,' Tony Pino said, 'but give me a drink anyway.'

"So I got them a drink, and Tony Pino belted it down. And then he got up and he said, 'I'm half loaded.' So they left, and I couldn't have cared less.

"So I went back to bed. And someone started knocking on the door again. I got up and opened it a little. There's Tony Pino, so I said, 'Who is it?'

"He said, 'Tony.'

" 'Tony who?'

" 'Pino,' Tony Pino said, 'Tony Pino.'

" 'Oh, hello, how are you? Come on in,' I said and opened the door. 'Have a drink.'

"So now we were alone, and Tony Pino was probably getting annoyed because my face was trying to copy his, do that twitch. So we're just sitting there like a couple of nuts.

" 'A friend of mine told me to look at you,' Tony Pino said.

" 'Oh, what friend is that?' I said.

" 'Mike.'

" 'Mike? Oh, sure, Mike. He's a good friend. How is he?'

" 'He's off getting seasick. He wanted me to ask you if you wanted some work.'

" 'What kind of work?'

" 'Didn't Mike tell you, dammit!'

" 'If he did, I forgot.'

" 'I take petes, that's what I do. I got the best goddamn crew that ever was, and I don't need nobody along who don't know that.'

" 'Oh, I guess you don't need me along then.'

" 'Jesus Christ, fella, you're giving me a lot of heartache.'

" 'Have a drink?'

" 'I don't wanna goddamn drink. I wanna know if you're any good and if you wanna come along.'

" 'Well, you won't know if I'm any good until I do come along, will you?'

" '*Do you wanna come along?*'

" 'With you and who else?'

" 'I'm the one who's supposed to be frying you!'

" 'Okay, what you wanna know?'

" '*If you're coming a-goddamn-along to take a pete with me and Sandy!*'

" 'Sandy who?'

" '*Sandy Richardson!*'

" 'Oh, that Sandy. I hear he's a nice guy. Who else?'

" 'You'll see when you get there, mister. Now you coming along or ain't you coming along?'

" 'Sure, I don't mind coming along. When?'

" 'I'll tell you when. I'm boss, and I say when and where. We all split even, but I'm boss, understand? You got a pair of gloves?'

" 'Oh, sure.'

" 'Well, make sure you bring them and a handkerchief. A big handkerchief. How much notice you need?'

" 'A day.'

" 'How do I reach you?'

" 'By phone. I'm here every morning. Call around twelve.'

" 'What about afternoon or night?'

" 'Call Jimmy O'Keefe's.'

" 'Well, if someone calls you there by the name of Stretch, that's me.'

" 'Stretch? I thought you was Tony Pino?'

" 'I am Tony Pino. Stretch is my secret name, so you know who the hell wants to talk to you.'

" 'Oh, well, make sure you use it. I wouldn't want anyone to know it was you who was calling. And never drop by O'Keefe's, okay?'

" 'Why the hell shouldn't I if I feel like it? It's a free country.'

" 'Well, if you drop by, don't say hello. You're bad for my reputation.' "

John Adolph "Jazz" Maffie bore many reputations and lived up to most. Born of immigrant Italian parents in the Jackson Square area of Boston's Roxbury section, young John Adolph was remembered best by neighbors for being easygoing, a dutiful son, a practical joker and, above all, an excellent athlete. Few rivals could best the Roxbury Eagles when their fullback was listed as No. 27 "Maffie" Adolph. Certain lingering fans of the brief and bygone eleven insist No. 27 could punt a pigskin sixty to seventy yards with uncanny regularity or carry half a dozen tacklers across the goal line with his flap-eared helmet flapping and a cigar clenched between his teeth. A few folks, not many, recall that Adolph worked at a shoe factory bench beside his father. More remember him as being an inveterate gambler since he was in knee pants; recalling that when only twenty-three he was a partner in the Columbus AA Club. The Columbus AA was no competition to neighboring drinking clubs such as the one Joe McGinnis operated at nearby Egleston Square, but you could shoot a comfortable rack of pool on any of the three tables in the single garage-sized room or readily find a seat in the poker game behind the screen in the corner. One or two people remember Maffie peddling dollar bottles of hooch back in Prohibition; many more recall him as a frequenter of the better speaks and restaurants in town, remembered that he was a spiffy dresser and always had a fat wad in his pocket and a pretty girl on his arm. In that jazzy era he qualified as a jazzy fellow—which may account for his nickname.

On March 6, 1941, he was drafted into the Army. His tour of

duty kept him stateside, where he made a minor killing playing
cards and betting the ponies. Maffie was discharged on September 11, 1943, returned to his Boston haunts and most particularly
Jimmy O'Keefe's restaurant—a popular watering hole for politicians, athletes, detectives, gamblers and a goodly segment of
well-regarded hoods. He married a former Jimmy O'Keefe's
waitress, took an apartment in Brighton, slept late every morning he could, pulled a string or two which resulted in his obtaining rare high-priority wartime papers, which in turn allowed for
the purchase of a brand-new chromeless Oldsmobile at Broni-
gan's Auto Showroom. Then one afternoon, while having a
shoeshine, he was approached by a guy who said, "Hey, you
seen Augie?"

"Oh, no," Maffie replied, "I haven't seen Augie for a couple
of days. But don't worry, he'll be along."

"When you see him, give him this, okay?"

Jazz accepted the $200 intended for Augie the Bookmaker and
a few minutes later was approached by a friend of the first bettor—who also handed him a bet for Augie.

"I forgot all about it, and I didn't bump into Augie," Jazz relates. "So the next thing I knew, I got myself four hundred
bucks because Augie disappears for a while. That's how I became a bookmaker. If the horse those two guys bet had come in,
I would have been something else."

Jazz Maffie earned a reputation as an honest and lethargic
bookmaker. Never try to find him before noon, then go look in
Jimmy O'Keefe's or wander up the street to Marie's or
McNiff's. If he knew you and if *you* approached him, Jazz might
take your bet. If he turned you down, he'd probably buy you a
drink. Above all, Maffie had the reputation of being as nice a guy
as you'd ever meet.

There was another side to him, which few people knew about.
On April 16 and 25, 1925, fourteen-year-old Jazz was brought to
court but never convicted on two different arson charges. On
December 2, 1926, he was found guilty of breaking and entering
at night and subsequently sent to reform school, where he
served ten months and two weeks. A 1927 larceny arrest was set
aside.

"Oh, I got into some trouble with the police when I was a

kid,'' Jazz admits. ''But all of that was more for adventure than money. I liked money, and I did some stealing to get some. But half the fun was the thrill, the adventure. If you don't have adventure in your life, you're dead.''

Maffie's adult record prior to going into the Army shows nothing more serious than two drunkenness arrests and a $10 and $5 fine for being present where gaming implements were and gaming on the Lord's day. He found additional adventure by being involved in at least two respectable robberies—armed robberies in 1940. Mike Geagan knew this and told Sandy Richardson. Said that with or without a gun, Jazz Maffie was a potent guy.

''Nobody ever impressed me much or scared me for as long as I can remember,'' says Jazz. ''My father was very strict, and his word was law when I was young. Maybe he scared me when I was young. But he was the only one I would do what he told me to do—some of the time.

''So when I ran into Mike Geagan and he told me some of the things Tony Pino had done, I was almost impressed. Maybe if I hadn't met him, it would have stayed that way.''

Pino was less than impressed by Maffie.

''The man acted like he couldn't remember his own name,'' Tony recalled. ''I was desperate for hands, but not that goddamn desperate. I told Sandy to look around for somebody else. Sandy told me that wasn't his job and that nobody else was around. So I knew I was stuck with the fella for at least one job sooner or later. I was hoping it was later.''

Big Steve tried again. The clerk came back in the room. Big Steve smiled and pointed to the jumbo-sized lunch bucket on the top shelf, took out his billfold, removed the nine $1 bills.

Mary handed Tony the list of supplies she needed for the new apartment, cocking a finger, warned that nothing must be stolen, demanded that he bring her a receipt for the most inexpensive of items.

Two hundred and seventy-five dollars is what the Winchester matron stated, cross-armed on her porch. Costa revised his bid to an even two hundred. Three hundred was the return quotation.

Pino watched Aunt Elizabeth pack the last of his "double" lunch into the jumbo-sized bucket, concurred he should go on a diet, kissed the woman on the cheek, took the lunch pail down to his apartment, removed the six sandwiches, two pieces of pie, four apples, two oranges and thermos, put in a pair of binoculars and the empty milk bottle he had boosted some days before, replaced as much food as he could, snapped shut the lid, stuffed the remaining sandwiches in his pocket.

At work on his delivery route he told the driver he had a chance to get laid in the coming week by a "beautiful" married broad, got a promise that for a few extra bucks he could get off between 8 and 10:30 P.M. when he had to.

After work that morning he walked to the tall wood-façaded office building on Pearl Street, tripped the lock, climbed the creaking steps to the fifth-floor single-room office. He chose the window desk to the right, seated himself in the darkness, hoisted up the lunch bucket, opened the lid, placed the two remaining sandwiches neatly down on the blotter, spun the cap off the empty milk bottle and placed both the bottle and cap neatly beside the sandwiches, removed the binoculars, put them to his eyes and focused out the window and across the construction site and parking lot at the Congress Street façade of the Chamber of Commerce building. All the upper windows were dark. Light flowed from the marble lobby and spilled out into the parking lot. Pino took off his watch, placed it on the blotter, checked the time. It was 5:02 A.M. He began eating a sandwich.

At 5:07 A.M. two men angled forward in the lobby. At 5:12 lights went on in a line of upper windows. A bridge adjustment was made. The room behind the first window to the left was empty except for a desk and three filing cabinets. At the rear was a door. The glasses jumped to the adjacent windows. A coatless man with spectacles was standing over a long table. His hand reached down, tickled the top. He inspected his finger, then departed through a door at the rear of the room.

The glasses shifted down to the marble lobby. A Brink's guard and a spectacled man in an overcoat and tasseled ski cap were getting on the elevator. Pino zeroed in on the janitor. He walked forward to the Congress Street end of the lobby and began unlocking the glass doors. The time was 5:18.

The binoculars swept up, came to rest on the long table. Paper money was being stacked along one side by the coatless man with the spectacles. Another spectacled, coatless man was seated opposite counting bills—counting with the rapidity and precision unique to trained cashiers. A third man, wearing a gray dust jacket, was seated at the table end, binding piles of currency with what appeared to be paper strips. Once the stacks were bound, he stuffed them into a gray cloth sack which had a small padlock dangling from its mouth. Pino glanced at the wristwatch on the blotter. It was 5:22.

The glasses moved back along the counting table, then up to the rear of the room. A fourth man, most likely the one who had gone on the elevator with the Brink's guard, was coming through the door. He wore a dust jacket, a green eye visor and glasses and was carrying a metal tray and book. The newcomer exchanged a few words with the men around the table, moved on to the next room and settled down at a desk. One of the coatless men brought him a stack of currency.

The binoculars skipped to the door at the back of the room which held the big counting table. It seemed to be made of wood. No extra locks or chains were evident. The rear doors in the adjoining rooms all appeared to be ordinary.

Pino kept his eyes pressed hard to the binoculars with one hand as he lifted the milk bottle with the other, unzipped his fly and relieved himself.

The glasses tilted down, picked up a white armored Brink's truck pulling to a stop in the parking lot. A uniformed guard got out, locked the cab, placed the key in the right-hand pocket of his jacket, pushed through a glass door, strode up the marble lobby to the wall phone on the right and lifted the receiver.

The three men seated around the large table continued their counting and stacking. The eye-shaded man sat in the adjoining room making notations in a book. The lobby phone was back on its wall cradle, and the driver was gone. The door behind the large table opened. A guard Pino hadn't seen before stood in the frame holding several white cloth money bags. Each had a piece of paper attached. The man in the dust jacket rose from the table, went to the guard, shook his head, removed the sheets, then led the way out of the room.

Seven minutes later a guard Pino hadn't noted previously stepped off the elevator and, carrying a gun, came forward down the lobby, moved through the Congress Street door, moseyed over to the rear of the armored truck, leaned his weapon against the wall, took out a pack of cigarettes and lit up.

The binoculars kept skipping between the smoking guard and the marble lobby and the upstairs offices. Four and a half minutes elapsed before the driver and the guard who had entered the counting room appeared in the lobby, pushing a portable cloth hamper. The driver moved around in front and helped open a glass door as his companion wheeled the hamper out.

The exterior guard heeled out his cigarette and went to the rear of the white armored truck, leaving his rifle behind. He lifted his jacket flap, raised a waist chain, inserted a key and pulled open the metal door. Pino kept count. Eleven packages, nine in cloth sacks and two bound in paper, were loaded on before the sentinel guard closed and locked the door and disappeared around the other side of the truck. The driver strode to the cab, reached in his right-hand jacket pocket, retrieved a key, opened the door, got in, leaned across and pushed open the opposite door. The sentinel guard climbed in. The engine turned over and was gunned. The armored vehicle's wide headlights glimmered momentarily, then sent strong beams out through the predawn haze.

A phone call from Stretch came into Jimmy O'Keefe's at 4 P.M. on Friday. Jazz was told to be at a corner location in three hours. He walked up Massachusetts Avenue, bought some handkerchiefs and a pair of suede gloves, returned to O'Keefe's for dinner with some friends who planned to make a night of it. At 7:15 he excused himself from the table on the pretext of having to collect a rather large bet and walked to the rendezvous site. Pino and Richardson were already waiting in the white flower truck.

"What t'Christ are you wearing?" Pino asked.

"A suit," Jazz replied as he got in. "Like it?"

"You're going to work in goddamn Sunday clothes?" Tony uttered in disbelief.

"Don't worry. I won't get them dirty."

Richardson drove to the textile company and parked in a back alley. The three got out, with Sandy carrying the satchel of tools. Once in the office where the safe was, Pino opened the satchel and told Maffie to look around.

"Okay, how do you think we should operate?" Tony asked.

"Oh, I better stand over there and watch the front hall." Jazz replied.

"How come over there?"

"Because if you're going to peel—"

"Who says I'm going to peel?" Tony interrupted. "Who says I ain't going to blow hell outta her?"

"If you were carrying nitro, we would have all blown to hell the way that satchel was getting swung around coming in here."

Richardson cleared his throat. Pino opened his satchel, removing a corner wedge.

"Why don't you move the pete out where you've got more working room?"

"You think somebody can move that pete, do you?" asked Pino.

"Why not?"

"Because all three of us put together couldn't budge that monster half an inch."

Maffie shrugged, walked to the corner, seized the safe by the diagonal corners, pushed and pulled and began a rhythmic rocking and, inch by inch, rocked it into the center of the room.

Pino inserted the wedge and began prying up the metal without daring to look at Richardson.

Jazz Maffie was back at Jimmy O'Keefe's by ten, buying drinks for friends without a smudge of dirt on his clothes and $1,800 richer. Tony Pino was already at work on the Stop and Shop delivery truck. Sandy Richardson would soon be overseeing the crap game at the waterfront hall.

Stretch left a message at Jimmy O'Keefe's restaurant.

"So I went to meet him ready for work," Jazz Maffie states.

"When I showed up, Tony Pino was by himself. He wasn't ready for work. Tony Pino wanted to talk. I guess he was lonely. He told me about all his problems. The next time I showed up he did the same thing. I couldn't make sense outta half of what he was saying. He told me about some old woman who was holding him up on a car and about some cop asking about him over at work.

"Tony Pino was supposed to tell the people he worked for he had been in prison, but he didn't do that. He told me he had to go paint the new apartment him and his wife had. His wife wouldn't let him boost the paint, and that musta killed him. Tony Pino can't take a drink of water without boosting the cup. He told me something else about paint. He saw some painters going into a joint somewhere. Who the hell cared where they went?

"So when Tony Pino left messages, I didn't answer them anymore. That made him leave more messages. One night he sent some guy [Jimmy Costa] over to Jimmy O'Keefe's to find me. So I gave the guy the swerve."

Pino sneaked into the bakery, stole a half dozen rolls and two freshly laundered sets of white baker's working clothes.

Maffie reached out from under the blankets, lifted the receiver from the ringing phone and answered.

"This is Stretch," Pino's voice said furtively.

"Oh, how are ya?"

"I been trying to reach you for days. Where you been?"

"Oh, I've been around, but I haven't been answering phones."

"Why the hell not?"

"Some guy was hanging around Jimmy O'Keefe's pretending he was you, so I been avoiding him."

"Whaddaya mean, pretending he was me?"

"He told everybody his name was Stretch, but I knew he wasn't you."

There was a short pause on Pino's end. "I need you tonight."

"Saturday?" Maffie asked.

"That's tonight, ain't it?"

"What time?"

"Seven."

"Oh, well, I can't do it at seven. What about later?"

"Whaddaya mean, you can't do it. This is big business."

"I have to take my wife somewhere."

"Well, take her and sneak away."

"Oh, I can't sneak away from there. Everybody will notice if I tried to do that."

"Where the hell you going, the coronation?"

"Bowling."

"You can't run a goddamn corporation if people go bowling when you need them the most."

"I thought we agreed I'd get a full day's notice before you needed me."

"I've been trying to goddamn call you for a full day!"

"Oh, well I been avoiding this other fella who was pretending he was you."

"That was my brother-in-law, and I sent him to get you 'cause I couldn't get you any other way!"

"Oh, well, nobody told me who he was."

"Okay, okay. We'll set it up for tomorrow!"

"Sunday?"

"Sunday follows Saturday, don't it?"

"As far as I know. What time on Sunday?"

"Seven."

"Oh, I can't do that. I go have dinner with my mother and father every Sunday night. Never count on me for Sunday night."

"Next goddamn week then. Monday or Tuesday."

"Oh, well, you see, I'm going to New York. I won't be back for maybe ten days."

Costa and Pino opened the bureau in the Savin Hill garage, put the hydraulic jacks into the burglary tool satchel. Tony got into the front seat of a recently stolen station wagon and hoisted the satchel onto his lap. Costa opened the garage doors, came back, drove the wagon out, stopped, went and locked the doors, got back in and headed for Boston. Richardson was picked up at a street corner behind South Station.

"I think this was the first pete job I went along on," Costa relates. "One of the first, anyway, and the reason he took me wasn't because of any promise—there wasn't anybody else to take. It was a Saturday night.

"So I park and we go into this joint out at the end of Massachusetts Avenue not far from Boston University. It's probably eleven at night, and we go up to the third floor where the safe is. Tony peels the door in nothing flat, and there inside the pete is this metal box. It's like a safe inside a safe, this metal box. It's welded in there. So we put the hydraulic jacks inside the door, wedge them between the walls of the safe and rip the box free. The [inside] box is too strong to get open. Tony packs up his tools and runs downstairs. Sandy and me lug the box to the window and throw it. The box smashes on the sidewalk and won't open again. We put it in the wagon and take it back to Savin Hill. Tony goes to work with the flame. Puts the torch to it. We get it open, and it only has thirteen dollars inside."

Tony Pino was fired from Stop and Shop—ostensibly for not reporting beforehand that he was a parolee. During his eight weeks of rehabilitated labor he had earned an average weekly salary of $90—net a total of some $600. During the same period he amassed nearly $6,000 from boosting and safe theft. His largest expense was $5,000 given to a lawyer for deportation matters. His physical assets included a half-remodeled set of burglar's tools, a partially furnished apartment without a phone at 3 Fuller Street in Dorchester, a stolen panel truck, an unoccupied, unfurnished, partially painted apartment at Egleston Square, ninety-nine business cards without any address or telephone number, and a 1938 Chevrolet sedan for which he had just paid $325—a bright fire-engine red Chevrolet sedan.

CHAPTER SIX

Mike

Mike Geagan ducked under a beam of filtering light, righted his agile 170 pounds to its full five feet eleven inches, moved cautiously over the creaking floorboards and up to the end of the dark hallway. He surveyed the pair of doors, trying to remember what he had been told, reached up to his blue knit watch cap and retrieved a piece of paper tucked in the fold. A penlight came out of a pocket. He snapped it on, examined the instructions, replaced both paper and light, stepped before the door on the left. A honed edged pick was silently eased under the lock tongue. He slowly twisted the knob and abruptly threw open the door, shouting, "How they hanging, Captain?"

The seated figure in the unlit room dived to the floor.

"Hey, is that any kind of welcome for your lieutenant?"

The sound of crawling was the only response.

"It's me, Mike."

There was no answer.

"Tony, I'm back on leave."

"You goddamn dumb chicken fucking son of a bitch, you wanna go giving people heart attacks," echoed Pino's harsh whisper.

"Where the hell are you?"

"Under the desk—where any sane person would be in this condition."

"Jesus, I didn't mean to scare you that bad."

"I heard you all the way from the street!"

"Then what're you doing under the desk?"

"Looking for something."

"Come on up. I brought you a present."

Pino crawled from under the desk and stood. "Whatcha brought me?"

"Irish whiskey," Geagan held out a bottle.

"Irish?" Pino took the bottle with his right hand.

"Jameson's. Drink this and your troubles will be over!"

"Okay, I'll drink yours, and you drink mine." Pino's hand came around from behind his back holding a milk bottle.

"What kind's that?"

"One hundred percent American/Italian piss. You snuck in on me while I was taking a pee, you fucking dumb potato eater."

Geagan laughed, took the binoculars from the desk, lifted them to his face and trained them out the window. "So that's the Brink's outfit, is it?"

"Who the hell told you about that?" a urinating Pino demanded.

"Sandy."

"Did Mr. Blabbermouth Richardson tell you about your bookie friend?"

"Jazz? He told me the trouble, okay. I'll straighten him out. Where's the pete?" Geagan asked, shifting the binoculars from window to window.

"Right behind the door behind the big table."

"Mary, Mother of Jesus," Geagan gasped, peering through the glasses.

Pino shook himself off, zipped his fly and capped the milk bottle. "Whatcha seeing now?"

"They're loading a big tin box right onto the back of a truck. We could jerk it from them on roller skates."

"Stop looking down there and stop thinking pistols," Pino barked. "Look upstairs where the pete is. Only that's not what I wanna know. What I wanna know is, are you back in town to do some honest thievery or are you just gonna sit around getting soused?"

Geagan lowered the glasses in the darkness. "I'm the lieutenant, ain't I, Captain?"

Thirty-year-old Michael Vincent Geagan was born in Boston of Irish immigrant parents; reared under the shadows of the commonwealth's oldest penal institution, Massachusetts State Prison, in the city's oldest section, Charlestown; grew up on the streets of a neighborhood which in terms of opportunity and poverty was no better or no worse than Costa's North End or Richardson and Pino's Southy.

At the age of eight he won a school award for exemplary deportment and scholarship and then, as if to neutralize the honors, went on a rampage that included breaking into railway cars to steal coal and potatoes and that ended in his first arrest and conviction for malicious injury to real property. By the age of nine he was a confirmed drunk. A year later he was brought into court first for auto theft and then for being a stubborn child. His first larceny arrest came when he was fourteen—the theft of two baskets of grapes. Sometime between his fourteenth and fifteenth birthdays a friend gave him a pistol.

"Having a gun was your strength," Geagan explains. "People do what you tell them then and don't get hurt. I never thought of using it. I never did hurt anyone with a gun."

At the age of sixteen he was committed to the Shirley School, a reformatory, for armed robbery. More experienced inmates taught him the advantages of shotguns and tommy guns, explained the finer points of jewel theft, hijacking and B&E. On being paroled in June, 1926, eighteen-year-old Mike went to see a guru safecracker known as the Silver Fox or Professor—the same Professor who took Tony Pino under his wing two years later.

Michael Vincent Geagan's first love remained the stickup. He partnered with different Southy gunmen. Hard jobs were pulled. He gained the reputation of being a "hard" or "potent" guy. He liked that. He was called a dangerous guy—a moody and unpredictable drunk with a gun. He differed with that. He liked to travel. He combined business with pleasure and perpetrated holdups in Rhode Island and Connecticut and New York. He bought a new Ford every year. He was Irish, and he liked Irish stories and Irish songs and Irish whiskey. He liked reading. He liked being alone. He respected people he considered strong. He respected people he considered intelligent. He respected the institutions of family and church. He lived at home with his parents until he was married at the age of twenty-four. He was picked up by the cops as he drove away from the church with his bride and Jimma Faherty and spent his wedding night in jail with Faherty. Long before that day he was always giving up crime.

"I wanted security, and there wasn't security in stealing. Not the way I was doing it," Geagan explains. "When a chance came along to be a lineman for the telephone company, I took it. It paid less than where I was, driving a truck, but there was a future with the telephone company."

One day after work, Mike ran across an old Shirley School alumnus, Jimma Faherty, in a Southy saloon. Jimma liked two- and three-day drunks, liked guns better than Mike did. They rekindled their friendship, got soused together, pulled a few stick-ups together. A third man was needed for one particular job. Jimma brought in a pal who also had a reputation for booze and pistols—Sandy Richardson.

On an evening in 1930 Richardson took twenty-two-year-old Mike Geagan to Southy's Alfred E. Smith Club, better known as the Gun Club, and introduced him to twenty-three-year-old Tony Pino.

Mike's respect for Tony's criminal mentality was immediate. In Geagan, Pino, who fancied himself as a tough guy, instantly found a real live hero. As far as Tony could see, nothing much scared Mike. Each man flattered the other. Each man was partial to flattery. In Tony, Mike saw the possibility of combining theft and financial security. Geagan joined forces with the fledgling Pino/Richardson/Faherty crew but didn't give up his telephone company job.

Mike had practical safecracking experience and soon became the number two man on clouts. An organizational ability began to show. Geagan took charge of personnel and left Pino free to concentrate on spotting and casing and planning. The crew's efficiency—and profits—increased. Tony dubbed Mike his lieutenant. Mike proudly referred to Pino as Chief or Captain.

A schism developed. Mike and Sandy and Jimmy wanted the crew to take on more stickups and hijackings. Tony was opposed. A compromise was reached. All four men were free to pull whatever outside jobs they liked with whomever they liked as long as it didn't disrupt the pete clout and burglary schedule dictated by Pino.

Eight months later Geagan and Richardson were arrested in connection with an October 16, 1934, $12,742 robbery of the Treasury office at the Brockton City Hall. Sandy was cleared for lack of evidence. Mike was found guilty. On February 26, 1935, he returned to his old neighborhood, entering Massachusetts State Prison to serve seven to ten years for assault with intent to murder, plus twenty-eight to thirty years for armed robbery. A year later Richardson and Jimma Faherty joined him—as the result of armed robbery. The entire crew was reunited behind bars when Tony Pino arrived in 1938. All four concurred they wouldn't be doing time if they had stuck together and listened to Pino. While at Charlestown, they resolved that when they got out—and if they should return to crime—Tony would be boss, even when it came to armed robbery.

On December 16, 1942, Geagan was transferred from Charlestown to the State Prison Colony at Norfolk, Massachusetts, where the inmate roster read like a Who's Who of eastern seaboard criminals. His chances for parole prior to 1955 seemed remote. No offers of early release were made to Mike or any other convict volunteering to be a guinea pig for the U.S. government's experiments with an artificial blood plasma that could be used on the battlefield.

"The thing could kill me tomorrow if I could do something for my brothers and for someone else's brother and my country," Mike states as his motive for submitting to the test.

The cow blood, as Geagan termed the synthetic, was transfused into some thirty convict-volunteers. The aches were immediate, traveled through the body like a "jolt of electricity," culminating in a sensation of "blowing up and exploding." Mike almost dropped on the spot. Others did. Some went temporarily blind. Some were afflicted for life. A twenty-four-year-old convict by the name of St. Germain died; he subsequently had a Liberty ship christened for him.

The results of the synthetic blood plasma experiments at Norfolk were never made public. The guinea pigs, along with volun-
teers who hadn't been injected, were soon released from prison.

Mike Geagan won his freedom on July 28, 1943, under Chapter 222, a commonwealth statute referred to as the Cleary Act,
which had been enacted to aid the defense effort by prematurely
releasing convicts for essential military activities. Geagan met
the condition by enlisting in the Merchant Marine.

Many longtime friends question Mike's claim that the artificial
blood transfusion left no debilitating effects.

"I knew something was wrong right away," Pino asserted. "A
fella don't sneak up on ya in the dark when you're peeing like
that unless something's wrong. I'm not saying it was a big
change, but I could see it all right. We went over to Bickford's,
and I can see he was acting like he was asleep. Dreamy. I
thought he was half drunk, but that wasn't it. He was dreamy
from the cow blood. But it wasn't bad. It was a little change.

"So I tell him all about the scores I have ready to go. That
woke him up. And when we go out to take them places, he was
as good as new. The old Mike. Maybe better than old Mike.
Mother of God, the four of us [Pino, Richardson and Geagan on
the inside; Costa driving] musta taken ten petes in six days.
Three on Sunday. I figure my share comes to ten or fifteen grand
alone. And the boost got hot as hell that same week, so there
was another five hundred.

"So when Mike's gotta pull out and go back on the Coast
Guard boat, it don't make no difference, see what I mean? I'm in
business better than ever. I got working capital and can buy all
them tools I need. My spirit and my confidence is up. Everywhere I look I find another score. I can smell 'em. I can look
through brick walls and find 'em.

"When I hear Jimma's [Faherty] getting out of the can, that
does it. Now I'm really cooking. I'm getting more done in one
day than some people do in a year. I even got the apartment
painted. I even got Jazz straightened out. The Chevrolet that
crazy woman sold me don't have a decent set of tires on it, but
the rest of the world is wonderful. When things is going your
way, you gotta take advantage of 'em. I'm takin' so much
advantage there ain't time to sleep."

Pino's endless days of boosting and safecracking and spotting and casing and tending to assorted trivia was indicative of future modi operandi. So was something else—for almost three weeks he had forgotten Brink's. And that affected Jazz Maffie.

"Sandy Richardson asked me why I was giving Tony Pino the swerve," Maffie relates. "I told him the guy was driving me crazy talking about nothing and I didn't want to work with him. I didn't need the money, and I didn't need Tony Pino calling me up all the time. He called me up at Jimmy O'Keefe's eight times in one day. I told Sandy Richardson if he ever had something himself to call me up.

"So Sandy Richardson drove me over and showed me all those armored trucks parked in front of Brink's [Chamber of Commerce building]. He told me never to tell Tony Pino he said so, but he and Tony Pino were going after Brink's pete. That was interesting—"

Interesting enough for Maffie to say he would work with Pino and Richardson on the stipulation that Sandy be his sole liaison with the crew and that he have the prior right to reject any proposed score he wanted for whatever the reason.

Pino and Costa excused themselves from Sunday dinner at Tony's parents' home in Mattapan, got in Jimmy's LaSalle and drove a mile away. They pulled into a garage behind a large house, jacked a Buick up, took off the brand-new rear tires and left the garage with the Buick still on blocks. Ten minutes later they rejoined their relatives at the dining-room table.

Big Steve boosted the receipt. Costa filled it out. Mary studied it the next day, agreed the sewing machine Tony had purchased had, in fact, been purchased—let it stay in the still-unoccupied apartment at Egleston Square.

Sandy managed to get into the subbasement at the Chamber of Commerce building, found no vault belonging to Brink's or anyone else.

"Okay, I'm sliding the console out the front door of the shop with my foot, see what I mean?" Pino said. "I'm moving into the new apartment and don't wanna show up empty-handed. Mary ain't moving in till the weekend, so I wanna get this new radio console. I'm looking forward to sitting in my new living room and listening to Fibber McGee and his wife, Molly.

"So I got the console out the shop door with my foot. Jimmy and me pick it up.

"So we're on the boost, see. Boosting this console. I get it out the door with my foot, and Jimmy and me pick it up and start running away with it—and that stupid brother-in-law of mine. goes and drops it."

According to Costa, Pino dropped it.

"We were backing up across the street carrying this radio when a car comes speeding up," Jimmy relates. "Tony's all bent over with his ass sticking out. This car almost tears his ass off. Tony gives a jump and yells like you never heard and grabs his ass. And the radio console goes flying. And I don't know why he's bellyaching about it the rest of his life. For chrissakes, we went right out and boosted another one that same afternoon."

The second set was defective.

On a Wednesday afternoon in November Pino entered the Chamber of Commerce building dressed in a suit and tie and a recently boosted overcoat.

"If you can see a pete, you can take her," Tony explained. "And we ain't seen her, but we know she ain't in the cellar. So that means she gotta be upstairs in that office of theirs. Behind the door in the back of the room with the counting table.

"Okay, I'm a respectable businessman, and I ride the elevator. I go to the floor below Brink's and check the fire stairs. Look 'em up and down and go down 'em. Check 'em all the way down. If anyone asks, I'm gettin' exercise.

"So what I see is some painters working on the third floor. *Psst*, that's it!

"I go running home and take the white baker's costume of mine and throw paint on it. I come back Saturday morning looking like an Italian painter. I got a bucket and brush, too—the ones I used to paint the new apartment.

"Okay, I start going up them stairs, start up the winding marble staircase in the lobby. There ain't other painters along the way, and that ain't luck. I planned it, see what I mean? The Chamber of Commerce ain't gonna pay painters double time on Saturday if they can help it."

On the second-floor stairway Pino heard voices, sneaked up to the third-level landing, peeked around the corner, saw a group of electricians at work, beat a rapid retreat. The following Tuesday he was back on the stairs in his painter's disguise.

"I go right around noon," he explained, "when the legitimate painters go eat their lunch. Okay, there ain't no electricians on the third floor. I keep going up. It's good. No one around. Then I get a case of the jitters. This is a million-dollar proposition. I hear my heart pounding. I'm huffing and puffing, too, 'cause these stairs is steep. But I gotta go on, rain or snow.

"Okay, now I'm on the Brink's floor. I feel myself going again. Getting them jitters. It's a tense time. There's nothing there but me and the door. Now I'm right at it. I open the door a crack and peek in. A goddamn hack's sitting right there in a glass cage holding a goddamn shotgun. I take it on the arches like some kind of hurricane."

So much for burglarizing the Brink's vault.

"Okay, the clout is off, but there's no use crying over spilt milk. And the milk ain't spilt that much anyway, know what I mean? I still own them people. Brink's belongs to me."

Pino waited behind the steering wheel of his parked Chevrolet, searched the predawn Thursday morning darkness of Post Office Square. A light was on in the windows of the FBI office, but nowhere else. There was no movement on the street. He reached down on the seat, opened his lunch bucket, removed the empty milk bottle and binoculars, unwrapped a sandwich and took a bite. Two tiny white dots appeared in the rearview mirror, jiggled and grew larger. He put the food aside, started the engine, let it idle. The pair of dots expanded into wide beam headlights. A rumbling was heard. The Brink's truck carrying the metal box passed. He waited until the white armored vehicle was a hundred yards beyond him, then switched on his own headlights and followed. Two blocks ahead the Brink's truck drove into Dock Square and veered right. Pino reached Dock

Square and veered left, but not before squinting off to the side and seeing the armored truck drive off along Moon Street. The following Thursday morning he was parked several blocks beyond the opposite side of Dock Square. He watched the truck come up Moon Street and head into the Callahan Tunnel.

BOOK TWO

GOLDEN EGGS

CHAPTER SEVEN

Jimma

Jazz Maffie left the men's bar at Jimmy O'Keefe's restaurant shortly after sunset. On his way out he told the hatcheck girl he was going up the block for a few minutes to pay off a winning bettor. To take his calls. That he'd be back soon. Once in his Pontiac he drove to Amory Street in a section of Boston known as Roxbury. He parked and walked around the corner to Egleston Square.

"Oh, I know that neighborhood," Maffie explains. "My people had a place about ten blocks away. So I go around to Tony Pino's house for this meet. The reason I came over was Sandy Richardson said Jimma Faherty was out of the can, and they were going to make a meet about Brink's.

"So let me tell you about that meet at Tony Pino's house. I'm going to try to tell you everything about it because you won't believe everything that happened. I still don't.

"Tony Pino had this new apartment at the corner of Washington and Columbus Avenue. The first-floor apartment. I went in, and Sandy Richardson introduced me. He said, 'Jazz, this is Jimma Faherty. This is Tony Pino's brother-in-law, Vinnie Costa, who works with us sometimes and sometimes he doesn't.' I met Tony Pino's wife, too, Mary Pino. I don't think they were married yet, but everybody called her his wife. Mary Pino was a very nice woman, and she brought us coffee and whiskey. You could see that she was bigger than Tony Pino. Not fatter. Mary Pino had a good figure. She was taller than Tony Pino.

"So the only one who wasn't at Tony Pino's apartment was Tony Pino. The rest of us talked about this and that, and it wasn't easy. Tony Pino's apartment was right under the elevated tracks, the elevated that ran along Washington Street. When a train came by, the whole joint roared and shook. There were a lot of trains that night.

"Let me tell you about Jimma Faherty. He was sitting in the chair next to mine, and he wasn't talking to anybody. He was sitting there, wearing carpenter's overalls and a hat and reading a book. I looked down and saw that he was wearing shoes, too. He had shoes okay, but he didn't have socks. So I watched him read for a while, and then I said to him, 'Hey, is that a good book you're reading?'

"He said, 'It's not a book, it's poems.'

"I said, 'Oh, no kidding.'

"He said, 'No kidding.'

"Then he said, 'You want me to read you a poem?'

"I didn't know what to say because he was very sincere and polite. So I said, 'Why don't you just tell me what they're about?'

"He said, 'Swans.'

" 'Swans?'

"He said, 'Have you heard about the great Grogan?'* or somebody.'

"I said, 'No, I haven't. Who's the great Grogan?'

" 'A great Irish poet.'

" 'Oh,' I said. Then I said, 'What makes him so great?'

"He said, 'Swans follow him around.'

"So I thought I had two nuts on my hands. I already knew Tony Pino was a nut, and there's this guy in overalls and a hat and no socks talking about swans tailing people.

"I lit up my cigar and tried to pretend I wasn't there. There was nobody to talk to because Sandy Richardson was sitting and sleeping and Vinnie Costa wasn't in the living room. Mary Pino

*Gogarty.

wasn't there either. So I sat there listening to the elevated trains. I put my cigar in the ashtray, and when I went to reach for it again, it wasn't there. I looked around, and then I looked at Jimma Faherty. He was still reading and smoking my cigar. What are you going to do, call a cop? I took out another cigar.

"Tony Pino came running in the room, and I started smiling. He was wearing a green doorman's uniform with big brass buttons and gold braids on it. And he was wearing a green doorman's cap that was too big and almost came down over his eyes. He told Vinnie Costa to get Mary Pino out of the house, and then he ran out as fast as he ran in. He didn't say hello to anybody. Vinnie Costa went into the kitchen, and all kinds of shouting started. All this time the elevated trains were shaking hell outta the joint, but you still heard the shouting. And when the door slammed, you heard that. So the door slammed, and Vinnie Costa ran through the living room and out the front door. Tony Pino, Vinnie Costa and another guy came back in pushing a big refrigerator they just swiped from somebody. Only Tony Pino let the other two guys do most of the work. Most—hell, he ran back outside. Vinne Costa and the other guy pushed the refrigerator off to the kitchen. Tony Pino came back in carrying two big suitcases. I looked around, and I thought I was going nuts. Nobody was paying attention. Sandy Richardson was still sitting up snoring. Jimma Faherty was reading about swans and smoking my cigar.

"So Tony Pino put the suitcases down in the corner, and the guy who helped move the refrigerator went home. Vinnie Costa came in the room, and Tony Pino said the meet had come to order. He started yelling at Sandy Richardson for sleeping, and he told Jimma Faherty to put away the swans.

"Tony Pino tried getting the meet going, and I can't keep a straight face. Tony Pino didn't sit down when he talked. He hopped all over the living room in his green uniform and waved his arms. He had the hat on, too—the big one—and he had to keep pushing it up so he could see. I looked at Jimma Faherty. He was slouched down in his chair and had his arms folded over his chest. One eye was closed, and the other was flicking like it was falling asleep. Sandy Richardson had trouble keeping his eyes open, too. Vinnie Costa was looking at the ceiling. Every now and then Vinnie Costa would interrupt Tony Pino and correct him. And don't forget, trains kept roaring by.

"So I sat there acting like everything was normal. And you want to hear the first thing Tony Pino talked about? He talked about buying gasoline. Us buying, him selling. Tony Pino was working at the gas station across the street, at Tony's Socony. He was pumping gas, and he wanted us to all buy our gas from him. But he didn't tell you that like any human being. He had to tell you about giving Tony Socony fifteen hundred bucks under the table and being a silent partner in the joint and they were going to give away dishes if you bought enough gas and had a lube job.

"Tony Pino finally got around to talking about all the scores he spotted. It was the longest list you ever heard. Tony Pino didn't only tell you about a score. He told you everything about a score like he told you everything about buying gas. He told you how he was riding on a Stop and Shop truck when he found this one or how he was walking down the street after he got fired and found that one. He told you what he was wearing and what he had for dinner.

"So Tony Pino went on and on, and some of the scores sounded good—some factories and warehouses and office buildings. Some were plain nuts—an ice-cream parlor and a dog kennel. I started thinking that every joint Tony Pino walked past he wanted to hit. I knew I was right when he said he wanted to go right next door and rob Joe McGinnis' place. That's when I said, 'Hey, do you know who Joe McGinnis is?'

"Tony Pino said, 'Who the hell cares who he is, he's got a safe, doesn't he?'

"Everybody in Boston knew that Joe McGinnis was the crookedest guy in town. Joe McGinnis had contacts everywhere—and Tony Pino knew it, too. So I said to Tony Pino, 'Have you ever met Joe McGinnis?'

"Tony Pino said, 'I've seen him around.'

"I said, 'Well, why don't you go and take a second look at him? A nice long look?'

"Joe McGinnis was the meanest-looking rogue ever born. A great big baldheaded guy who was built like a bull and just as strong. He could tear a person apart with his bare hands, but he liked using a baseball bat better.

"That's when Jimma Faherty opened both eyes. He told Tony Pino they had to leave Joe McGinnis alone because Joe McGinnis and Mike Geagan were good friends. Tony Pino said if they were friends, Mike Geagan would have told him. Then the fight started between Tony Pino and Vinnie Costa.

"Vinnie Costa told Tony Pino that he was there when Mike Geagan told Tony Pino about being a friend of Joe McGinnis'. Tony Pino heard that and went crazy. He yelled at Vinnie Costa and called him every name there was. Vinnie Costa kept looking at the ceiling and wouldn't change his story. Tony Pino got redder and redder and shouted louder and louder. I never remembered seeing a man get that mad that fast. I remembered thinking it was a good thing Tony Pino didn't own a baseball bat. He was ready to do damage.

"Sandy Richardson got up and said, 'Let's forget it." It was the damnedest thing. Only those words, and Tony Pino was calm again. He acted like he forgot all about the argument.

"Tony Pino went right back to talking about the scores. When he finished, he asked which one I was interested in.

"I said, 'Oh, I'm not interested in any of them. I thought you knew that before I came over.'

"Tony Pino started to get red again and said to me, 'Then why the hell did you come over at all?'

"I said, 'Because I thought you were going to talk about Brink's!'

"Tony Pino damned near choked. He wanted to know how I knew about Brink's. I told him I'd been hearing about it all over town. I was sorry I said that. Tony Pino turned white as death. He sat down in a chair and started breathing heavy like he was going to have a heart attack. I started to worry, but Sandy Richardson signaled he'd take care of it. Sandy Richardson began to tell Tony Pino that he told me about Brink's, and that's when the crash came. The floor jumped, too. It felt like one of the trains had hit the house. I jumped up and looked around. The refrigerator was laying on the floor in the doorway, and Mary Pino was standing behind it, kicking it. Tony Pino jumped up, too, and asked her what she was doing. Mary Pino said she was going to kick the refrigerator right out into the gutter because it was stolen property. Tony Pino swore it wasn't stolen. He said he bought it and had a receipt. She's already called the store that the receipt was from, and they said they didn't carry refrigerators. She called Tony Pino this and that and told him to get rid of the refrigerator. Tony Pino gave up easy. He said okay, he'd take the refrigerator away in the morning.

"So Tony Pino was up on his feet and walking around. He wasn't white or having a heart attack anymore. He wanted to know where I heard about Brink's. Sandy Richardson said he told me. That's when Tony Pino started telling us about Brink's. Telling us everything. The whole story about spotting the metal box and using the office to spy on them. He said he went up to their joint and found out we couldn't get to the safe. He said Brink's was still going to make us all rich, that he was tailing some trucks.

"Jimma Faherty told Tony Pino to be careful around Brink's trucks. Jimma Faherty said that Brink's was always trying out brand-new gimmicks so they wouldn't be robbed. He said he heard that Brink's used radar on their trucks to keep people from following them. Tony Pino asked what radar was. Jimma Faherty said it was a new secret weapon the Navy used to sink submarines. Tony Pino wanted to know where Jimma Faherty heard all this. All about Brink's and radar. Jimma Faherty said he read about it in the prison library.

"Tony Pino said we should all go home and think about which score we wanted to hit. He said they'd have another meet soon to decide which went first. He told me I could be in on Brink's if I wanted. Be in even if I didn't want to go on any of the other jobs. I said I'd think about it. And that was the end of the meet.

"Oh, wait, there was one more thing. Everybody started to leave Tony Pino's apartment. I was out in the hall, and Tony Pino grabbed my arm and said he wanted to talk privately. We went back in the living room and he said, 'What size do you take?'

"I said, 'What are you talking about?'

"He said, 'Suit size. What suit size do you take?'

"I said, 'Oh, I take a forty-two. Forty-two long.'

"He said, 'You look like a forty regular to me.'

"I said, 'Well, maybe I lost some weight, but my arms didn't shrink.'

"He said, 'When you lose weight, your arms always shrink.'

"So I was standing there thinking of something else to say, and Tony Pino ran over and opened a big suitcase I saw him bring in earlier. He started throwing out suits on the floor, looking at sizes and throwing them away. He came running back, carrying two suits. He held the jackets up to me and said, 'See, I told you they fit.'

"I said, 'Well, let me try them on.'

"He said, 'Don't you trust me?'

"Well, I don't want to call a man a liar in his own home, so I said, 'I'm not calling you nothing. But maybe my arms didn't shrink as much as you think?'

"He said, 'If you don't try them on, you can have them both for thirty dollars.'

"You want to know something? That wasn't a bad price. So I told him I'd think it over."

Jimma Faherty had a propensity for getting arrested; he had been booked for nine offenses as a juvenile and twelve more as an adult. Jimma Faherty had a propensity for being convicted; he had spent twelve and a third of his thirty-three years in penal institutions as a result of twelve specific counts.

Jimma Faherty had a propensity for drinking. When he and Sandy and Mike and Tony were all together on the old crew, he outdrank Richardson and Geagan two to one. Jimma occasionally went out on a job soused; once he was so crocked he brought along a machine gun, thinking it was a .32 caliber pistol. Jimma's favorite legitimate part-time job was bartending.

Jimma Faherty had a propensity to lose articles of clothing when he got drunk. Given a few drinks on either side of the wall, chances were good he might soon be without a shirt or socks or shoes or all three or more.

Sober or not, incarcerated or not, five-foot nine-inch, 150-pound James Ignatius Faherty had a sense of humor and gift of gab that was rivaled only by his intelligence. Indications are his IQ neared the 160 quotient. Drunk or not, Jimma was the official debating champ of Charlestown Prison, as well as the official inmate designated to accompany visiting VIPs around the institution.

Jimma Faherty had a propensity for reading. Poetry was a

passion. So were scientific books and magazines, particularly those dealing with guns and explosives. It was, therefore, not surprising that Jimma had found an article on radar.

Everything the crew was doing stopped. All the safe clouting and spotting and planning and meets. It was the holiday season, and as was true in the past and would be true in the future, Tony devoted himself exclusively to the Christmas Boost.

"I make my year's expenses, know what I mean?" Pino said. "If I don't make anything all year, I can pay for my rent and necessities from the Christmas Boost."

This particular season Tony, Jimmy Costa and Big Steve netted approximately $7,000 per man for three weeks' work.

Predawn the first Thursday morning in 1949 Pino was positioned in the shrubbery off a sidewalk in East Boston. The Brink's truck emerged from the Callahan Tunnel. Tony raised his binoculars, studied the white armored vehicle as it slanted right onto Paris Street and headed for the Chelsea intersection. No wires or antenna could be seen, and the magazine article Jimma Faherty had given him stated that radar systems required antennas.

The progenitor of the money-moving industry, as well as the armored car, can technically be traced back to May, 1859, when in Chicago, Washington Perry Brink purchased a horse and wagon and had painted on the buckboard's side, "Brink's City Express." The venture prospered and for the next sixty-one years remained a local Chicago operation almost exclusively dedicated to general cartage. Isolated incidents of Brink's moving money occur as early as 1891, when a bulk payroll, believed to belong to the Western Electric Company, was transported. The following sixteen years saw the company expand these services to include not only bulk payroll delivery, but making up pay envelopes for certain customers and in some instances delivering them to individual employees, plus shuttling currency between banks. Introduction of government-sponsored low-rate shipping via parcel post and the emergence of Dr. Frank Allen in the company hierarchy helped shift Brink's away from general cartage and onto the money-moving specialization. A 1917 payroll robbery of a Brink's open touring car in which one of Dr. Allen's sons was killed accelerated research for a safer means of transport.

The first truly armored car was put into service in 1923. Windows were made of the newly perfected bulletproof glass. Light-gauge boiler plate steel was used for construction since the low-powered combustion engines of the day couldn't propel heavy vehicles. Even so, it was a rolling fortress. Brink's had a symbol—and the instrument which was to dominate the future money-moving market.

Any pretext the company might have for being anything other than a transporter of cash and valuables was quickly dropped. Between 1923 and 1927 Brink's opened twenty-seven U.S. branch offices from Los Angeles, California, to Boston, Massachusetts [which began operations on August 25, 1925], plus one in Montreal, Canada.

In 1927 the first all-risk insurance policy ever to protect armored car service was issued to Brink's with coverage of $2,500,000 by Commercial Union Assurance Company Ltd., London, England.

Ninety days later, on March 11, 1927, a Brink's armored truck with trailing convoy car set out for the Terminal Coal Company in Cloverdale, Pennsylvania. About twenty miles outside Pittsburgh the lead vehicle tripped a guide wire stretched across the road. Buried explosive charges detonated. The three-ton armored truck was blown into the air and crashed back to earth upside down. A second explosion, meant for the convoy car, went off ahead of schedule. The car careened but could not avoid the crater left by the first explosion. It pitched in head first, knocking all the guards unconcious. An ambushing gang of robbers swept down from the hills, gathered up the payroll valises and escaped with $103,834.38. Miraculously, none of the personnel in either vehicle was seriously hurt. Police quickly apprehended Paul Jawaski, a known murderer and wanted fugitive, and other members of the infamous Flathead Gang. All were either imprisoned for the robbery or executed for previous homicides. Thirty-eight thousand dollars in buried loot were recovered and turned over to Commercial Union Assurance, which had sent Brink's a check for $103,834.38 three days after the robbery.

The explosion pointed up a weakness company experts had long known about and were in the process of correcting: The armored car rode on a wooden frame and floor. More sophisticated engines and technology allowed for redesign, including an all-steel frame and armored steel floor. The robbery resulted in new security techniques for the vehicle's crews. Routing of a money shipment must not become predictable. Measures to spot surveillers were instituted.

"So I'm reading all about how after they put in steel bottoms and retrained them crews, nobody ever took a Brink's truck again," Tony Pino related. "I'm reading about it first up in the library in Providence, only they don't have much about it. I wanna know about Brink's trucks having radar, and all they wanna talk about is that president, Alden [Allen], I think his name was. The guy used to be a veterinarian. What wonderful things he done for the company, which I'm sure he did. Or they tell you about how they got fifty or sixty offices by then.* [Fifty-eight in the United States, six in Canada.]

"Now I gotta go elsewhere, see what I mean? Libraries where Boston cops don't spot me. Providence ain't got enough. So I start going to other towns, other libraries. And they don't have much—or nothing. So that's how I get to Harvard. I go closer to home. I go to Harvard over in Cambridge. No cops are gonna figure a thief for going to Harvard Library. And Harvard ain't gonna figure no crook is coming in with a divinity student ticket. You can always tell a student, but at Harvard you can't tell a divinity student. They're the craziest bunch you ever seen, so I go over to where they live and boost one of the tickets—library cards. I forget which was which.

"Now I'm a student. I'm studying about Brink's. Reading everything they got. Wait a minute! Something's wrong here. This magazine is saying how slick these guards are, but the fellas I been watching over at Brink's are sloppy and careless. And they're older than they're supposed to be. I figure it out. It's the war. Them slick young Brink's fellas is probably out fighting the war.

"And I don't find nothing about radar, and that's when I get

*For complete list and dates of Brink's subsidiary companies see Appendix A.

my break. I'm over looking up 'radar' in them files of cards they got, and some young engineer student is looking it up, too. We start talking about radar. He tells me no matter what, you can't work radar without an aerial. On a truck you even gotta have it, know what I mean? The Brink's trucks don't have them kinda aerials.''

It was ideal crooking weather—drizzle and darkness. Pino sat behind the wheel of the idling fire engine red Chevrolet and squinted out through the wiper-swept windshield watching the intersection of Paris and Chelsea streets in East Boston. Earmuffs pronged down on his porkpie hat. Binoculars, an empty milk bottle and a lunch bucket rested on the seat to his right.

Hazy headlights and a dark outline of the Brink's truck carrying the metal box appeared on Paris Street. The truck pulled to a full stop at the corner, then turned left and accelerated along Chelsea Street. Pino followed, maintaining a distance of about 200 yards. The silhouetted armed vehicle lumbered on several miles, then bore left along Saratoga Street and made another left onto Revere Highway [then Route 1, today Route 1a].

Increasing rain prolonged the morning darkness and deterred traffic. Only a dozen and a half vehicles passed Pino's red Chevrolet and overtook the moderately accelerating white armored truck. Tony used the incidents to vary position. Sometimes it would be he who passed a car ahead, only to drop back when another from behind overtook him, then to move up again. He was certain the precipitation would leave his headlights blurredly unidentifiable to any guard watching from the peephole in the rear of the Brink's truck.

The route continued north through the town of Revere and, as blackness dissipated to mawkish gray semidawn, on along the silhouetted towers and balls and runs of pipe latticing and the hulking tankers moored beyond a line of gasoline refineries.

The Brink's truck disappeared into a miasma from the Lynn marshes. Pino speeded up. He emerged from the fog just in time to see the square white back of the armored vehicle diminishing up Route 107. The red Chevrolet braked, skidded into a right turn, zoomed ahead and then, after a quarter of a mile slowed to a more leisurely pursuit.

Once atop the Saugus River Bridge, Pino glanced off to his

right. A rain-swept vista of lighted windows in a red brick factory and office buildings spread as far as his eyes could see. Pino needed no sign to tell him the complex belonged to General Electric. His hunch that this was where the metal box would come to rest was immediately contradicted. The Brink's truck drove past the entrance, steering a straight course up Western Avenue.

Once beyond a small business section, the white armored vehicle turned left. Pino pulled up to the curb and parked at the corner of South Street. The view across Western Avenue to the corner around which the Brink's truck had driven was obscured by a cluster of trees. He got out, strolled up the sidewalk and gazed off to his left. The street the white armored car had turned into was actually a private road leading past a guardhouse and open gate and on toward a maze of high red-brick factory buildings. Farther ahead the Brink's truck was backing toward an opening in a structure to the left. A fourth of the way in, it stopped. The driver got out.

Pino crossed Western Avenue and walked casually toward the complex, looking for some company sign or name painted on a building. None could be seen. He neared the guardhouse and open gate, noting that workers were passing by unchallenged and without displaying credentials.

Pino increased his pace and strode through the gate. The guard was reading a newspaper. He continued up the roadway and peered into the opening where the Brink's truck stood parked. The metal box was being pushed across the garage floor behind.

"Say, fella," Pino said, stopping a passing workman, "where do I find induction research?"

"Induction research?"

"Yeah, you know, them gizmos that keep telling submarines where they are. I work on them down in Virginia. They sent me up here to help out."

"You better ask over at personnel. Two buildings up to your right."

"They said I'd see induction research right when I come through the gate," Pino took a slip of paper out of his pocket and feigned reading it. "See a sign saying induction research. This is Massachusetts Development Company, ain't it?"

"This is General Electric."

"I thought I seen General Electric back down near the river."

"That's General Electric, too."

"You got two different operations in the same town?"

"It's all part of one. This is mainly administration and pay-master. Some manufacturing. Down near the river is mainly manufacturing."

Sandy Richardson elbowed his way up to the bar and squeezed one shoulder through.

"My God, it looks like New Year's Eve in here," he commented to a man swaying on the stool to his right.

"Only payday friend, payday." The semidrunk stared at Richardson's pea coat and knit watch cap. "You a sailor?"

"Merchant mariner."

"Lemme buy one."

"Sure you can afford it?"

"When you work for GE, you can afford it and more," the semidrunk replied, flagging his pay envelope, then using it to get the bartender's attention.

"Pay pretty good at GE, huh?"

"The best. Not a man in this room with take-home of less than a hundred and a half. And tomorrow morning, when the boys get off the night shift, then you'll see genuine spenders."

"They pay even better on the night shift, do they?"

"Yup."

"Never heard of a place paying on Thursday night and Friday morning. How come they don't pay Friday afternoon like everyone else?"

"They do. They pay the morning shift."

"Then when do you work?"

"Afternoon shift."

"Three shifts? Christ, you must have five thousand guys working here."

"More. I hear it's around twenty thousand. Hey, Apples. Apples! Goddamn ya, Apples, give my sailor friend here a drink, will ya?"

"What'll it be?" a bartender apparently named Apples yelled over.

"Gin and Coke," Richardson shouted back.

"Hey, Apples, how many guys you think GE's got working for it altogether, twenty thousand?"

"Twelve thousand two hundred!"

"Can't be that little, Apples."

"It's twelve thousand two hundred. Half the boys from paymaster drink right here. They told me."

A man down the bar differed with both opinions. He said he worked in personnel and that GE employed 26,000.

The Brink's truck reversed gears, backed halfway into the garage at the GE plant, stopped at an angle. Pino sat up against a building across the way, munching a sandwich, as the driver got out and headed to the rear of the truck. A Brink's guard remained in the cab. Four men, two who were definitely armed, came forward from the rear of the garage. The two with guns deployed took up sentinel some twenty paces apart, just beyond the rear of the truck. The two other men and driver disappeared from Tony's view momentarily, then reappeared, rolling the metal box toward the rear of the garage. The pair of armed men followed slowly after, turning and looking about.

Several hours later Pino climbed the steps to the floor above the garage. Once in the lobby he determined this was the paymaster's office and that it was too well secured to attempt going after the estimated $2,500,000 Brink's had just delivered by safe theft.

CHAPTER EIGHT

The Snitch

It was a matter of "golden eggs"—a master plan evolving from the simplest of logic. The crew had given up aspirations of cracking the vault they'd never located at Brink's. The same was true for the vault Pino never found at General Electric. And because the exact whereabouts of both safes were unknown, the idea of armed robbing either premises was eliminated.

There was a possibility of taking the estimated $2,500,000 in payroll by holding up the Brink's guards and making off with the metal box when it was either being loaded on at the Chamber of Commerce building or being unloaded in the GE garage. The security Pino had seen at GE wasn't insurmountable. At the Chamber of Commerce building it was, in the minds of the crew, negligible.

But at this particular time Tony was short on experienced hands. Sandy was definitely available, but Maffie was still difficult to deal with. Jimma Faherty, who had helped the crew's fortune soar his first three weeks home, had taken his share of the safe clout loot and gone off on several long benders. Even if Jazz and Jimma did come into the fold, that would bring crew strength only up to four hands. Pino needed more than four.

Manpower to the side, there was another consideration.

"You don't wanna scare the duck that's laying them golden

eggs, see what I mean?" Pino said. "Mother of God, every one of them trucks I been watching load up was carrying golden eggs, see. Every one of them packages was going to petes somewhere. And maybe all the petes could be took!

"Let me explain something to you. We weren't in no position to take that box at Brink's. Someday we would be. But once we did that, Brink's is through forever. We killed the duck. All that loading routine I seen—them sixteen packages going on one truck and the ten going on the next—that's gonna change. They'll change the guards and where the trucks go to. Everything. And they'll be watching for us, too. So we wanna keep away from Mr. Brink's. We want him to go on snoozing like he's been all along. We just wanna find out where the trucks is dropping them golden eggs. Don't never forget, I spent a good couple of months watching them trucks load up in the morning. And that's all bonus time, know what I mean? They do their loading before the sun comes up in the morning. So I can watch 'em an' still get in an honest day's crooking somewhere else.

He began in the bonus hours, went back to Brink's before sunrise, chose Tuesday, Wednesday, Thursday and Friday mornings. He counted money sacks and boxes and other containers being loaded at both the Federal and Congress Street doors of the Chamber of Commerce building. Armored vehicles were designated by the number of "packages" they carried—15 Truck Wednesday, 8 Truck Wednesday, 7 Truck Thursday, 12 Truck Tuesday. Only he didn't select the 8s and 7s for following, kept to the 10s and above.

And the tailing of the trucks didn't go as easily as it had with the GE box out to Lynn. It was a block or two at a time; then he would return the next week for another block or two; he would be waiting ahead of a truck one Thursday, pull in behind it the next Thursday. One Tuesday morning truck required two months of tailing before he followed it farther than a mile and a half from Brink's.

Nor was the surveillance limited to one truck per morning. When he had followed the 5:30 Wednesday truck far enough away, he didn't have to pick up its trail until 6:30 or 7 A.M.; he was able to follow the 5:45 for twenty or thirty minutes before.

It was not unusual for Tony to tail three trucks on one particular morning. As each truck was tracked farther away from Brink's and the center of Boston, choices had to be made. On Wednesday mornings 17 Truck received highest priority. Then came 14 Truck. Tuesday was 11 Truck with no backup. Thursday became 19 Truck. And Friday—Friday was the prize of prizes, the goldenest of eggs in Pino's universe—48 Truck.

Then Mike Geagan returned from the Merchant Marine for good, and the crew became exceedingly busy on other scores, many that required early-morning casing. And Pino gave up trailing the Tuesday and Thursday trucks. Then the sun began rising earlier.

"It's broad daylight, and I still ain't got nowhere with Wednesday Truck, know what I mean? I'm on a long road where they can spot me easy. So I give her up till next year. I'll come after her while it's still dark. I give them all up except for Forty-eight Truck [Friday morning]. I make up my mind and tail her no matter what."

At 4:35 P.M. eastern war time, Friday, April 12, 1945, President Franklin Delano Roosevelt died in Warm Springs Georgia, from a cerebral hemorrhage. Whether because of grief or shame or respect, or for other reasons, the crew remained inoperative for several weeks, then scored a factory safe for about $9,000.

As it would be in future years, crew activity was curtailed with the onset of warm weather and longer hours of sunlight. Jazz Maffie began rising early so he could get in a full thirty-six holes at the golf course. Richardson continued his daily stint down at the docks, looked forward to spending more time with his family. Faherty told Sandy he was going to use the summer to dry out and pulled a partial vanishing act. Costa knew there would be no respite from the boost with Tony and Big Steve over the summer, but his time would be free enough to open negotiations for buying a small dress manufacturing company and to look into a lottery franchise.

For Pino it was time to form another partnership.

"So I'm working over at Tony's Socony [Tony Gaeta's Socony oil service station directly across Columbus Avenue from Pino's apartment], filling tanks and changing people's oil, and one day Barney [thirty-six-year-old Joseph Silvester Banfield] shows up. Barney's the nicest guy you ever want to meet. I done time with him a couple of times. Reform school, I think. And he was in Charlestown.

"Barney was the best man I ever met with trucks and cars. His brother used to have a fleet. Barney's a drunk, too. He gets so goddamn drunk Joe [McGinnis] has to chain him up in the cellar. Don't laugh. Joe chains him to the cellar wall with bear chains 'cause Barney goes too cuckoo when he drinks; if you don't chain him, he'll vanish for two weeks and maybe hurt himself.

"So Barney tells me [over at Tony Gaeta's service station] that he's working for Joe McGinnis. I can't avoid Joe McGinnis, know what I mean? You go outta my back door and cross the street, and there he is in front of the package liquor store [Iberschied Liquor Store] hosing down his car. Joe McGinnis is the cheapest son of a bitch there is. And the crookedest. He makes me look like Rockefeller.

"So Joe and me's got what you could call a grunting relationship. When I pass him, we grunt at one another.

"I don't know what day it was, but Barney wants me to meet Joe. So he takes me over to Joe's bottle club [J.A. Club]. The club's right around the corner from the package liquor store. Joe and his wife live above the liquor store.

"So Joe says he heard about me, and I tell him I heard about him, too, and he asks me if I wanna do a little business. We gotta lotta mutual friends, Joe knows I can spot and open anything. Joe's gotta lot of important connections down in Providence and New York—places like that and out in the Midwest. What he wants is the two of us to work like experts, see, tell other people how to rob a joint. Somebody'll send us blueprints, and I'll figure out how to take the pete. The best way. Joe says we can work for both cash and get percentages, too. So I agree. That's how we started doing business together.

"And guess what the cheap son of a bitch did—he made me pay for the drink he invited me to have."

Among their mutual associates was James V. Crowley, the Boston detective for whom Pino was suspected of being an in-

formant and whose number one source for underworld information was Joe McGinnis.

When Adolf Hitler's death was reported on April 30, Tony
had followed the 48 Truck as far as Somerville, less than five
miles from 80 Federal Street. Nazi Germany's unconditional
surrender to the Allies, May 7, had found him a mile beyond
Somerville on Route 28. In mid-July, as President Truman met
with Winston Churchill and Joseph Stalin in Potsdam, Pino was
watching 48 Truck drive through Stoneham, Massachusetts
(some eleven miles north of Boston on Route 28). He had tailed
the armored car three miles farther to the outskirts of Reading,
Massachusetts, by August 6, when an atomic device dubbed Little Boy was detonated over Hiroshima. The subsequent August
15, V-J Day, the Brink's truck was observed leaving Reading.
While the United States battleship *Missouri* lay at anchor in To-
kyo Bay preparing for the formal Japanese surrender on September 2, Tony Pino was crouched behind a manure pile on an
abandoned farm off Route 28, seventeen miles from Boston.

During the fall and early winter of 1945 the crew's fortunes hit
a postwar high in the Boston area, and 48 Truck was abandoned.
The majority of safe scores ranged between $5,000 and $8,500
and the schedule had expanded to include several holdups in the
$10,000 category. Geagan had taken charge of personnel prob-
lems, which left Pino free to spot even more work.

After the Christmas Boost layoff so many jobs were being
found that extra hands were often brought. For the larger thefts,
the crew turned to a pair of New York City area criminals who
had worked with them in preprison days. Young Stanley Gusciora of Stoughton, a former inmate with Tony, Mike, Jimma and
Sandy at Massachusetts State, was the favorite recruit for the
smaller jobs.

Whether they were regular or "extra" crew members, the
take was always divided evenly among the men participating in
the specific robbery. All scores Tony found, which were by far
the majority of those perpetrated by the gang, had to be first
offered to the regular crew. If the regular crew members rejected the project, Tony was free to do with the location whatever

he chose. Often he merged regular crew members and outside hands to do the job. More often than not, he turned a rejected score over to McGinnis, who "sold" it off to other gangs of local crooks. That was another business Pino and Joe had formed— score selling.

In mid-January Pino was driving away from a Cambridge mansion he had been casing for a possible theft of silverware when he spotted a Brink's truck pulling into a side street.

"I hadn't tailed one of them sweethearts in months and couldn't figure out what she was doing over here, see?" he stated. "This ain't the kind of neighborhood that they deliver to. Especially at night. So I follow her a block or two. She pulls into this alley, and I drive past. I see her park in front of a low garage building.

"So I drive around and park and come walking back from the other side. Other side of the alley. Okay, the truck's gone, so I look inside this long garage building—it's long like the old stables they used to have.

"Bang, there I seen 'em all lined up. Brink's trucks. I know I got their garage, and I'm watching this janitor they got. This fella's moppin' up in between the trucks. He goes into the back, and fast, I open the door and sneak in. The first thing I see is a board nailed up on the wall with the keys on it."

The keys to the armored trucks.

The crew's continuing heavy schedule of Boston area thefts dissuaded Pino from returning to his tailing of 48 Truck which would have taken him too far from the city. Instead, he picked up where he had left off the previous late winter; he began following four different Brink's armored cars: one on Tuesday, two on Wednesday mornings, one on Thursday mornings.

By the beginning of February, 1946, he had grown very interested in a Thursday morning truck which left the Federal Street entrance of the Chamber of Commerce building at approximately 7 A.M.* In the course of almost one full year Tony had tailed

*Pino's estimated time of departure.

this armored car along Atlantic Avenue and into Kneeland and then onto Albany Avenue and out toward Hyde Park. He had seen it cross a small bridge and stop at a shoe factory to drop off a money sack. Two weeks later he observed it delivering money sacks at the B. F. Sturtevant factory in Hyde Park. Fourteen days after that he was following at a safe distance as the truck pulled to a stop at Dedham Square.

Richardson gazed into the rearview mirror. The Brink's truck from Sturtevant was parking down the block at Dedham Square. The guard and driver got out of the cab, locked the doors, walked to the rear of the armored chassis and unlocked and opened the back door. A guard jumped down and waited while the door was relocked.

The trio strode across the street and entered a restaurant.

"Jesus," Sandy muttered in disbelief.

"They done it four Thursdays in a row now," Pino said. "Each time they stay inside longer having their coffee. Last time they didn't come out for forty minutes."

Richardson turned casually, peered longingly at the crewless armored truck parked at the curb.

"Think maybe we can mask her?" Pino asked. "Put up wood blinds like we were street workers or something? Sewer workers. Then we take out our equipment and open her up like a can of soup."

"Anthony, there are times I think you're criminally insane."

"Yeah, ain't it wonderful?"

"Assuming we could detain the guards, exactly what equipment do we have to open her? Dynamite?"

"This here, Mr. R." Pino dangled a key in front of Richardson. "It fits their back door."

"Where did you get it?"

"From Mr. B.'s garage. Snuck in and copied it off the board they got. Have a copy of every key for every truck they got."

The Thursday morning Brink's armored car scheduled for Sturtevant and Dedham Square pulled off River Street, crossed a trestle and came to a stop before its first delivery of the day—a small factory. The driver unlocked the rear door. A guard jumped out, holding several sacks. The door was locked after him. Once the two men were on their way toward the building, Pino and Richardson sneaked out of the shrubbery, inserted a key and quietly pulled open the armored door in the rear of the vehicle. Pino reached inside, grabbed the first item he touched and bolted back into the foliage. Richardson calmly relocked the door, then tore off after his colleague.

"Son of a bitch," Tony muttered, going through the contents of the single white bag as Sandy drove away.

"Son of a bitch what?"

"There's only thirty-five hundred in her."

Nothing appeared in the newspapers concerning the theft of $3,500 from a Brink's truck. No change in armored car scheduling or personnel was noted at the Chamber of Commerce building in the early-morning hours. The number of packages observed being loaded onto each truck remained what it had been in previous days.

"Okay, it ain't so surprising Brink's swallows the loss, see what I mean?" asks Tony. "They don't wanna tell the papers they got knocked over 'cause that'll be bad for business. Scare off new customers and maybe lose a couple they already got. And they don't wanna tell the cops neither, 'cause then their insurance company will find out and jack the rates on 'em. So they swallow the loss.

"What surprised the living hell outta me is they don't do nothing about it. The first thing you're gonna do if somebody's been following your trucks and snitching 'em is change the routes and put on different loads. Brink's don't do that. They keep the routes and loads the same. If Brink's figure a hack screwed up and lost the package, you'd expect them to change the hacks around. They didn't. It was all the same guys on the same trucks."

After a ten- or twelve-day wait Tony and Sandy sneaked up on a Tuesday morning truck which had stopped to make a delivery. They unlocked and opened the back door and snitched a money bag containing $5,100.

Again nothing appeared in the papers. No change in routing or loading or personnel was seen.

The first phase of robbing Brink's had begun—a phase which, by itself, would net the crew nearly $400,000*—with the bigger money yet to come.

---

*Brink's Incorporated states all its records for this period are gone and would make no comment regarding the Pino, Richardson, Costa allegation that money was stolen in this manner. Insurance companies covering this period would make no comment. Police records indicate no reported loss.

CHAPTER NINE

Light and Heavy

By the first week of January, 1946, a Tuesday morning Brink's truck had been followed to the end of its route, the value of individual deliveries estimated and the premises of several deliverees cased. By February the same was true for a Wednesday, Thursday and Friday morning truck. In mid-February the first safe belonging to a Brink's customer was cracked by the robbery team and $7,300 taken.

Again, there was a wait. This time the theft was given a few lines on the back pages of the paper, but no change in Brink's routing or personnel was observed.

The safes of three more Brink's customers were rifled. There was still no variance in armored truck procedure. Four safes were cracked in one week.

"We weren't selecting joints that got payroll deliveries," Sandy Richardson points out. "Those Thursday and Friday deliveries. There were several ways to tell it was payroll. Brink's made up payroll themselves and often delivered them in long flat metal trays. We'd also been in the joints they delivered to, so we could often tell if they were getting payroll or something else. If you hit a joint right after they got a payroll from Brink's, the cops might put two and two together.

"We went after the regular deliveries. Places that needed a lot of cash on hand to conduct their business. That meant if Brink's delivered on Tuesday, we could go in on Wednesday night and take the pete. That's what we were doing that winter. Hitting joints like that. We were hitting so many other joints around that time—joints that had nothing to do with Brink's—that I guess the cops never got suspicious.''

By the time the days grew longer and the warm-weather hiatus began, an estimated twenty Brink's customers had been robbed by the crew.

The spring and summer of 1946 saw Pino make substantial additions to his collection of costumes.

"Now when it comes to work, thievery, I need a whole different set depending on which operation I'm pulling. We was starting to burn a lotta petes then, see what I mean? Not peeling 'em down like I like, but putting the acetylene torch to her because of the new hard metals they're using. You turn on the torch and sparks start flying. So what I do is go follow this Red Sox umpire. Follow the big suitcase he travels with and grab it. I mean it, I boosted a real suit off the umpire. Instead of wearing his wire mask I used the regular acetylene mask. But I used his protector [chest protector] to keep the sparks from burning me— only one night they burned up the protector because it wasn't fireproof. Mother of God, you never saw such a mess. All that black smoke from the burning mattress stuffing.

"One of my favorite costumes was the frog suit, the rubber suit our Navy frog fellas used in the war. Now the reason I needed one of those was because I got stuck in the holes, know what I mean? When you're up against a great big pete, a walk-in vault, you don't peel her, you burn her. And sometimes you don't burn all of her. What you do is cut a neat round hole in her door and crawl in and take the money. Well, I was putting on weight, and once or twice when I tried crawling in, I got stuck. And once when I got in; it came time to get out and I got stuck again. That was the scariest. I'm trapped in a stranger's goddamn vault, and the sun ain't far from coming up. I tried getting out through the hole frontward and backward, and nothing worked. I'm desperate now. So I take off all my clothes and back up to her. Stick my legs through. The other fellas grab my legs and and lug and tug and finally, plop, I'm through. I musta left three pounds of my ass on her. So I try going on a diet and I don't lose a pound. I try using ladies' corsets and the thing they advertise in the books [trusses and male girdles advertised in comic books], but they make me wider than I already am. Then I see a movie about these frog fellas blowing up a ship from underneath. So I go down to the Navy and boost one of their rubber suits. I had to boost two or three before I found one I could half get into. Then it's so tight I'm walking around like the mechanical man, but it pushes my gut up to my chest. I can crawl in them holes if I have to.

"Now my favorite costume was the tamer's. I take my grandson to see the circus, and afterward we go around to look at the elephants. While he's looking at them, I go boost the tamer's costume, lion tamer. It's gorgeous. All yellow and gold, but I got no place to wear it, know what I mean? There's no place when I'm on the bend, and they'll laugh if I wear it at Sunday dinner. And I don't dare wear it when I'm spotting. When you're spotting, you wanna blend into the neighborhood and become invisible. Look like everyone else around there. There ain't many neighborhoods full of tamers in Boston. So I got nowhere to wear it except at home. After Mary goes to sleep a couple of times, I get up and put it on for a couple of hours."

Pino's most extensive collection of contraband apparel was employed solely for spotting.

"I could be a milkman or a busboy or hotel doorman and two dozen different other people. I liked being a chef because of the early hour of the day they gotta go to work. They come in early to bake the rolls, so I grabbed one a them big puffy hats they wear and the apron and whole shebang. Garbage men is good, too, because people ignore you. When's the last time you looked the garbage man in the eye? You didn't 'cause nobody does. You turn away and ignore the fella as fast you can. So when we go back to opening the tin cans [unlocking Brink's trucks] in the fall, I'm a garbageman a lot.

"Now there's limits to who I'll be," Pino insisted. "I'll go just so far and not a foot beyond. I draw the line on cops and priests. You never see me being a cop or priest.

"You usually only wear the costume when you're spotting on

your feet, when you're walking around the district. When I'm
spotting from the car, I just wear regular workman clothes and
nothing elaborate. I'm a workman on his way to work who happened to drive past. Or a salesman. Salesmen is good, too, because they're always driving past someplace. When I was out
chasing that truck [48] across the field the summer before [sum-
mer of 1945], I had these farmer's overalls and straw hat on because of the fields. I had a fishing pole, too, in case anybody
stopped me. Looking at me driving past, you'd think I was a
farmer. Stopping and talking to me, you could tell I was going
fishing.

"What I'm trying to explain is the father of necessity. You
grab a costume for the work at hand and stay up on things. When
things change, you gotta change along with it. A crook don't live
in a vacuum. He's gotta be more on the ball than anybody if he's
any good. The stock market goes down, and that changes some
big company in Arizona, and maybe that changes some joint in
Boston I been looking at, see what I mean? It's all a part of free
enterprise. Things is gotta move ahead and change, and if you
ain't ready to change with it, you shouldn't be a crook.

"That's why I was so goddamn busy with costumes in '46 and
'47. There was lots of changes. There was lots of crazy things
happening."

Fall began, and Brink's customers became a staple on the
crew's agenda. Pino industriously followed new armored trucks
every morning of the week to ensure the supply of golden eggs.

On the side, Tony and Sandy continued to open the back of armored cars and snitch money bags.

"What the hell you letting all this stuff sit and rot for?"

The department store auxiliary shipping clerk looked around
at the little fat man in glasses wearing a porkpie hat and long
white dust coat and holding a clipboard. "It isn't rotting."

Pino pointed to the stacks of boxes and cartons on the loading
pier. "This batch is all supposed to be shipped out as fast as you
get it, ain't it?"

"It will be, sir."

"Will be ain't good enough, mister. It's supposed to be gone."

"We can't ship unless we have trucks. I'm waiting for trucks."

"Why the hell you waiting on trucks when you're supposed to use the wagons?"

"Wagons?"

"Where the hell you been, fella? The company hired half a dozen wagons to help. Look, there's one waiting now."

Pino yelled and waved. A station wagon driven by Costa pulled up. Big Steve jumped out. The temporary-assistance shipping clerk helped them load the vehicle.

The Christmas Boost was on. All other crew activity was off.

Demand was outdistancing supply during the winter months of early 1947. Many Brink's customers had their safes rifled for a second time. A handful for a third time.

Pino returned to tailing 48 Truck.

"It's nothing but goddamn fields," Tony complained to Richardson and Faherty as the three had dinner at the Egleston Square Diner several doors down from Pino's apartment on Columbus Avenue. "It's straight goddamn road, and nothing but farms and fields on both sides, and I gotta lay flat on my stomach and watch the goddamn truck like I was some kinda Indian."

"What happened to the fishing pole?" Jimma asked, rubbing a neatly cut square of thin, tough roast beef into the black/brown gravy.

"I got the pole right with me, and I got on the farmer's overalls and straw hat, but I can't stand up and be seen," Tony explained. "There ain't a goddamn fishing pond in ten miles. Where the hell was I?"

"On a stretch of road that leads only to Andover," Richardson replied.

"Only my ass," snapped Pino. "There's Route 62 cutoff up a couple of miles, and then there's 125 [route] slantoff."

"Then, Anthony, why not simply go up ahead of both cutoffs, and if the truck doesn't pass, you can work yourself back?" suggested Sandy. "My hunch is she'll pass. I feel she's heading for Andover."

"Me, too," said Faherty without bothering to look up from his plate. "She's heading to Andover."

"I can't do that because there's no goddamn place to hide my red Chevrolet," Tony replied, "and I ain't laying on the ground no more because I got a cold and arthritis. That's why I gotta borrow your car next Friday."

"My car is having a new transmission put in, and I doubt it will be ready Friday," Richardson explained.

"And I don't have one," announced Faherty through his mouthful. "—They came and repossessed it."

"Whaddaya mean repossessed?" demanded Pino.

"I couldn't meet the payments."

"You made over fifty with us in the last eight months alone," Tony asserted.

"And if I made fifty, that means you made twice that much," Jimma countered, "so why don't you shock us all and go buy a new car?"

"I got expenses, for chrissakes," Tony bellowed. "And I don't have to be laying in the field anyway. I'm doing it for you fellas. Now you don't wanna be no help and be selfish, that's your business."

"Try borrowing Mike's Ford," someone suggested.

"I used it once already," said Tony. "And I used Jimmy's a couple of times, too, and the cheap son of a bitch Jazz is holding onto his Pontiac like it had tits."

"What about your aunt's?" was another suggestion.

"Unh-unh. She charges me by the mile."

"Well, there's a stevedore down at work who has a '34 Chrysler he doesn't use much," Richardson recalled. "It runs, but it's a wreck."

"Anything that moves and ain't bright red'll do."

"I'll talk to him."

Pino leaned forward, dug his fork into the mound of cold mashed potatoes and brought a heap forward, dropping a large gob on his napkin-covered belly. "Great food, huh?" he commented as he swallowed.

"Tasty," Faherty, who was blotting up the gravy with an end of bread, answered.

"Great, huh, Sandy?"

"Worst goddamn food I've ever looked at in my life," Richardson said.

"What the hell are you talking about? Look at Jimma, he's cleaned off everything but the enamel on his plate."

"Jimma would eat mud if you put gravy on it," Sandy proclaimed. "Anthony, you have an uncanny know-how to find the filthiest restaurants with the most ungodly food."

"All this joint needs is a good scrubbing, and it'll look real high class."

"And how do you plan to decontaminate what's cooking in the kitchen?"

"What you getting so smart-assed about this joint for?"

"Because, Anthony, it oughta be burned to the ground. And why, might I ask, are you defending this garbage dump?"

" 'Cause I own it!"

"Own it?"

"Yep, I bought every inch of her.* And what a steal. Got it for under two Gs."

"What in the name of God do you need a joint like this for?"

"To have property and make a legitimate dollar. Once I give her a good scrubbing and add some salt and ketchup, they'll be standing in line. Don't worry, Sandy," Pino said in dead earnest, "you're in on it."

"I don't want to own one rotten slat of it."

"Nobody owns any of her but me. But I'm staying open twenty-four hours a day, so you and Jimmy can work here between your other jobs."

By the end of June Tony had discarded his fishing pole and farmer's overalls, emerged from the fields and follows 48 Truck to a textile mill in Shawsheen, Massachusetts, where he saw two guards deliver money sacks. Sandy Richardson followed up and

---

*Records show Pino listed as an employee, not owner or operator of the diner. According to Pino, the lease was drawn in Tony Gaeta's name; originally both he and Gaeta put up $1,000 per man to take over the operation and not long after, he allowed Gaeta to keep the $1,000 he had invested in the Socony service station in return for total control of the diner.

estimated that the delivery contained a payroll of roughly $80,000. Friday after Friday through July, August and September the white armored car rolled on, with Tony on its tail and Sandy several weeks behind. A total of twenty-nine packages was left behind at the three mills in Andover—twenty-nine with an estimated value of $800,000. As the crew took out its burglary equipment and began using the longer nights of September to its best advantage in the immediate Boston area, the estimate for the payroll delivery to Lowell, Massachusetts' Amoskeag Mills was placed at nearly $720,000. By the time the team ran out of safes and picked up their pistols the final stop on 48 Truck, Billerica, was given a value of $500,000.

At 7:45 A.M., Thursday, October 30, 1947, the day before Halloween, Brink's armored car personnel delivered a weekly payroll to the second-floor paymaster's office in the three-story general manager's building of the Sturtevant factory on Damon Street in Hyde Park. The Brink's guards returned to their truck and drove away. Ten minutes later five men wielding sawed-off shotguns and pistols and dressed in either dungarees or work clothes emerged on the stairway leading down from the third floor. Three of the quintet wore Halloween masks, one held a burlap bag up before his face, and the fifth had blackened his face with cork.

Once off the staircase and on the second floor, the bandits went to the telephone switchboard, pointed shotguns at the two female operators and ordered, "Pull all your plugs and get out of there." The pair of terrified women disengaged all switchboard wires. One of the bandits moved down the hallway to act as lookout while the remaining four herded the two phone operators into the main office, where fifteen employees were beginning their day's work. The staff, thinking it a prank, gazed on the masked men with a degree of amusement or annoyance. One of the gunmen expertly brandished his sawed-off shotgun and harshly said, "What do you think this is, a Halloween party?" The employees quickly realized their mistake and raised their hands.

"We don't want to hurt you," the holdup spokesman warned. "All we want is the cabbage. Everyone lie down on the floor."

The office staff complied. Two gunmen stood over them, keeping a watch on the rest of the suite, while the last pair of bandits hurried for the mail room. En route they ran into an employee who had just left his traffic division office.

"Get on the floor," the man was told, "and you won't get hurt. We want the cabbage."

The employee remained upright and immobile, staring at the pair of bandits, one masked by a burlap bag and the other by burnt-cork-darkened features. "We're not fooling, mister," the holdup man warned loudly. "Get on the floor."

The traffic man obeyed, and the two bandits strode into the mail room, where eight persons were at work. They, too, were commanded to lie on the floor. The woman in charge of the mail room also thought the two men were playing a prank. Her opinion changed when a gunman grabbed her roughly by the arm and ordered, "Get down on the floor before you get hurt." The eight-person mail room staff obeyed.

The pair of bandits cut across the mail room, walked up to the unlocked door of the vault room, turned the handle, pulled and entered. The burlap-masked robber trained his gun on the five employees who were in the process of filling pay envelopes and demanded, "Drop what you're doing, and turn around and face the wall."

The staff turned away from three tables laden with money in boxes and bags and moved back to the wall. The bandit whose face was darkened with burnt cork stationed himself near the vault room door, where he could keep watch on the employees lying on the mail room floor, while his companion began stuffing bills into the burlap bag. Vault room personnel were continually warned, "Keep facing the wall. No one is going to get hurt if you keep following orders."

Nine-year-old Joanna Manartto walked up Damon Street, pulled open the main entrance door to the general manager's building and entered. "I went to the plant to get twenty-five cents from Daddy for my lunch and our school Halloween party," the child subsequently explained. "I went to the reception desk where the policeman who is always there gives me candy. The policeman said, 'You wait here, honey, and I'll get your daddy for you.'"

Sixty-two-year-old Sturtevant guard John Cheefer started up the steps for the second floor in search of Joanna's father, Anthony Manartto, a plant employee who worked in the second-floor heating and oil conditioning department. When Cheefer reached the second-floor landing, he was slugged in the chin and knocked down by the fifth bandit, who was standing sentinel there.

"Stay down, mister," the gunman warned. "Don't move and you won't get hurt."

Little Joanna went on to explain what followed: that, as she waited in the ground-floor reception area, "I heard a loud man's voice say, 'Get back there, you.'

"A plain, fat man with a real gun came down the stairs. After him came a man carrying a big bag over his shoulder. The man with the bag and the other one ran outside to a car—a black shiny car. Then four more men all came down, and they were all carrying guns. And they all drove off with the door partly open.

"The third man was also fat. The second man with the bag was thin."

Pino denies that he or the crew had anything to do with the Sturtevant robbery. He lies. Tony, Jazz, Mike and Sandy were all involved. They had crossed the field behind the plant before daybreak, sneaked inside and hidden upstairs until after the delivery was made. Their getaway was clean. The $109,000 stolen made it the largest cash stickup in the Boston area and not too far off the mark of what many considered to be the national cash theft record: $427,000 at gunpoint taken from the Ruble Ice Company of Brooklyn back in 1935.

At approximately nine fifty the next morning, Friday, October 31, Halloween, and while the Boston Police Department was launching the largest manhunt in its history, a Brink's truck made a payroll delivery to the American Sugar Refinery Company in South Boston. Ten minutes after the vehicle departed, Jimma Faherty, Stanley Gusciora and two other extra men Pino had used from time to time approached the building, wearing masks and carrying pistols and shotguns, stuck up a guard standing outside, marched him into the company's 47 Granite Street entrance, missed seeing telephone operator Barbara Green, who was obscured from sight in the switchboard cubbyhole, prodded their captive along a thirty-foot stretch of first-floor hallway and ordered him to make the correct turn. One of the gunmen posted himself at the hallway corner. Barbara Green began dialing the number for Police Station House 6. Three armed robbers burst into the paymaster's office, still holding the guard captive, shouted and yelled and cowed a staff of about thirty female employees into a corner. Two of the gunmen kept the prisoners covered as a third, whose head was covered by a burlap bag with eyeholes, walked directly to the cashier's cage, pointed a gun at paymaster Albert Mamaty, who was making a call, and said, "Get the hell off the phone."

Mamaty faltered. The armed thief pulled the receiver from his hand and hung it up. Barbara Green waited as the phone at Station House 6 kept ringing.

Several burly company workmen walked into the office for paychecks. The gunmen subdued them, but not too easily, and finally locked them into a small room, saying, "What's wrong with you guys, this ain't your money we're taking."

"Where's the box?" the burlap-masked robber at the cashier's cage demanded of paymaster Mamaty. Another of the armed thieves pointed to a metal box containing small envelopes. Burlap Head grabbed it up.

Station House 6 still didn't answer. Barbara Green dialed Devonshire 1212—the police emergency number. An officer answered. She reported a robbery in progress just as the four masked men ran past, rushed out of the building and jumped into a car driven by Jimmy Costa.

The getaway was successful. The total take was $29,000 in cash—of which Tony Pino, who was not present, received a full one-sixth share for having "owned" the score.

CHAPTER TEN

Last of the Eggs

The American Sugar stickup, on the heels of the largest Boston heist in history—Sturtevant—added insult to injury, allowed the press corps to coin the phrase "Halloween Robberies," but did little to intensify what was already the largest manhunt in memory for both the city and the Commonwealth of Massachusetts. State troopers were placed on full alert, and roadblocks ordered for all main highways. In Boston itself the police department unleashed its favorite weapon as it had never been unleashed before—the SP or suspicious person pickup in which any suspect could be apprehended or questioned or detained without ever being officially placed under arrest. Geagan, Richardson, Faherty and Stanley Gusciora (a Pino extra), were all SP'd and questioned and released. Tony, who was almost never SP'd in situations like this, owing to the offices of detective Jim Crowley, was also brought in.

"Mother of God, it was awful," Tony attested. "They grabbed me on the street and took me to the basement at the police station and made me strip down to my skivvies. My skivvies was dirty and had holes in 'em. Them rotten sons of bitches didn't gimme a chance to change into something respectable."

Pino was grilled by Jim Crowley; after swearing he knew nothing of the double robberies, he was let go. Crowley spent extensive time talking to his number one informant, Joe McGinnis— who Pino swears knew nothing of the heists.

On either Thursday or Friday, November 6 or 7—not November 8, as the papers would later print—Crowley arrived in Manhattan, along with Massachusetts State Police Lieutenant James F. Conniff. The pair of out-of-towners huddled with several old friends from the office of Manhattan DA, Frank Hogan, then went over to the Edison Hotel in midtown and planted a handful of electronic listening devices on phones in the rooms occupied by certain underworld money changers. The taps brought results. One of the money changers was seized and taken to the DA's office. After a grilling by Assistant District Attorney William P. Sirigano, the suspect broke down, stated that Sam Granito had come to him several weeks earlier, saying he was going to Boston and "pull a big stickup," that Granito was soliciting the changers' future aid in converting "small bills into large ones." The informer went on to say that Sam had returned from Boston a few days earlier, not only announcing the stickup was a success, but displaying newspaper clippings of the Sturtevant heist as well. Granito's crowing to the money changer allegedly included the names of four accomplices—"Happy Joe" Bellino of New Jersey and a trio from the Boston area—Pino, Costa and Michael Geoghegan, AKA Geagan.

Jim Crowley knew Granito well. He knew that Pino was arrested with Granito during the abortive robbery at Rhodes Brothers on Thanksgiving Day in 1937 (he believed that Sam, not Tony, was the boss of that ill-fated operation), knew that Granito had served time at Charlestown with Pino and Geagan, knew that Granito and Geagan had served on the same Merchant Marine ship during the war. Crowley may have known something else—something Pino found hard to admit: that approximately ten days before Sturtevant, Joe McGinnis may well have seen Granito entering Pino's apartment on Columbus Avenue.

On Sunday, November 9, Joseph A. Bellino, a convicted jewel thief, was arrested in Newark, New Jersey. Crowley and Conniff participated in the Manhattan apprehension of Samuel S. Granito, leaving the seizure of Pino, Costa and Geagan to Boston area police. None of the fifteen eyewitnesses, employees and victims at either Sturtevant or American Sugar could identify Mike, Tony or Jimmy as holdup men. Geagan was released almost immediately. Costa was held for a short time while detectives tried to convince him to testify against his brother-in-law. Pino remained incommunicado and under arrest for thirteen days in lieu of $50,000 bail until a young criminal attorney by the name of Paul T. Smith was able to secure his release on November 22.

Pino never stood trial, but Joseph "Happy Joe" Bellino was extradited and did go before the jury, only to be found innocent. Sammy Granito, who had also been extradited, pleaded not guilty, was identified in court as the gunman whose mask had slipped during the Sturtevant robbery, was convicted for armed theft and sentenced to serve sixteen to twenty years at Massachusetts State Prison.

"I'm telling ya, the man they sent away for doing it didn't do it!" Pino hotly avowed. Nevertheless, Tony, Sandy, Mike and Costa would, in the future, take a small percentage out of many a strictly crew-related haul and set it aside for Sam Granito.

James V. Crowley was publicly and departmentally credited and lauded for breaking the Sturtevant case—Boston's largest armed robbery. The detective remained convinced that Tony had participated in the stickup but apparently didn't believe he was the boss of the job; he would never fully forgive the garrulous pete man for having lied to him, could never fully conceive of Pino possessing the capacity to organize and direct a fair-to-middling criminal operation, let alone the ultimate in a slick, smooth, sophisticated caper—Sturtevant.

Crowley and other investigators would never solve the American Sugar armed robbery, wouldn't be told until after the statute of limitations had run out that Pino, though not actually participating in the heist, had found, cased and "sold" the score to Faherty, Costa, Gusciora and two extra men for a full share of the take.

More surprisingly, the Boston police and officials of the money-moving company, while realizing that Sturtevant and American Sugar had each been held up only minutes after receiving a payroll shipment from Brink's, never connected the two Halloween robberies to a conspiracy involving the following of armored trucks.

Fear of impromptu police surveillance forced a cessation of crew activity, even abbreviated Pino's annual Christmas Boost, but then as the new year of 1948 got under way, Tony, Mike, Sandy, often Jazz and Jimma, quite often Costa and Stanley Gusciora went back to what they did best together. Brink's delivery operations were resurveilled, and although little change in procedure was noted, the robbery ring displayed an antipathy for company customers. New armored trucks were being surveilled—but not those belonging to Brink's. Pino had grown interested in another money-carrying operation in the Boston area.

Had someone been observing the robbers' public styles during this same period—as Pino professed to have feared and the others professedly doubted—little that was unusual would have been seen. Faherty vacillated between working part time as a bartender or stevedore or electrical handyman or janitor, usually could be found sometime during the course of most any winter's night wandering drunkenly about without a topcoat and often without a jacket—occasionally without shoes or a shirt. Geagan appeared religiously at the docks each workday morning, as did Richardson, who in January had traded in his 1946 six-cylinder Oldsmobile and, through the auspices of a finance company, had bought a baby blue brand-new 1948 Oldsmobile 98. Barhopping and semiserious drunks remained Sandy and Mike's favorite nighttime sports. Jazz Maffie continued to rise at noon, leisurely spend the afternoons at his ex officio office—Jimmy O'Keefe's restaurant—making book or socializing, staying on into the evenings and having dinner there with his wife and friends. More often than not Gusciora would drop by Jimmy O'Keefe's during the course of a night; more often than not he'd be accompanied by some attractive young lady-around-town or his latest pal—a smooth-moving, smooth-talking street thief with a pronounced lisp named Specs O'Keefe, who was not any relation to the restaurant's proprietor.

Early February had seen Maffie have an exceptional run of gambling luck, winning $9,000. By the beginning of February he had lost it all—and more. As April neared, the small clothing factory Costa had purchased the year before went bankrupt.

The big news in the spring of 1948 dealt with Pino. Not only had he broken down and bought a new Buick, but he had also taken over as cook at the Egleston Square Diner—replete in a boosted white puffed chef's hat and stolen white surgical gown.

"The food was starting to go to hell," Mike Geagan recalls. "Tony's cooking didn't taste bad when we were in the joint. Anything that isn't rat poison tastes good when you're in the can. On the outside it could croak you. It was croaking us at the diner, but we had to be there. That's where we made our meets—at Tony's diner at night. We wouldn't all come in together. We'd drop in one by one and get the news. Maybe that's one reason Tony kept the joint open all night. We could drop in anytime and get the news.

"The clientele was getting worse than the food, worse than the coffee even," Mike goes on to say. "A man could get badly damaged in there with the element that was coming in. Motorcycle guys and the like. They'd tangle with truck drivers who were steady customers. All our friends who were crooks stopped coming in there because of the blood. They called it the Bucket of Blood.

"The only one who could keep order was Mary. I was sitting next to her at the counter when a punk gave her some lip and—*powee*—her fist shot past me and knocked the chump cockeyed."

Pino assessed the situation differently. "I was having trouble with cooks, that's all. They kept passing out on me—from drink, not the smell of my food. I was cooking up the best pot of stew in town, and the coffee wasn't as bad as people was saying. And them motorcycle fellas wasn't so bad after you trained 'em. I kept a two-by-four under the counter, and after a few weeks they behaved.

"Now one a them motorcycle fellas give me one helluva scare," Tony admitted. "I'm in there all alone behind the counter, and I hear him outside gunning his motorcycle and waking up the world. It's maybe three in the morning. I only see his back, and when he comes in and up to the counter where I am, he has his head down. All I see is his leather back. Now he raises up his head and goes *Grrrr*. Mother of God, I damned near jumped through the roof. Not from the *Grrr*, see what I mean?

Grrr don't frighten nobody. What scared hell outta me was the gorilla face he's wearing. He's got on one of these rubber masks that was starting to be sold then. Rubber masks that go right over the head and make you look like a gorilla. I thought a goddamn gorilla had come up to me for a cup of coffee. It was gruesome. I never saw anything like it before.''

Mary Fryer, her four-year-old grandson and Tony Pino set out on a June trip. Their first stop was Atlantic City.

"So I'm walking with Mary and my grandchild down that boardwalk there,'' Tony related, "and we see all these penny arcades where they gyp you. So we go in and take a look. Now one of the first things I spot are those masks like the motorcycle kid scared me with. Hideous-looking rubber items. And they didn't only have gorillas you could pull down over your face, they had everybody—Chinese and Boris Karloff, too. So while Mary and my grandchild are looking in the other direction, *pfft*, I boost two or three. Stuff 'em under my coat. Every arcade we go to the next day I boost a coupla more.

"Now we go on down to Baltimore, and Mary and me get married [June, 1948]. When we go out to celebrate, I see more of them masks in the novelty stores. So I grab 'em.''

Brink's had provided many a golden egg for the robbery crew over the previous two years. Five delivery routes had been followed from beginning to end, two more partially and, as a result, according to Pino's estimate, individual safecracks and stickups of customers serviced by the armored money movers had netted the thieves between $600,000 and $700,000—exclusive of Sturtevant [$109,000] and American Sugar [$29,000]—and another $350,000 to $400,000 from the pilferage of many sacks from parked trucks.*

*These are strictly Pino's assessments. Richardson and Maffie, while conceding the crew robbed Brink's customers during this period, would give no further details. Costa, who was privy to most every side deal made by Tony, believes the $350,000 to $400,000 from pilferage is 50 percent too high, confirms that the other estimates, to his memory, are accurate

Pino further stated that approximately seventy safe thefts and stickups were perpetrated against approximately forty-five different Brink's customers but would name only a dozen of these robbery victims.

By the time the winter thieving season of 1948 got under way, there was still many a lucrative score left on the Brink's routes. A few involved safecracking. The balance required armed robbery.

Not that the thieves were averse to a stickup, if potential returns warranted it. But many of the regular crew members felt the robbery team had run out its string of luck with Brink's, opined that sooner or later the police and company officials would have to realize what had been occurring—might have already done so—and were surreptitiously watching both the trucks and customers' premises. If risks were to be taken, let them be taken elsewhere. Pino, for example, had tailed armored cars belonging to another money carrier in the Boston area, had spotted an estimated $3,000,000 in betting receipts being driven away from a local racetrack in a private car occupied by only two men.

Tony's contention that every available golden egg be plucked from the nest before Brink's was finally abandoned was overridden in a late September meet at his apartment. He kept sniping away in the weeks that followed, buttonholing fellow crew members at every opportunity to press for a continuation with Brink's. In mid-October an accommodation was worked out. The crew would kill the duck that laid the golden eggs forever. They voted to pull a score that would force Brink's to change almost every aspect of their operation and, therefore, discourage Pino, for all time, from ever venturing near the company again. They agreed to arm-rob 48 Truck of the estimated $2,000,000 in packages as it loaded up at the Chamber of Commerce building.

Brink's Incorporated would make no comments on whether one dollar was stolen from parked trucks or the premises of customers during this period. Nor would they say how many customers they had in the Boston and northern New England area where Pino claims the bulk of the robberies occurred.

The Boston Police Department, while providing no actual records, confirms that at least eight of the robbery victims named by Pino had indeed been robbed. Seven of the thefts were believed to be unsolved. An arrest was made on the eighth, but there was no conviction.

CHAPTER ELEVEN

48 Truck

Suspended in darkness, noted by heavy haze, a pair of shimmering beams descended, enlarged and intensified and slowed, came to a stop, after several seconds went off. Maffie waited for the clanking metal, then stepped out of the alcove. He could see the cab of the Brink's armored truck and departing driver's silhouette in the glare of light splashing out through the glass doors two blocks up Federal Street. Before crossing over to be on the same side of the street as the parked truck, Jazz watched the man enter the Chamber of Commerce building. He waited in the doorway for three or four minutes, saw a Brink's guard carrying what looked like a rifle emerge into the slight splash of light and post himself—gun raised across his chest—beside the truck. Maffie adjusted his workman's cap and jacket, stepped out onto the sidewalk and started walking toward the sentinel.

"It was five thirty or six [A.M.], and I'm walking at the guy," Maffie relates. "He stood there with his gun, and I'm walking toward him dressed up like a *jabone* truck driver. I walked straight at him, and he don't give me a burn. I see two more hacks inside the lobby pushing the money cart for the doors, and they don't give me a burn either. Nobody bothered with me. I kept walking. I walked right past the guy and his rifle, and he kept on acting like I wasn't there.

"So I keep going up Federal to where Tony Pino's hiding. Tony Pino's been watching this whole thing because it's his goddamn crazy idea. When I got to where Tony Pino was, he said, 'What'd he do?'

" 'Oh,' I said, 'he shot me with his gun.'

"Tony Pino got all excited and said, 'Where'd he get you? Where'd he get you? I didn't hear no shots. We better get outta here!'

"What I wanted to say was he shot me three times and killed me with a silencer, but you can't do things like that with Tony Pino. His sense of humor went down with the *Titanic*.

"Anyway, we knew the hack outside would be easy to grab, but we knew that anyway. I watched him the year before. What I found out walking down the street was the hacks inside were pushing the money truck off the elevator sooner than we expected."

Other things that had been observed the year before were noted again a week later as the spotting continued. A week after that the final plan was worked out.

Pino would drive the paneled flower truck; drop Maffie off at the Federal Street corner above the Chamber of Commerce building; continue on and turn down Congress Street; drop Richardson, Geagan and Faherty a block below the Chamber of Commerce; swing around and turn into Federal Street and back into an alley two blocks below the Chamber of Commerce; park and let Gusciora off. 48 Truck had maintained an immaculate schedule in the previous weeks of casing and was expected to do so again. Gusciora, costumed as a window washer, would already be walking up Federal Street when 48 Truck turned in, starting for the Chamber of Commerce building on the near sidewalk. On seeing 48 Truck's headlights, Maffie would step into Federal Street, starting down for the Chamber of Commerce doors on the far sidewalk. Richardson, Geagan and Faherty would be crossing the Congress Street parking lot, stationing themselves in the darkness so they could see through the glass door and up the lobby to the elevators. By the time 48 Truck had parked and the driver and gun-toting guard got out and the driver went into the building Maffie and Gus would be only about ten yards from the truck. Once Richardson, Geagan and Faherty saw the driver enter the elevator, they would move up near the doors and wait. Gusciora would pass the truck, wheel around and disarm the rifle-carrying guard. If there was any trouble in the subduing, Maffie, who would be crossing the street behind the truck, could lend a hand. Gusciora would handcuff the guard and slap tape over his mouth. On seeing Maffie signal through the far glass door, Richardson, Geagan and Faherty would enter the Congress Street end of the lobby and hurry past the elevators, descending the stairs just beyond the elevator. When the driver and guard, who had been upstairs, got off the elevator and pushed the cart of packages past the stairwell, Faherty, Geagan and Richardson would move in from behind and capture the pair. Sandy would push the cart on out through the door while Geagan assisted Faherty with taping the prisoner's mouth and applying handcuffs. Once Pino saw Sandy emerge with the cart, he would drive hell-bent for leather up the street and pull in in front of the glass doors. Maffie would help Sandy load while Gusciora led the captive sidewalk guard into the lobby and turned him over to Faherty. By this time Geagan would be on his way out to help with the loading. Faherty would take the third captive down to the bottom of the stairwell and handcuff him to the railing to which the other two Brink's truckmen were handcuffed. Gus would go out and help Mike, Jazz and Sandy. By the time Faherty got outside the loading would be finished. He would get on the truck with the others, and Tony would make the getaway.

Orders went out for all crewmen to desist from any type of crime and prepare their alibis. In traditional prescore procedure, not even Pino would go near the Chamber of Commerce building until the night of the strike. 48 Truck would be taken in fourteen days—Friday, December 10—at the onset of Pino's usually sacrosanct Christmas Boost season.

The Christmas Boost officially began on Monday morning, December 6, 1948, as Big Steve and Tony drove away from Boston. There was no particular reason for their selecting their first target, other than that Pino happened to be driving through Arlington en route to the first scheduled shoplifting site in Lincoln, Massachusetts. As a matter of fact, there was every reason for the pair of holiday boosters not to stop in Arlington, particularly not at the R. W. Shattuck Company. They had pilfered the premises so many times in the past it was almost a joke. As a matter of fact, they laughed when they saw the Shattuck storefront come into view. With a touch of evil glee, they decided what better place to launch their Yule thievery season.

Pino pulled to the curb, left the motor running. Big Steve got out, walked into Shattuck's. Nothing of value was easily accessible. Rather than leave empty-handed, the booster slipped a package containing one dozen golf balls under his coat and started out. Tony waited until his partner was back in the car, released the emergency brake and shifted gears. Before he could accelerate, policemen blocked his way. Tony swore he didn't know Big Steve, that the stranger must have climbed into the wrong car. Big Steve swore he didn't know Pino. At the December 8 hearing in the Third District Court of Eastern Middlesex, Tony was charged with stealing a dozen golf balls of value less than one hundred dollars. He pleaded not guilty. The Court convicted him of larceny and on December 24, 1948, the Court passed sentence of one year's imprisonment in the House of Correction. The decision was immediately appealed. Tony's lawyer was optimistic, believed the jail sentence could be reduced to a probation. Pino wasn't too sure, but at least he was free until a verdict was handed up.

The time, to the best of everyone's knowledge, was shortly after 5:15 A.M. the first Friday in January—Friday, January 7, 1949.

Pino dropped Geagan, Richardson and Faherty beyond the Chamber of Commerce building, continued down Congress Street, took a right, then after traveling a short block, pulled another right into and up Federal Street, stopped, backed up into the alleyway, cut the engine, let Gusciora out. Neither Tony nor any other crew member had been in the area since the last Friday in November, but that didn't strike anyone as unusual. In the past, after final casing, the robbery crew had stayed away from certain targets as long as six weeks before moving in to score.

Gusciora, window washer's bucket in hand, moved down the far sidewalk.

"The timing's gotta be perfect, see what I mean?" said Pino.

The Kid's [Gusciora] gotta be on the street when the truck starts down [Federal Street] or else the driver and guard'll get suspicious. Okay, so the Kid's moving up the street on the Chamber of Commerce side, and way up past Brink's [Chamber of Commerce building] I see a fella pass under a streetlight and hope to God it's Jazz.

"Like I told ya, it's dark out, but from the slow goddamn way he's moving I convince myself it can't be anyone but Jazz. Now I got two of 'em moving slow. And only one of 'em's supposed to be on the street. Jazz don't make his move till after the truck gets parked. He comes out after the driver goes in. So he ain't supposed to be where he is, and Gus's getting down too close. He's only supposed to walk so far and wait in a goddamn doorway. And then Gus stops altogether. He's standing on the goddamn street too close, and he's stopped. Then it hits me. The truck ain't arriving like it should. The goddamn truck's late. Oh, Jesus.

"I tell myself maybe they changed the schedule some, see? We ain't been around this joint for a month. But that shouldn't make no difference. I been watching this goddamn truck three years, and it splits the second right in half. It ain't never not been on time.

"So now I'm counting seconds by the beat in my throat 'cause that's where my heart jumped up to—my throat. It's stuck up there choking me. I'm trying to wave at Gus to keep going because that's what he's supposed to do if things get screwed up. He's supposed to keep going. Not a goddamn thing's right, including Jazz—he's still out there, and the goddamn guy is standing still, too.

"Now I'm waving at both of them to get outta there. I damn near honk the horn. Now I see Jazz start walking down the street, and I almost faint. If the fellas out back [Richardson, Geagan and Faherty] see him pass the door, they might start moving in. They can see right through to Federal from Congress. If the truck shows up now, they're going to get us all out of position. The driver's gonna see people all the hell over the place who shouldn't be there, and even if he don't notice nothing, they're outta position for what they gotta do.

"Now I look down there and see the worst: Jazz's stopped

and Gus had started to move. Jazz is just standing a half a block from Brink's. Now the goddamn Kid does the same thing. He stops a half a block up on the other side. The goddamn truck comes along right now and sees that, and it's curtains.

"That does it. I start up the floral truck and head down for Brink's. I'm praying the truck don't come by and spot me. They never seen the floral truck around here. But once I pass, Jazz and Gus see me, and they know what it means. They start walking again. Jazz is walking the right way for a change—away from the joint.

"I pick up all the fellas where I'm supposed to get them if things don't come off. We're all in the truck saying to one another what the hell's happening? What the hell's gone wrong? Do you think somebody spotted us? Do you think somebody tipped them? Why the hell didn't the truck show up?"

The reason was that Brink's Incorporated had moved—as a matter of fact, had moved on December 8, 1948, the same day Pino and Big Steve were arraigned for the theft of a dozen golf balls.

BOOK THREE

THE GOLDEN

DUCK

CHAPTER TWELVE

North Terminal Garage

Copps Hill is a place of history. Sloping upward from pier dotted waters to an altitude of fifty to fifty-two feet at old Boston's northernmost extremity, it commands a fine view of the Charles and Mystic rivers to the north and west. Along the hill's northern crown is the spot where, in 1630, John Winthrop and his Puritan followers from plague-stricken Charlestown across the river landed their longboats and stepped ashore to begin colonization. Over the same waters traveled by Winthrop, but in an opposite direction and 145 years later, on April 18, 1775, Paul Revere was rowed by two colonists to land and a horse.

A prerevolutionary burial ground, shaded by venerable elms, where many of America's first patriots were laid to rest under slate markers, is settled on the crest of Copps Hill. Many of the headstones bear shot marks from British muskets which used them for target practice during the English siege of the city. Beneath the cemetery segments of tunnels that formed the fabled Underground Railroad are believed still to exist.

Down the southern slope, below the burial ground, Old North Church punctuates the sky, its reconstructed steeple rising like a cautionary finger above an industrial and residential complex. Moving clockwise from Old North, other vestiges of early America are evident among the four- and five-story frame dwellings that line a labyrinth of thin, often abrupt colonial streets.

151

The cloistered community, unwelcoming to outsiders with no business there, is called Little Italy.

Hull Street descends northwest from the burial ground to the crown, a narrow avenue that retains a semblance of Federal and revolutionary atmosphere in the area to its right, ends at a two-way Commercial Street which runs parallel to the river. Snowhill Street rises from the eastern base of the hill, ascends in a slightly southern direction, passes the burial ground and intersects Hull Street, veers further south in its descent to Little Italy, stops at another narrow prerevolutionary avenue, a bottomland thoroughfare called Prince Street, which lies generally parallel to Hull Street on the east.

Copps Hill originally may have been fifty-seven to fifty-nine feet high. During the late 1700s the slopes and crest were shaved somewhat to provide earth for the construction of a street around the hill's eastern and northern crown. In 1806 work began on filling in Mill Pond, which lay to the west of Copps Hill and to the east of Beacon Hill. When the reclamation was completed five years later, Beacon Hill had been lowered by 111 feet. Copps Hill also contributed to the pond fill, went on giving up soil. By 1840 the crest was seven feet lower, but a far greater loss was suffered by one of the sharper faces. Beginning at the promontory intersection of Hull and Snowhill streets, all the rise along the northern side of Snowhill down to Prince Street and all the rise immediately to the west along Hull Street down to Commercial Street had been sliced away, leaving a sheer perpendicular drop of forty to forty-five feet near the summit. What was left on the floor below comprised a long stretch of level ground which formed a rectangle between parallel Hull and Prince Streets and intersecting Commercial Street to the north and ended in a canyonesque triangle as Snowhill Street veered southwesterly between Hull and Prince streets at the opposite end. It was to the rectangular section of the tract, a location not far from where John Winthrop and his colonizers debarked to found the city in 1630, that Tony Pino, in January, 1949, would eventually and circuitously find his way.

"Now we're driving away [from 80 Federal Street], not knowing what's what," Pino related. "We got our fears aroused. That truck [48 Truck] has been arriving religiously every Friday, and now it don't. The crew's saying, 'You think we got spotted? You think we got tipped? You think they found out and are coming to arrest us?'

"Now I'm back at the diner, uneasy. I'm making the coffee and figuring if Brink's smelled us out and missed us at Federal Street, I'm gonna have visitors. But what can they do, see what I mean? They can't dump you in the can for harboring criminal thoughts. No visitors show up, and I start to concentrate. If they didn't pick us up in the truck and they didn't come to arrest us after, then maybe they don't know nothing about nothing. But where the hell's the [48] truck?

"I'm going mentally cuckoo. I'm not interested in nothing only this unsolved mystery, because I wanna know what happened here. This is a fortune gone down the drain—a million and a half bucks going down.

"I go into town. I go over at eight or nine (A.M.) The place is swarming. I see armored trucks up and down Federal Street like there always is, but not one of 'em belongs to Brink's. These are trucks from other companies that haul payrolls.

"Okay, now I scram outta there. That's a bad part of the country. Lotsa cops is always around. Lotsa Pinkerton fellas live down there, too. I'm a well-known criminal personality. I can't afford being seen here.

"I drive over to Cambridge, to where they got their garages— the joint I went into to make all the keys to their trucks. I take one look, and it hits me. There ain't a goddamn truck anywhere. The lousy sons of bitches snuck off in the night and didn't leave no forwarding address.

"So I know we're in the clear, see? People don't pack and move away because a bunch of thieves is after them. They move to better themselves, and that's got me concerned. Wherever they've gone can be a tougher joint to crack. That truck [48] can get itself loaded up in a goddamn castle behind a ditch instead of out in front like on Federal Street. For all you know, they may even start switching the loads around. Instead of putting on forty-eight packages, maybe they'll put on two. I got a million and a half bucks involved with this company. I can't afford no changes.

"So I gotta find out where they snuck off to. I gotta find out fast before the fellas get fed up and kiss it off, but that don't mean I can pick up the phone and call Mr. Brink's up and say, 'Hey, this is Ireland and you won the sweepstakes. Where the hell you expect me to send the money?' You don't do things like that because what if they got one of them new kind of electric phone gadgets that can check your voice?"

Pino's best recollection is of spending the weekend simultaneously cooking at the diner, worrying about the strategy to counteract his golf ball conviction and devising a plan of action for locating the missing Brink's Incorporated. On Monday, January 9, he was able to hire a full-time chef. Tuesday saw his lawyer appeal, for the second time, the judgment for conviction of the theft.

Either Wednesday or Thursday afternoon, January 11 or 12, Tony drove to a small manufacturing plant not far from Mattapan. In days gone by he had seen a Brink's truck drop off a package here, and he knew that this was the last delivery of the day. Tony's professed strategy depended on the armored car company's not having changed any of its procedures. If the plant near Mattapan was still the last location on the delivery route, Pino need only tail the departing truck, which he hoped would lead him to Brink's new garage. Once the garage had been found, he need only return there early in the morning and follow any truck. Any truck would be going to pick up a payload at the new offices.

"So I'm out near Mattapan, and you show up right on schedule like you always do," Pino related. "Now I'm on your tail. I tail you back to Boston. I stay maybe fifty or sixty feet behind, and you're heading toward North End. I ain't never seen you come this way before. Okay, we're on North Washington. Shadow's coming around a corner. I slow and look out my window. I see another truck [Brink's] sitting there in a gas station. I'm turning onto Commercial Street, and I see another truck pulling out. I know I gotcha. I know the garage's gotta be right around here somewhere.

"Okay, you're up ahead, and you slow it down. I slow it down. You're right in front of this big garage on Commercial. I think that's where you're going, only I get tricked. You go to the end of the garage and pull a right. I'm back about thirty feet, so I speed it up and take a right, too. You vanished. The road [Hull Street] goes right up the hill, and there's nothing on it. I keep going up. I'm on the side of that building, see? That garage building [whose doors he had just passed on Commercial Street]. And the building's built right into the hill [Hull Street side]. I see a big garage door on the second floor and another up on the top [third and last level]. I look in 'em both and can't see much, but I figure you are in one or the other.

"I pull right past the building and slow down near the cemetery [Copps Hill burying ground at the intersection of Hull and Snowhill streets]. I can see down the hill from there. I'm looking in my mirror and see another truck [Brink's] coming up. It turns in the first door. Now I know you're on the second floor. I get outta there and go home."

North Terminal Garage was the registered name for the three-story, 54-foot-high, concrete structure occupying the northeast end of the excavation below Copps Hill. The front of the building in which Pino now believed Brink's housed its armored trucks was generally considered to be on Commercial Street—a two-lane avenue running in a northwesterly direction at this point. The northeastern wall of North Terminal Garage was, as Tony noted, erected flush against the old hill slice and ascending Hull Street. The lower garage door on Hull definitely led into the second floor of North Terminal; the second door, nearer the hill-crest, offered egress to the third and top floor. The opposite side of the building stood on level bottom ground, rose up parallel to narrow Prince Street. Both Prince and Hull were one-way thoroughfares going in the same direction—from northeast to southwest away from Commercial Street. The rear of the square concrete building faced onto an asphalt-covered, acute-angled, triangular playground. The longest side of the tract was walled by the sheer Copps Hill cut which apexed at the Hull/Snowhill streets intersection, then descended along Snowhill to the Prince Street intersection. The Prince Street side of the playground was several feet below sidewalk level and protected with a metal chain-link fence. A cluster of small tenement buildings stood in the Snowhill/Prince Street corner of the triangular and paved expanses.

In a fashion, North Terminal Garage was an interloper in a predominantly residential sector of North End. Not that other businesses weren't nearby. Going left on Commercial Street from the front of the garage, the trucks took only two short blocks to be at the merging intersection of busy Washington Street, as well as beneath the overpass for the Charlestown Bridge. On the other side of Washington, Commercial became Causeway Street, and a causeway bearing Route 1 ran overhead. On ground level, two blocks west of Washington Street and between rows of steel support girders, was the common entrance to both North Station and the Boston Garden. Across overpass-covered Causeway Street from the indoor sports arena/railway terminal was an almost uninterrupted line of shops and restaurants.

Leaving North Terminal Garage and following Commercial Street to the right, around the seaward northern base of Copps Hill and on to where the thoroughfare became Atlantic Avenue, one would encounter first a police station, then a mounting number of piers, waterfront warehouses, industrial buildings and dockside restaurants.

The panorama directly beyond the Commercial Street doors of the garage building was more picturesque and remote. A wide expanse of well-tended grassland lay between the thoroughfare and shoreline fronting the Charles River. Rising up to the left was the Charlestown Bridge. In easy viewing distance across the river was Charlestown.

To the rear of the triangular playground behind North Terminal, via either Hull Street up over the crest of Copps Hill or Prince Street around the southwestern crown, lay a maze of narrow prerevolutionary avenues—some short, some twisting, some intersecting others at odd angles. Compressed tightly together along every sidewalk of every street on these inland slopes and aprons were four- and five- and six-story apartment houses, many dating back to revolutionary days, many poor or adequate or excellent facsimiles of the Federal style, almost all bearing the scars of rigorous wear.

At the lower end of Prince Street, approximately four short blocks south of the playground side of North Terminal Garage and along the building-jammed eastern crown of the hill, ran the Broadway of Little Italy: Hanover Street.

It was just off of Hanover, probably near the corner of Tileston Street that Pino parked his car when he returned that night to North End.

"Okay, I get out and start walking," Pino related. "It's about seven fifteen at night, and all the families is eating their spaghetti dinner. Even if they ain't, it don't matter. I'm dressed like a truck driver, and I know this neighborhood good. This is where my brother-in-law [Costa] comes from. Lots of other friends come from here, too. Italian friends. It's all Italian around here. I'm dressed like an Italian truck driver, so what the hell.

"I go up on the hill [Copps Hill], see? You can walk from one end of that hill to the other in four minutes, so it isn't much of a climb. It's dark as hell all over. All these streets is narrow as hell because Paul Revere built 'em. He forgot about the lights. That's why they're the best crooking streets in the world.

"Let me tell you about them streets and this neighborhood. Remember that Frenchman fella, Pepper k'Moka? Well, you go see that movie of his [*i.e.*, Pepe Le Moko in *Algiers*]. You take all the white houses in that town of his [Algiers] and paint 'em green or yellow or red, and that's what you got right here. A stranger ain't got a chance around here, and neighbors ain't gonna help you much. A thief could hide in here five years and never get pinched. A lot have. The cops'uv been looking for the bookie joint back of Prince for ten years and never found it. The biggest bookie joint in the state.

"Okay, we're up the top of the hill. Hull and Snowhill. And there's buildings all around, but it's dark as hell. It's darker where I am 'cause the cemetery's right behind me. People got lights on in their apartments, but that don't ruin nothing. The streets stay like they should—dark.

"Now I cross Snowhill and get over on Hull. On the right side of Hull, only we should be on the left side 'cause that's where the garage is. I go over to the left side. Get on the sidewalk there. Before you get to the garage, there's this gate, brick gate—over on the left, too. I go to the gate and give her a burn. I see these steps, and then I see a terrace and more steps and

another terrace. Whatcha got here is a big staircase with three
terraces going down to the park [playground to the rear of garage
building between the base of the hill cut and Prince Street]. They
go way the hell down because it's a helluva drop. You fall off
here, and it's fifty feet before you hit bottom.

"I don't go down to the terrace, see? I see lights come out
from the back of the garage building. Up on the second or third
floor. This whole building's windows. Windows run all the way
across it. Two and three stories of windows, and every one covered by them heavy wire grates. 'Cause of the angle up here, I
can't see what window is lit up back there. It's a couple of them,
though.

"Okay, so this terrace goes down to the park in the corner; it's
right in the corner between the cliff and the building. I look up at
the roof. It's an easy climb. Maybe only eight feet. This side of
the garage is buried in the hill, so it sticks up eight feet over it.

"Now, I'm going down the hill [on Hull Street]. I get up to the
first door [top level of garage building]. It's wide open, and I
don't believe what I see inside. They got the bare light bulbs
burning in there, and not too many of 'em so it's kinda dim, but
what I see is armored trucks. Only they ain't Brink's trucks.
They look black 'cause of the poor light. But if they were white,
I woulda known it. 'Mother of God,' I tell myself, 'I got two
goddamn money companies parking trucks in this place.' I make
a mental note to myself to come back and steal all their keys and
keep going down the hill.

"Okay, I'm coming up on that second door [the lower of the
two doors through which he had seen two Brink's trucks enter
earlier in the day]. I go past and give her the peek. That light's as
rotten as upstairs, but I can see trucks, okay, only they ain't armored or white. They got ordinary trucks, and some are parked
in there, but nothing from Brink's. I can see way across the garage. There's a big truck door in the back that's closed. I figure
it's probably a metal slide door. I gotta hunch that's where
Brink's hides her trucks, but I don't do no stopping.

"I keep going down to the corner [where Hull meets and ends
at Commercial] and keep right going across into the park [grassy
tract of land beyond Commercial leading down the bank of the

Charles River]. I'm circling, see? I circle around out into that
Park and keep the peek on the garage door they got there in front
[ground level on Commercial]. The doors open a little, and I see
a guy sitting right inside at a desk. It's dark behind him 'cause all
they got is one or two of them twenty-five-watt bulbs burning.
But I can see a couple of trucks and cars parked between them
pillars. Every floor I looked into so far has them cement pillars
holding up the roof. You gotta park between 'em. So I'm looking
at what's parked between 'em down there, and it ain't nothing
that belongs to Brink's. I give a peek to all them windows upstairs, too. The ones covered by the wire. There ain't no light in
none of 'em. The joint's a morgue.

"Now I do another thing. I take a look up Commercial. Under
the bridge [elevated approach], 'cause that's where the Garden
is. There's a lotta traffic, but none of it's coming this way. All
them cars are going on the bridge or back over to Hanover Street
to eat at them good Italian restaurants. Nobody's coming this
way. Only one or two cars come this way. That's good. This territory's empty as death."

Pino angled forward, crossed Commercial Street, took to the
sidewalk beyond the partially open garage door, came to the end
of the building and turned left into Prince Street. The narrow
one-way avenue struck him as being narrower than Hull Street,
possibly because it was sparingly lit. The somber wall of North
Terminal with its three tiers of grate-fronted darkened windows
rose to his left.

A façade of wood or brick apartment houses pressed from the
opposite side of the street, stretched as far as the eye could see
before slanting around to the right. One streetlight stood in front
of a tenement building door a good distance from the Commercial Street corner, a second much farther down on the garage
side. Both lamps were dim, and a degree of additional illumination spilling out of apartment windows didn't increase visibility
to any appreciable extent. The brick and spottily asphalt-covered street and the two thin bordering sidewalks was a shadowy
place. With the exception of a pair of cars parked along the
right-hand curb, it was a desolate place as well.

Tony ambled forward, keeping to the sidewalk adjacent to the garage. Not far from the corner he passed a pair of closed doors—one metal and large and apparently meant for vehicles. The other was also metal and smaller.

"It was a people door that second one," he explained. "I don't bother with either one of 'em. I keep going. I ain't seen a goddamn person on the street yet. And I ain't seen a car driving by neither. The only way you know people live around here is because you see lights in their windows and hear 'em talking every now and then.

"Okay, I keep going along the building. It's as long as a goddamn football field.* Now I'm getting up near the end of her, and I spot this old lady up ahead. I know she's old 'cause she's kinda bent over and ain't carrying nothing. She heads into that little store up there. Over to the right there's this alley [Lafayette Street], and on the corner there's some dinky little candy store. I can see that now 'cause I'm closer. That's where the old lady goes.

"Now I see the second door. Maybe ten feet from the end of the building. I see her and I gotta stop, see? She's a people door and she's metal and pasted right on her is the signal [Brink's symbol: a shield]. Up on top of the door is the address, 165, but right there on the signal it says Brink's and eighteen something. Whenever it went into business.

"I can't take my eyes off that door. I gotta think, too. I know Brink's is the chintz of the world. They ain't gonna spring for no goddamn fancy signal like this unless there's a reason. I can't figure out what the reason is.

"I ain't gonna play with metal doors, see? I didn't bring my picking tools along, and even if I had some, I'm not touching that door. It's probably wired straight to J. Edgar Hoover's desk in Washington."

Pino walked a few steps, paused until the little old lady left Peppy's candy shop and started back up the street, then continued to the end of the building. Light spilled down into the playground from the grate-covered windows in the rear of the

---

*Not exactly—the measurement for the Prince Street side was 255 feet, the Hull Street side 312 feet, playground side 266 feet and the Commercial Street side was 231 feet.

garage structure. He saw two young boys descending the stepped terraces at the Hull Street end of the paved recreational expanse.

Tony loped forward along the metal fence siding the playground without looking back, passed the two apartment houses at the end of the block, turned left onto Snowhill Street and started climbing the hill. Once he was beyond several more apartment dwellings, his view of the back of North Terminal Garage was obstructed by a high brick wall. Back atop the promontory at the Snowhill/Hull Street intersection he still couldn't find a vantage point which offered a good view of the illuminated grate-covered windows.

Tony stepped back and looked down Snowhill Street. No one could be seen. He hurried around a Hull Street gate leading to the top terrace, scurried across, clambered onto the brick wall stretching the length of Snowhill and, on his hands and knees, started crawling. Five windows on the second tier of the garage, stretching in a line from near the Prince Street end of the building to a point midway into the playground, were illuminated. One or two people could be seen moving about inside. Tony was still too far above the second level to have a rewarding observation angle. He crawled farther down the wall top. A man in a white shirt was sitting at a desk behind the third window from the right. Tony crawled a little farther. Something was going on in the last window to the right, but he still couldn't see exactly what. He crawled farther. Then farther still.

"Mother of God, it was a glory. Here's a Brink's guy with his arms full of packages, and where'd you think he's taking them? He carries them right into the vault. I spent all them years over at Congress trying everything to peek in their pete, and now by climbing on some rotten fence I'm staring her right in the face. The vault's standing wide open, and this fella's carrying money into her."

And as Tony Pino had said long ago on Congress Street: "If you can see a safe face to face, you can crack her."

CHAPTER THIRTEEN

The Twenty-Pound Mask

Seven grate-covered windows were illuminated, not five, as had been seen several nights before. All were in a row along the second floor at the rear of North Terminal Garage, began at the Prince Street corner and stretched to the middle of the concrete building, to a point midway above the playground as well.

Shortly before 6 P.M. the light in the narrowest of the seven windows, a high, thin one closest to Prince Street, went off. Moments later a man wearing the uniform jacket of a Brink's guard emerged from the ground-level metal door at 165 Prince, the door closest to the playground end of the weather-stained structure. Pino rose from the doorway down the street in which he had been sitting, tucked the lunch pail under his arm, crossed to the opposite sidewalk, rounded the corner, trudged up to the top of Snowhill Street, turned left, passed through the roofless brick gate, descended to the third and lowest and widest terrace, seated himself up against the Snowhill Street retaining wall, took out and began eating a sandwich, kept his eyes on the line of six lit grate-fronted windows.

At approximately 6:45 P.M. the light in the window farthest to the right, the one almost directly in the middle of the building, went dark. The head of a man could be seen moving across two larger windows to the left. It disappeared. Lights went off in the

162

three windows closest to Prince Street, leaving only two windows in front of which the man had passed illuminated.

Pino jammed the partially consumed sandwich into the pail, scrambled to his feet, hurried across the terrace, bounded up the steps and across the middle terrace and up the final staircase to the topmost terrace. His intention was to hurry back down Snowhill and see who left the building through which of the two doors on Prince Street. The upper terrace led directly onto Hull Street, and no sooner did he reach the abutting sidewalk when headlight beams turning out from the second-level garage doors, blinded him. He jumped back behind the building corner. The car passed. The man seated beside the driver wore a cap with which Pino was familiar—the standard hard-beaked uniform cap of Brink's armored car personnel.

He watched the car take a left onto Snowhill, then descend from sight between a line of low apartment houses and the burying ground's ancient retaining wall. He walked a few steps farther, turned right, strode down Copps Hill on Snowhill Street. When Snowhill ended at Prince, he crossed over to the far sidewalk, sat in the recessed doorway he had used an hour earlier, gazed off beyond the street and playground and kept his eyes fixed on the two remaining lit windows in the rear of the building—particularly the one to the right, the one behind which he had seen the open vault several nights earlier.

The silhouetted form of a man appeared up the block, a man in a cap. Pino could not mistake the outline of this uniform hat either. It was a foot patrolman turning into Prince from Commercial Street. The officer meandered forward, checked the first two doors of the garage building and continued on as Tony stood up, pressed back against the wood door of the apartment house, felt behind him, found and turned the knob. The door opened, and he kept it open a bit. The policeman reached the North Terminal door at 165 Prince, gave it a casual try, then angled across the street, heading for the same sidewalk where, eight buildings down the street, Pino was hiding. Tony eased the door behind him wider open, stepped back inside, waited for footsteps to pass. None did. Several minutes had elapsed, perhaps as many as five, before he cautiously poked his head outside. The policeman was gone. He gazed off across the playground. The vault room window was dark. So was the one beside it. The time was approximately 7:50 P.M.

In the course of the three more surveillances Pino noticed that the last light to go off in the second floor line was always in the fifth window—the window through which he had seen the vault. This, he concluded, meant that Brink's final operation of the day was locking money and valuables in the vault for overnight safekeeping. This hypothesis was reinforced when he observed that on Tuesday the vault room window went dark a full hour earlier than on Thursday or Friday—and any good crook knew that weekend payrolls were far larger than beginning-of-the-week payrolls.

There were other things to be seen. Shortly after the vault room window went dark, two or three men left the building through the door on Prince Street closest to the Commercial Street corner—the one numbered 165. The two or three men had always left Prince via Commercial. The foot patrolman wasn't observed again, not between 6:30 and 10:30 P.M. on Tuesday, Thursday and Friday at least.

Of utmost importance was the possible existence of cleaning personnel and night watchmen in the Brink's office. The hack or watchmen might not turn on the overhead lights to make rounds, might very well use a flash beam. Cleaning people would simply turn on the lights. Pino had looked for precisely this, but between the time the vault room went dark and 10:30 P.M., he had not observed the vaguest indication of battery- or generator-powered illumination behind the line of grate-fronted windows over the playground.

The weather was foul beyond working possibilities. Mike Geagan, his yellow oilskin, hip-hugging fisherman's boots and yellow nor'easter already splattered with rain, tugged the yellow storm cap down over the front of his face, lowered his head, moved out from the safety of the pier warehouse and slogged out into the gale. He caught up with the group of longshoremen near the storage building just inside the main gate, but because their faces were all but hidden under tightly pulled hoods, he couldn't tell which one was Richardson. Only after entering the low concrete floor structure where the perennial crap game was in progress was he able to locate Sandy and take him right back outside.

"What's the word from Tony?"

"Haven't heard from him," Richardson, still a one-third owner of the dice game inside, replied.

"It's been a week."

"I know."

"I better give him a call," Mike suggested.

"I've been trying. Nobody answers at the apartment, and all I get over at the diner is some drunk who keeps hanging up on me."

"Maybe he's in trouble."

"I'd say no. I'd say he's probably on to something."

"The Brink's?"

Sandy's hooded head nodded. "I wish he'd forget that goddamn outfit. I wish we could wash it off his system for good—just bend him over and shove a hose up his behind and wash it for good."

"Hot water or cold?"

Stalled headlights spanned the Charles River atop the Charlestown Bridge. Distant honking was audible, but generally obscured by the roar of heavy fast-moving homeward traffic on Commercial Street. Between 5 and 5:15 P.M. three Brink's trucks were noticed going up Hull Street and turning into the second-level door. Few vehicles were observed using Prince Street, nor was pedestrian traffic movement particularly large. The peak period was from 5:20 to 5:35 P.M., when twenty-odd men and women were seen entering the various buildings between the Commercial Street corner and down beyond the entrance to Snowhill Street. On no occasion were they seen taking out keys to unlock the front door of the apartment houses. In no instance did they seem to notice a short, stocky man in a soft hat, leather jacket and baggy trousers walking along the sidewalk, watching them enter through doors.

At 7 P.M. Tony was standing on a rooftop of a building opposite the playground watching the lights go out in the first, second and third large windows nearest the Prince Street corner of North Terminal Garage. The fourth window was partially illuminated. The fifth window—the one fronting the vault—remained lit for another twenty minutes. When it went dark, so did the fourth.

Jazz Maffie sipped a cup of after-dinner coffee at his usual table in Jimmy O'Keefe's restaurant and announced he would be going to the basketball game at the Boston Garden.

"I'll go with you," his wife said.

"Huh?"

"I said, I'll go to the basketball game with you."

"Oh, well, I only got one ticket."

"Buy another."

"Oh, sure. But you see, I'm sitting with the boys."

"If I sit and have dinner with the boys every night at this table, why can't I sit with them at the basketball game?"

"I didn't think you liked basketball."

"I always liked basketball. You always took me to basketball games before we were married."

"Hey, look, there's Danny. I think I'll go buy Danny a drink."

It wasn't because Jazz was trying to avoid a confrontation with his wife or because he wanted to talk to Danny that he excused himself from the table. He had seen Gusciora enter and head for the bar. Gus was no unfamiliar face around Jimmy O'Keefe's. The young, burly, smiling ex-convict was in several nights a week—usually accompanied by an attractive, if not somewhat flashy, young lady—of late usually a lady as well as Specs O'Keefe. Tonight he was settling for a lady alone.

"How are you?" Jazz asked, ambling up to the bar. "Can I buy you a drink?"

"Sure, thanks," Gus replied, then introduced Stella to Maffie.

Stella had on long, dangling metallic earrings—the type that tended to tinkle on the slightest movement. Stella didn't talk all that much, but she was very given to smiling. When she smiled, she usually giggled. When she giggled, she usually nodded her head.

"Heard anything from Stretch?" Gus casually asked after the drinks had arrived.

"Oh, no. I haven't heard anything from Stretch," Jazz answered. "Have you heard anything?"

"Who's Stretch?" Stella asked.

"A friend," Gus explained.

Stella smiled.

"I haven't heard anything either," Gus complained. "I think it's time we should hear. After all, we haven't heard anything for maybe ten days."

"Oh," Jazz said, nodding.

Stella nodded.

"You think he's in good health?" asked Gus.

"Oh, if he wasn't in good health, we woulda heard," Jazz assured. "He's okay."

"If he's okay, I think he should let us know. I can't sit around this long. I've got other opportunities with other people."

"Have you tried getting hold of his relative?" Jazz suggested.

"I called over at the Bucket of Blood," Gus said, referring to Pino's Egleston Square Diner, "but the phone's disconnected."

"Oh, they must have torn it off the wall again." Jazz laughed.

Stella laughed.

"They're always fighting over at that joint," Jazz explained, "and ripping the phone out."

"If Stretch is okay and he has nothing on, I have to take these other opportunities," Gus declared.

"Well, you know how Stretch feels about other opportunities getting in the way of his opportunities."

"Then he should let a person know one way or the other."

"I'll see what I can find out."

Jazz winked at Stella as he left.

Stella blushed and lowered her head.

Maffie didn't take Gusciora's ultimatum all that seriously. He, like all crew members, was aware that Gus and his newest pal, Specs O'Keefe, had been pulling a string of petty stickups and keystering parked cars in the jewelry section of town. Jazz doubted that much could dissuade this activity, wasn't particularly concerned despite the fact that the majority of holdup victims were bookies who ran crap games. Maffie knew that several game operators, particularly Tommy Callahan, had let out word that Gus and Specs lay off or else, but this didn't bother him either. Gus could take care of himself on the worst of days. Nor was Jazz impressed with Pino's constant ranting against Specs O'Keefe for corrupting Gus and making him into an ordinary street thief. He knew what everyone around town knew, that Tony Pino and Specs O'Keefe went back a long ways together, had begun robbing together when they were five or six years old, had grown disaffected, were constantly bad-mouthing each other. Nonetheless, Pino knew that O'Keefe was a pretty good thief, had even used him on the American Sugar job; he grew enraged when after the heist Specs went around town complaining about Tony's getting a full share for doing nothing but turning the score over to him and the others.

Jazz wasn't particularly anxious to hear from Pino, not if it was about Brink's. He felt that the crew had pressed their luck in rifling company armored trucks and scoring customers. Smart money dictated forgetting the joint altogether.

"Come on," he told his wife on returning to the table.

"Come on where?" she replied.

"To the basketball game."

"What makes you think I want to see a basketball game?"

"You just said you wanted to see a basketball game."

"Only when I'm invited."

"Well, I'm inviting."

"Because I asked you to. When the invitation's your idea, I'll go. Have a good time."

Once at the Boston Garden, Maffie tried phoning Richardson. There was no answer at either Sandy's home or the crap game. He dialed the diner. The number was temporarily out of service.

The new cook had gotten drunk and passed out. He'd done it before. This time he remained unconscious two full days, and that's how the phone happened to get disconnected. Pino first took over in the kitchen, darted between the stove and pay phone on which he persistently called the Seamen's Home urging them to send over another chef. The man who finally arrived was missing a right leg, and was already drunk on arrival. Nickels and dimes clicked down, yellow pages turned, and numbers were frantically dialed for the Salvation Army, Hibernian Home or anything that sounded like a repository for inexpensive labor. Even the most philanthropic or desperate of institutions didn't respond favorably to the fifty-cents-an-hour offer. Mary refused to work in the kitchen under any circumstances. Jimmy Costa turned down an initial tendering of $1.10 an hour, remained indifferent over a thirty-six-hour period, saw the figure rise to $3.50, countered by demanding a guaranteed week's emergency salary of $100 for a total of no more than two hours in one day. Pino threw a metal ladle at him. Costa, as a result, upped the base to $150 for the week—payable in advance.

Tony never would have paid this under any condition, except that he had closed the diner the second morning and gone over to Brink's, had seen exactly what he wanted to see—early-arriving armored car crews entering the main-floor garage on Commercial Street and going toward two different routes upstairs: one in the back of the garage, one over to the right side along the Prince Street wall.

He had hurried back to the diner and called Costa. In desperation he agreed to Jimmy's terms. Jimmy refused to come over until the cash was received, rejected the suggestion that the money be left with Joe McGinnis, compromised on Tony Gaeta, whom he trusted somewhat more. Pino ran the cash over to the Socony service station across the street, had Gaeta call Costa to say payment had been made, then hurried back to the diner. The phone was ringing. Tony answered. It was Costa. He wanted Tony to apologize for throwing the ladle at him. Tony swore and hollered and hung up. Ten minutes later he called Jimmy back. He apologized. Then he tore the phone from the wall.

The light went off in the fifth window, the vault room window. The entire back of the garage was dark. The time was 8.

"Okay, I'm sitting in that doorway on Prince. I keep my eyes on that door up near the corner—up near Commercial. That people door. Right after the light goes off I see these three fellas come out the door like they always do. I been around here a lot so I know that now. They come out and go around the corner [from Prince into Commercial Street].

"I get up and get going. I got nothing incriminating on me, see? No tools. No wallet. I left my wallet in the car. All I got are the car keys.

"Now I make the climb. Go up on Snowhill. I go up casual. I keep watching the windows for hacks or cleaning ladies. I haven't seen any of their lights ever, and I been here maybe eight times already.

"Okay, I walk up the hill and down [on Hull]. I take the corner and walk right close to the building. I walk right past the garage door on Commercial. The door's open, and I don't see any fella sitting at the desk. I keep going to the corner [at Prince], then turn around and come right back. I see inside from another angle now. There's no fella anywhere.

"Bang, I duck inside quick—inside the garage door. I get back in the shadows. I move around behind them newspaper trucks. It's all shadows in there 'cause there's only one little bulb up in the ceiling. I keep close to the wall [parallel to Commercial]. Now I turn and keep close to the other wall [parallel to Prince].

"Okay, I'm moving slow and easy. And I'm looking, too. Not for hacks 'cause they can't see me back here. I'm looking out for oil ponds on the floor. You don't wanna step in no oil or grease and leave a trail to where you're going.

"Right away I'm near the doors—the pull-down garage door and the people door.

"I look over the door [people door]. I don't see no wires. I put on my driver's gloves and try her. She opens right onto Prince street. Now I know for sure it's the door down near the corner I just seen them three fellas come out of.

"Now what I do is set the lock, see what I mean? Fix her a little bit so she'll stay open. Be ready in case I gotta come through her in a hurry. The reason I do this is the steps. The steps going upstairs is right there. I come down them steps fast, I don't wanna go running around back through the garage. I wanna come out the faster way—through that door.

"Okay, the door gets fixed, and I'm all set. I look over the steps going upstairs. Look for oil and grease, and it's goddamn hard to see because it's dark over here. I check the bottom of my shoes 'n' make sure they didn't pick up no oil or grease. Okay, I start up step by step and slow, so I don't make a sound. One by one and easy. Now I'm out of view of anybody in the garage downstairs. Up ahead it's darker and darker. My eyes adjust fast, though . After all, it ain't the first time in my life I been up a dark staircase. Step by step and cautious I keep going.

"Now I'm up at the landing. I stop and look around in the dark. There's a little bit of light coming from upstairs. From down the staircase that keeps going up to the next floor. But it's ordinary street light from outside. It must be coming through some window high up. Nothing to worry about.

"Now I look in the other direction on the landing. I turn [with his back to Prince Street] and right ahead is like a little hall with two fire doors facing one another. Big metal slide doors. Okay, I stand there in the dark. I look over the fire door to my right. That's the one facing the back of the building. It's got tracks up on top and on the ground. That's what it slides on, these tracks. It's got little wheels on top and bottom that run along on these tracks. I look her over good again. I look for wires. Bugs. Electric eyes. I look for sneaky pictures [hidden cameras], too. I don't see nothing, but that don't mean it ain't there. Brink's ain't moving from one place to another without a reason. Without making some improvement. I gotta figure every extra modern precaution's been installed. All that Buck Rogers stuff that's getting fashionable.

"I keep looking her over. Kneeling down and standing on tiptoe. I don't find nothing. So I give the slide door a little jiggle. A back-and-forth jiggle, not a sideways jiggle. It jiggles a little, but nothing happens. If they got bugs on it, they ain't for back-and-forth jiggles, but I don't expect that anyway.

"Okay, I go for the test. It's the moment of crisis. There ain't no way of avoiding it. I gotta find out. I get all prepared. Suck in. Bang, I slide the door open and slide it right back shut and tear the hell outta there. Run down them steps and out the door and up Prince Street. I'm outta there like I'm in the Olympics. I get way the hell up the block and sit down in a doorway. I'm bushed, and my heart's doing a hard pound. Jumping right through my jacket. I'm sitting, watching to see what goes off. What alarms ring. Who comes running. What lights go on upstairs. I'm far enough up [Prince Street] that if people come running, I can vanish without no trouble.

"So I'm sitting and waiting. Nothing goes off. No alarm I can hear. No lights go on in any of the windows. I stay sitting. Maybe a sneak alarm went off right in the police station or some private joint [agency]. No one comes. No one drives up and rushes inside. Nothing happens for fifteen, maybe twenty minutes.

"So I get up and go back a second time. Go in through that Prince Street door. I fixed the lock on that door before, so I go right through it and right up them steps. I go up to the fire door. The slide door I just tried. Real, real easy I slide it open an inch or so. I peek in, and there's nothing but black. Easy now, real easy, I slide her open more. I step through—and what the hell ya think is facing me? Another fire door. I'm in a tiny hall between them two slide doors.

"So now I gotta check it out like I done the other. It's got wheels on the top and bottom, too. I don't see no wires or nothing. I give it a jiggle. When it jiggles, it squeaks. The first door squeaked, too, when I rolled it open more. But this one squeaks on the jiggle, not the slide. I haven't done no sliding yet, but I know from what I've done it ain't locked. Now I get ready. And I probably take more time getting up courage. This second door can explain why nothing's attached to the first door. I mean, if you got two doors, which one ya gonna put the bug on? The second, that's which one. In all my experience, I never come across more than two fire doors in a row. I come across two before, but never three. So if this second door leads anywhere, it's got the best chance of having the bug.

"Okay, I get all prepared again. I get up to that door. Bang, quick slide it open and back shut. Fast. I jump back out and slide the first door shut, and *pftt,* I'm down them stairs and out the door I fixed. Only I unfix it on the run. By run, I don't mean a real run like a relay race. I mean moving as fast as you can without drawing attention. It's a helluva strenuous thing.

"I'm outta there and up on Prince Street like a flash—slow flash. I sit down in the doorway. I'm panting bad. I'm watching, too. No alarms go off. No lights go on. No cars come racing up with cops or security people. I'm exhausted from all the running up and down. My energy supplies are empty from all the fright. I get the hell outta there.

"I go home to sleep. Only I can't sleep. I keep trying to figure it out. If nothing went off, if no lights went on, then those slide doors weren't hooked, bugged. That means they probably don't go nowhere near Brink's office. That's what I think on the one hand. On the other hand, there's just so much space on that second floor. Brink's is up there somewhere, I know, 'cause I looked into their counting room. I saw her vault with my own eyes. It's gotta be up there someplace."

Twenty minutes after being repaired, the phone behind the counter rang.

"Diner," Costa announced on picking up.

"Jimmy?" Geagan's unmistakable voice asked.

"Yeah."

"You call?"

"Yeah."

"What's on?"

"Stretch wanted you to know he found that missing friend."

"Me and the redhead will be over."

"Come if you want, but it won't do no good. I don't know much, and he's gone."

"You say he found him?"

"Right next door to where I grew up."

"What else?"

"He says it looks like a miracle."

"He visited him face to face?" Mike asked.

"I think he's got that on his mind for tonight."

"If he hasn't been in, why all the talk about a miracle?"

"Hey, I only know what I know."

"What the hell do you know?"

"He's been running in and out like a crazy animal. Busy as hell. He's supposed to cook, see? The cook keeps getting drunk. The Salvation Army keeps sending over more and more drunks, so he's gotta give me guaranteed wages in advance and then—"

"Never mind about the goddamn cook and wages," Geagan interjected. "What's going on?"

"I'm telling what I know and how I know it. We get this other cook yesterday and Tony—"

"Did he tell you he was going inside?"

"He didn't say nothing!" Costa shouted back.
"Then how did you get the idea?"
"Because he swiped a bag. Boosts a goddamn paper bag from his own goddamn restaurant!"

Two men in overcoats emerged from the Prince Street door, stood chatting in the darkness, then walked the few yards to Commercial Street and disappeared around the corner. Fifteen minutes later Pino was fixing the lock of the door through which the pair had just departed—from the inside. He crept up the staircase, on the lookout for grease or oil, did the same on the landing, put on his gloves, carefully inspected the fire door to his right and eased it open. The rollers on the track below squeaked.

"Okay, now all I got in front of me is that second fire door," Tony relates. "The one that squeaks more than the first one. I look her over again. She's okay, too. So I take hold of her and easy, real easy now, I slide her a little. Open her an inch. I peek through. It's dark as hell in there. Merciless dark.

"I wait, and it's hard to adjust 'cause it's so dark. Okay, now I get ready. I take hold of her again, and bang, I slide her open and duck right through and give a dive. I dive through the air, and I hit and scramble right under a truck there. I'm laying as flat as I can under her. I let my eyes adjust, but I can't see nothing from under here.

"Okay, I slide back out and sit behind her. I'm panting like a mad dog. My eyes get adjusted. I see a little bit. I'm sitting against the wall. I'm staring at the ass of the truck I was under. Parked right there next to her is another truck. An armored job. A Brink's job. I'm in their garage or a garage that's got two of her trucks. The truck I'm sitting behind's a Brink's, too.

"I don't move from a sitting position except to take out the paper bag. It's one of them twenty-pound brown paper bags you use for grocery shopping. I take it out of my back pocket and sit right back down on the concrete floor. I start unfolding the bag real slow. Layer by layer and slow. More than slow because paper makes noise when it gets unfolded. I can't make no sound. So one layer gets unfolded slow. Then I stop. Then I unfold another slow. . . . I'm trying to give you a sense of time passing.

"Okay. I got it all unfolded. I reach inside and open the bag up. Then I put it over my head. I feel where my eyes are and poke two holes. Holes to see through. Now I got a mask.

"Why I need a mask on this operation is because of sneaky pictures [hidden cameras]. They can have sneaky pictures hidden all over the place. Ultrareds and all that.

"Now I got my mask on. Only I punched the holes too close. I'm looking out kinda cross-eyed. Now I crawl around the truck on my hands and knees. That ain't as easy as you think because you gotta keep your head straight up. Drop your head, and the paper bag falls off. You try crawling with your head straight up, looking out cross-eyed?

"I crawl around to the front of the truck, and now I get up a little more. Get up into a crouch. It's goddamn dark, but I can see pillars. Concrete pillars that hold the roof up. They're all over the place. Over at my left is the slide door I come through. Then there's a little bit of wall and then a garage door. It's closed. Then more wall and then another Brink's truck. From what I see, Brink's trucks is parked along the wall right across from where I'm crouched. I get up more and looked over at my right. It's too dark to see much except them pillars.

"So I take first things first. I get down low again and crawl over to the first slide door. It's still open. I crawl through and open the second slide door a crack. I put in one of the wood blocks, the slanted blocks. I put it at the bottom and slide the door closed. Now it's wedged up a tiny bit, so I can get out in a hurry. I do the same thing to the second slide door. I wedge it, too. I crawl back to the front of the truck.

"I look over all the trucks ahead of me. There's a big open space from where I am to those other trucks—the space for the door [garage door]. Then I'm off and going, crawling on my hands and knees like John Wayne does in war movies. I get in behind the first truck. Then I get up. Get up slow and cautious. I peek into the front seat of the first truck. I peek into the front seat of the second truck. I'm looking cross-eyed half the time, but I'm peeking all the same. Whatcha gotta watch out for is hacks sleeping. Lots of hacks go to sleep in trucks instead of patrolling like they're supposed to. That's what I'm looking out for. Sleeping hacks.

"I look in the back of the trucks and the front. I go from truck to truck along that wall. Maybe there's six or seven trucks. Maybe more. I sneak up on each one and look for hacks. All the trucks is Brink's. Some is parked nose first. Some is parked ass first. Now down at the end I see there's another big door. Garage door. But it don't look like it's used much because trucks are parked in front of it. That's where the last trucks are, in front of this door. And right beyond that last truck I see this hall. A dark thin hall.

"Now I gotta take the hall. I move in on my hands and knees. I'm feeling as I go. With my hand. Right away on my right I feel this door. It's open and I go in slow. Now it's darker than dark, and I bump right into something. It's a toilet. I'm in their goddamn crapper. So I back outta there on my hands and knees.

"Now I'm back in the garage, and I'm crawling along the crapper wall [parallel to Hull Street]. I come to the end of it, and it goes in. The wall shoots off to Hull Street. So I can figure out they built the crapper right out into the garage. It's like a big shithouse standing there. Now I crawl in behind it, into the wall running along Hull. I can see equipment and a truck parked up on a jack. This has to be their repair shop. The part of the garage where they fix their trucks. So real slow I peek in the truck. Front and back. No hacks.

"I'm back on my hands and knees going for a line of trucks parked out in the middle. I'm cutting right back across the garage [toward the Prince Street side], and that's where these trucks stand. Parked between them concrete pillars. I crawl up on each one and peek for hacks. I don't find nobody. The joint is mine. I looked over all the trucks, and there ain't no one.

"I'm getting a neckache, see what I mean? I been crawling all the hell over, keeping my head straight up so the cross-eyed mask don't topple. I been looking up for hacks and down for oil and grease, trying to keep my head straight. But I don't know I got this neckache till I stand up. That's when it hits me.

"So I'm standing out in the middle of the garage with a neckache. Now I see what I couldn't see from the other side of the garage. There's a wall running the whole length [parallel to the playground]. I walk around a truck to get a better look, and I damn near die of shock. A goddamn rotunda's staring at me. I dive back down. I don't know what I was thinking, but nothing happens. I crawl around and take a better peek at the rotunda. It's a glass rotunda sticking right out in the middle of the wall. A goddamn guard booth. It's dark inside. I keep staring at it and start noticing it's not as dark as I think. There's some filter light coming through. Like on the staircase out front, some light coming from a street somewhere. No direct light.

"So I sit down and think it over. You build a rotunda so a guard can sit in it. And if a guard was sitting in it, he would have seen me. But nothing's happened. That means two things. Either the guard's sleeping down low in the rotunda or somewhere nearby or there ain't a guard. Now I'm up in a crouch. I run across the floor on the crouch and hide behind a concrete pillar, only that ain't much hiding. Those pillars are so skinny you can damn near put both hands around them. I look over the rotunda from here. Now I run back to the wall I started from [facing Prince Street], and I almost fall over dead. There's a whole line of trucks I never seen. And there's another goddamn rotunda, too. A square rotunda right in the corner [of the wall parallel to the playground and the wall parallel to Prince Street]. But this rotunda's smaller, and I can't see no window in it. All I see in it's a door. A closed door. So that's not gonna give me no trouble.

"So now I gotta check out these new trucks. Peek 'em one at a time. I get down to the end, and I see what happened. This wall they're against [parallel to Prince Street] only runs halfway back into the garage. Then it cuts off and goes back [toward Prince Street] to where I started. So you figure there's gotta be something on the other side of that further up. Maybe offices.

"So I check these trucks, and it's clean. My escape path's okay. I got a clear shot at the fire door. I move back between two of the trucks. Then I keep low and run out into the middle of the garage. I duck in between two trucks there. Now I'm right across from the big rotunda in the middle of the wall [wall running parallel to the playground]. I feel around the floor and find a little pebble or two. Maybe a small chip of cement that feels like a pebble through my gloves. I move up closer behind a pillar. I take another deep breath 'cause I may be going out of here like a blast. I toss a pebble at the rotunda. Clink, it goes and nothing happens. No sound. No light going on. I toss another pebble. Clink and nothing.

"This makes me brave. I stand up a little bit straighter and look this wall over. Next to the rotunda is a few feet of wall and then a door. Then it's all wall to the rotunda in the corner. Looking the other way, you got the rotunda [in the middle of the wall], then more wall all the way down to what looks like another door [in the same wall]. So it's the first time I've seen this other door [near the Hull Street corner of garage]. I sneak back down there. The door's closed, and I get up close. Then I see this is only a half a wall. It's like a pen [animal pen] down here with a door in it. It's probably a storage area of some kind, so I don't bother with it no more.

"Now I'm back in the middle of the garage. Back behind a pillar facing the center rotunda. Clink, I throw another pebble. Nothing. That does it. I move right up on the rotunda. It's got one long window facing me and two little side windows sloping into the wall. We stand looking at one another, and I look in. There ain't nobody there. But like I explained, a hack could be sleeping behind it. I can make out there's a small room behind it and off to the left there's a door. That's where the light's coming through. Filtered light coming through that door. So I can see there ain't no hack sleeping in the small room. That don't mean he ain't sleeping somewhere nearby, though. Maybe right behind the door where the light's coming through.

"I move back a ways. I look over the rotunda, and I look over the door to the right. Now I see something else. Something low and black. I sneak up on it. It's a cooler. A cooler for your pop and Coca-Cola. Now I'm back looking at the door and looking at the rotunda [the rotunda in the center of the wall]. The reason that rotunda got a side window on it is so the hacks can see who's going into that door. That means this is the main entrance for drivers unless I'm a hundred percent wrong. No driver's going to be pushing those money hampers through the door in the corner of the room [the door in the rotunda at the corner of the garage]. This is gotta be their Golden Gate right out here in the center. And if a hack's sleeping somewhere right now, it's gotta be right around here, too.

"So I walk right back to the rotunda and knock hard on the window. I run across the floor and duck in between two trucks [parked against the inner wall running parallel to Prince Street]. I wait to see if somebody answers. See if lights go on in the rotunda. See if somebody opens the door and looks. Come out to see what all the noise is about. I'm crouched, and I'm waiting. Nothing happens. Nobody comes out the door."

And if someone had come into the rotunda or opened the door beside it?

"They woulda had an imagination. I coulda heard the footsteps coming and ducked further behind the trucks where nobody could see me. Whoever come out would think he'd had an imagination that somebody knocked, know what I mean? You open a door and see that there's nobody there, you think the knock you heard was an imagination."

When no one came out to have an imagination, Pino moved back to the door beside the rotunda in the center of the wall.

"It's a big heavy door, and it looks like it's metal or thick wood. I figure it for metal. I look it over for wires. Look up on top and around the sides. There's nothing. It was clean. Now I squat down and look at their lock again. It's a Schlage. The cheapest one you can buy.

"Now I get up and give a second lookover for wires. Trip wires. Alarm connections. I don't find 'em. I give a light rap on the door and get back behind the trucks. Nothing happens. I go back and give a harder rap and get behind the trucks. Nothing happens again.

"So I'm back at the door. I'm standing there figuring nobody's around, but I can't be sure there ain't secret wires on that door. Secret wires get tripped all kinds of ways. Sometimes knocking on the door don't trip 'em. So I get all set. This is critical. I get on my mark. I give the doorknob a hard twist and tear out. I go running back and open both slide doors and take out the block. I close the doors and tear down them steps. I got the blocks in my pocket and I'm taking off the paper mask and folding it. I'm tearing down the steps, putting the paper mask in my pocket, too. I unfix the door [downstairs on Prince Street] and get the hell outside and up the street. I'm sitting and watching in the doorway up the street. Watching for something to happen.

Nothing to Christ happens. I don't understand it. I get up and go around the corner for my car, not understanding why these people don't have some kinda alarm.''

While walking toward his car, Pino took the paper bag mask from his rear pocket, tore it to shreds and paused to drop the pieces down a sewer.

CHAPTER FOURTEEN

The Kiss

It was Pino at his obsessive best or worst, his compulsively most thorough or overthorough or ridiculous thorough. The North Terminal Garage building totally monopolized his thoughts and time. How long the mania would last was problematic. He was mercurial in undertakings such as these, but for the time being he couldn't get enough of the building. The Brink's garage itself was left alone, not entered again, temporarily forbidden territory. Nearly all else above and below and abutting was systematically covered or penetrated, watched, crawled through, felt, smelled, listened to. He found that the second floor of the garage building was divided into four sections of which Brink's took up the southernmost, or bottom quarter above at the corner of Prince and the playground. Entering the double fire doors to his left, coming off the staircase he always took, he saw a garage housing additional Brink's trucks, some of which were apparently used for large or long-distance hauls. The large garage door between this section and the one Tony believed was Brink's main garage was always kept closed and locked. The adjacent garage door on the wall parallel to and farthest from Prince Street was usually locked. On occasion it wasn't. He had walked through into the large common garage on the other side, a common garage running along Hull Street—an area he computed as accounting for half the space of the entire floor. He had been up on the third floor, seen rows of parked green armored cars belonging to the United States Armored Car Company, took time to search for vehicle keys. He had been on the roof. He had spent considerable time in the first-floor garage opening onto Commercial Street, had located and studied a second door which he believed led up to Brink's—the door far back in the space and over near the Prince Street/playground corner. Everywhere he went he found the ubiquitous rows of thin concrete pillars. Everywhere he went the lighting was poor. Seldom at night did he run into people, though on one occasion the lights of a car in the process of parking near the end of the second-floor common garage caught him unawares. Nowhere at night— between eight and ten-thirty—and with the single exception of the fellow who occasionally sat at the desk inside the Commercial Street doors had he run across any watchman or cleaning people. That didn't mean they didn't exist in the one section he had avoided to date—Brink's.

So he took to the roofs above and along Prince Street, lay there long hours watching the darkened windows for light, remained prone until ten-thirty and sometimes eleven and saw nothing to indicate hacks or cleaning people. And when after a ten-day hiatus he reentered the Brink's section of the garage through the old familiar route, donned his paper bag mask, peeked into each truck and the windows of the two guard cages along the parkside wall, he still found no indication of hacks or maintenance personnel. He did however receive a shock when he reinspected the door beside the center rotunda.

"I thought I was seeing things," said Pino. "That last time I looked her over it didn't have no window in it. I swear to God it didn't. But now it does. Jesus, I tell myself, maybe they're starting to change things. Put in new stuff.

"It ain't a big window. Just a little slit window up on top. A peek window. So I look into her and can't see nothing but dark. Now I get close to the lock, the cheap Schlage. It looks like the same one I seen before, so maybe I missed the window. I tell myself this ain't the time or place to be getting sloppy."

Pino raised his fist and began hitting hard on the door, then darted behind a nearby truck. No light that could be seen went on. No alarm that could be heard went off. He returned to the door, dropped to one knee and stared hard and long at the lock. He reached up, gave the knob a twist and waited. No alarm was heard. No light went on. He put an eye even closer to the lock. Then he left.

"They've got to have some kind of alarm there," Richardson commented as he drove Pino toward the Savin Hill plant.

"I know they gotta, but they don't. I told you I burned her high and low. Twice I burned her."

"And you knocked on the door you think goes into the offices?"

"I did everything but hit it with a baseball bat. I damn near twisted the knob right off and nothing. I can't get a sneeze from them people."

"Perhaps the door doesn't go into the offices?"

"It can't go anywhere else, Sandy. There's just so much space on that floor. I go another twenty feet in that direction, and I'll fall out a window."

Richardson pulled to a stop on a side street. He and Pino got out and started walking for an alley.

"Anthony, if that door goes into their offices, it must have an alarm on it."

"Well, if it does, it's in the lock. But I never heard of no one hooking up a ten-cent lock."

"Then maybe that's exactly where it is. Perhaps that's why they installed a cheap lock, to catch the unsuspecting?"

"If you ask me, Mr. Brink's put in that lock 'cause he's a chintz." Pino reflected for a minute. "Every time since I started watching 'em, they been chintzy and screwing up. Maybe they moved over to this new joint 'cause it's got cheaper rent. They got two goddamn rotundas up in that garage of theirs with no visible hacks in them. They got no hack out in the garage, too. Maybe they're too goddamn cheap to pay their hacks night rates. They're too goddamn cheap to put anything on them slide doors. Christ, they won't even spring fifty-watt bulbs in their garage. Whoever heard of a garage for twenty-grand trucks with only a twenty-five-watt bulb in it?"

Richardson unlocked the garage door to the Savin Hill plant, followed Pino in and slide-bolted the door shut. Tony snapped on the light—a twenty-five-watt bulb.

"Good God," Richardson uttered at seeing large cardboard cartons stacked three and four high on every available foot of space around the panel truck and cache of recently stolen lawn mowers.

"Yeah, we need a bigger joint," Pino announced, squeezing past a wall of cardboard. "I already been looking."

"Anthony, do you mind telling me what these boxes are and where they came from?"

"Cigarettes. Barney's been smuggling them in the state but don't want McGinnis to know, so I took some off his hands."

"Barney doesn't do anything without that skinheaded bastard knowing."

"Joe's okay when you get to know him."

"He's a goddamn crook and thief, and I don't want to know him."

Pino circled the last mound of contraband cigarettes and reached the rosewood cabinet containing his burglar's tools, lock cylinders and array of costumes. "You know something, that lock of theirs could be wired after all," he told Sandy, "but not the way you think. Not to the alarm. That turret had two slanted windows on the sides. Slanted so you can see the door. That maybe means the hack inside pushes a button, know what I mean? He sees somebody come up to the door and knock. When he sees who it is, he pushes a button and the lock opens."

"All I know, Anthony, is that you've only been in their garage twice," Richardson replied, "and maybe you caught them on an off night. Maybe those guard cages are manned most other nights."

"Then they gotta be sitting there in the goddamn dark," Pino countered, slipping a finely honed ice pick in his pocket. He reached up to the cabinet's upper shelf and removed a flat, square industrial flashlight affixed with shoulder straps—one he had boosted from a night watchman's office some months before. "I'm telling ya, Sandy, I know what should be and shouldn't be. I know they should have that joint locked tighter than a drum. But I've been living in that neighborhood at night, and what my eyes see and my logic says are two different things.

They're keeping her wide open. I can't say what goes on after ten thirty [P.M.]. I don't think it's much. Up to ten thirty you never seen anything more wide open in your life."

"What do you want me to tell Jazz?" Sandy asked.

"Don't tell 'em nothing till we got this thing whipped." Pino took down two wooden wedges, then closed the rosewood cabinet. "I don't want nobody to know I'm in ten miles of that joint."

"Anthony, none of the crew's had any word from you for nearly three weeks."

"Stall for an even month, okay?"

"Go easy if you get at that door of theirs, Anthony," Richardson cautioned. "If Brink's had a bag of tricks, that's where they'll start springing 'em."

"Sandy, if they gotta bag of tricks, even money says they bought 'em cut-rate."

The first metal-fronted fire door squeaked open in the dark. Pino stepped through, with a gloved hand set one of the wooden wedges in the floor tract between the wall and door edge. The door was eased shut—almost shut. The second fire door, the one that squeaked more than the first, was then inspected, eased open, affixed with a wedge and, after Tony had stepped through, rolled closed—almost closed.

"See what we got here?" Pino asked. "Both them doors look shut till you got right on them. It's just open wide enough to get your fingers in and pull 'em open if you're in a hurry. Wedging them doors only saves you a second or two in opening them up, but when you're running for your life, it can save you ten to twelve years. I'm carrying an ice pick. An ice pick is a burglar's tool. I can get four to six for possession of burglar's tools."

The short, dumpy leather-jacketed thief with a paper bag mask covering his upright head sneaked along the lines of armored trucks standing between slim concrete columns, cautiously peeking into cabs and through rear slit windows that were darker than the nearly absolute darkness of the garage. The probe required close to half an hour, terminated in the Hull Street corner of the wall closest to, and running parallel to, the playground. There was an open door here through which he looked before on other visits. He looked now, found nothing to warrant concern, was tempted to explore beyond the closed door. Didn't.

He moved along the wall, stopped, rose, trained the eyeholes against the slanted glass siding the rotunda, sidestepped to the larger pane in the front. The blackness beyond was not total: over to the left it had diluted to a heavy gray. He moved on, past the door immediately to the right of the rotunda—*the door*— reached the glass-fronted guard booth in the Prince Street/playground corner. He gave it the burn. Nothing appeared suspicious.

He backtracked to the center rotunda, faced that door there— *the door*. He dropped to one knee. The erect paper bag moved forward. Stopped.

"I'm staring at that goddamn dime lock," he says. "I start thinking Sandy can be right. Maybe the sonsabitches rigged a goddamn cheap dime lock, know what I mean? They're trying to sucker me. They're letting me pound on the door and turn the knob and run all the hell over without nothing happening. They're getting me overconfident on purpose. They'd give me anything out here I want. All they're waiting for is me to touch that lock and bang!, it's the Fourth of July. Treacherous, rotten bastards.

"What's gotta be done gotta be done, see. That's the way it is. Okay, I take out the pick—my ice pick with the tip I honed down to needle size. My hands is steady as hell—I'm a brain specialist. I got the pick up and raised. I get all set. I'm standing up now 'cause this is a two-hand job. I'm going to be running, too. I got one hand on the knob. The pick's in the other. *Pfft!* I open the lock and open the door and real fast shut her and take off. My legs are short, see, and they're pumping up and down, and my head's straight up 'cause a the twenty-pound sack, and I hit the cracks in them slide doors on the run. I don't bother with no wedge blocks. I leave and tear down them steps and take off the twenty-pound sack and get through the door. I don't check nothing. I keep going. The alarm goes off now, and I'm dead. I'm on my way to Italy forever and Mike and Sandy got themselves a crew all to their own.

"It's the fastest moving I've done. I get to the doorway and al-

most collapse of exhaustion and terror. I'm goddamn coughing,
trying to find my breath. Some thief, huh? The cops pull up, you
won't hear their sirens with all my coughing. I'm so goddamn
weak I won't be able to get up and beat it onto the roof. Anyone
shows, that's where I go—through the door behind me and up
over the roofs.''

No lights went on in the line of seven windows above the playground. No light went on anywhere in the back of the building or
along the Prince Street side. No foot patrolmen or police cars
appeared. Nothing. Fifteen, twenty minutes went by, and nothing.

Pino reentered the building through the Prince Street people
door, reset the wedges on the second-floor fire doors, was soon
standing, rumpled paper bag over his head and honed ice pick
poised, at *the door.*

"*Pfft,* I got her open again. I jump inside and close her. Mother of God, it's dark. Wherever I am it's dark without relief. And
I can't move much either. I'm inside, and I don't know what
they got in here. They can have all them electric eyes planted
low along the boards [floorboards]. They can have bugs buried
right in the cement [floor] so pressure sets 'em off. That's why I
brought the flashlight around my neck, but I don't turn it on the
regular way. The electric eyes don't pick up nothing that's fast,
see what I mean? They gotten be broken, and fast light hitting
'em don't do it—don't break 'em. That's why I give her the *pfft-
pfft.* I turn on my light fast, and I turn her off fast, *pfft-pfft.*

"So I'm standing there not moving, looking over the floor.
Trying to figure out what kind of alarm they got around here and
where the hell I am. I *pfft-pfft* along the boards. There ain't no
electric eye down there [to his right]. Now I bend way down and
feel the cement, feel for alarms they got buried. I don't feel
nothing. I got a little tiny piece of floor that's clean, so I get
down on my hands and knees on her. That's how I start going—a
foot or two at a time. *Pfft-pfft* her and feel her. You don't wanna
break no speed records here. When I'm about five or six feet
down the boards, I start feeling out further. Start getting myself
out into the middle some. Now I got three or four feet cleaned
out there. My island's getting bigger. I go back and start *pfft-
pffting* the wall. All the way up the wall in that area. It's a pain in

the ass, this slow going, but you gotta have patience. I got all the patience there is. That's why I'm still alive. But you don't take no chances because of that. Only one hidden wire or sneaky picture, and you're dead. Them things don't take up much space, and I gotta lotta dark to cover."

Pino reached the corner of the wall nearest Prince Street, searched along the adjacent wall, eventually reached the other corner nearest the playground side of the building and determined he was in a long rectangular chamber, perhaps twenty feet in length and six in width. Eventually he reached a second door. It was directly opposite the one through which he had entered, and it stood slightly ajar. Nothing much could be seen in the continuing darkness beyond. *Pfft-pffting* and feeling of the doorframe and door edge produced a new revelation.

"The goddamn lock's rigged," Pino explained. "It's another goddamn dime job, and they rigged it only not on the lock itself, see. Where the wires run to is the latch. The latch's in the frame, the tongue of the lock fits into the latch—that's what keeps it locked.

"So now I gotta figure out. It's like I told Sandy. This door's open a little, see? If this was alarm rigging, whistles woulda gone off already. And I didn't open the door—it was open like this when I got here. So all you gotta ask is why you'd have wires running to the latch if it ain't for alarms. To open it, is why. What we got here is one of them electric opening jobs. Press a button somewhere, and this lock opens itself up.

"Now I get over to the other wall—the wall running between the door I come in and the door that's rigged. I see a window in the wall. When I peek her, I'm looking into the rotunda. I get way over, and I could look out this window and right through the rotunda and out the rotunda's other window—the window that goes into the garage.

"So now I play a hunch. I go back to the first, the door I come through to get in here [opening into the garage]. On this side I can see she's rigged, too. A wire goes into the latch. It's an electric opening job like the other one.

"See how it works? A hack gets out of his truck and comes to the door [leading from the garage to the room]. The hack in the rotunda looks him over. If he likes what he sees, he presses a button and the lock opens by itself. The truck hack comes in the room. The hack in the rotunda can give him a second peek now. He looks out that little window in the side. If he still likes what he sees, he presses his button and the second door pops open. The door that's a little open now.''

Pino continued his investigation of the room. By and large it was barren. One or two lockers were up against a wall. Three or four wooden chairs were against another.

"They got this bulletin board on the wall, and I can see some names on it. They're roster names for which hack is supposed to work what days. I'm in the hacks' room. This is where the hacks wait for their trucks to get loaded. Maybe it's where they bring the money in and out from too.

"Now I own this room. Know everything about it. It's safe. But I don't go no further. All this took me time. I figure it's ten or ten-fifteen when I finish. This joint is only safe for me until ten thirty. I only checked her out for hacks and cleaning women up to ten.''

The phone refused to stop ringing. A nightshirt-clad Pino finally woke up, got out of bed and answered.

"Hey, Tony," Jimmy Costa said urgently, "you better get the hell over quick.''

"Over where?''

"Over where I've been for almost a week. Your lousy diner.''

"You make the stew like I told you?''

"I don't know how to make stew, Tony. That's why I'm calling. I put—''

"Anyone can make stew for chrissakes. I put all the meat and vegetables in for you myself, didn't I? All you got to do is turn on the flame.''

"I did turn on the flame, and that's how the fire started. Tony, we had a fire in the kitchen. I burned up the stew.''

"You done what, mister?''

"Burned up all the stew.''

"How much stew?''

"All the stew!''

"Both potfuls?''

"Both.''

"Mother of God, that's forty-five dollars' worth of profits in them. How could you goddamn go and burn 'em up?"

"I been telling you for three goddamn days I don't know how to cook stew."

Trapped amid prospects of millions upon millions of dollars in vault room money and possibilities of continuing $45 stew losses, Pino hardly hesitated in picking the immediate over the imminent. He ran over to the diner and was away from Brink's for two full days while he stayed on at the diner cooking.

A twenty-pound paper bag rose up in the darkness, peered into the rotunda window and moved on. A honed tipped pick slid between the door and jamb, touched against a metal tong and depressed it. Reinspection of the guardroom was cursory; of the second, slightly ajar door leading farther in the direction of the playground, painstaking. A gloved hand reached out; two gloved fingers pulled gently, coaxed the door open wider. The hunched-shouldered figure dropped down on its knees, tilted its square head slightly forward. Unseen eyes peered down through torn holes in the paper. All was dark. The hunched shoulders swayed backward. The square head raised cautiously, guarded, so as not to fall off. The unseen eyes looked upward. Light, so diffuse as not to be total or in shafts, wafted above, etched out the unmistakably straight outline of the top of a wall, a wall parallel to the door and perhaps eight feet away, a wall perhaps eight feet high, perhaps ten feet high. Below this edge line, all was as dark as ever. Looking up again, tracing the edge line back and forth provided some estimate of the enclosed space to be investigated. Far to the left, perhaps twenty to twenty-five feet to the left, a second edge line ran at right angles to the first. The area above the second edge line was not entirely open, was covered by some sort of heavy-duty screening, which reached up to the ceiling.

Some six or seven feet to the right the first edge line collided into solid black, a ceiling-high wall.

Pino started into the darkness to his right. Began on his hands and knees, felt the floor, *pfft-pffted* along the base of the wall. Almost immediately he reached a corner. On turning the paper bag, and head underneath, he collided with an object. The gloved hand reached out, felt the hardness and cold, gently searched out the edges, determined that it was metal and square and on rollers, stood three and a half or four feet high. The fingers probed farther back along the top; the wrist bumped under something, went farther, got stuck, retreated without difficulty. The fingers came out, rose, moved forward, gained only a few inches, found a wall, lowered, felt the molding, skipped along, soon determined that there was a door four feet high and three and a half feet wide there, that the cold metal object was protruding from this door. The chest-suspended flashlight was gripped. *Pfft-pfft.* The metal General Electric money box. If not the GE money box itself, one that looked identical and was standing two-thirds of the way through the door.

More crawling, feeling, *pffting-pffting* onto the corner, the back wall over which light drifted, the eight- or ten-foot-high wall. A partially opened door was reached. The floor beyond was dark for several feet, then lightened into a visible cement floor. This door was passed by, the wall beyond only beginning to be examined when Pino could see more visible floor off to his left. It became evident that he was in a large L-shaped room, the shortest leg being the dark recess in which the box had been found. The longer leg of the L ran back toward the garage, ended at a wall in which there was a closed door. A door he could plainly see. Much of the wall parallel to the money box wall also ran beyond the shadows and into the weak, diffuse light. A counter ran along it. Above the counter were louvered windows. Some five feet above the windows the wall ended. Where the wall ended, an endless expanse of sturdy metal grille screening began, a barrier which ended at the ceiling.

Pino went home, returned the next night and, foot by foot, hand pat and *pfft-pfft* by hand pat and *pfft-pfft*, became satisfied that no hidden microphones or alarm-triggering devices were embedded in the cement floor, that no electric eyes scanned the area, that no "sneaky pictures" were poised to photograph trespassers.

Though he did not know the company-designated name, he was in the counting room, concluded on his own that the counters and louvered windows along the screen-topped three-quarter wall parallel to Hull Street were used for one thing and one thing only—counting money. This put a chill to him, a rush, an effusive excitement. Time was running out, safe time in which he knew the chances of guards or cleaning people appearing were minimal. But he was drawn, hypnotically, toward the door ahead of him. Not the closed door to his left at the end of the room which he correctly assumed opened into the rotunda, but the door beside the counter in the screen-topped wall facing Hull Street. He knew that he must go through. He knew that he could not resist going through.

And he became careless. He didn't bother to check the door before touching it. There was visibility over here in this section. Weak light, but light enough to look for wires or devices; somewhat stronger light from the other side after he coaxed the door almost completely open. He entered without as much as a glance at the frame. If he had looked down, he would have seen wires running along the floorboard. If he had looked down, particularly in the direction he was heading, he would have seen a metal button rising up out of the cement—an alarm button. But the paper bag tilted upward; the eyes behind it were transfixed.

An errant mist of unhurried street light brushed against the grille-fronted window, seemed to lose purpose and cohesion on entering, managed to reach and penetrate a high, wide gauze screen metal wall slanting across the front of the room, continued aimlessly on a ways, then gently spread itself out at the base of an eight-foot-high, eight-foot-wide, twelve-foot-long rectangular box—a box which, farther back in the gloom, a motionless, round-shouldered, bag-headed silhouette stood staring at.

Pino shuffled forward, stopped, studied the structure again. Again he slid his foot in preparation for a step. The toe glanced off something. He jumped back, knelt, lowered an eyehole. The metal tit poked up from the cement maybe half an inch. A stomp button. A stomp button to a floor alarm. The paper bag rose and slowly shook from side to side. A stomp button was the most primitive of alarms in his opinion. In his opinion he could have stepped right on it with no adverse result. Stomp button alarms were what the name implied. You had to stomp hard to set them off. He had run across ones where you literally had to jump on

Tony Pino at Boston's Suffolk County Courthouse in September, 1956—as a defendant in the Brink's robbery trial.

Boston Herald America

View along Prince Street to North Terminal Garage Building, 1950. Elevated tracks in background run along Commercial Street; entrance to Lafayette Street is on the left. On the night of the heist, the rigged getaway truck was parked some six feet farther down the street than the car shown in this photo.

Hull Street side of the building in the wake of the robbery. Arrow in foreground points to end of Snowhill Street which descends Copps Hill to Prince Street. Brinks's truck can be seen emerging from second-level garage, where Pino first saw a company truck enter in January, 1949. *Boston Herald American.*

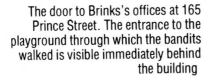

The door to Brinks's offices at 165 Prince Street. The entrance to the playground through which the bandits walked is visible immediately behind the building

Playground and rear of North Terminal Garage Building from atop apartment house on Snowhill Street. Prince Street can be seen to the left. Lower steps and landing of three terraces ascending to Hull Street-Snowhill Street intersection is to right. It was from this rooftop and one to left (not in photograph) that Pino surveiled Brink's offices and operations. It was from rooftop to left that Costa gave signals to gang members descending steps. Behind the "fifth window" (actually the sixth from the left on the second tier) lay the vault room.

Closeup of three windows (numbered one, two, three by the gang) fronting Brink's counting room. Mike Geagen moved up behind window to left, received the signal from Costa that the safe was still open, then led the other robbers on to the vault room. *Boston Herald American.*

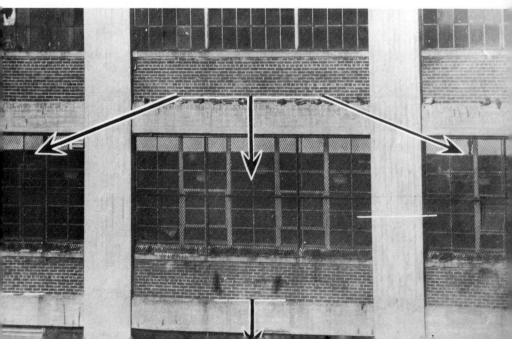

Model of interior of Brink's offices used by prosecution at 1956 trial:

1. Sliding metal doors through which Pino first entered premises
2. Garage
3. Control room referred to as "the rotunda" by Pino
4. Corner guard booth
5. Door to guard room which Pino tested and later used to enter offices
6. Guard room
7. Check-in room
8. Vault room
9. Vault
10. Check-cashing room
11. Payroll-wrapping room
12. Counting room
13. Money-room cage
14. Door for G. E. box
15. Front corridor
16. Executive offices
17. Men's washroom and lockers
18. Supply room
19. Garage supervisor's office
20. Front stairs

THE BOSTON HERALD

6 A. M. EXTRA

Nine Bandits Steal $1,500,000,
Leave Another Million at Brink's

BIGGEST ROBBERY IN U. S. HISTORY

5 Armed Guards Bound, Gagged

Victims Tell How Gang Cowed Five

150 Police 'Brass' Confer on Holdup

FIN COM ASKS Police Blast Brink, $95 JOB CUT Charge 'Inside Job'

Truman Calls For Showdown On Civil Rights

STEEL PLANTS CURTAIL AS COAL STOCKS SHRINK

Biggest Manhunt Seeks 'Cream of Crime World'

The Boston Post

EXTRA

We cannot control the evil tongues of others, but a good life enables us to disregard them.

9 GUNMEN SEIZE OVER A MILLION DOLLARS IN CASH IN HUB HOLDUP

Brink's Armored Bank Truck Company Victimized in Nation's Biggest Robbery---Bandit Gang Makes Clean Getaway After Leaving Another $1,000,000 Behind---Masked Robbers Tie Up Five Armed Guards---Flee in Single Car---All Identically Attired---Money Intended for Pay Rolls Today

DIES AT RADIO BRIDAL SHOW

Mother of Bridegroom Stricken on Coast-to-Coast Hookup in Which Roxbury Girl Marries

FAYE EMERSON DIVORCE FINAL

Star and Elliott Roosevelt Now Free

Highlights of Holdup

Robbers Pass Through 6 Doors and Up Flight of Stairs to Reach Treasure in Vault

GUARD HELPLESS TO FOIL ROBBERY

Tab. Post Reporter He Didn't Have Chance to Reach for Gun ---Couldn't Believe His Eyes

WALLACE IN AID BID FOR CHINA REDS

CASH TALKS!

$20,000.00 in CASH PRIZES

1st Prize $2,500.00 CASH
See Page 19

GALLAGHER & BURTON'S

NOW HERE

The day after the robbery the Boston Police Department dressed nine men in costumes similar to those worn by the thieves; they also retraced the suspected route of the gunmen through the Brink's offices. Most press photographs of the demonstration were cropped to include only seven men. Except for the chauffeur's cap left behind in the vault room, the FBI was never able to determine what became of the actual costumes and masks or where they had been obtained. *Boston Herald American.*

Exterior of the vault

Interior of the vault.

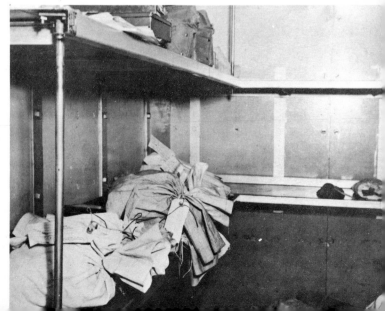

Interior of vault, showing sacks on shelf that were left behind by the robbers.

These official police pictures were made in reenactment of the Brink's robbery. The men tied up are those who were working on that fateful night. In the top picture are Thomas Lloyd, foreground, and Charles Grell. In lower picture are James Allen, left foreground, and Sherman Smith, extreme right. *AP Wirephoto*

Chauffeur's cap, rope and adhesive tape strips left behind by the robbers the night of January 17, 1950. The FBI lab in Washington, D.C., examined these items but could find no clue to the identity of the thieves. A nationwide investigation of manufacturers, wholesalers, and retailers failed to provide information on the origin of these objects. *Boston Herald American.*

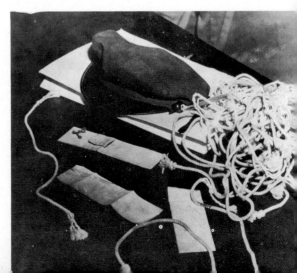

Boston Police Department plainclothesmen and uniformed officer listening to hold-up victim Thomas Lloyd (third from left) in vault room shortly after robbery. Man in cap and jacket (second from left) is believed to be from American District Telegraph, the company whose alarm system provided security to the premises. Lloyd and the four other Brink's employees confronted by gunmen never agreed on how many masked assailants had surprised them. All five victims state that each of the invaders was approximately the same height and weight. *Boston Herald American.*

Officials examining metal door leading into second floor offices of Brink's in wake of the robbery. It was determined that the perpetrators had keys for this door as well as the doors at the bottom of the stairwell (165 Prince Street entrance), but no one knew how the keys had been obtained. *Boston Herald American.*

REWARD
$100,000

has been offered by BRINK'S, INCORPORATED, Chicago, Illinois, "for information leading to the Arrest and Conviction of the Persons involved in the Holdup of the Office of Brink's, Incorporated, 165 Prince Street, Boston, Massachusetts, on January 17, 1950." The person or persons to whom the reward shall be paid and the amount will be determined by a specially designated reward committee.

If you have any information concerning the identity or the whereabouts of any of the perpetrators of the robbery of Brink's, Incorporated, at Boston, Massachusetts, on January 17, 1950, please communicate with the undersigned or with the nearest office of the FEDERAL BUREAU OF INVESTIGATION, U. S. Department of Justice, the local address and telephone number of which are set forth on the reverse side of this notice. The telephone number can also be obtained from page one of your telephone directory.

If such information leads to the arrest and conviction and/or recovery of money, the FEDERAL BUREAU OF INVESTIGATION will, if specifically requested to do so by the person furnishing information, advise the Reward Committee of the information so furnished.

JOHN EDGAR HOOVER, DIRECTOR
FEDERAL BUREAU OF INVESTIGATION
U. S. DEPARTMENT OF JUSTICE
WASHINGTON, D. C.
TELEPHONE NATIONAL 7117

The international media was accused of creating a "carnival atmosphere" in the days following the Brink's heist, but police and the five victims were not reluctant to meet the press corps. Marked and partially captioned photo shows the January 18, 1950, press conference held in the Brink's garage where company officials Eugene Murphy and Otto Plank (center at microphone) along with an insurance executive announce $100,000 reward offer. In upper right is door to guard room which Pino picked open to first enter offices. Later in the day NBC's fledgling television division used this garage for what may have been the first on the scene newscast of a crime. *Boston Herald American.*

Above left: Section of the dump at Stoughton, Massachusetts, where getaway truck parts were found in March, 1950. Man to the left is believed to be BPD Liuetenant James V. Crowley. The FBI still ponders why the truck was cut up rather than simply abandoned. Right: Pieces of truck recovered by FBI.

Above: 617 Tremont Street, Boston, where part of the Brink's loot was found concealed behind wall panel in June, 1956. Right: Portion of money found at Tremont Street address.

Boston Globe headline, January 12, 1956. *Copyright © 1956,* The Boston Globe

Stanley Gusciora

Joseph Sylvester Banfield

Chief defense council Paul T. Smith (left) conferring with Joe McGinnis (center) and Jimma Faherty in a guarded room during Brink's trial, August, 1956.

Eight members of the Brink's gang at the Suffolk County Courthouse, Boston, in August of 1956. Left to right: Jimma Faherty, Mike Geagen, Sandy Richardson, Joe McGinnis, Tony Pino, Jimmy Costa, Jazz Maffie, Henry Baker.

1973 portrait. Jimmy Costa, seated. Standing from left to right: Tony Pino, Jazz Maffie, and Sandy Richardson.

the button for activation. From the look of the metal tit, this alarm in this room was the cheapest and least efficient of the generally inefficient species. What's more, it wasn't meant to trip up interlopers. Stomps were internal security to be used by employees.

Pino couldn't dally with the button, didn't. Sweat had risen on his bag-covered face. His ticlike smile was flashing with such rapidity that even he was aware of it. The big shadowy "room" off to the right inside of this room was his sole concern. This huge box anchored in a base of concrete eight inches to a foot higher than the floor.

He stepped past the button, circled around in front of the "room," stood back and gazed. There was more light here. Still shadowy, but enough to see by. The front wall of the box was constructed of large cinder or concrete blocks. A wide metal ramp lay at its base, gently rose to the bottom of a three- to three-and-a-half-foot-wide door, a metal door. A heavy metal door six feet high and fronted by large lap-over hinges on top and on bottom. A heavy painted metal door latticed by two unpainted metal rods running into and through protruding metal cylinders. In the middle, in the exact middle of the door, was a spike-metal wheel. It was the vault.

"Mother of Sweet Christ, what a sight. What a piece of furniture. Oh, it was something. I coulda cried to begin with, but when I see painted on her face, 'built in 1875,' well, maybe I did cry. Back then, in 1860 or 1875, they didn't have the fancy new metals that are around today. The stuff back then was banana skin. Peel or burn her, but no nitro.

"There's something else on her, so that's why I gotta be careful. There's this sign that makes my work easy. Pasted right on her is a warning from ADT [American District Telegraph]. Touch this pete and you're up shit creek is what ADT's telling me, we got the beauty covered with all our alarms. We got her bugged.

"That ain't gonna stop me, see. She's breathtaking. Breathtaking and delectable. She's so gorgeous I'm overcome. I take off the sack. I go up and plant a kiss. Give her a smacker. Not a hard one 'cause I don't wanna set off that ADT bug, but a good loving smack to tell her I'd be back real soon to take care of her good."

The calls grew frantic, were eventually abandoned. Pino drove over to the longshoremen's office, learned that Sandy hadn't been in for two days. A tip at Cassiday's Café led to the Head House Bar, where Richardson and Faherty lay draped over a table.

"You drunk?" Pino demanded.

"Sleeping," came Sandy's mumbled and belated reply.

"You're goddamn sloshed!"

"Unh-unh. Goddamn sleeping," Faherty added.

"Don't tell me what you are! I can see what you are. You're both goddamn pie-eyed and sloshed."

"Incorrect," Richardson mildly objected, trying to raise his head. "We were goddamn sloshed an hour ago. Now we're sleeping."

"Up the rebels," Faherty rejoined.

"Up yourself and look at me!" commanded Pino.

"You do the honors," Faherty suggested to Sandy.

Richardson raised from the table, sat semierect and swaying.

Pino studied Sandy's bruised and eye-flickering face. "You're a goddamn drunk and a goddamn disgrace. You're nothing but a drunk street brawler."

"We . . . were not brawling," Richardson tried to explain. "We were set upon by unknown assailants. Ask Mike."

"Mike ain't here!" Pino barked.

"Oh, they musta kidnapped the poor fella. Well, ask Jimma if we weren't set upon."

Pino stared angrily at the snoring Faherty and then back at Richardson. "Because of your horrid conditions, I ain't gonna tell you why I came over," he warned.

Richardson yawned, nodded and started teetering forward. Pino caught him by the lapel and forced him back in the chair.

"Don't you have no sense of pride?" Sandy was asked. "Don't you have no ordinary curiosity?"

"Curiosity? About what, Anthony?"

"Our partner."

"Which one?"

"Whaddaya mean, which one? How many do you think we got?"

"So many I can't count."

"This is our biggest one—that's which goddamn one!" Pino shouted. Then, realizing he shouted, he sat down and leaned forward. "Our legitimate one," he explained. "A fifty-fifty partner, only we take both fifties, see? Sandy, we just gone into business with Mr. Brink's."

Richardson squinted dimly at Pino. "We've been in business with him for two and a half years."

"Yeah, but now he's selling out. He's giving us the keys and full title."

Sandy cleared his throat. "Are you saying, more or less, Anthony, that you got through his door?"

"Got through the door? Mother of God, I moved in. I took rooms with a bath. Sandy, I kissed her!"

"Kissed who?"

"A luscious lady with an unbelievable shape. You won't be able to keep your hands off her."

"Anthony, what are you talking about?"

"I found the pete. I went up and laid a smacker on her."

"You kissed a safe?"

CHAPTER FIFTEEN

Rooms with a Bath

Sandy didn't have to be on Hull Street at 5 P.M. to see the last Brink's truck of the day turn in from Commercial Street, to see the driver shift gears and gun the engine, to watch the truck groan and creak, ascend the slope and turn again, this time into the second-level garage. He didn't have to see that because Tony Pino had told him all about it, and they didn't get there in time to see it anyway. They didn't get there in time to see the foot patrolman come around the corner from Commercial Street and check the three North Terminal Garage doors along Prince before departing the area via tiny Lafayette Street. But Tony told Sandy all about the cop, explained how the tour was over by 6:15 P.M. every evening except on Friday, when for some inexplicable reason he showed up an hour later.

This was Richardson's first visit to the joint, the first time Pino would be taking any crew member in—a Cook's tour deluxe, with no small dosage of histrionics provided. Sandy arrived in time to see the light in the fifth window over the playground go off, was then told to watch Prince Street, did and saw two men emerge from the door nearest the Commercial Street corner. He had to run to keep up with the jubilant, high-stepping Pino as they climbed Snowhill. Rather than enter the building via Commercial, Tony followed a new route, one he had established during the four days following his discovery of the vault room—into and across the second-floor common garage on Hull Street, past the door to the auxiliary garage used by Brink's, exiting by the pair of sliding fire doors at the other end, then opening and wedging the two squeaking sliding fire doors leading into the Brink's garage itself.

Pino no longer used paper bag masks, no longer bothered with peeking each truck. So confident was he of the terrain that he ran along explaining in full voice, not whispers, all that he had found in the section in bygone days.

There was no reason for him and Sandy pulling their bandanas up over the bottom of their faces and sneaking up on the rotunda—other than the suspense of it all. Pino had quit checking the window since the night he found the vault. He allowed Sandy the honor of using the pick to open the door into the guardroom. Once through the door on the other side of the room, Richardson got on his knees as instructed and followed Tony through the small door in which the money cart had been found. The space they came out in, fronted by a metal screening, was called the money room cage by the company. Pino had searched it several nights earlier, as he had done with the large counting room into which they now walked. The large chamber was amply il-luminated by street light coming in from the two large and one small fronting windows. Here, between the cage to the money room and windows, stood three double rows of back-to-back desks and one single row. They crossed back to a door beside the money room cage, entered and followed a long hallway lead-ing toward Prince Street and came out in a small lobby. To the left was a metal door; to the right was a guardroom window. Straight ahead were windows looking out over Prince Street.

Sandy was told this was as far as Tony had come in his search and screening of the territory. More rooms existed to the right—behind the guard booth window and the door in the long hall they had just come down.

Pino led the way back into the money room cage, under the small metal box floor door and out into the L-shaped money room itself. A door was opened at the garage end of the longer end of the L. Richardson stepped into what the company called the control room and Pino referred to as the rotunda. The long fronting and two short siding windows provided a complete view of the unlit garage. Pino pointed to a set of buttons to the side of the counter which ran under the windows. These, he said, were the buttons that electrically opened the door leading into the guardroom from the garage, as well as the door that led from the guardroom into the shorter L section of the money room. Particular attention was given to the metal ring near the counter. Sandy knew what it was on sight, a pull alarm—hook a finger in the ring and pull and the alarm goes off. "My God, it's a cheap variety at that," Richardson commented. "Not cheap, the cheapest there is," Pino rejoined, "and I've found three more of them in other parts of the joint."

They left the control room by the side door facing Hull Street. Once through they were standing in the garage end of the vault room.

"Anthony, needless to say, was having the time of his life conducting his tour," says Richardson. "It had been a shock so far, a total shock. Brink's was absolutely wide open. The alarms they had were a laugh, and the locks in their doors were pathetic. What was more deplorable was that they kept all the doors inside open. Except for the door to the guards' room, everything else was left open. When Anthony showed me the stomp button, it was worse than deplorable. After all, Brink's is paid millions of dollars to guard other people's money, and here Anthony and I are running around through the joint like two kids in a deserted ice-cream parlor. There's no excuse for that. I was upset, and I don't know why I should have been. We'd been watching this company for four and a half years, and they were screw-ups from top to bottom. When I start putting together what I saw up here, adding cheap alarms and cheap locks to the fact that no guards are present and no other security is apparent, you can easily reach the same conclusion as Anthony. Brink's is a chintz."

Pino continued his tour of the rear of the vault room, picked open a cabinet lock and showed Sandy a small arsenal of rifles and handguns, then picked open a second and smaller cabinet affixed to the wall. Keys for every Brink's truck hung from nails.

"Anthony had made copies of most of these keys years before," says Richardson. "That's what we'd been opening up their trucks with. But it was still a sight. Everything was so far.

"The section of the room we were in was dark. Both Anthony and I had penlights with us, but we were only using his. He showed me several of the money carts they had there. These were new to me. The money trays and the sacks on the counter weren't. You might say I'd come across them in the course of other Brink's business. The General Electric box was out in this area, too. This is the big metal box on wheels that started it all—the one Anthony spotted back in '44. Needless to say, the box and trays were empty, but I imagined how they would look full.

"We gave the box a playful shove. It squeaked when it rolled.

"Anthony, of course, had saved the best for last. He had intentionally led me around the long way and got me fascinated with other things in the joint. It was easy to be fascinated.

"When we came around the corner, or what I thought was a corner, I was flabbergasted. There was the vault. As Anthony put it, 'luscious to behold.' I estimated she stood somewhere of eight feet high and about nine or ten feet wide in front. The front was built out of concrete block. The door reached right up to the top and was possibly three and a half to four feet wide. The door, of course, was dialed shut and had a heavy opening device on it—two bars across, one down the middle.

"If you can believe something right out of my own character," Sandy confides, "I repeated what Anthony had done. There we were, standing in the dark with only the playground lights to see by, and I became the victim of an irresistible compulsion. I walked up and kissed a metal safe.

"I kissed her carefully because she was obviously bugged. We had, in our travels, learned that smoke undeniably leads to fire. The signs attached to the safe usually tell the truth. I had no doubt that ADT had a bug somewhere on her. If we could beat the bug, I was certain we could burn or blow up the safe with no difficulty. We'd tangled with ADT alarms before, and I was pretty sure we could find this one and put it out of business. In fact, we started searching her then and there.

"We had a brief discussion first about electric alarms—wireless alarms. From what we'd seen, Brink's wasn't going to spend an extra penny if they could help it, and wireless alarms are more expensive.* We went on the assumption that wires would be hooked in somewhere.

"I got up on the chair. I had little choice. Anthony was so corpulent a [chair] leg could buckle from his weight or he could have a more difficult time balancing over in the corner. I had situated the chair on the lip in the corner of the two safes. Did I mention the small safe? At the far end [garage end] of the big box, the vault, was a smaller safe—probably a utility safe for ordinary company business. It was pressed right against the big box and was high itself but not as high as the big one. It came right over the lip. The big box was elevated a few inches on a cement platform. I would say the platform came out eight or ten inches beyond the box. That was the lip I was trying to set the chair on. Only three of the legs would fit, so I began over in the corner where the small safe was—the corner between the big box and small safe. If the chair rocked here, which it did, I could brace myself on the small safe. Only Anthony could come up with a situation like this.

"I began feeling around the top of the big box and vividly recall a chuckle. I recall turning around and seeing Anthony sitting on the counter flashing his penlight off and on when he was supposed to be looking for wires.

"I watched him for a minute and whispered, 'Anthony, what the hell, might I ask, are you doing?'

"He went right on sitting there, chuckling and flashing his penlight off and on. I might add that Anthony is by no means a chuckler.

"I must admit I got pissed off. Here I am up on top of a chair, trying to balance on three legs while I'm feeling around in the dust for wires, trying not to leave marks in the dust—and there's Anthony down there having the time of his life. I believe I said something eloquent like, 'Is this lunch hour or are you partaking of another comic book?'

" 'Oh, a real funny comic book, Mr. R.,' he said back. 'Come by and look for yourself.'

"I managed to jump off the chair without breaking my neck

*This was an incorrect assumption.

and wiped away footprints from the seat. I put it back near the counter where we had found it. I mention all this because it occupied my time. For a moment or so I completely forgot Anthony likes nothing better than topping one surprise with another. And if you think there was nothing up here that could top seeing that vault and Brink's criminal indifference to security, you're wrong.

"Anthony hands me a clipboard he had taken from the wall. That's what he had been chuckling over. My penlight is flashing off and on, and I'm stupefied. Schedule sheets are clipped to the board. Schedules telling exactly what trucks are going out of Brink's every day and exactly how much each delivery is. Each delivery was specified and itemized—eight hundred thousand dollars to be delivered to such-and-such a factory at seven on truck whatever . . . fifteen grand to be delivered to such and such a bank at seven forty-five on another truck. It's right there in front of me on these sheets. Everything. Everything we spent years trying to find out by tailing trucks and hanging around dropoffs is marked down.

"I'm sure you can see the obvious impact of this on us. I'm standing there in front of the box on a Tuesday night. The top sheet on the clipboard is for the Wednesday morning deliveries. Everything that is supposed to be delivered, therefore, has to be in the box at this moment. I ran my fingers down the list of each delivery—the column that had the dollar value of each delivery. I remember it added up to four million seven hundred thousand dollars. Almost five million dollars was sitting and waiting less than five steps away."

"Hello, who is this?" Jazz Maffie asked as he picked up the phone at Jimmy O'Keefe's restaurant.

"Stretch," Tony Pino whispered, "this is Stretch."

"Who?"

"Stretch!"

"I don't know no Stretches."

"What the hell you mean you don't know no Stretches?"

"Listen, whoever you are, the only Stretch I know is in the can."

Maffie hung up, lit a fresh cigar and waited beside the cloak room. The phone rang, was answered by the hatcheck girl, who then handed the receiver to Jazz.

"Hello, who is this?"

"It's the only goddamn Stretch you know, and I ain't in a goddamn can," Pino bellowed.

"Yeah, well how do I know it's the same Stretch I used to know?"

"You know by listening to my fucking voice!"

"I got a cold. I can't hear too good."

"You come meet me at the regular place in twenty minutes and you can see for yourself!" Pino shouted.

"Hey, you think I'm a sucker, whoever you are? I don't go anywhere till I know who I'm going to meet."

"Then how the goddamn hell you ever gonna know it's me if you can't tell my voice and won't go and look?"

"Oh. You got a point," Maffie said. "I'll tell you what. You describe yourself."

"Describe myself?"

"You know, tell me how you look."

A long pause ensued.

"I'm five eight," Pino finally said.

"The guy I know is shorter."

"Okay, so I'm five seven."

"Thin or fat?"

"In between."

"You ain't the guy I know!"

"I'm chubby, not goddamn fat!"

"In the face or all over?"

"You can't be chubby in one place. When you're chubby, you're chubby all over."

"You're starting to sound like the guy I know. You have any relatives I might'uv met?"

"How's a brother-in-law sound to you?"

"Sounds good, depending on what he does for an honest living."

"He used to be a presser and takes care of a diner, and he just went bankrupt in the women's clothes business. Now, for the love of God, do you know I'm me?"

"Oh, sure. How you been, Stretch?"

"The goddamn question is where the hell'uv *you* been? I been calling all over."

"Oh, I been right here all the time."

"Then why didn't you pick up the goddamn phone?"

" 'Cause I thought it was a setup. I thought it was somebody imitating you."

"Why to Christ would you think an insane thing like that for?"

"Oh, well, I thought you got pinched. I figured the only reason I hadn't heard from you in four weeks is you was pinched and went to the can."

"Well, get your ass over to the regular place. I'll pick you up at the regular place in twenty minutes."

"Oh, I can't meet you then."

"You gotta meet me then. Listen, mister, and listen good." Tony lowered his voice, spoke slowly. "I'm making you a part of history. The other fella can't get over tonight, so you're gonna be number three, see? The third man in all the world to see something history's gonna be writing about soon."

"I don't want nobody writing about me!"

"They ain't. Not about you. They ain't gonna know."

"I think you oughta let the other guy go third."

"I told you, he ain't available. Now be there like I said."

"Oh, well, listen, Stretch. I have something to tell you. I been talking to some other people. You know, talking to them about this and that."

"You saying you're quitting us and joining up with another crowd?"

"Oh, I haven't definitely joined up. We're just talking it over."

"I don't believe what I'm hearing. I don't believe you're selling us out."

"Well, I thought we was out of business. After not hearing from you all this time, I thought you was in the can. Me and the Polish guy started making other arrangements."

"Gus, too?" Pino yelled. "You can't do this to me. We're ready to move. We got to go on something hot right away."

"Oh, well, I can't guarantee nothing, Stretch, but out of old friendship I'll do you a favor and have a look."

The door leading from the common garage on Hull Street to the auxiliary garage in the front of the building used by Brink's was closed. Pino backtracked, led Maffie down the hill, around the corner and into the ground-level garage on Commercial Street.

"Oh, I heard all about Tony Pino walking around under a shopping bag. Sandy Richardson had been keeping me and Gus posted ever since Tony Pino told him he found the pete. I wasn't burned up about Tony Pino not calling for so long himself, but Gus was some. Gus was a funny guy, too, so we decided whoever Tony Pino called first would give him a hard time. He called me first.

"When he couldn't get in the first door, I told him I wanted to go home. When we got up to the slide doors [leading to Brink's garage from the ground-floor stairway] and they squeaked, I told him everyone in town must've heard the squeaking and I was getting out of there.

"Tony Pino was talking a mile a minute and being polite. He told me how we were all going to be millionaires the rest of our lives and all of that. He was doing everything he could to keep me there. It was killing him that I could walk away without seeing what he had to show me.

"Let me tell you something—I was impressed. Everything I saw when I got up into the joint impressed me. Even if I was impressed, I wouldn't show that I was. When other people don't get excited about what Tony Pino is excited about, it makes him really crazy.

"So when I walked over and saw the pete, I looked at it without even a smile and said, 'This is all you got to show me?' Tony Pino about fell over when he heard that. I even think he started hopping up and down. He has a funny little hop dance he does, up and down, when he gets out of control. He did that dance, and he said, 'You big dumb cluck, you big this and that—.' I keep playing this indifference, but it's hard to keep a straight face. Tony Pino always makes me smile.

"I think I almost smiled, so I said, 'Hey, this is all nice, but I gotta go back and have my meet with those other people. The ones I may go into business with. We have some work to discuss.'

"Now that about collapsed Tony Pino. He started talking to himself about big, something about if you wanted a big job, he'd show me the biggest. Tony Pino went over beside the safe and takes off a clipboard. He brought me this clipboard and said take a look.

"I use my [pen]light and looked at the clipboard. It's got a list of every shipment and how much it's worth. Now I don't pretend I'm indifferent anymore. I add up what's in the safe every day of the week. The smallest is three million and change, and the biggest is over six.

"Tony Pino saw I'm impressed and he said, 'Well, are you impressed?'

" 'Oh, sure, I'm impressed. This is something,' I said.

" 'Then kiss it.'

"You know what crazy Tony Pino wanted me to do?" asks Jazz Maffie. "He wanted me to go over and kiss a safe. Hell, I don't even kiss my own wife if people is looking."

"Tony knew better than to ask me to kiss anything," asserts Mike Geagan. "We went in through the upstairs garage [via the Hull Street common garage]. My first thought was stealing a couple of the trucks there. Tony had keys to all of them. Steal a couple of their uniforms, too. You put a couple of our men in their uniforms, in there late in the day, and they won't know you don't belong there until it's too late. That was my first impression.

"When we got inside and I saw the clipboard, I forgot the stickup. On one night alone they had seven and a half million in there. On another night it was six. The two smallest nights were three and five. That was worth taking time for. It was worth seeing if we could beat the bug and blast the safe open.

"I always felt we had to blast," Mike asserts. "This was a big box made out of old steel. It wasn't hard to cut, but it was slow. The sides were in concrete block, so we'd have to burn through the door. That door could be two foot thick. That's a long burn through any kind of steel—two feet. Tony and me talked about the new methods of burning—the latest torches. We kept that on the shelf. The first thing was killing that bug. Finding the wires and cutting them off.

"When I went in, there were parts he hadn't been to. Sandy and me gave him a hand after that. Every night one of us was in with him. Never two of us. The rule was never more than two men inside at one time."

"We got out into their front hall. The big metal door was on the left. It went down the stairs, two flights, to the front door [165 Prince]. We didn't touch that yet. We kept on going down looking for wires. We got underneath the place in the basement. We had to be careful with the wires down there. Wires from all over the building were down here. ADT is a sharp outfit. They've been at the game a long time. Best there is with alarms. They know how to trip their own wires. Have their alarm wires bugged, too. We had to look for bugs on bugs."

T&T was the acronym used. Jimma Faherty had extended another T, TT&T—Tony's Tour and Tony's Talking Tour, respectively. Jimma, the fourth crewman to take it, had entered the building by the Commercial Street garage. Stanley Gusciora, fifth, came in by way of the second-level common garage on Hull Street. For both men the tour really got under way once the squeaky twin fire doors into the Brink's section of the garage were opened and wedged. There can be no doubt that for both men the junket definitely deserved an extra *T*. Tony's travelogue was uninterruptable and, because much more, if not all, of the premises had been scouted by this time, far longer than suffered by Geagan.

Both Jimma and Gus in their tour had to wear handkerchief face masks and gloves. It would never do to go the easy, short way while the harder, longer was available—not to Pino in his puffy prime. Jimma and Gus, each in his turn, got down on their hands and knees and followed Tony under the half door in which the money box had once sat, up behind the money room cage, out into the vast counting room and into the corridor leading toward Prince Street.

A door to the right was entered before the end of the corridor was reached. This was new territory, space scouted and proclaimed free of bugs only days before. All had windows looking out onto Prince Street. First came the general office and then the manager's office and then the superintendent's office and the supervisor's office. The girls' washroom and, beyond it, the girls' locker room were also visited.

The next leg of the TT&T began back in the corridor leading from the counting room. To this point, Tony had seldom lost a chance to condemn the cheap locks in every interior door along the way, to point out not only that they were cheap, but that the doors were either kept open or unlocked. Here, at the door leading from the end of the corridor into the small front lobby facing onto Prince Street, he guardedly called for caution. "This one the dumbbells sometimes lock, so what we'll do—" The door was opened, and a wedge affixed at the bottom to keep it from closing. The door to the left of the lobby was metal. It was always kept locked. Another wedge came out.

The metal door opened onto a three-story-high stairwell. Just beyond the concrete landing was a flight of concrete steps leading down toward the playground side wall of the building, a half flight ending at a small square landing. The steps here, also concrete, descended in the direction of the Commercial Street side of the building. The stairwell prompted silence and caution from Pino. Once he had reached the landing at the bottom of the second half flight of stairs, he pointed at the metal door and whispered that this was the main door, the one on Prince Street numbered 165 and to which the Brink's shield was affixed. This door was never to be touched. Yes, Tony had scouted it for wires already and found none, but you still couldn't be sure. If Brink's were to use a second trick from its bag anywhere else besides on the vault, it would be here. "I'm telling you again," he told each man in his turn, "never touch it."

The second-to-last lap of the TT&T began back upstairs in the counting room. The trespassers kept low and angled toward the windows overlooking the playground, were right up against the windows when they passed through the Dutch door—the unlocked and open Dutch door—and into the payroll wrapping room.

At the opposite door of the payroll wrapping room, Tony again signaled for total silence, got down on his hands and knees and, for no requisite reason except effect, crawled out in front of the slanting wire barrier.

There on the other side of the grillwork loomed the vault.

This then was the TT&T, the psychological device Pino would forever credit with convincing Faherty and Gusciora not to abandon Brink's. Forever the others would dismiss this boast out of hand. The briefest of peeks at the pete sitting there, they would avow time and time again, was enough to divert the most pious of cloth toward the rankest of thievery.

The meet, as best can be remembered, was made in either the first or second week of February in Tony's living room. Mike was there, and Jimma and Sandy and Jazz and Gus. It was evening, and Mary served whiskey along with the coffee and cake. Mary left, and Tony brought the meet to order. The six of them, he intoned, were "setting sail on a spectacular piece of work." They would have to pull together and do what had to be done. He certainly had. Fifteen times in five weeks, he told the gathering, that's how often he'd been inside Brink's. On four or five other occasions or maybe six, he'd been outside peeking the joint. Since the aborted grab of 48 Truck on Federal Street he'd been up at North End "every single night"—well, not every night; there'd been some trouble with a cook and Jimmy Costa. Jimmy had burned up $45 worth of stew. But he'd been there *almost* every night, and oh, the wonders he had beheld. He began relating the wonders.

"Nobody said it wasn't wonderful," declares Mike Geagan, "but Tony forgot we'd been in there and seen for ourselves. He forgot he had told each of the men what he went through.

"Tony's the greatest crook that ever lived. He's a genius. The Captain. We worked for him and did what he told us to do. Sometimes he overdoes and gets off the track in his enthusiasm. You have to get him back on the track.

"I got things back on the track. I didn't have to tell the men Tony was right about the B&E. We all knew we were going after the biggest haul of all. When you do that, you need as much time as you can have. You don't want to rush like you have to with pistols.

"I told the men—that's before we got started—I told them I thought the six of us could handle whatever there was to do. I still do. Six was all we needed to grab her off either way.

"I told the men that anything we said between us in that room

stayed between us and nobody else. I didn't want anyone shooting off their mouth. We went through that with another big haul
[Sturtevant]. Right when we were ready for the clout, word
started spreading around town. We almost had to call it off.

"This was the biggest thing of my life and any of theirs. This
was seven million dollars that we knew of. We could all quit and
be set for the rest of our lives on that. I was quitting. No one had
the right to spoil it for the others. I was the one who said if anybody opened their mouth, we should give them the death."

No concrete suggestion came up for detecting the bug other
than what was being done at present. Tony would continue looking for wires. Should this effort fail, all seemed content with Pino's assurance of coming up with alternative plans for neutralizing the alarm.

Discussion turned to methodology and personnel for opening
the vault. Peeling was totally out of the question. They could
peel for two full days and nights and still have half the layers of
metal to go on a box this size.

Burning was a sure bet, but a slow bet. The standard butane
torch would possibly take as long as five hours cutting through a
vault door as thick as Brink's. There was another consideration
here. Tony was primarily a peeler. He'd worked with torches all
right, but not on anything so huge as to require five hours of
flame. He wasn't even sure if five hours were the maximum
assessment or if butane was the most efficient fuel under these
conditions. Mike and Sandy didn't know either, and they had always been the backup burners on crew torch jobs in the past. To
burn and burn correctly, chances were that an outside expert
would have to be involved—if not to sit under the tent erected at
the vault door and wield the torch, then surely to give advice on
equipment and technique.

Explosives were a possibility, but even with nitroglycerine—
the minimal amount of soup needed to blast a box of this propor-
tion—the resulting concussion might shatter all the office windows running over the playground, send shock waves out into
the immediate neighborhood, causing even more destruction; it
could result in policemen and firemen hurrying to the scene prematurely. Once again, none of the five crew members gathered
in Pino's living room could be sure this would or would not oc-

cur. Tony had handled nitroglycerine before, and so had Mike, and on occasion Sandy, but never in amounts even close to what was being speculated on. For safety's sake alone, a blast job of this magnitude could not be undertaken without the physical presence at the vault of an expert blow man. An outsider.

Pino offered another possibility. What about the kids from New York City, the ones he and Mike and Sandy and Jimma had done time with at Charlestown? Those crazy chemical students who knew how to freeze a pete with liquid oxygen and then walk up and crack away the door like a block of ice? Those kids who had *already* made a couple of million bucks down around Manhattan, walking up and chipping away solid metal petes with an ice pick? If they were talking about bringing in outsiders, why not get hold of them? If they were not interested, maybe they'd give the crew the formula so they could do it themselves?

Once again, not even Pino was sure the liquid oxygen worked or that it currently was being employed by the chemical students. Gang members had only heard that this was the case, heard thirdhand of a rather startling series of exploits, including the freezing of entire alarm systems in preparation for an ice crack. Tony liked to believe rumors of a grandiose nature such as these but, when it came to his own domain, talked more than he acted. Anyway, bringing in the chemists would mean two men, not one additional man, with whom to split the biggest haul of all.

Tony turned the discussion back to burning. Since it seemed unavoidable that an expert would have to be brought in, why not find one who knew something about those newfangled high-power electrical torches that postwar technology was credited with perfecting? Nobody said they had to give a commitment right now, but why not talk to one of the fellows who knew about it if he could find him? Sure, why not, everybody seemed to agree.

Deployment of manpower would follow the usual lines. All six would carry in whatever equipment there was. Jimma and Sandy would assist Tony and Mike with the burning, Jazz and Gus would guard the premises. If an extra specialist were along and five hands were not needed in setting up, Faherty would prematurely join Maffie and Gusciora. Specification on where peeks would be kept would be made later by Pino and Geagan. All hands would help with loading on the loot and equipment.

Tony brought up Costa's name. No matter what method was finally employed to crack the safe, the six regular crewmen would have their hands full. Therefore, a seventh man should be assigned to drive—Costa.

Costa had certainly proved himself behind the wheel of a car. But some one or other in the living room pointed out they might not need an extra hand to drive—not if they entered the premises by the shortest route possible, pulled their vehicle into the second-level common garage of Hull Street, drove across the auxiliary garage used by Brink's, opened the door between the auxiliary space and main garage and pulled right up and park in front of the guardroom door.

Someone else pointed out that burning equipment, regardless of what was finally selected, would take up so much space that a car couldn't possibly be used. Not unless, of course, one car was used for the equipment and another for the five robbers. Pino agreed that he didn't want to use two cars but pointed out no final decision had been reached in regard to burning. The possibility still had to be explored. In the end they might decide on nitroglycerine. You could certainly fit all the men and nitroglycerine into the same car—driven by Costa. Gus and Jazz politely let it be known they weren't riding in any car carrying nitroglycerine no matter who was driving.

Someone else asked the most obvious question. Forgetting the equipment, how was it physically possible to fit seven men and $7,000,000 into the same car?

One way or another, a truck would be going to Brink's. And Jimmy Costa wasn't any great shake wheeling a truck.

"Anthony, when he gets excited at meets, often says the first thing that pops into his mind without thinking about it," says Sandy Richardson. "That's when most of the outrageous ideas come out. Even if the others laugh, he'll argue for them a few minutes and then give it up. Sometimes he'll keep an outlandish idea hot for a few days, but not often.

"What I'm trying to imply is you don't take everything Anthony says seriously. I admit, sometimes it's hard to know if he's serious or not. On top of everything, he kids around a lot, particularly when meets are at his joint. So do the other guys—kid around.

"I don't think he was serious when he brought up that thing about half a gallon of nitroglycerine and seven guys all in the same car. At least I hope he wasn't.

"And I think he always knew we had to use a truck. In fact, once we got onto trucks, he made the best suggestion of all: grabbing one of those newspaper trucks [Record-American] parked in the downstairs garage and using that. No one around the neighborhood would think twice if they saw one of the newspaper trucks driving in or out.

"All Anthony was doing was putting in the pitch for Jimmy Costa. He wanted Jimmy in on it, and we all knew that. As I remember, he put in the pitch again. He said even if Costa didn't drive, we needed him on the outside peek to be on the lookout for cops or other people coming into the joint when they shouldn't be.

"It wasn't a matter of greed with me not letting in extra men. Maybe it was to some of the guys, but I don't think so. I didn't care how many ways we split the haul just so every guy pulled his own weight. If we needed a guy outside or if we needed a driver or another torchman, that was okay with me, but we were getting ahead of ourselves. I said for myself, if we needed Jimmy, we'd use him when the time came, but there were other things we needed first.

"If we needed anything, we needed a bigger plant. We'd have to take the stuff someplace and count it, and Savin Hill wasn't big enough. Anthony said he'd think about it.

"I started to get a drift of the idea when Anthony said he had a brainstorm. He said we'd have to get the best driver there was for the truck, and he had just the man. He brought up Barney's name. I didn't know Barney* well, but he had a good reputation with a truck. He was a nice guy, and I liked him, but I knew he belonged to Skinhead [Joe McGinnis]. I didn't know Skinhead from a hole in the wall, but I knew enough about him to know he was the biggest cheat that ever lived. Anthony did business with

*Joseph Sylvester Banfield

him, I didn't know what kind, but that was Anthony's business. I didn't want Skinhead anywhere near us, and that meant keeping Banfield away, too. But it never came to a vote that night. Someone else said it was too early to talk about truck drivers.

"When we broke up, we knew we had to find that bug. We were pretty sure we'd have to bring in one or two extra guys, but we didn't know who they would be or when. If we didn't find a way to kill that bug, we'd have to change all our plans—go in on the heavy."

Before the first meet concerning the big haul was terminated, a second warning was given that not one of the attending participants breathe a word about their plans. All six conspirators concurred wholly. The penalty for such an infraction was firmly set at death.

The legal address for the tract of land in Dorchester opposite Franklin Park was 780 Blue Hill Avenue. Nearest the street, nearest Blue Hill Avenue, and in the right-hand corner of the property, stood a three-family house. Farther to the left on the property were lines of stores. Between the house and stores was a driveway which ran back to a garage in the rear of the plot. Alongside the garage was an old barn. The owner of the garage was eighty-two-year-old Tomasso Soracco. Soracco lived around the corner at 16 Wales Street. It was at this address that Tomasso's daughter-in-law, Alma, answered the door on February 3, 1949.

The visitor was tall, gaunt, properly dressed and polite. He had come to inquire about the vacant garage at 780 Blue Hill Avenue. How many cars did it hold? Alma collected and recorded rents for some of her father-in-law's property but wasn't acquainted with the garage. Tomasso was summoned. "Three cars," he told the visitor. The old man wanted to know the stranger's name. "Callahan Brothers," was the answer. The old man wanted to know what kind of business Callahan Brothers was in. "The building cleaning business," Callahan Brothers answered. What did Callahan Brothers mean by that? the old man wanted to know. They cleaned the inside of buildings out, Callahan Brothers explained. How much was the rent? Callahan Brothers wanted to know. Forty dollars a month, the old man explained. Did he want to see the garage? the old man asked Callahan Brothers. That wasn't necessary, Callahan Brothers explained. Callahan Brothers said he would take the garage. The old man told Callahan Brothers that his daughter-in-law, Alma, would take the rent. Callahan Brothers explained to Alma that he was going to Florida for a much-needed rest. Callahan Brothers asked if he could pay an additional two months' rent in advance. Alma said yes. Callahan Brothers gave Alma the money in cash. Alma gave Callahan Brothers a receipt saying that the rent for March, April and May had been paid. Alma gave Callahan Brothers the key to the garage.

Callahan Brothers was Barney Banfield, who turned the key and receipt over to Tony Pino.

"That new plant had nothing to do with Brink's, see?" Tony insists. "I was gonna get a new plant for Brink's all right, only this one wasn't it.

"Let me tell ya what the place on Blue Hill was for, okay? I was getting back into a lot of my other business and needed a bigger joint. Sandy and me and Jimmy were grabbing lots of refrigerators and TVs and power lawn mowers, and we needed a big joint for them. That garage over at Savin Hill couldn't hold 'em all. Barney and me was bringing in some cigarettes from New Jersey, too. Not McGinnis, just Barney and me. McGinnis and me had a lot of our own business going good then, but not cigarettes. Joe didn't know nothing about Barney and me.

"Okay, now what happened is Barney tells me about this guy, Sam the Toy Man. An old friend. Sam the Toy Man uses the big barn back there on Blue Hill, and one day he tells Barney about a garage being free come March. So I give Barney the money to go rent it—pay a coupla months in advance.

"He rents it for outside business, know what I mean? Not Brink's. I ain't even cased the whole joint yet. I'm still down in the basement looking at wires. And nobody knows about it like we agreed. No one but the five of us."

Not quite the truth. Over the threat of imminent death Pino had told Costa everything there was to know about Brink's—had taken Jimmy into the premises and on the QT given him the TT&T; had alerted Banfield to be ready to drive for the "biggest thing you ever heard of"; had hinted to Joe McGinnis that something spectacular was in the offing.

CHAPTER SIXTEEN

Skinhead

Joseph F. McGinnis was born on August 19, 1903. He grew up in Providence, Rhode Island. His father was a Rhode Island cop. His mother never cut his hair and dressed him as a girl until he was seven or eight. His two prettiest frocks both had ruffles and velvet and could be worn only on Sunday, when his mother would take him to mass. Sometimes she would take him to two masses on the same morning to show him off. His father objected to his son's being dressed as a girl. His father had fights with his mother over this. His father had fights with his mother over her thriftiness—over the fact that she wouldn't spend money on anything but Joe. His mother cried after a fight. His mother died when Joe was still very young.

When Joe McGinnis grew up, he shaved off all his thinning hair long before he became prematurely and totally bald. He moved to Boston, where he had lived for a short period during his late teens. His first wife was well publicized as being one of Boston's leading madams. He was cheap, wouldn't spend a dime on anything. He loathed clothes, usually was seen—depending on the weather—in a T-shirt or dark turtleneck sweater with the same pair of inexpensive plain dark trousers. As far as anyone knew, he owned only one suit, which was worn only on Sunday when he went to mass. He never missed mass. Sometimes he went to two masses in the same day. As far as anyone knew, he seldom smiled, and he seemed to dislike everybody with the exception of his second wife. He smiled with her, often appeared to be gentle when he was with her. They were rarely seen publicly together anywhere other than mass. He detested anyone who treated a woman, let alone a wife, shabbily. He hated cops and the law as few men have ever hated cops and the law.

Joe McGinnis' first recorded arrest came on June 2, 1919. It was for robbery and was filed without prosecution. Four days later a Boston juvenile court ordered him to be committed to the Shirley School for idle and disorderly behavior. He moved back to Providence, and by the time he was twenty he had been fined a total of $200 for two different larceny convictions, served four months in jail for another larceny conviction, plus almost three full years in state prison for robbery. During Prohibition he moved quickly up the bootlegging ladder from peddler to distiller to importer. In 1933, the same year he had to pay a $15 fine for making a false statement on auto license application, McGinnis, with a partner, purchased the J.A. Café at Egleston Square, Dorchester. Five years elapsed before he was arrested again—and subsequently served six months at the Hampden House of Correction for carrying a revolver. McGinnis' final arrest, on February 21, 1938, was his first federal violation—a narcotics violation—and made the front pages of Boston papers, where he was referred to as "the husband of a once notorious vice queen." The ring he was publicly linked to allegedly trafficked in a million dollars' worth of smuggled dope a year. On May 26, 1938, he was found guilty of conspiracy to violate narcotics laws and sentenced to fifteen months in "a penal type institution."

Despite this public record, little was actually known about McGinnis. The Boston police, as well as underworld sources, believed Prohibition had made him many times a millionaire, yet Joe's style of living belied any hint of money. The J.A. Club and his liquor store were both modest enterprises, and his apartment around the corner was plain. God only knows Joe wasn't a spender. A favorite story among the crew was of the time Joe stole an entire car to get a battery for his own car. Another dealt with his being too cheap to spend twenty-five cents for a car wash, and this could easily be verified by driving past the package liquor store where he hosed down his car once a week—weather permitting.

Revenue agents kept an occasional eye on Joe because they believed, but couldn't prove, he was still bootlegging—was continuing to distill liquor someplace. The FBI knew of him as well, believed, but couldn't prove, that he was a partner with Raymond Patriarca—the alleged boss of New England organized crime—in the Islander Hotel in Providence, Rhode Island.

It was this supposed association with Patriarca and other Providence big shots that greatly added to McGinnis' criminal prestige. Joe had come from that city and unquestionably knew many of the reputed overlords, probably not as well as did Ben Tilly, (Benjamin Franklin Tilly, alleged operator of a jewel theft ring and a childhood friend of Pino's) but well enough to spawn a persistent rash of rumors of his being a well-connected crook. Rumors begat rumors, and Joe didn't seem inclined to negate any of them, not if he could use them to his own best illicit advantage. And he usually did.

McGinnis was generally considered a prominent figure in Boston's highly disorganized underworld; a potent guy, who on his own was strong as a bear and didn't need a baseball bat to knock you down the stairs but used one just the same because he was also as mean as a bear; an A-one organizer with the capacity to spot and perpetrate the biggest of scores; possibly Massachusetts' leading fixer because dozens of politicians and police officials and maybe a few feds and judges were on his payroll; the official link between the Boston and Providence mobs and those in Chicago, Cleveland, Detroit and maybe half a dozen other Midwestern cities; a master fence; a master money changer; a near criminal genius if you like.

Of course, there were some close to McGinnis who dismissed most of this as malarkey; who wrote Joe off as three-fourths bark and one-fourth bite. Police Lieutenant James Crowley did. But not all that many people could get halfway near Joe to begin with. In regard to business it was next to impossible to know what Joe was about. His personal life and background were a far deeper mystery. Only Joe knew the details here, and he wasn't the type to confide in anybody—unless, of course, he happened to forget himself in the presence of a fellow thief as penurious and crooked as himself.

"He opened up twice in my kitchen, know what I mean?" said Pino. "It's only a couple of steps from his house to my back door, and he's always coming over for something when I'm having my breakfast. I don't know why he always picks then. Maybe he wants to see what I'm eating.

"So he comes in this one time and says, 'Why are people always saying I do damage?' I tell him, 'That's 'cause you go around hitting them with baseball bats and knocking them downstairs.'

" 'That only happened that once,' he tells me, 'and I didn't damage him. He got right up and walked away.'

"See what was happening? Joe didn't like everybody whispering he was a killer.

"Now the second time is when my mother and father musta been over," Pino recalled. "Joe runs into 'em in the kitchen before they left. They talked to Joe a couple of minutes, and then they left. Now I get along good with my mother and father. We loved one another, and Joe musta seen that. So after they go, he says how nice they are. Then he tells me about his own father. He says everybody got it wrong about his father. He says he don't hate cops because his father was a cop or because his father argued with his mother. He says he hates cops 'cause they fired his father, made him go tend a bar someplace. They kicked him out for no good reason, and he worked all his life for 'em. And when they kicked him out, his mother suffered 'cause there wasn't any money. His mother died 'cause of it—'cause they were poor. That's why he hates cops.

"Now that ain't all. He tells me the goddamn thing about being a girl. His mother thought he was a girl and put him in dresses. Joe said he didn't mind 'cause it made his mother happy. He said he did everything to make his mother happy, and when she cried, it damn near killed him when he was a kid. She cried 'cause they didn't have no money 'cause the cops fired his father. When she cried, she got unhappy about the crying. It killed her to cry in front of her kid. She thought it made her look bad—weak. Joe told me the last time he ever cried was at her funeral.

Tony Pino didn't think Joe McGinnis weak in the least. In fact, he thought Joe was the toughest guy he'd ever met. Tougher even than Mike Geagan. Tony Pino didn't care that nobody, absolutely nobody except himself and the second wife of

McGinnis, had anything nice to say about Joe. He liked him. In fact, Tony Pino looked up to Joe McGinnis. He thought Joe McGinnis was the biggest and best crook he'd ever met. Far bigger and better than himself. Tony Pino not only trusted Joe McGinnis, but damn near adored him. Joe McGinnis was his hero. He believed the worst about Joe McGinnis—which, in Pino's mind, was the best.

And after Tony brought up Joe's name at two different meets concerning Brink's, Sandy Richardson started to grow uneasy.

"Okay, I'm steaming," said Pino. "I go all over the goddamn building looking for wires. I'm gonna find 'em no matter what. I go up on the roof looking. I look on the top floor [third] and down in the first [Commercial Street garage]. I'm out in the hallways and up and down every staircase in the joint. They got staircases all the hell over. One right next to Brink's on the other side [nearest to Hull Street on the playground side of the building and going up to the second-level common garage].

"I'm cooking. Nothing's gonna stop me. Most of the time I spend looking in the offices [Brink's offices]. I gotta check out every wire going outta the joint. And there's lots of 'em. They got five of them no-good cheap pull boxes [pull alarms] in there. One in the rotunda [control room] and one out near the pete. Three more in the joint. I'm on the crawl seeing where the wires will take me.

"And when you're on the crawl, you don't waste time. You keep the peek on everything. I gotta learn how these people operate. I'm starting to know Brink's better than Brink's knows Brink's, see what I mean? These working people they hire come in and do their job. They're only concerned with what's on their own desk. They become oblivious. I ain't oblivious. I've been on my hands and knees learning. Examining every goddamn inch. I know what's under the desk and in it, too. I got a mind like a camera. I can't remember everything I read in books, but looking over a joint, I don't forget nothing. I don't let nothing pass and remember forever. It's a natural talent."

Pino also had a talent for forgetting to tell others all that his mind's eye had photographed or, if too much time lapsed between the seeing and relating, jumbling certain facts. Both these tendencies became more pronounced when a mass of data was being mentally recorded, as in a situation such as the casing of Brink's.

Whether Tony was aware of these flaws, had consciously tried to correct them by telling Jimmy Costa his every last experience shortly after they occurred, is conjecture. But Jimmy, except for activities involving Joe McGinnis, knew nearly everything Pino was about. The crew had been in the habit of going to him for the latest details on the group's operations.

Sandy, for one, didn't have any delusions that Tony hadn't told Jimmy everything about Brink's already, but before the second meet he pointed out to other crewmen that if anyone could keep up with, and make sense out of, Tony's multinefarious doings, it was Costa. That was one of the reasons for suggesting Costa be brought in on the job.

There was other discussion relating to Costa before the second meet. But who was kidding who? Tony Pino wanted him in, and Tony Pino was running the show, had always run the show, had almost always got what he wanted.

There was little discussion at the second meet in Pino's living room. The haul would be divided into seven equal parts, and Jimmy Costa would have one of them. He was unanimously voted in as the seventh man.

Henry Baker's name was mentioned along with Barney Banfield's at this meet. Henry might be getting out of prison sooner than anticipated, it was learned. Not only was he a friend and working associate of all but Gusciora, but he was, to the majority's way of thinking, the best sneak thief in the business. Henry could open anything there was to open. No one was quite sure what had to be opened besides the vault at this juncture, but Maffie, Geagan, Faherty, Pino, Richardson and now Costa said Henry should be brought in on the great haul if he was available. As he had done with the vote on Costa, strapping, amiable Stanley Gusciora smiled and nodded and said, "Anything you boys want."

If you have your outside man, Costa, and possibly a top pickman like Henry Baker, why not wrap the whole thing up and take care of the wheel? That was Pino's logic at the second meet. Let's bring in Barney Banfield. We can find that bug any minute now. There's no sense in finding it and then sitting around waiting while we go arrange for a wheelman, wait around for a wheelman to grab a truck and get it tuned and in shape. Let's bring in Barney and have everything ready. And even if the bug isn't found, we're gonna take that lady anyway—and right away—so what the hell's the sense of not being prepared? There ain't a better fellow for the job than old Barney.

That's when Joe McGinnis' name came up for the first time. Barney, somebody said, certainly is a nice fellow and a good wheel, but he belongs to Joe McGinnis lock, stock and barrel. No way can you bring Barney in and leave Joe out. And Sandy Richardson, for one, wanted no part of Skinhead. No way can you even tell Barney what you have in mind without him telling Joe McGinnis.

Every way, Pino argued. He did some business with Joe, didn't he? He knew Joe better than anybody, didn't he? Well, Barney and he were in on lots of things together that Joe didn't know anything about. Tony Pino would swear on a grandmother's grave that Joe wouldn't know a thing about it. Sandy said no to Barney. Mike said no. Jimmy wouldn't vote. Jazz and Jimma were indifferent. Stanley smiled and nodded and said, "Whatever all you boys want."

Tony Pino was irate and said it wasn't the worst thing in the world to have Joe McGinnis himself in on the score, that Joe could be a big help if you let him.

Sandy Richardson picked up on this and during the third meet, when Pino again hammered away at bringing in Barney, picked up on an idle comment concerning the counting, processing and distribution of stolen loot. It had always been a crew practice in the past, and had been agreed to in regard to the impending Brink's haul, that all "bad money"—new bills whose serial numbers ran consecutively and therefore could be easily traced—was destroyed, usually by burning. For safety's sake big bills in good money—old, used currency—should be broken down into small denominations. The gang was aware the Sturtevant robbery had been partially solved when a money changer in New York City ratted to the police that he had been contacted but not used for a big score up in Boston, had sung about being told by Sam Granito that Pino, Geagan and Costa were in on the haul, had led to Sam's conviction.

"If we had had someone reliable like Joe making the change, that man wouldn't be in the can today, but you guys are too hard-nosed to listen to reason," Pino had commented to Richardson's disgruntlement.

And a little while after that, when the discussion turned to the best ways of disposing of bad money, Pino let it slip that Joe had a surefire way for laundering new bills—processing them in an ordinary washing machine with some type of ink or dye which made them appear old and used.

Sandy, Maffie, Richardson and Costa again voted firmly for destroying all bad bills. Jimma Faherty went along with Gus, who said, "Anything all you boys want."

The question of a plant came up at the third meet, and Tony said he was still looking around for one, ran down a list of people who had plants he might be able to take over, a list that included Joe's name.

Sandy Richardson picked up on this mention as he had picked up on the early ones but didn't say anything at the time or afterward, when he and Tony drove over to North End, pulled up on Hull Street, turned into the second-level common garage of the North Terminal building and parked. He carried the box of graphite Pino gave him all the way across the auxiliary garage used by Brink's, listening to Tony complain, not always in whispers, about having to pay cash for the graphite, recount his unsuccessful try at boosting it off a shelf behind the counter while two clerks stood nearby in the hardware store.

He couldn't talk once they had passed through the pair of fire doors leading out of the auxiliary garage.

Pino slid back the first of the two squeaky fire doors opening into the regular Brink's garage. He knelt down, tore open the box top and carefully sprinkled graphite on the tract, and rubbed some under the door edge. He rose and moved the door forward a few inches, then back. Forward and back several more times. The graphite began doing its job, grinding into the tract and rollers, smoothing them, killing the squeak. Back and forth over a longer area, and longer. Soon the first door glided open and shut in total silence. The second fire door was processed with graphite. Soon it too skimmed between its tracts, making almost no noise.

"The cheap sons of bitches oughta pay me for what I'm doing for 'em here," Tony crowed, on examining his handiwork. "I'm putting up the real estate value, see?" he told Sandy as they started across through the rows of armored cars parked between the columns in the dark. "Making improvements in their property for nothing. Remind me to steal an extra hundred grand from 'em for this, okay?"

A sound of approval rose somewhere deep in Sandy's throat, but no words were spoken—not as they entered the picked door of the guardroom, not as they turned left and walked across the unlit money room, turned right and walked across the unlit vault room, turned left and walked across the unlit payroll wrapping and counting rooms and on into the dark corridor and through the door to the right.

Only after they had been in the unlit general office, looking out onto Prince Street for quite some time, had searched through filing cabinet drawers, had stood reading folder contents with the hope of finding some information on the alarm wiring connected to the vault did Sandy get around to mentioning what was sticking in his craw.

"What's that gorilla got on you, Anthony?"

"Which gorilla?" Pino asked while *pfft-pffting* his penlight on pages of company correspondence.

"The skinheaded one."

"Hey, don't call him Skinhead, okay, Sandy? He's sensitive."

"Snakes in the grass are sensitive, but that's no reason to say they don't have tails and bite."

"You got Joe all wrong."

"Anthony, it's not very easy to get him right. There's nothing right with him."

"Don't go listening to all those goddamn rumors. You don't even know the man, and you're accusing him of things he ain't even thought about. People say terrible things about Joe 'cause

they're jealous. They make him out to be some kinda rat and—"
Pino caught the slip, realized Sandy had as well and cleared his
throat.

"You said it, Anthony, not me."

"Okay, I'm gonna tell you something nobody in the world
knows except you and me. Joe gives Crowley some dirt every
now and then 'cause he gotta make it look good, see what I
mean? Joe owns Crowley, but he gotta make it look the other
way—like he's the cop's pigeon. So he gives him something on
some punk. So what? Punks is punks, and Crowley does what
he's told to do. He gives Joe all the inside stuff and stays outta
the way."

"What about you and Crowley?"

"Oh, Detective Crowley comes and sees me all the time,"
Pino readily admitted. "He thinks I'm his pigeon, too. He thinks
he's smarter than me any day of the week. He believes anything
I tell him, and not one fucking word of it's ever been the truth."

"That's a risky game, Anthony. A slimy game."

"Eh? It pays the rent and keeps you outta the can. So far none
of us are in the can, are we?"

"You still haven't said what Joe's into you on." Richardson
persisted.

"Nothing, I told you, nothing!"

"You wouldn't be pitching him if he didn't have something.
Anthony, I know you. You've pitched Skinhead two meets in a
row now."

"I ain't pitching nobody, and nobody owns me. Joe and me is
friends and neighbors, that's all. And we do a little business on
the side."

"A little?" Sandy queried. "I hear it's a lot."

"What are you, a goddamn priest in the box?"

"I don't need the box. I've got eyes and ears and listen to
what reliable people have to say. I've listened to you in your
own living room."

"Stop shouting at me!" Pino shouted.

"You're the one who's shouting."

"Well, you cut it out, and I'll cut it out. Look, Sandy, Joe and
me live in the same neighborhood. You want me to ignore neigh-

bors? I'm seen with the fella. So what? That don't mean we're sleeping in bed together. I do some business with him—that don't mean nothing either. I like the man. I like you, too, and I'm seen with you. That's all there is to it. Nothing.''

"Then you don't want him in?'' Richardson asked.

"All I goddamn want in is Barney,'' Pino exploded. "But you goddamn guys don't wanna believe that. You hate Joe so goddamn much for no reason you'll let the whole ship go down. Okay, you wanna do that, fine. You think you can go out and get another driver as good as Barney, fine—go out and get him.''

"What's Skinhead got on you, Anthony?'' Sandy asked again, evenly.

"Nothing. Honest to Christ, nothing. I just want Barney.''

"If we bring in Barney, what's to keep Skinhead from knowing?''

"Barney'll clam. I swear on my grandmother's grave he will.''

"How's he going to keep Skinhead from grabbing his share?'' asked Richardson. "I hear Skinhead goes through his pockets at night.''

"I'll work it all out, Sandy. You get me Barney, and I'll take care of Joe. Come on, let's hit the other room.''

Drawers to cabinets in the manager's office were opened; papers came out and were *pfft-pffted.* Nothing relating to the ADT alarm was found. The search continued to other parts of the room.

"Hey, don't tell me you're the president?'' Pino commented on seeing Sandy seated behind the manager's desk.

Richardson righted himself slowly, looked quizzically in Pino's direction and carefully folded his hands on the blotter. "Only the president sits here. Every schoolchild knows that. Is there something I can do for you, my good man?''

"How about a job?''

"If you're asking for a job, sit down. Presidents don't talk to people who stand up over them.'' Pino drew up a chair. "Now, am I to understand you wish honest employment with Brink's?''

"I think you desperately need me.''

"Brink's needs nobody!''

"I can save you lots of money.''

"My good man, a million here and there is nothing to us big companies. The important thing is experience and character. What's your experience?"

"Nothing nobody can prove."

"Ah, that's what we like to hear. May I inquire into your particular specialty?"

"I'm very good with money and safes."

"Your own or other people's?"

"There's something about other people's that gets up my dedication."

"You certainly sound like you belong here with us. We money carriers feel the same way. How's your character?"

"Never been sick a day in its life."

"You certainly sound like the upstanding young man we've been looking out for. When could you start?"

"Right now."

"In the middle of the night?"

"That's when I do my best work."

It was nearing 10 P.M. when Pino and Richardson abandoned the file search, walked back across the general office and into the corridor, went left along the corridor to the door on the right and out into the counting room. Rather than take another sharp left, going into the Money Room Cage, crawling through the money box door into the short L of the checking room as he usually did, Tony followed the playground side route. Rather than crouch down as he always did when he was moving along the wire-covered windows, he stayed erect. This was foolish. Even though the rooms were unlit, their shadows might still have been noticed from the outside. But Pino was often careless when he was preoccupied.

"You don't like Joe, do ya?" he asked, stopping beside the last double row of counting room desks.

"He's a phony and a cheat, Anthony. He cheats his own."

"I got something on my mind, Sandy. Something very important to me, and I ain't asking you to do nothing one way or another besides hearing me out. I wanna know what you and Mike has got against bringing Joe in on this job?"

"For the love of God, Anthony, the man's a leech, a bloodsucking scavenger. He takes over everything he gets near and sucks it dry and screws it all up. He's done it to friends of mine time and time again. To friends of yours, too." Richardson hesitated, then deliberately, if not menacingly, asked, "Have you told him about this?"

"I haven't told him nothing. I'm just finding out how you feel."

"I don't want him in two thousand miles of anything I'm on."

"Okay. Now supposing he didn't take over. Supposing he does what he's told like everybody else? How'd ya feel then?"

"There's nothing he can do for us, Anthony. Don't you understand? He can't carry his own weight. He's of no use."

"There's lots of things he could do for us. Mother of God, he's got plants and the best connections in the state. He can handle the count and change the bills. He can even do the financing and if you—"

"Financing?"

"This is gonna cost a fortune before we're through. Joe can put up all the money—and—"

"What the hell are we, a bunch of crippled welfarers? We have our own money, and we'll pay our own way! Tony, don't you understand? Can't you see? There's nothing that baldheaded louse can do for us except fuck it up."

"He's already done something big for us. He called up the ADT and—"

"How the hell does he know about ADT?"

" 'Cause I told him about it."

"You could have your goddamn head blown off for that."

"He don't know what for. He don't know what for. All I told him is I got something big that's having trouble with the ADT. So he calls the ADT, and you know what he has 'em do? They're putting outfits in his store. Both his stores is gonna have them ADT systems. Once he gets 'em, we can see how the hell they work and kill the one over here. Now that's goddamn good thinking, ain't it, Sandy? That's big-time thinking, and it was all Joe who thought of it."

"I don't care if he buys ADT and makes himself president of it. I don't want him around."

"Look, Sandy, I think I can make a hell of a deal. Get two for the price of one, see? I can get us both Barney and Joe for the same share. They'll only take one share between the two of 'em.''

"Which means Skinhead will take all the share and let Barney go begging.''

"Who the hell cares how they operate between themselves? We get the benefits.''

"You asked me, and I'm telling you how I feel. No, I don't want that big bald prick around.''

Pino nodded, grabbed up the box of graphite he had set on the desk, led the way through the Dutch doors and payroll wrapping room and out the slanting grille wall fronting the vault room. He gave the box to Sandy, reached through the wide gauge screen and tripped the arm of the lift lock. The grille door slid back. The pair entered the vault room proper.

Tony went over, picked up the clipboard, *pfft-pffted* and checked out the next day's schedules. Quick calculation told him about $6,000,000 were currently in the vault. He motioned to Richardson that it was time to leave, entered the L-shaped check-in room, spotted the portable metal money box, stopped at it, beckoned Richardson over and took the box of graphite.

"I gotta have Joe in," Tony announced, kneeling down. "I owe him.''

"Then he *is* into you," Sandy replied.

"Not in the way you think. You know my deportation?''

"Don't use deportation on me again, Anthony.''

"It ain't again. It's the same goddamn deportation they been hounding me for since I came out. And that goddamn lawyer of mine screwed up. I laid out twenty-one grand so far and made every secretary and office boy over there rich, only the big shots won't play ball. The governor slammed the door in my face. He won't give me no pardon. But Joe's got a way of getting to 'em. Joe's working on it.''

"And he told you he's either in on this or forget the pardon?'' Richardson replied contemptuously.

"I told ya, he don't even know about it," Tony snapped. "But I don't want him giving up. He's my last hope, Sandy. He's the only thing between me and Italy.''

"You rotten son of a bitch. Brother, you're a rotten son of a bitch.''

"Yeah. But you gotta do what you feel in your heart. You're the only one who can help with the other fellas. If you want Joe in, you can get the others to go along if you want to, huh?"

"They're all grown-up men. They all think for themselves."

"Sure, but none of 'em hate Joe like you and Mike do."

"Let me think about it."

"Sure." Tony was down on the floor, applying graphite to the wheels of the metal box. "Hey, lift up the other end, will ya?"

Richardson complied. Tony spun the pair of free wheels, added more graphite, then had Sandy lift the other end and repeated the process on the last pair of wheels.

He got up and rolled the container forward and back once. The wheels, which had been nearly squeakless before the application, now were completely silent.

"I was just mad enough to want to get my mind off things," Richardson recalls. "I guess I did it with the box. The graphite made it roll smoother. First Anthony pushed the box around and then rolled it over to me. I stood with it there and gave it a little push. Anthony took it back and rolled it around again and pushed it back to me. Let it roll free over to me. I pushed it somewhat further this time. Then we got silly. Anthony started going *choo-choo* when it was his turn to push it. I did the same thing when it was my turn. We kept taking turns. We shouldn't have been doing it because it was careless. But carelessness often leads to carelessness. Nobody was more careless than Brink's. So there we were, running around in the dark pushing the metal box and going *choo-choo*."

"I own the joint," Pino had once said, shortly after entering past the guard room door. "I live there. I can't get enough."

And so it was and continued to be between the time the last lights in the vault room went out and the last guards were seen leaving until 10 to 10:30 P.M. Finding file information which would lead to neutralizing the supposed alarm on the vault itself was uppermost, but other areas were scouted out as well, many things learned. Pino continued to be the most addicted to the nocturnal probing, hardly missed a night. But Richardson and Geagan and Maffie and Gusciora and Costa were also caught up in the often-meaningless casing. Theoretically, only two of the gang were allowed to enter at a time. Pino almost always was one of the two intruders, but sometimes an extra man showed up. Sometimes four went in at the same time. Sometimes the ever-suspicious Tony relegated two to go in, then sneaked in later to spy, to make sure they were doing what they were supposed to.

Much of what went on was careful and calculating. Much of what went on was not. Much was a direct violation of the crew's own rules of safety. Tony and Gus never should have parked in the public garage section of the floor, and they knew it. Jimma Faherty did them one better. He drove right into the auxiliary garage used by Brink's and parked—drove in and parked a stolen car. Often, as Pino and Sandy had done, other men walked right past the windows overlooking the playground when they should have crouched. Often penlights were flashed on and off without being masked—in plain view of anyone who might be looking into the window. The washrooms were used, the toilets flushed. The phones were used, usually by Faherty, who seemed to prefer making personal calls from the instrument in the vault room itself. Pino, who originally put a stop on using premises phones, worked out a ring signal on which he could call in to the men assigned the casing for that night. Documents taken out of a file were often replaced in the wrong order. When a sign was read on the company bulletin board soliciting contributions for a wedding present for one of the drivers, Gus and Costa each put a dollar in the cup below, bringing the total take up to $2.75. The gang had gone through the wastebaskets looking for discarded data, knew that no one emptied the trash at night, but still shouldn't have left an empty whiskey bottle in one. Men smoked on the premises when they knew they shouldn't have, knew that even if they masked the red top glowing in the dark, the smell of smoke might linger. The men were absolutely certain no hacks would show up before 10:30 P.M. but had little idea of whether one might enter after that time, so they shouldn't have remained until 11 or 11:30 as they often did. The main route for entering the office had almost exclusively become via the Hull Street second-level common garage, but few, if any, of the gang were careful to see if any outsiders were around. They usually wandered right in and up to the slide door going to the auxiliary garage used by Brink's vehicles, carrying on a conversation. If the door was closed, they slid it open. There was a lock latch on the door which Pino had broken. It had never been fixed. The men hardly ever bothered to pull up their handkerchief masks once they were past the bauxited pair of fire doors fronting the Brink's main garage. They always wore their gloves but sometimes didn't even bother to bring a handkerchief. Less and less were they speaking in whispers when roaming the premises. They often congregated in one room and held bull sessions at which the laughter was raucous. On one occasion Gus hid behind a desk and, when Jazz walked by, jumped out and yelled, "Stick 'em up, I got ya." A noisy chase followed, and after Maffie got his hands on the prankster, a grunting and laughing wrestling match took place. In short, the gang was acting as if they *did* own the joint. There seemed to be no good reason why they shouldn't. As Costa observed, "You coulda set a time bomb off in there and nobody in the world would care."

Through it all a great deal was learned about the Brink's offices and procedures. Four of the five pull alarms were located. Personnel files were read. So were assignment rosters. The gang had a pretty good idea of just how many people worked in any one office during the course of the day and what they did. They knew how many men were assigned to what truck for the following day, exactly where each delivery was made and how much it contained. They became aware of "sealed packages," a service the company rendered and in which the customer turned over a delivery for shipment without specifying how much it contained or what it contained. The gang knew when each individual truck was gassing up or staying at the service station for a more serious overhaul. They knew from reading an assignment sheet that during the day there was a garageman assigned to take care of the trucks parked in the garage, he was usually finished about 5:30 or 6 P.M. There was no information concerning cleaning personnel either during the day or at night. During the day a guard was assigned to the front guard booth looking into the main hall in the second-floor lobby. The name for the center rotunda in the garage was control room, and a man was assigned to this—during the day. The guard booth in the corner of the garage, the one with a door in it leading to the garage, was manned only on certain days. Nothing could be found concerning any guard's being present in any booth at night after closing. Nothing at all could be found regarding night watchmen.

Despite all the effort and searching, nothing at all had been found indicating how the bug on the vault could be neutralized. But a letter was found stating that one definitely did exist.

"It was my weakness," Mike Geagan asserts. "I never should have let them in. All we ever needed to take that place, either way [B & E or heavy] was seven men. Not even seven. Six of us could have done it. Costa was as much a part of us as anyone, so it was only right he be there. That could have been seven. But the other two men—we didn't need them. Tony was the boss, and I knew he wanted them. Tony had made us all money, but I went along because he wanted it. I didn't have anything against those two men, but we didn't need them. The more you have along, the better is your chance for word getting out. You can't get mixed up with too many men doing things there's no need for. You can lose control. I felt bringing them in could be a disaster for us all. I should have said that and stopped it."

Pino had managed to get Richardson, Geagan and Costa's approval beforehand and was in the process of outlining—for the consideration of Maffie, Faherty and Gusciora—the proposed guidelines of acceptance. Barney would drive and take care of transportation—on the heavy if it came to that. Joe would underwrite all expenses and—

It was at this point that Barney and Joe walked into Pino's living room. Tony would swear afterward it was a mistake, that they were supposed to wait until they were voted in and then come over. This, of course, was a lie. He planned it as it occurred. And once they were at the meet, specific plans began being discussed before anyone could object.

Joe announced the ADT alarm system would be going into his two businesses within several days. If that didn't work, he had another plan. Tony announced no wires could be found for the bug but that he had another system for killing the alarm.

Joe and Barney stayed until the meet broke up. Tony contacted Jazz and Jimma and Gus the next day, apologized for Joe and Barney's walking in unannounced and then asked if they wanted the pair along on the haul. Jimma said okay. Jazz said, what the hell, which meant okay.

Good old well-liked easygoing Gus said, "Whatever the other boys want," then for the first time he told Tony Pino what he wanted in return—who he wanted to come on the crew.

CHAPTER SEVENTEEN

Specs

Swimming, swimming for this goddamn life in the harbor, trying to escape the detention house on Deer Island, swimming in
the water in the middle of the night, swimming like a madman
and complaining every stroke of the way—that was the illusion
Joe McGinnis used at the meet to illustrate what a chronic bel-
lyacher Specs O'Keefe was. Haberdasher of disaster—was the
malapropism spit out to warn what a chronic bad-luck guy Specs
O'Keefe had been to all who had known him in the past, would
unquestionably be again in the future. That anyone with half a
brain and half an eye and only one arm and no legs who owns a
grocery can make it pay off—even Ben Tilly makes that grocery
store of his pay off—but not that dope-eating queer was a com-
parison used to put across what a chronic loser Specs O'Keefe
had been.

Well, Joseph James O'Keefe did bellyache a lot and did have a
grocery store fail, just like the real estate business and several
other legitimate undertakings failed, and it did seem that those
close to him, with the possible exception of Gusciora, were star-
crossed, and every time you looked back over your shoulders
there he was swimming like a madman in the middle of the night,
trying not to go under for good, but did that make him any less a
crook? That was the attitude of some of the other crewmen at
the meet.

And when Specs was on the lam after that escape from Deer Island and met and married Mary Gerst, he hadn't lied to her about being a crook, as Joe McGinnis claimed—he merely forgot to tell her what he usually did for a living. And when he went back with her to the Midwest, didn't he give it his honest all to get on the straight and narrow once again? Do you think any man who loves his wife and adopted son is going to let them be in need? And just because he never stayed with them after he brought them back to Boston didn't mean he loved them any the less, as Joe McGinnis accused. Some guys just aren't born to be monogamous. And why doesn't Joe McGinnis make up his mind? One minute he's calling Specs the scum of the earth for running off and womanizing with Helen Whatchamacallit and in the next breath he's saying Specs himself is womanish. And anyway, does that make him any less a crook?

Being nearly forty-one years of age and standing five feet seven and weighing about 150 pounds and having a gaunt, sallow, pinched face, Joe O'Keefe wasn't exactly an Adonis. He seemed to have worked extraordinarily hard to find a girl, some nights seemed to work every joint in town from Jimmy O'Keefe's restaurant down to the lowliest semi-hook shop trying for a pickup. But Joe McGinnis, like many other underworld denizens, professed that this was only show. Specky was thin, wiry and light on his feet. He also possessed a slight lisp. Rumors of his being "womanish" persisted. McGinnis not only repeated and elaborated on these but recounted homosexual experiences O'Keefe supposedly had when he was in the can.

And it was possible, as Joe McGinnis claimed, that Specky wasn't always a stand-up fellow. Maybe because of all his problems, maybe because of his small physical stature, he dogged it a wee bit too much. Specky did seem overly concerned with passing himself off as a tough guy—a movie-type tough guy replete with tucked-in elbows and thrown-back shoulders and the best and latest in gangland suits and overcoats. Overcoats seemed important, or at least many of the crewmen recall he wore them a lot. So maybe Specky felt he had to act like a tough guy to prove a point; maybe he challenged the wrong guy every now and then and had to back down. Maybe he developed a great big ego to con himself into being tough when he wasn't. Maybe he was scared silly half the time, and that's why he went on the attack every now and then, suddenly became cocky and abrasive and aggressive. A lot of guys in town were laughing at him to begin with, and a lot that counted didn't even know who he was. That could be good for crew purposes, Specky being dismissed as a third- or fourth-rate crook, being ignored as a joke. My God, the man made one of the most spectacular escapes ever when he swam off from Deer Island, and nobody who was anybody even seemed to notice. Sure, that all could be good for the crew, but it didn't do Specky's self-respect all that much good.

Specky probably did smoke pot every now and then, or at least Gus, who smoked pot, told a couple of the gang guys Specs smoked, but it's hard to say if he was addicted to opium and heroin, as Joe McGinnis claimed at the meet. His father had been a hack, for a time the acting master at the very house of correction on Deer Island from which Specs had once escaped—but not at the time he escaped. And sure, Specs was close and loyal to him and to his sisters and brother, just as he was close and loyal to his pals, such as Stanley Gusciora. That didn't mean he was trying to hide something, as Joe McGinnis insinuated, did it? Sure, everybody around town knew Specky had somewhat of a temper when he thought about it, and could become emotional when he didn't think about it, and his sister and brother were often recalled as being emotional in public, but did that mean, as Joe McGinnis finally came out and said, that insanity ran in their family? For chrissakes, family members could be close and spend time together for reasons other than hiding the skeletons of five generations of babbling maniacs in the attic—look at all the time Pino spends with his family for chrissakes.

And who the hell cared if Helen Whatchamacallit, the woman for whom Specs had deserted his loving wife and adoring adopted child, was or was not a prostitute, did or did not have a massive case of the clap? Joe McGinnis, who was once married to the number one hook shop operator in town, should be the last guy going around throwing rocks. Nah, forget all that back-alley gossip. Mike Geagan had known Specky nearly twenty years, and the same was true for Sandy and Jimma. Maffie had been friendly with him since 1945, drank with him every now and then over at Jimmy O'Keefe's. Specs was no less human than the next fellow. All that counted was his being a pretty good thief. But was he?

O'Keefe's first arrest, when he was six, came in the company of another six-year-old neighborhood boy, his best friend—a roly-poly Italian immigrant boy named Anthony Pino.

"I told you we was all part of the same bunch," Tony acknowledged. "O'Keefe, his older brother and some more. We all went to the same school and church over in Southy—John Andrews School and St. Monica's Church.

"Now, what most people don't know about O'Keefe is how he got his name [nickname]. They think you call him Specs because he wore glasses or something, and that ain't it. He got it 'cause when he was a little kid, he was always mooching bananas from the peddler, see what I mean? He'd go to a food peddler and beg for old bananas to eat. Old brown colored ones with specks on them. 'Got any speckled for me today?' he was always asking the poor unfortunates. Pretty soon he became a speck himself. He was Specs.

"So the thing I brought up at that meet was all about that record of his," Pino went on to say. "It was as long as your two feet. All our fellas been stealing as long as O'Keefe, and they don't have even half the pinches O'Keefe got. Not two of 'em together has as many pinches."

Specky's police record covered a thirty-five-year career in crime which was definitely far lengthier than any other crew member's: thirty-three arrests on thirty-seven counts; twenty-one convictions, which resulted in eight reformatory, correctional institution and prison sentences; one escape from incarceration; at least three violations of parole or probation; two returns to detention for such violations; and no less than fifty SP pickups. The offenses themselves included four breaking and enterings and larcenies, five plain larcenies, one plain B&E, two attempted B&Es, one carrying a pistol, one armed robbery, one assault and battery and one possession of burglar's tools. Almost everything was of a minor nature, and local cops didn't even rate O'Keefe in the upper echelon of street thieves.

Nobody attending the living room meet was aware of O'Keefe's actual record, nor did they know he was still on parole. All they knew was that Specs got pinched often. And yes,

Geagan and Richardson and Maffie suspected he couldn't do time well, but they seemed to overlook this.

Pino's general, somewhat lackadaisical accusation that O'Keefe wasn't of the caliber required for the big haul was dismissed on several counts. Tony had used O'Keefe on the American Sugar caper, had grown incensed when Specs later complained about Pino's receiving a full share of the take for not actually participating in the heist; for merely turning the job over to another group to rob. The crew got a sort of kick out of Pino's getting beet red and flustered and calling O'Keefe every name in the book, and then, when O'Keefe heard about what he was being called, he started saying a few more things himself, which got back to Tony and only made him all the madder, started off a new round of epithets.

"The thing that got Tony the maddest is when Specky called him the Pig," Jimmy Costa says. "Specky always tried to be neat, and he liked to eat in fancy restaurants even though he couldn't afford to. He used to tell people about his good table manners and the plays he went to see. It drove him crazy that every crook in town respected Tony and that Tony was making so much goddamn money when he couldn't pay his rent. He used to tell people what bad table manners Tony had and how sloppy he lived. That's when he called him the pig the most.

"Tony was jealous of Specky, too—that was over Gus. Tony had this thing about bringing in young guys on the crew and teaching them. He acted like their father, maybe because he never had any kids of his own. He did it with a couple of guys in the old days, and he tried doing it with me and tried doing it with Gus. Tony didn't like Gus running around with Specky as much as he did. They were close as brothers and spent all their time together.

"I think what Tony worried about the most was the trouble with some crap game guys [most likely the Callahan Brothers—specifically Tommy Callahan]. They'd been warning Gus and Specky to stop sticking up their games. Gus and Specky didn't stop, and they [the Callahans] came around and talked to Joe and Tony. They said the only reason they hadn't done damage to Gus was he was a friend of Tony's. They said enough was enough, so Tony said he'd talk to Gus and try and have him stop.

When he talked to Gus, he blamed Specky for the trouble and tried to get Gus to keep away from Specky. Specky was telling Gus the same thing—keep away from Tony. He told Gus that Tony would rob him blind.

"I tell you something, Specky used to act like he was in love or something when he was around Gus. He giggled like a goddamn girl around Gus. He was always buying Gus' cigarettes for him or lighting them. A couple of the guys came back one night and said they saw Gus and Specky in Jimmy O'Keefe's restaurant and that Specky was cutting Gus' steak for him. Can you imagine?

"Anyway, Tony and Specky were fighting over Gus like he was some kind of dame. If you ask me, Gus loved it. If you ask me, he was playing one off against the other."

Grinning, easygoing, six-foot-tall Stanley Gusciora did display a previously unnoticed ability if not to play one gang member off against the other, to get what he wanted from the crew. He had waited patiently while Costa, Banfield and McGinnis all had been promoted by Pino and discussed by the others. He had patiently and pleasantly gone along with whatever the boys wanted and cast his vote of approval for each of the three. He let it be known that if the others wanted Henry Baker in on the job, that was okay with him. And when it was learned that Henry wouldn't be paroled as soon as previously anticipated, he made his move. "Why don't you bring in my partner, he's as good a sneak as is around," And Gus definitely said "my partner," and everybody there definitely knew that his partner was Specs O'Keefe and that Specs O'Keefe wasn't all that bad a sneak thief compared to what was around.

When Pino said there had to be a full discussion and full vote on the matter, Gus said, "Sure, whatever you fellows want, but I want O'Keefe in on it—and if he can't come along, neither will I." That was the hold card. Everybody wanted Gus along.

So the regular crew and Costa and Banfield suffered Joe McGinnis' one-hour-and-forty-five-minute harangue against O'Keefe and absentmindedly listened to Pino's halfhearted ten-minute warning about Specky's propensity for getting arrested and SP'd and then all voted as they knew they were going to vote even before they showed up: Richardson, Maffie, Geagan, Faherty and Costa for acceptance, McGinnis against, Banfield and Pino abstaining and Gus not present but counted as the sixth aye ballot just the same.

Specs O'Keefe was the tenth man officially to come in, and if Joe McGinnis' thunderous prediction that the crew was courting disaster wasn't heeded, it should have been.

The grain of the wood was beginning to rub through, exposing the improbable, nearly inconceivable, yet pervasive texture of the robbers and their intended enterprise. Within the course of five days, often with amusement and often with indifference, the regular crew added one full-fledged alcoholic to their roster of one nearly full-fledged alcoholic and two excessively heavy drinkers, not far from the border line of alcoholism. They had also knowingly reunited two old friends, Specky and Tony, who hadn't been getting on well for some time. More than that, they had brought together two men they weren't wholly sure of: one whom they suspected of being a police informant and they didn't personally like; the other who they more or less agreed couldn't do prison time well—two men who loathed each other.

Joe McGinnis rode the T&T; so did Barney Banfield. Pino was at his effusive best as he led the ninth and eighth gang members, respectively, through the premises. Joe, who had been un-characteristically garrulous at the meet concerning Specs O'Keefe, was his usual quiet self, but was not in his usual outfit. His trousers were still the same old dark ones, the sweater was the same dark turtleneck, but over the sweater was a dark suit jacket Tony had never seen before. Over the baldhead was a dark wool pulldown seaman's watch cap. Tall, gaunt Barney was in a soft hat, neat two-button suit and armless gray V-neck sweater. All three conspirators were wearing what Pino had only recently ordered to be standard footwear—soft-soled shoes that wouldn't squeak. As was always the case when Barney and Joe were together, Barney stayed in the background—a foot or two to the rear of Joe.

Joe wasn't all that impressed by how smoothly the graphite made the twin fire doors slide open. Joe didn't smile or frown or show any reaction when Pino made him push the graphite-pro-cessed money box. He grunted indifferently as he read the clipboard which showed that some $5,000,000 was due for delivery the next day, was probably in the vault at this very moment. He did, however, seem more interested with the names of individual customers and the amounts they were slated to receive than the overall total.

"Joe said we oughta copy those names so we could rob them later," Pino related. "I didn't tell him that's what we'd been doing for two years 'cause that's none of his goddamn business. So what I told him was no, no one copies down names 'cause those names belong to the fellas, the regular crew. That's their property unless they say no, they don't want it.

"So Joe bellyaches about that. He says everything we find in the joint oughta belong to everyone. I say what belongs to Julius Caesar belongs to Julius Caesar, and that's how it's gotta be—fair or unfair.

"Joe grunted, but there was nothing he could do about it, see?"

Before departing, Joe stole two pads of paper and a box of paper clips.

Costa scurried over the rooftop along Prince Street opposite the North Terminal Garage building. It was 5:30 A.M. The lights in the fifth window on the second floor over the playground came on approximately fifteen minutes later. He moved farther along the rooftop and raised his binoculars. The angle still wasn't right.

The next morning at around the same time he tried the door at 109 Prince Street, the first building beyond the playground on the same side of the street as North Terminal Garage. It was open, and he entered. The stairs creaked. He slowed his climb, carefully stepped on the outer edges of the boards. He reached the first landing. A radio or television set was heard playing behind a door. A woman's voice called out to lower the volume. The steps creaked on the way to the next landing. Someone could be heard gargling behind a door. The steps continued to creak, and a dog started barking and growling. He continued up. The door at the top of the staircase was unlocked. He pushed it open and walked onto the roof. He ducked under a clothesline and crawled up to the edge. The lights in the second, third,

fourth, and fifth windows of the second level across the playground were on. He raised the binoculars and focused in on the
fifth window. His angle was perfect. Two men in shirt sleeves
and wearing glasses were pulling open the heavy door on the
vault.

"Okay, now I'm up on the roof [109 Prince Street]," Pino
said. "We ain't gonna find no wires that do us any good inside,
see what I mean? That whole idea fell through. We ain't gonna
kill the bug by cutting no wires 'cause we can't find no wires to
cut that go to the box. That's why I come up with this new plan.
That's why I'm up on the roof over the park."

"It's maybe six o'clock in the morning and still dark out.
Okay, I got my German naval glasses with me. The ones that
was on submarines. Now I pick 'em up and look in that fifth window of theirs. That's the one where they got their vault. Behind
the fifth window. Okay, I'm gonna get her numbers, see? I'm
gonna watch what numbers they turn on the [vault] dial and get
the combination. When I got the combination, I got the pete. All
I need's the goddamn combination, and Brink's is as good as
gone."

How can possessing the combination be of value if the alarm
system to the vault isn't neutralized?

"Mother of God, you got that combination, you drive everybody hi-sterical, see what I mean? You take that combination in
your hand and you sneak into Brink's, go right up to the safe.
Now you look at the number [where the vault dial is set], and
now you look at the combination you're holding. You use the
combination, and *pfft*, open the safe and close it right up again.
Close it tight and spin the combination back to the number
where it was set, and then you tear the hell outta there. You go
up the block and sit down someplace they can't see you. What
happens? Everything happens is what happens. Once that door
pulls open, alarms go off all over the world, and everyone comes
running. Cop cars come running. Detectives come running. The
marines land and come running, rushing right up into Brink's,
and whatta they find? See what I mean? The safe is locked. No
one broke the safe. There it is shut, with tumblers set just like
they left it. They open the safe. Every last goddamn penny is

where it's supposed to be. So everyone goes home, and ADT figures something went wrong with their wiring or something and then checks it all out. Nothing's wrong, so ADT goes home, too, and then you sneak right back in, open up the safe, shut it and set the number right, and tear out all over again. *Pfft*, what happens? The alarms go off and the whole goddamn world comes racing back in again, only nothing's been touched. Now's the time someone starts in getting hi-sterical.

"Now we get 'em—'cause either ADT puts in an alarm we can beat or we keep up with the tripping. Keep opening and shutting the door. Even if we can't beat the alarm, it don't make a difference. We get them to such a state that everybody's ignoring the alarm. The guy at ADT's board hears the alarm go off and says, 'Oh, Jesus, there's Brink's going crazy one more time—the hell with them. I'll send someone over in the morning.' He ain't gonna call the marines 'cause they died of mortal weariness weeks ago. All they gotta hear is that Brink's went off again and they're under the covers.

"So there it is. We just walk in one night, trip the alarm, close the door and go back out on the street and watch. When nobody shows, we go back upstairs, open the safe for good and clean her out. Don't even leave that one penny behind. Close the safe back shut and put the dial in place. The next morning the repairman [from ADT] shows up and experiences a surprise: a very empty feeling."

McGinnis and O'Keefe met face to face at a full membership meet in Pino's living room. If the five-foot-seven conspirator was aware of the harangue the large, burly, baldheaded six-footer had launched to keep him off the job, Specs didn't show it. O'Keefe was docile and conciliatory—as sweet as cherry pie, you might say. McGinnis was also cordial, but one or two of the fellows noticed that he didn't address Specky all that much, and when he did, he usually looked at Gus. Even McGinnis liked Gus.

Pino tried to do most of the talking but got off the track a lot. Geagan often got him back on the track. Costa often interrupted to correct a fact or two. McGinnis often butted in.

Among other things, McGinnis said he'd have those ADT

alarms in both his stores shortly, and then he'd find a way to kill them. Joe told everyone he was very good mechanically, repaired his own clocks. But if he couldn't figure out how to neutralize the devices, he knew a former MIT graduate who could—a guy named Sullivan. Pino announced that he was working on a revolutionary, surefire scheme to neutralize the alarms on the vault, something that had to do with getting the Brink's people hysterical. Someone suggested that they forget the B&E and go in on the heavy. No one else agreed. Try the B&E first. Try everything to take it on the clout and, if everything failed, then bring out the pistols, seemed to be the consensus.

Geagan managed to raise a few more issues on which everyone concurred: Tony Pino and only Tony Pino was the boss. No one gave orders except Tony. Tony's official liaison was Jimmy Costa. Only Costa could pass on an order given by Tony. If Tony wasn't available, all information any crew member obtained would be given to Costa.

The one dictate twice repeated by Geagan and twice agreed to by the assemblage was this: Anyone letting out word of what they were up to, either by intent or by mistake, would be killed.

The meet broke up without O'Keefe's being given any particular assignment other than accompanying Gus to the joint in what was now becoming routine and general reconnaissance.

When Specs finally did get a specific nod, it was for what might be called a shit detail.

"Tony Pino wanted to know what went on in the joint late at night," Jazz Maffie related. "He'd only burned the joint until ten or ten thirty [P.M.]. He sent Specs O'Keefe and me over there first. We were supposed to stay there all night and see if any hack showed up. Stay there until three in the morning. We got in the back of a truck [Brink's]—a truck over near the repair section. When we looked out the peephole they have in the back of the truck, we could see most of the garage. Well, we couldn't see much because it was dark, but if somebody came in with a flashlight, we would have seen them.

"So we were laying there, talking about this and that and taking turns looking out the peephole. I don't know, maybe it was two or three o'clock and Specs was at the window. He gave me a poke, and I got up and looked out. So we see this shadow of someone sneaking in. You can only see a shadow, but the shadow's so fat you know it could only be Tony Pino checking up on us. So I said to Specs, 'That little son of a gun. We're going to teach him a lesson for not trusting us. Come on, this is going to be good. We're going to drive Tony Pino crazy.'

"So Specs O'Keefe and me got out of the truck and sneaked along one wall while Tony Pino was sneaking along the other. He was going in one direction, and we're going in the other on the other side. He couldn't see us over there because it was dark and he was too busy trying to find what truck we're in. We heard him going, '*Psst, psst*, hey, you guys. Hey, Jazz, Specs, where are you? This is Stretch. Where are you?'

"We snuck out of there and went down a ways and waited on the street. We're watching Brink's from up Prince Street and after a while we see Tony Pino come running out that far door near the corner [of Commercial Street]. He's coming our way, and you can't see his face because it's dark, but you could tell from the little hops he makes he's madder than hell. He went hopping off down Lafayette Street, and Specs O'Keefe and me went right back into Brink's and got back in the truck.

"So maybe another hour after, Tony Pino come sneaking back in the garage looking for us. Specs O'Keefe and me knew he'd probably been to Jimmy O'Keefe's and every other club he thinks we ran to. So this time we let him find us, and he said, 'Where the hell you two been?' We said, 'Right here looking for hacks.' Tony Pino started almost shouting and said, 'Like hell you have. You been out drinking is where you been.' We said, 'We been right here all the time, and we found that hack you were worried about. A little round hack came through an hour ago with a cold. He musta had a cold,' we said to Tony Pino, 'because he was making a sneezing noise, a kinda psst, psst. But even if he gets better, don't worry about him. He's so dumb he looked right in where we was hiding and didn't even see us.'

Jimmy Costa was sent into Brink's. He remained inside an armored car until 4 A.M. without seeing a single hack.

The dim streetlamp partially illuminated the man in the bulky overcoat standing at the door of 165 Prince Street. He searched in one pocket, then another. He stood for a moment scratching his head. He hiked the overcoat and reached down into his trousers. Something was found, thrust toward the door. No sooner had the man disappeared into the building than the light in the high, thin, narrow window closest to the Prince Street corner of the North Terminal Garage building went on. A moment later the one small window and two large windows on the second level in the back of the building were illuminated—the ones Pino had numbered one, two and three because at night, when he usually watched the offices, the narrow window was always dark; it was the staircase window. Several moments elapsed, then the fourth window was lit, spilling a degree of light behind the fifth window—enough to see a man crossing in front of the slanting grille screen wall fronting the chamber. He seemed to pass right through the barrier. The vault room was illuminated.

Pino crept closer to the edge of the roof atop 109 Prince Street, lay prone, brought up the German naval binoculars, trained them down over the playground at the fifth window and began focusing in on the vault room. The double layers of wide-gauge wire mesh, the one grating the window itself and the grille wall some feet back inside, posed a problem. But after sliding over a bit, changing his angle slightly, he was able to get a fairly clear view of the vault door. He tried to focus tighter, to zero in on the combination; then he heard footsteps—loud footsteps coming up the stairs behind him.

He jumped up, bounded across the roof, leaped up on the adjoining roof at the corner of Prince and Snowhill streets and made his escape.

"Hey, where were you?" Jimmy Costa asked, walking into the diner sometime later. "I went looking for you up on the roof, but you weren't there."

The stairway light went on first, then the ones in the first, second and third windows. Several minutes passed. The fourth window and fifth window remained dark. The light in a sixth window went on.

"What the hell's that?" Sandy Richardson asked.

"Must belong to the place next door," Pino explained.

"They wear Brink's uniforms in the place next door?" asked Sandy.

Pino put down his sandwich, took the German naval binoculars from Richardson, lay prone at the roof's edge and focused in on the sixth window. A small office could be seen behind the grating. A man in coveralls was standing over a desk, pointing down at something. The man standing beside him was definitely in a Brink's uniform.

"Jesus Christ, I musta missed a room," Tony admitted aloud.

Joe McGinnis hadn't uttered a bad word about Joseph Specs O'Keefe since that nomination meet several weeks back. In fact, the bigger Joe had behaved rather well toward the smaller Joe right along, had even started looking at him when he talked. And McGinnis didn't seem in the least bit angry or vindictive when he walked into Pino's kitchen that morning and said he had just talked to Detective Crowley and Detective Crowley had said that another one of his "contacts," Crowley's contacts, had said he'd overheard a girl named Helen Whatchamacallit telling a girlfriend that her boyfriend had *taken her into a joint, actually taken her into a physical premise,* that he told her he and *some pals were going to hit for seven million bucks. Seven million. Some pals.*

McGinnis told Pino that Crowley told him the "contact" didn't have any idea where the score was. Crowley had said that Helen Whatchamacallit was a god-awful liar to begin with and hard nut to crack if you wore a shield, so he wasn't all that concerned, but he wondered if Joe had heard anything about a big haul? Joe told Tony he told Crowley, no, he hadn't heard anything. And then he told Pino that Crowley said the Whatchamacallit broad had a string of keepers a mile long and the one she's been shacked with the most was Specs O'Keefe and that he, Crowley, knew that Specs O'Keefe was as god-awful a liar as Whatchamacallit and couldn't be in on anything bigger than hubcap heists, but he wondered if Joe knew anyone else Whatchamacallit was seeing, maybe a big timer from out of town. Joe told Tony he told Crowley, no, he didn't even know Whatchamacallit, so no, he didn't know anyone she was seeing from in town or out. Well, it's probably nothing to worry about anyway, McGinnis said Crowley said. The only place you'll find seven million dollars in this burg is over at the Federal Reserve, McGinnis said Crowley said. Joe told Tony that Crowley told him, "But if you hear anything, let me know, okay?"

McGinnis related all this to Pino in a low, controlled, even-tempered voice. And without the least bit of rancor he also said something to the effect of let's damage the queer rat once and for all, huh? Whaddaya say to shotguns?

"Now that's when I start realizing Joe McGinnis could be a menace," said Pino. "I been getting along good with Joe, and I liked him a lot. And I went along with him when it came to not letting in O'Keefe, but that was for a different reason. I didn't want O'Keefe in 'cause we didn't need him and 'cause I knew he couldn't do time without having a nervous breakdown, that's all. It was nothing personal, see what I mean?

"Let me tell you something, O'Keefe ain't my favorite person, but he's in on the job and holding his own. Once a man's on the job, you let him alone. But Joe was getting out of self-control. He had this hard-on for O'Keefe that wouldn't go down. He don't know how to put his personal feelings on the side for the good of all of us. What's happening is he's coming in with a pack of lies that don't add up to two cents.

"So now I call McGinnis on his lies and tell him to keep them to himself. If he don't like O'Keefe being in on the thing, he can go and hand in his resignation.

"But I got the other problem, too. I got an obligation to the fellas, see. I don't wanna keep no useless rumors alive and go starting trouble. But I gotta let 'em know something's been said. And I gotta make it clear to O'Keefe to keep his trap shut around women. One of McGinnis' spies sees Specs saying hello to a nun, Joe'll probably says he's selling out to the Pope."

Tony believed he told Mike something to the effect of the cops hiring some new women rats who sat around bars drinking and getting crooks drunk so they could hear, suggested to Mike that somebody should warn O'Keefe to watch what he said in public. Mike recalls that he told Jazz that Tony told him that Helen Whatchamacallit was getting drunk a lot and mouthing off and that somebody should tell O'Keefe to clam up. Jazz recalls that he told Gus that Mike told him that Tony was hopping mad because Specs was getting drunk a lot and bragging in front of dames in some bar and that somebody should talk to O'Keefe about keeping quiet.

A day or so later Jazz told Mike and Mike told Tony that Gus had taken the matter up with O'Keefe and that O'Keefe had said, "Sure, whatever you boys want."

Pino and Costa, costumed as electric company repairmen, walked up Prince at 2 P.M. on a Monday afternoon, stopped at the metal bearing the Brink's crest and number 165—a door Tony knew was always kept unlocked for entering and departing office personnel during the day. Costa inspected the doorframe as if looking for wire. Pino unscrewed the lock tumbler, replaced it with a "slug" or "dummy" from his vast collection of tumblers.

"Tony went around the corner and down to this locksmith on Hanover Street," Costa states. "An old Italian guy—I think his name was Remo. I go up the block and watch the door to make sure no one spots the slug. Tony has his key made and comes back. We go up to the door again and switch it around. Put the regular tumbler back in."

Later that night two would-be robbers entered Brink's through the front door.

CHAPTER EIGHTEEN

Trips to Washington

The sun began to set a little later each evening, rise a little earlier—and the bug loomed larger than ever. Tony, under the alias of a McGinnis associate named Russo, went over to Andrew J. Lloyd Company's Washington Street store and for $99.75 in cash, purchased a Bausch and Lomb Spotting Scope, a telescope with which he hoped to accomplish what the binoculars had failed to do—get a view of the numbers on the combination dial as the Brink's vault was being opened in the morning.

Gusciora and Specs O'Keefe assisted in the removal of at least two more tumblers from Brink's—the metal door at the top of the entrance steps leading up to the company lobby, the door leading from the lobby into the long hall—waited inside the premises at night while Tony drove off to have keys made from the tumblers. In at least one instance he drove off to Dorchester and used a key man named Jake Dana.

And a long ladder was carried across the rubble, hoisted onto the stage of an abandoned movie palace and set in place. Pino climbed the rungs while Costa held the base and lashings were cut and the silver screen came crashing down, was gathered up and transported to the recently whitewashed and window-covered garage at Blue Hill Avenue and was laid out and scrubbed with soap and water.

And Barney and Jimmy Costa spotted a massive electric company repair truck outfitted with a hydraulic tower, and Tony, dressed as a woman, came back late at night and cased the vehicle in a company parking lot and felt this is what was needed for the burn—that the huge semi could somehow be backed down into the playground behind Brink's and the tower raised and the high voltage line and burning equipment passed through the fifth window and right up to the vault. But no one else agreed.

Then there were non-Brink's matters, some good, some bad. Pino's December 8 sentence for the theft of twelve golf balls not only had been reduced to a year probation, but now the entire case had been filed and therefore couldn't affect his deportation. The crew's regular thieving was going well, and the boost couldn't have been more lucrative. And on the negative side, on the very predawn morning Tony was planning to use the telescope for the very first time . . . .

"The goddamn cook gets drunk," Pino exclaimed. "The cook who's been making the wonderful fifty-nine-cent family stew over at my diner. So I put away the spyglass and run over. He's lying out in the middle of the sawdust floor in the kitchen, and I see his shoes is missing. Both his shoes. He's lying out in the middle of the sawdust with socks that don't have no toes in them sticking up. So I feel around in the sawdust. I find one of the shoes, but I can't find the other one. It's nowhere. I look at the big pots of stew and say, 'Oh, my God!'

"I get out the big ladle and go up to the pot of stew cooking on the stove. There's two big pots of family stew, one on the stove cooking and the other sitting in the sawdust cooling. There's nothing in the one on the stove, so I go after the one on the floor. I put the ladle in and sense something. Out comes his goddamn shoe.

"Now I got a predicament. The diner's full of customers waiting for their family stew. Little kids and whole families waiting. So I taste the stew that had a shoe in it. It's not bad. I dump in a coupla bottles of ketchup and some peppers. Now I serve a little up to one or two customers I don't know so good. They love it. I serve it all up. The customers tell me they never had such good stew. So I forget everything and stay there a couple days till the cook sobers up."

* * *

The motion-picture screen was painted by Pino to resemble a red-brick wall and was raised and rigged to the ceiling some ten feet inside the garage doors at the Blue Hill plant. It now constituted a "fake" wall which could be raised or lowered by guide ropes at the side—it would be kept lowered even after a vehicle had entered, would not be raised to expose the remaining two-thirds of the garage until the doors had been firmly closed and locked.

And a dog, a very small dog, raced out across the tar paper and grrred and grabbed hold of a cuff and grrred harder, tugging at Tony's pants leg just as he had lain down at roof edge to use his telescope on the Brink's vault opening. The next time Pino came to the roof he brought dog candy he had been forced to purchase, and that did the trick, but he still missed the vault opening. And the next time, as he was just about able to make out the markings on the combination dial, a cloudburst occurred. The time after that Joe McGinnis sneaked up on him. And a time or two after that Gus and Maffie sneaked up to see how he was doing. But it didn't make any difference. The telescope wasn't strong enough to pick up the markings clearly. "Mr. Russo" returned the spotting scope to the Lloyd Company and received a rebate check—a check that was cashed at Joe McGinnis J.A. Café, Inc.*

Emphasis shifted to tunnels, those tunnels running under Boston which might carry the alarm wires between Brink's and American District Telegraph's office at State Street. Nothing of relevance could be found in the library. Tony, with Costa, took to the sewers near the alarm company's headquarters, found little of merit and ended up by sneaking into the office building's subbasement.

Tubes and cables were seen in profusion, but there was no way of knowing which, if any, ran between ADT and Brink's.

"So I sneak from the subbasement right into the regular basement," Pino stated. "I see where their alarm room is; only I

---

*Lloyd Company records indicate the rebate check was dated January 24, 1949. Pino insists he used the eyeglass until late February and possibly into early March.

can't tell what cable hitches in where. I go all through the building and can't tell.

"Okay, now I tell the fellas we only got two choices when it comes to tunnels. We can blow all the wires up right in ADT's basement or outside in the sewer near Brink's. The only thing with that is we don't know if we got the right wires. We never found wires going to the pete."

Joe McGinnis suggested that if someone could get into ADT's executive offices, perhaps information relating to the alarm installation at Brink's could be found.

Gusciora and O'Keefe received the assignment, gained entry to the main floor of the building, read the tenant directory board, sneaked up to the third floor and into the offices of American District Telegraph and in a file drawer marked "B" found a folder titled "Brink's—Commercial Street" and brought it back to Pino's apartment.

"And whaddaya think's the first thing I come across when I start looking through it?" Pino asked. "It's a letter or something from the insurance company showing the Brink's is insured for five million. We already know that from reading their mail back at Prince Street. And whaddaya think's the next thing I find? It's this letter Brink's wrote to ADT. Brink's is bellyaching about the cost of the alarm. I think it was sixteen or nineteen dollars a month, and Brink's was saying they was getting robbed and wanted it cheaper. But the big thing is the name of the alarm. The alarm on the pete. It's called a phonet. Now we know what the hell we're looking for, a phonet."

Pino and McGinnis brought the file to a former MIT student and supposed electrical/mechanical expert by the name of Sullivan. Sullivan scanned the contents, found no way of beating the bug with the enclosed material, suggested that he go to the U.S. Patent Office in Washington and see if he could pick up the plans on the phonetalarm.*

The night after they had stolen it, Gusciora and O'Keefe sneaked back into ADT and replaced the Brink's file. Sullivan traveled to Washington.

*Phonetalarm, the actual name of the sound detection device first patented in 1925 by Richard M. Hopkins, longtime chief engineer for American District Telegraph.

"Okay, this MIT expert comes back from the patent office, and he's loaded down," Pino stated. "He's got plans and blueprints, and he can tell you everything you gotta know to build a phonet. Everything about how it works. The only thing he can't tell you is how to shut it off. It's wireless. Electronic."

Sullivan made two more trips to Washington and the patent office. Neither journey provided information on neutralizing the bug.

The days were much longer by now.

Tony Pino made two decisions: to sell the diner as soon as possible and, after the summer layoff, to take Brink's on the heavy.

CHAPTER NINETEEN

Night or Day?

The light in the fourth grate-fronted window went off. The man in the muffler and square-shouldered Brink's jacket and stiff-beaked cap walked past the three illuminated windows fronting the empty counting room. He stopped near the door in the rear. The first, second and third windows over the playground turned dark.

Attention shifted to the tall, narrow window nearest the corner of the building, nearest Prince Street—the stairwell window. Unfailingly it had gone black only moments after the counting room was deelectrified. Now it didn't.

The binoculars skipped back over the darkened windows. A light went on in the fourth—in the payroll wrapping room. The man in the cap and square-shouldered uniform jacket was searching for something. He reached for something. The light went out. Almost instantly a light flared behind the third window—the light from a match. The binoculars bore in. A square-shouldered and capped shadow stood just inside the grating. A bright tip glowed near its top, then lowered, raised again, glowed again, lowered. The shadow moved along the second dark window, stopped in front of the first dark window. The red tip rose once more, glowed hot once more and disappeared. And the shadow, too, disappeared.

The lights in the stairwell window went out. The guard in the square-shouldered uniform jacket and hard-beaked cap emerged from the door at 165 Prince Street and started up toward the Commercial Street corner.

The binoculars rose and swung up along the rear of the building, stopped on the one window that was still illuminated, the fifth window, and focused in. A gaunt, balding man in shirt sleeves stood at the wall counter to the right, making notations in a ledger. Several paces farther back and to the left a second jacketless man, resting on a knee directly in front of the open vault, lifted a white cloth money sack off a cart, held it close to his spectacled eyes, lip-read something from the attached pink sheet, then handed the bag to another coatless man standing just inside the vault. The man standing in the vault and the man kneeling before it both were wearing holsters and guns. The man at the counter to the right didn't seem to be armed.

A fourth Brink's employee, also in glasses, emerged from the door at the rear, stepped forward to the counter running along the left-hand wall of the vault room, picked up a spindle and began searching through the impaled pile of yellow pages.

"Now that's the fella who should always have his pistol on him but don't," Tony said. "That fella just came in from the rotunda. He's the rotunda guard, so there ain't no excuse for him not carrying his pistol. But like you see, he don't. I only seen him do it once. The fella who's there other nights never does."

"What about the fifth man?" Geagan, who was watching through his own pair of binoculars, asked.

"He's a long crapper. He's in the back taking that long crap of his. When he comes back, he'll go up and take over in front of the pete. That's his usual place. He don't wear his pistol either."

The fourth Brink's employee ripped one yellow page from the spindle and walked directly back through the door to the control room [rotunda].

"How long does he stay in there?" asked Geagan.

"You never know," Pino answered. "He keeps coming in and out when it suits him."

"So he's looking right into the garage half the time?"

"Yeah."

A fifth Brink's employee entered the room, sipping a Coke.

He, too, was in shirt sleeves. He carried no weapon. After putting the bottle down, he walked to the front of the open vault and took over from the man ⸱v' o was kneeling.

The fourth Brink's employee emerged from the rear, took a step or two, stopped and seemed to say something.

"He's the tough one, isn't he?" Geagan commented.

"If we come through the garage, he sure as hell is," Pino agreed.

"Even if we come in through the front, he can give us trouble," Mike said. "We have to get them all bunched together. We can't be taking four of them and have a fifth one walk in on us from that position."

The man in the control room did pose a difficult problem, but not the only one. At this early stage Pino wasn't sure whether the stickup should be perpetrated at night when the vault room staff was preparing to close or in the morning just as the office was opened.

Pino spent many long pre-daybreak hours along Prince Street, gave hard consideration to taking Brink's by sneaking in before dawn and waiting for the man who had the combination for the vault to show. But could the robbers effectively hide on the premises until then or would they be forced to seize, bind and gag each arriving company employee—employees who entered the upstairs offices through two different doors in the rear as well as one in the front. Tony concluded the latter would be the most likely circumstance. He had on certain mornings counted as many as twenty-five workers going in by the 165 Prince Street door alone before the vault was opened. And what assurance was there that when the man with the combination did appear, he'd ever, under the worst of coercion, open the vault for them? Were Tony and his crew willing to torture hostages to reinforce their threats? Were they prepared to find where the safe opener lived and wait until he left for work and kidnap his family— assuming he had one—and when he arrived at Brink's warn that the dear ones would be killed if he didn't comply? Were they willing to kill family members? Kill hostages?

Assuming they did get the safe open in the morning, what about the getaway? The streets in the Copps Hill area posed strategic escape problems at night and empty. After the vault had been opened and looted, it would be the beginning of rush hour; almost every avenue would be jammed with industrial and commercial traffic—it would be nearly impassable.

And wouldn't hiding on the premises and waiting for employees to show in the morning and sacking the premises be reminiscent to the police of what happened at Sturtevant back in 1947?

From the onset Pino leaned toward an evening heist, but could not entirely dismiss the possibility of a morning strike. Night or day a great many things were unknown. Many, many questions had to be answered and worked out.

"It was all on Anthony's shoulders," states Sandy Richardson. "He carried eighty percent of the load in the beginning. He found the joint and did all the difficult work and had most of the ideas, crazy or not. That was when we were thinking about a clout. When we changed over to the heavy, he did ninety percent and not one idea was crazy. He was at his best. He outdid himself. Nothing was wasted."

Geagan generally reinforces Richardson's observations. "My responsibility was the men. I'd lead the men when we went in. And make no mistake about it, Tony would tell me how to lead them. He would figure out everything, and Sandy and me would help him if he asked.

"When Tony cleared us all out of there and told us to stay away [from Brink's], that was all right with me. Tony had to look at it his own way. If he brought one of us along, it wasn't that we couldn't help him. He saw things no one else saw. Tony saw things like an artist sees things. Tony was the brainpower. Tony had no equal. Tony was a genius over there."

On February 4, 1949, Gusciora had been caught in a police gambling raid and paid a $10 fine for violation of true name. On February 9 he paid a $15 fine for violation of true name. On February 11, 1949, Specs O'Keefe was arrested and charged with assault with intent to rob. The arrest constituted a possible violation of his three concurrent paroles stemming out of the July 5, 1945, convictions for negligently operating an automobile, carrying a weapon on person in automobile and receiving firearms with knowledge of serial number removed. On April 6, 1949, the

Central Court found no probable cause for the alleged assault arrest. That same day O'Keefe surrendered to the authorities, and his original parole on the 1945 conviction which was to run until August 11, 1949, was reduced by almost three months when a new termination date of May 11, 1949, was set.

All this seemed to elude allegedly well-police-connected Joe McGinnis, but not long after, he stormed into Pino's kitchen with something he had found out.

"The goddamn turnip's a rapist,* understand?" intoned the burly skinhead.

"Which turnip?" Pino, who had once served time for abuse of a female child, managed to ask.

"How many turnips we got? The punk one, that O'Keefe."

"Joe, why you so interested in O'Keefe's pecker? All you been hollering over since the man came in is where he's putting his meat. The man's behaving and doing his job. Who cares what he does with his meat?"

"I don't like working next to a turnip rapist, understand?"

If Pino was irritably blunt in dismissing McGinnis' latest assault on O'Keefe, there seems good reason. Ever since the decision to go in on the heavy, he not only felt he would require every available gang member for the job, but also had a precise idea of their dispositions. McGinnis came into the operation on a firm stipulation he be nowhere near Brink's at the time of perpetration. Tony himself very much wanted to go inside for the stickup, but because of his easily identifiable size, Geagan and Richardson had ruled against this; they pointed out he had damn near been recognized from sheer bulk in the Sturtevant caper. Banfield would remain on the heavy where he would have been on the B&E—behind the wheel of the truck. Costa, never considered an inside man under any circumstances, would do the spotting and signaling and, if a follow car was utilized, would be the driver of that vehicle.

Therefore, the men going in with guns would be Geagan, Rich-

---

*On August 26, 1934, O'Keefe, under the alias of Fred Hale, was fingerprinted in the Detroit, Michigan, police station in regard to a statutory rape investigation. He was subsequently released on bond and apparently cleared of any involvement.

ardson, Maffie, Faherty, Gusciora and O'Keefe. Six actual armed robbers. Geagan remained convinced that four or five gunmen could handle the work inside. Tony agreed that four or five men might very well be able to get the drop on the vault room employees, but the concept of hauling away $7,000,000 complicated things. Mike and Sandy, both experienced long-shoremen, estimated that carting off such a large amount could take a full half hour.

A thirty-minute loading period was alarming to Pino. It was simply too long to keep a robbery in progress. Tony, for one, would have been happy if another reliable thief or two were available and upstairs with the six now assigned. Sandy, as a result of his concern over this perilous time span, urged that however the robbers came into the joint, the truck be pulled right into the Brink's garage and loaded up there. Barney saw no difficulty in turning a truck off Commercial Street, ascending the hill via Hull Street, pulling into the second-level common garage and right on through to the Brink's garage and backing and parking in front of the guardroom door. The gunmen inside could load, jump in and they could all leave together. The getaway route from the garage was heaven-sent: follow Hull Street a few hundred feet up to the crest of Copps Hill, take a left at the Snowhill intersection and follow one-way Snowhill a short distance down the waterside slope to Charter Street, turn left into Charter and, almost immediately, right into wide two-way Commercial Street and sprint for home.

For a time Pino subscribed to this plan. Day or night the Hull/Snowhill/Charter/Commercial Streets route had a minimum of traffic. But soon he grew uneasy over the thought of all the men and money being inside a truck that itself was inside a garage—far inside a garage that had only one exit.

In a morning escape that route could inadvertently be blocked by any number of incoming parkers who utilized the common garage. They would have to pass through on the Hull Street side of the building. Tony had always had a preference for loadings and getaways that originated in the open—on streets or sidewalks or even alleys—places from which there was a maximum chance for escape.

His alternative was Prince Street. If the truck pulled before the door at 165 to load, a follow car could cover its rear—could be parked up near the corner of Commercial, could pull out into the middle of the street and temporarily block intruding police vehicles, obstruct the way long enough for the robbers down at 165 to light out in any number of directions, vanish into the maze of narrow streets and clustered houses.

But even if the loading went well, what then? Prince was one-way. After leaving the door at 165, the truck would have to drive down several blocks and then turn into the heart of Little Italy— into a network of narrow, pedestrian-traveled, parked-car-lined streets.

"And the traffic will kill you over there," Pino pointed out. "That's where everyone in Boston comes to buy their spaghetti dinner. It's where all the restaurants are. It's busier at night than Boylston. You want the shortest and fastest way to a main street, a big, wide main street you can make some time on getting the hell away from there."

This description put Pino right back on Hull Street—leaving the second-level garage, going to the top of the hill, taking Snow-hill down to Charter and Charter out onto wide two-way Commercial.

Oddly enough, Prince Street also provided a shorter and faster route to Commercial. Cattycorner to the Brink's door at 165, just before the candy store called Peppy's, was an entrance to Lafayette Street. Lafayette ran only a short block and stopped at Endicott Street. Endicott lay parallel to Prince and ran one-way in the opposite direction. Once they were on Endicott the distance back to Commercial Street was only a few yards longer than the length of the North Terminal Garage building.

The problem here, as Banfield saw it, was that no regular getaway truck he had ever driven could make the sharp turn off narrow Prince Street and into narrower Lafayette Street at anything but a snail's pace. Even if you could turn, wheeling a bulky truck past the one or two cars usually straddling the curb in barely alley-wide Lafayette Street seemed impossible. The problem, as Sandy saw it, was that the robbery team upstairs in the vault room, instead of toting the money into the garage, would now have to haul it out the front of the room, through the payroll wrapping and counting room, on through the front corridor and front hall, through the first metal door, down two half flights of steps, past the metal and main door on Prince Street *and then* load it onto the truck. This not only was as long an alternative as existed, but was hands down the most susceptible to detection. The gunmen would be lugging $7,000,000 right across the windows that overlooked the playground.

Pino still preferred a street-side loading over the risks involved in escaping from the second-floor Brink's garage. He told Banfield to look around for some kind of vehicle which could negotiate a getaway via tiny Lafayette Street and carry $7,000,000 and the men.

In his talks with various crew members, Tony sounded cocksure about his plan, but at this juncture only one thing was absolutely certain: The six gunmen would be entering Brink's as the days grew shorter and the fall thieving season began.

The pull-down rubber masks Tony had stolen on his honeymoon and the three keys for Brink's doors remained behind in the Savin Hill garage. Almost everything else was transported across Roxbury to the larger garage at the rear of the property on Blue Hill Avenue.

"Barney knew where the plant was," says Costa, "because he rented it for us. But he didn't know what was in it. Tony never told him or Joe what we had in there, and he sure as hell didn't let them come in. Nobody went in there but Tony and Sandy and me."

And as far as Pino was concerned, nobody ever would.

For all practical purposes the crew did not have a plant for the Big Haul.

They had been there right under his nose. He had seen them departing in the evening, arriving predawn, walking alone or in pairs or even groups of four or five. He may have even watched four or five together climb or descend the triple terraced outdoor stairway rising up from the building's corner of the playground to Hull Street some forty feet above. He believed he had. His interest in the species in months gone by had focused on the times of goings and the comings, mainly the goings. He himself really didn't dare return to the area and watch again because the days were long, dawn too early, dusk too late. So he thought it through, recaptured and visualized. Forgotten aspects came into focus. No one on the streets could be remembered giving them a first glance, let alone a second. They were as indigenous as the cracks on the aging sidewalk or the peeling paint on the venerable wood façades, these Brink's guards and drivers, these ubiquitous strollers in their standard hip-length square-shouldered uniform jackets and hard-beaked caps. Cold or warm, rain or sleet or clear, their silhouettes had always been the same—had always been ignored. From what Pino could recall, they had always been ignored when they entered the door at 165 Prince.

And so, many important logistics for the Big Haul began to fall in place: The robbery would occur at night; entry would be made through the door at 165 Prince Street; pending the finding of a suitable truck, the loading would take place on Prince Street, if not inside the garage.

Maffie took out his golf clubs and started hitting the links almost every morning of the week with the advent of warm weather. His wife, Eleanor, didn't complain, simply gave an ultimatum. If he wanted her to continue getting up a full hour before the children did and fix him breakfast, then he would have to take the entire family on a motor trip before the summer was out. If not, he could fix his own breakfast. Jazz asked for time to think it over. Mike Geagan's wife wasn't as permissive. She was beginning to question her husband on his comings and goings—particularly at night. It had reached the point where Mike had to sneak his robbery clothes from the house a full week in advance of a job. On occasion the working togs were out and waiting, but Mike himself couldn't get out and had to miss a couple of good scores. He really didn't care. The Geagans had a brand-new baby daughter, their first child, and Mike liked to be home with her as much as possible. Faherty, well, Jimma loved the warm weather better than cold, didn't lose as much clothing when he went on one of his bouts—and he was going on quite a few and sometimes sticking people up when he was drunk as a skunk. Gusciora and O'Keefe were still pulling minor stickups whenever they got short of funding for their perpetual rounds of hoodlum watering holes with whatever women they could find. Sandy was content with working at the pier and being home for dinner and an evening with his wife and children. But his late-afternoon drinking with a couple of longshoremen buddies was markedly heavier; often not only was he dead drunk when he reached the dinner table, but he passed out during the course of a meal.

Joe McGinnis had exchanged his turtleneck sweater for a T-shirt. As always, the trousers were dark and apparently heavy. Sunday was still the time to don a suit and take his wife to mass. Thursday afternoons his shoes and socks came off while he hosed his car in front of the package liquor store. As always, Barney Banfield had to do the chamoising once the vehicle had been washed. In the early days of June he began making the trip across the street, up the short alley and into Pino's apartment more frequently.

"I was measuring the fellas for their costumes, and that knocked Joe out," Tony recalled. "You'd think it was a god-damn free movie, the way he wouldn't miss it.

"I'm measuring their heads and jacket size and shoe size, see. That's all the costume is gonna have, caps, jackets and rubbers. Anything that looks like Brink's [uniforms]. Not the rubbers. Brink's don't give their people rubbers.

"Now let me tell you about the rubbers," Tony went on. "Sometimes when we used to sneak into the joint and it was wet out, I made the fellas take off their shoes and knot 'em and hang 'em around their necks. That's so we wouldn't leave no marks on the floor. They had to walk in their stocking feet. Well, you can't do that on the big night, see. If it rains, you gotta go on it anyway, so if you got rubbers on, you're all set. But that ain't the real reason for the rubbers. You're wearing rubbers rain or shine because they don't make no noise when you walk over those floors in there. Some of the fellas have been wearing crepe [soles] in there, and crepe makes less noise than rubbers. But if you're wearing crepe and it starts raining, you slide all over hell. All we need is one of the men slipping and falling down on his way in.

"Anyway, Joe showed for the measuring of the fellas like I was running mass or a dirty dame show."

Those measured were the six designated gunmen—Geagan, Richardson, Maffie, Faherty, O'Keefe and Gusciora.

* * *

Richardson lay on the grass under a tree, watching Geagan approach from across the park. It was nearing dusk, and the lights from a nearby ballfield had just gone on.

"My God, look at that," Mike muttered just as he reached Sandy. Both men gazed off beyond the softball diamond. Tony Pino was striding toward them attired in shorts, a Hawaiian sports shirt and a wide-brimmed frazzle-edged straw hat.

"Think anybody will notice you?" Sandy asked as a somewhat panting Pino stood over them.

"Whatcha say?" Tony asked, plopping down.

"I said, do you think you might draw undue attention in that getup?"

"Naa, I got my dark glasses on, don't I?" Pino reached up and tapped one of the Polaroid lenses. "Pretty classy, ain't they?"

"How much *didn't* they cost you?" Geagan inquired.

"I didn't boost 'em, I bought 'em. Bought 'em when I bought some of the caps."

"Bought the caps?" Sandy repeated.

"I ain't stealing none of the stuff. Whaddaya think I am, crazy?"

"We think Henry's getting out," Sandy said.

"When?"

"Pretty soon. We don't know exactly, but word is pretty soon."

"Sandy thinks we should ask him in," Mike said.

"What if Henry don't want in?" Pino asked.

"He'll want if we ask," Mike replied. "If you ask."

"Well, sure, let's talk it over with the—"

"No talking with Skinhead, Anthony," Sandy warned. "The say is here with the three of us."

"Why the hell do you always have to call him Skinhead?" Tony snapped. "Don't I have enough heartache between him and O'Keefe without you taking out after him for no good reason?"

Richardson's intended rejoinder was thwarted by distant shouts and whistles. The trio of thieves looked up. Players were waving at them from the nearby night-lit baseball diamond. Pino rose, retrieved a rolling softball and awkwardly hurled it toward the infield.

"Who picked this spot?" Geagan asked, watching two of the players hustle toward the weak and misdirected toss.

"I did," Pino said. "Is something wrong?"

"You ever been pinched by a fed?"

Pino shrugged. "Not that I remember."

"Know any of them on sight?"

There was another shrug. "Maybe one or two."

"Know who you threw that ball to?"

"A fed?"

Geagan nodded. "A whole nest of feds. The men out on that field are all FBI."

Tony knew the towns and individual stores well. All had either been on his boosting or safecrack or burglary agenda in the past. But this time he was traveling alone, was paying cash on the line.

"Now the closest thing I can find to one of them Brink's jackets is them Navy pea coats over at the Army-Navy [stores]. So that's where I start driving [midsummer]. I take lots of trips. I got the hat sizes and the coat sizes. And I start with the coat sizes. The dark blue Navy pea coats is what I'm after first. I drive up to Worcester and Springfield. Oh, yeah, and Weymouth. I even go up to Manchester, where they don't like me. I give 'em some of their money back. I only buy one or two at a joint. I try keeping it to one so no one gets ideas. It ain't always Army-Navy, but some were. A lot of other joints were selling Navy surplus then. I think I got Jazz's coat first 'cause it was the biggest.

"I keep traveling, see? I drive from town to town. I get all the pea jackets and get one for Henry [Baker], too. I know he takes about the same size as Sandy.

"Okay, now I got all the coats over at Savin Hill and now I start driving after the hats. Them chauffeurs' caps. I remember where I seen Sears, Roebuck before and go there. Sears, Roebuck is trickier than Army-Navy 'cause I boosted the straps off 'em, but I go in anyway. When I go in there, I don't go asking nobody nothing. I don't ask for them hats, see? I see 'em or I don't. When the FBI comes looking later, they're gonna cover the world. I don't need ten different stores saying, 'Oh, yeah, a fat little guy came in asking for a hat like chauffeurs wear. Store people remember something they don't have in stock being asked for better than things they have. Sell it and put the money in the register and forget it, that's how they operate. You don't wanna make 'em insecure. You ask for something someone don't got, they start thinking about it in their mind. They can say to themselves, 'Why don't we have that in our store? Do you think we lost a sale and he went somewhere else to spend his money?' They make a mental issue out of it, see? They can get depressed over it. So you look to make sure they got it before you buy it. You see it on the counter. You buy something they got to sell without 'em thinking about selling it, and you're safe because all they're thinking about is how they're gonna spend the bonus they got for selling it."

The rule for the summer was: Keep away from Brink's unless Pino tells you differently. McGinnis obeyed, if for no other reason than he didn't like being seen there on any account. Mike and Sandy and Jimma Faherty kept away. Barney had to go down there once or twice to look over the streets, and Jimmy Costa had to go down to look over the roofs from which he would be giving the go-ahead signal. Gus told Jazz that he and O'Keefe had driven past one night with two girls, assured him they hadn't said a betraying word, but admitted they started giggling like schoolboys when they saw it again. Maffie himself couldn't resist driving by after having dinner at one of Little Italy's better restaurants—"just to make sure the joint didn't sneak away from us again."

The vehicle lot was enclosed by a locked cyclone fence and belonged to the Boston auto dealership firm of Lalime and Partridge, and as Barney drove slowly past late one evening, he told Pino "over on the last line," and Tony squinted out at the three-quarter-ton open-back Ford truck with removable side partitions and said, "She looks too small," and Barney said nothing bigger could get through Lafayette Street and Tony asked if any hacks were around and Barney said no, he'd been past a coupla times and he hadn't seen any hacks and Tony asked what's on the gate and Barney asked did he mean locks by that and Tony asked what the hell you think I mean and Barney said if he meant locks, yes, there was one on the gate and Tony asked what kind of lock and Barney said he hadn't looked to see what kind it was, so Tony said pull over for chrissakes and Barney pulled over and Tony got out and walked back and pretended to tie his shoe and looked at the lock while he was pretending.

"Whatcha find?" Barney asked Tony as they were driving away.

"Religious people."

"Yeah?"

"Yeah, Lalime and Partridge is very religious. They're letting God protect all them new trucks 'cause the lock they got sure as hell ain't."

A seventy-five-cent payment the next morning to a Dedham locksmith obtained a key guaranteed to open any variation of the locked model Pino had described. The test came several nights later and proved successful. Tony led the way through the new vehicles parked in the lot, did a take and stopped.

"Where the hell's our truck?"

"I don't see it," Barney replied.

"I know you don't see it. I don't see it, so why the hell should you see it? You think they got it inside?"

Barney glanced over the garage/showroom building and shook his head. "If it's not out here, it means they sold it."

"They can't do a goddamn thing like that. It belongs to us. It's our truck. We need it."

"More'll come through," Barney said as he opened the cab door of a new rig and began searching inside.

"Yeah? Well, what if one don't come through?"

"We take our business someplace else." Barney righted himself. "But they make it easier here," he said, dangling a set of truck keys he'd found under the floor mat.

Some believe it was earlier, right after the costumes were purchased, others that it was later, but all agree it took place in Tony's living room. The pea coats and the caps were there, and so were the majority of the six men designated to go into Brink's with guns. The guns weren't there because they hadn't been acquired yet, but Tony did bring over the pull-down full-faced rubber masks, many of which bore the features of Captain Marvel of comic book fame.

"Let me tell you something about Tony Pino and those masks and those caps," says Jazz Maffie. "We all had hats there that were supposed to be our size, but when Tony Pino gave me mine, it was too big. About a half size too big. Jimma Faherty's was a half size too big, too. I don't know about the other rogues, but I saw that and I thought, 'There goes Tony Pino screwing up again.' Tony Pino wasn't screwing up. He's the smartest little son of a gun born. He took out one of those masks and put it on his head and pulled it all the way down. Then he started crinkling it up, bunching it up over his face until it was sitting on top of his head like a headband. So we did the same thing with our masks after we put them on. When we got them up on our heads, Tony Pino had us put on our caps. My cap wasn't big now. It fit perfectly.

"So we're all standing in Tony Pino's living room in our jackets and with our hats on with the rubber masks rolled up under them," Jazz continues. "Tony Pino had a cap on, too. With a mask under it. Rolled up. That's when he started having a field day—putting on his show. Tony Pino started strutting around his living room to show how he wants it done. He runs a little bit with that funny hop of his. He takes a real long hop and comes down and squats like he's taking a crap and he raises the cap with one hand and pulls the mask all the way down with the other. Before the mask is all the way down, he takes the hand away from the cap and starts aiming like it was a gun. That's how Tony Pino thinks we should stick up the guys. He keeps hopping around doing that squat and pulling down the mask and shooting away with his finger.

"So now he has all the guys practice the same thing. We're all hopping around Tony Pino's living room pulling down masks and sticking one another up. Some rogues isn't happy just sticking up, so he starts grabbing. Pretty soon everyone's sticking everybody up and grabbing them too. The next thing you know the joint goes wild. Guys are running around going bang-bang and grabbing one another and rolling on the floor and laughing and kicking hell out of the furniture."

Just mention Henry Baker's name, and most of the crewmen couldn't help saying what a nice guy and good thief he was; they always seemed to point out that he was Jewish and in the same breath, point out that his being Jewish didn't matter a damn because he was such a nice guy and such a good thief. The cops didn't think Henry was all that good a thief, but as second-rate second-story men went, they rated him a pretty nice guy.

Five-foot-eight thin, thick and silvering-haired, Henry Baker *was* a pretty nice guy and a better than average thief in some respects. Pino, Richardson, Geagan and Maffie felt he had no peer when it came to opening locked doors. Henry seems to have opened quite a few in his day. He was also caught quite a few times. Of his overall total of twenty-two court appearances, ten had involved breaking and entering or burglary. He had been fined or jailed for offenses such as stealing an automobile or driving under the influence of liquor or operating an auto after his license had been revoked or having a revolver in the car, but five different B&E and larcenies plus one burglary and larceny convictions had resulted in his spending eleven years and five months in penal institutions. Forty-three year old Henry Baker had been as nice a guy in stir as out. He made a lot of friends doing time and grew friendlier with people he knew before. During his 1941–1943 sojourn at Massachusetts State Prison he was constantly in the company of Pino and Richardson and Faherty and Geagan.

He had worked as an extra on some of Tony's crews back in 1936 and 1937 but from that time on was usually in the can. Crewmen felt he was closer to Sandy than anyone, but O'Keefe knew him and liked him, and so did Jazz and so did Costa and so did Barney Banfield and so did Joe McGinnis. There was no trouble with his being approved by all, even though all weren't asked if he could join the crew. So on August 22, 1949, Pino and Richardson drove to the state prison colony in Norfolk and picked Henry up. No mention was made of the Big Haul during the trip back to Boston. Henry, after all, needed a little time to rest and be with his wife and children and get himself reestablished in the family's vending machine company. There was no doubt that Henry was now a part of the Big Haul, but you don't finalize something like that the minute a con gets out of the can. Henry, after all, had just served five years and three months for breaking and entering and larceny of rationed property.

The laundry delivery truck just happened to be parked beside Pino's Buick at the Socony service station across the street from the Columbus Avenue apartment. The driver just happened to have the rear door open and be stacking empty bags on the vehicle's floor according to size—according to five specific sizes—when Tony just happened to walk up and look over his shoulder.

"The big one is okay," Pino told the driver, indicating a regular-sized laundry sack, "but the small ones ain't small enough."

"How small you want?"

"About the size of a cigar case."

The laundry man thought for a beat. "We got something on that line ordered over at the steaming plant. How many you want and when do you need them?"

"How much you charging?"

"You taking the little ones and big ones both?"

"Depending on what you're charging."

"Twenty-five bucks for two dozen. You take two sizes, make it an even fifty."

"For goddamn empty bags you're stealing?"

"Hey, I take risks."

"I don't need two dozen of each size. I only need a dozen of each size."

"They come in two dozen, that's how they come."

"What kind of crap is that? They come how you pack 'em up. Whatcha trying to pull, mister? You think you're the only goddamn fella in town stealing bags from his own laundry company?"

"Nope, but I'm the only one who delivers 'em to your doorstep."

"I'll give you a sawbuck for everything."

"You'll gimme a sawbuck a dozen."

"Fifteen for the lot."

"Fifteen ain't worth my time of day."

"Split the difference?"

The driver thought for a moment. "When do you want them?"

The next day the driver delivered two dozen regular-sized heavy-duty white muslin laundry bags and two dozen envelope-sized string-mouthed gray linen pouches. The total cost was $17.50.

Joe McGinnis led Pino down into the basement, where he usually chained up Barney when Barney needed chaining up, and displayed the large sacks.

"They were bone sacks," Tony recalled. "The size was okay and I didn't mind the price either. Joe was asking five bucks each, but the dumbbell forgot he's paying for it anyway. That's our deal. What was wrong with the sacks was the printing. They had some stencil printing on 'em. Something about Brazil and some meat company. You don't wanna use nothing like that. Nothing that's marked."

Two different cars left Boston. One carried Pino and McGinnis, who were heading to a hotel in Providence to meet a gun merchant. Richardson and Baker were in the other car and drove to New York.

"We went up along the East River [in Manhattan]," relates Richardson. "The Lower East Side where they make burlap bags and this sort of thing. Henry stayed in the car, and I went into one of these places that said 'Big Bags,' used bags. I'd never been to this place before. I just picked one of many advertising on the street. They had signs on the building saying they sold bags. I picked one, and who the hell's going to know anything since I'm dressed in working clothes.

"I go up into this loft and I proposition this guy, one [of the businesses] that said 'Big Bags.' I bought a dozen of these big burlap bags. Like coffee bags, only bigger. Like big trash bags. Burlap. They were regular big bags such as on the docks. They were not threaded at the top. The regular big bags that were open at the top—almost, like I said, big trash bags. Not one was marked, had printing on them. As I remember, they cost no more than two dollars each. All twelve couldn't have cost more than twenty-five dollars. Henry and I drove back to Boston and gave them to Anthony.''

Henry Baker would be going in with the other six, thereby making a total of seven armed and masked gunmen entering the premises via the door at 165 Prince.

How they would reach that door hadn't been determined. How the truck would reach the area and where exactly it would drop them off were far from clear, and therefore, just how, where and when the go-ahead signal would be given weren't clear either. Pino still preferred the loading of the stolen money to occur at the 165 Prince door, but even this hadn't been totally set. So when Mike Geagan began rehearsing the masked robbers, he could only work on entry maneuvers and deployment and the surprising of the guards. Even when he took some of the men into Brink's late at night and acted out the entire operation—had himself and Henry Baker going under the half door and up to the rear of the vault room while the other men crept across the parkside offices to reach the grille walls fronting the vault room—he couldn't be sure what would be happening next. The actual stuffing of money into bags—who went into the vault itself first—could be designated, but where they took their sacked loot remained a mystery.

Many physical items had to be obtained. Tony didn't like the guns Joe McGinnis' contact had displayed in the Providence hotel, so pistols were still needed. No plant had been gotten, and as a result, plans for the count and processing and distribution of stolen money remained up in the air. No truck of the size preferred by Pino had been located yet, and Tony was beginning to feel that maybe they would have to make do with something larger. One small requisite was scratched from the shopping list when Gusciora and O'Keefe were sent over to Sears, Roebuck and stole some adhesive tape and window sashing with which to bind and gag vault room personnel, but as the days grew shorter and daylight savings neared an end and perfect crooking nights approached, a great many factors were missing—the most important being an overall plan.

*   *   *

Pino walked along the playground, glancing back over his shoulder. The lights burned in the stairwell window at the rear of North Terminal Garage, as well as in the six larger windows stretching across to the middle of the building on the second level. He turned and walked a few more steps and again glanced back. The light in the fourth window went out as he watched. He slowed his pace and angled across the street and glanced back up. The third, second and first windows went dark simultaneously. Pino stopped mid-sidewalk, turned around and watched the stairwell window fade to black and then a man step through the door at 165 Prince. Tony remained transfixed. He slowly raised his eyes. Only one window remained illuminated: the fifth window. Then he realized he had seen what he wanted.

They stood on the roof of 109 Prince Street the next night, four of them, Pino, Banfield, Costa and Richardson, standing bold upright with Tony closest to the edge, waving his arm and pointing. The fourth, third, second and first office windows went dark. Next to lose illumination was the stairwell window. Tony waved more frantically, pointed to the one window that was still lit—the fifth and vault room window—pointed down to Prince Street and Lafayette Street and up to the top of the hill and down to the terraced steps, back to the rooftop on which they stood. And the others saw it immediately and began to nod, and Barney even slapped Tony on the back. All the loose ends had been suddenly tied together, and a final plan worked out.

The truck carrying seven robbers would pull into Prince Street from Commercial Street and drive slowly past the building. If someone inside the truck saw that only the light in the fifth window was burning, they would know that everyone had left the building except the men in the vault room. They couldn't be sure the vault was still open, but at least they would have isolated their main target and only four or five employees. When they saw this, the truck would take a sharp right turn into narrow Lafayette Street and then another right turn into Endicott and another right turn into Commercial Street. Costa would be in a car following the truck from the beginning. He could see on his own if the lights were right—if only the fifth window was lit—

and if they were, he would follow the truck onto Lafayette and Endicott and Commercial. The truck would pass Prince and the front of the garage and turn up Hull Street. Costa would pull back into Prince, park, get out and start walking for 109 Prince Street. The truck would climb Hull Street, angle across the intersection at the top of the hill, turn left onto Snowhill and park right there. Costa, in the meantime, would have climbed to the roof at 109 Prince and with his binoculars could see if the vault was open. If it was, he could give some kind of flashlight signal. Maybe a signal wasn't even necessary. Maybe when the truck pulled in to park, the seven men would just automatically jump down and cross over to Hull Street and start down the terrace steps into the playground. Somewhere along their route across the playground Costa would give another signal, a signal saying whether the vault was still open or not. If it wasn't open, the men would turn around and go back to the truck. If it was open, they would continue on to Prince Street, open the door at 165, sneak upstairs and go to one of the windows in the dark counting room. Costa would now give them the final signal. If the vault was closed, they would turn around and go out. If it was open, they would deploy, simultaneously creep in the front and back of the vault room, stick up the employees, bind and gag their prisoners and begin their looting.

When the man in the back of the truck—and Tony now realized two people, a driver and rear spotter, would have to remain on the truck—when the man in the back saw Costa's second signal, the signal telling the men to proceed into Brink's, he would tell Barney to get going. Barney would drive the truck down Snowhill, take a left onto Charter Street at the base of the hill, take another almost immediate left onto two-way Commercial Street, drive back along Commercial to Prince, pull into Prince and park just opposite the Brink's doors. By that time the gunmen would just about be reaching the window in the counting room. If, at this juncture, Costa saw that the vault had been closed, he would give the appropriate signal, the men would turn around, sneak out of the offices, come out the door at 165 Prince, climb into the waiting truck and drive away.

Assuming the vault was open, Costa would wait until he saw the seven gunmen subdue the employees and begin their sacking before leaving the roof. His appearance on the street would be enough to let the two men in the truck know the robbery was in progress. Costa would return to the follow car parked near the Commercial Street corner on Prince.

The robbers inside would haul all the millions down to the area just inside the 165 Prince Street door. When everything had been amassed there, they would give some type of signal. The truck would pull in front of the door. The money and men would be loaded on, and they would leave the area via Lafayette Street. Costa would follow.

For the plan to work, Lafayette Street was a necessity. If, when they first drove past and saw the lights on in only the first window, the truck drove all the way up Prince and turned right on the first wide street and then came back to Commercial, valuable time would be lost. That first wide right up Prince would also bring the truck out into the heavy nighttime commercial traffic in the heart of Little Italy—possibly causing even more delay, a delay during which the employees might very well close the vault. No, from all that had been observed, ten to fifteen minutes seemed to be the average time the vault door remained open after the other offices were vacated. The timing on this heist would have to be split-second. Minutes could not be wasted. Lafayette would absolutely have to be used. The only truck that could get through Lafayette was the one Barney had spotted at Lalime and Partridge. The one that had suddenly disappeared.

On Friday, September 30, 1949, a convoy carrier of the University Overland Express Company pulled through the double gate in the cyclone fence enclosing Lalime and Partridge's car lot at the rear of 1255 Boylston Street, Boston, and made a single delivery—one 1949 Model 112 (chassis) six-cylinder heavy-duty stake body, three-quarter-ton green Ford truck.

Leo Fedor, new car foreman of Lalime and Partridge, was handed two sheets of paper by the carrier driver, a pink bill of lading from University Overland and Invoice No. C-110451C from the Ford Motor Company plant in Somerville, Massachusetts. Fedor checked the specifications contained in the two forms against the actual vehicle and made one notation of his own. He jotted down "432" on the bill of lading, 432 representing the digits of the ignition key number. The brand-new pickup truck was signed for and left to stand with some other 100 vehicles in the fence-surrounded Burns-Detective-Agency-protected lot.

The following morning Lalime and Partridge was informed that Leo Fedor was ill and would not be in for work.

For all intent and purposes the crew had a truck. Now all that Pino had to concern himself with was some lifting, some sketching, some rigging, some guns, a plant and, of course, the light in the fifth window.

CHAPTER TWENTY

Rehearsal

On September 9, 1949, Tony Pino received a "Full and Complete Pardon" on both counts of the 1938 convictions for breaking and entering at Rhodes Brothers in the daytime with the intent to steal, as well as possessing burglar's implements and for which he served two concurrent terms of six years and nine months at Massachusetts State Prison. A "Full and Complete Pardon" meant that these two convictions were technically stricken from the record. Technically Pino had now served only one sentence of more than one year in a penal institution. The existing law on which the United States Immigration Board had predicated their continuing action to send Tony back to Italy clearly stipulated the serving of *two* one-year sentences as the minimum requirement for deportation. The state pardon cut the ground out from under the federal government, which dropped its case against Tony. The full and complete pardon had been granted by both the governor and council. Signing in place of Governor Paul Dever was Lieutenant Governor Charles F. Sullivan.

"You wanna know where a thief's money goes?" asked Pino. "I'll tell you where it goes. Go ask his lawyers where it goes.

"I'm gonna give it to you straight how much that pardon cost me to buy. It cost me *fifty thousand dollars.* All I had and more,

277

see? I had to go begging and borrowing to make it all up," averred Tony, who since his release from prison in September, 1944, to date was responsible for an average of 180 thefts per year with an estimated aggregate value of $2,500,000 to $3,000,000 and of which his personal share came to approximately $400,000.

"Now I don't know who got all that money, see what I mean?" Tony said. "I don't know if the Governor took it or the acting governor had his hand out, too, or who the hell up there got rich off me. All my money went through lawyers. I had three lawyers, not counting Paul Smith. Paul Smith wasn't in on this. He only handled me for pinches and judges. And my other three lawyers only did the setting up. They got other lawyers to work this thing out. I paid my money over to the other lawyers. And the guys they bought off up on that hill [statehouse] was all lawyers, too. So who the hell knows who got what? They don't give you receipts when you do this kind of business. But fifty thousand dollars and one hell of a lot of lawyers were mixed up in this thing."

Despite disclaimers of poverty, obtaining of the pardon prompted subsequent expenditures—many of which were legal fees. Once Pino was sure he would beat the immigration action, he began investing in his future—letting his professedly nonexistent fortune go to work for him. No lawyers were required when he and Costa made a cash deal with a well-established lottery operator and his brother to open up the territory around Canton, Massachusetts.

This particular racket was commonly known as the Federal Reserve or Treasury Balance Lottery since the winning daily ticket was the one whose numbers were the same as the final number of the daily Federal Reserve Bank balance as printed in the local newspaper.

Pino and Costa's initial outlay was approximately $15,000, mainly to cover the cost of purchasing the physical tickets, hiring ticket folders and recruiting agents. The bank was not an out-of-pocket expense. They would simply have to stand good for any losses they suffered. No money was paid to two established lottery operators with whom they were affiliated. The pair would be provided with physical tickets at cost and share in the profits.

Pino and Costa's involvement in the lottery had both a positive and negative effect on the planning of the Big Haul. Jimmy, not surprisingly, was tied down with the bulk of the work, was totally responsible for recruiting agents up in the Canton area, couldn't be as readily available for Brink's activities as before.

Tony, on the other hand, found the perfect way to minimize the potential suspicion meets at his apartment could generate. He sped around Boston trying to find agents, talked to everyone he could, including Ben Tilly, and he now had the perfect guise under which to stay in constant and direct touch with each and every gang member away from home. Tony even convinced Richardson and Maffie to try to sell lottery tickets for him.

Acquisition of the Harbor Motor Terminal preceded involvement in the lottery and did require the services of a lawyer. The parcel of property lay adjacent to the U.S. Navy Yard in South Boston and belonged to the Commonwealth of Massachusetts. When it went for auction, Tony and his three partners—Jimmy Costa, a cousin and an uncle—seemed to be the only bidders. The estimated purchase price was $100,000. Legal papers drawn in October, 1949, showed that Tony purchased a one-fourth interest in the operation. Both Pino and Costa, another one-fourth owner, claimed they had to borrow the $25,000 required for investment. In truth, Jimmy put up his own money, and Tony put up the money for himself and two other relatives.

From the moment of purchase Harbor Motor Terminal became a second command post for the impending assault on Brink's. The phone in the gas station shack on the property was a much-used point of contact. Any of the gang members could drive in, buy gas and unobtrusively chat with whoever was manning the pump—Costa or Pino. Should longer and more direct conversation be required, Tony and a crewman could wander out into the vast much-used commercial parking lot, sit in a car and say what had to be said.

Toward mid-October a great deal was being said. Daylight savings time had ended. The nights were longer. The crooking season was under way. The crew in pairs and sometimes trios was sneaking back into Brink's to recheck the physical premises and contents. The locks for which they had made keys were the same. The other doors and locks were the same. The pull-down and stomp alarms were the same. The personnel records indicated the staff was essentially the same. Except for the vault door having been painted white* and the removal of a counting room desk, they found no changes of note. Costa was back on the roof at 109 Prince Street almost every night with his binoculars, watching the closing procedures in the windows above the playground, and he observed no appreciable changes from the season before. And away from the joint many other things were being done.

"Okay, I go over to Abe's place," Tony recounted. "Some fella named Abe, see, and he's in the auto business, too. I knew he keeps auto plates in his drawer. So it's late at night, and I have keys to his front door. I open the office, and I go in and open his desk and take the plates. One set of plates for a truck.

"Now I go pick up Barney. We drive over to Lalime and Parridge and open the lock on their gate 'cause I got a key for that, too. I got a key for Abe's, and I got one for Lalime and Partride. I'm in the auto key business tonight. Barney don't need no key 'cause he finds it under the mat.

"So Barney and me go in and put Abe's plates on the green pickup [Ford truck]. Barney starts the pickup and drives her right out of there. Maybe it's one o'clock at night. I get in my car and go over to where Barney is parked, waiting. I flash my lights and pull in behind so he knows it's me. I take the three-galloner out of my trunk and pour gas into the pickup. Now Barney's got gas to go where he's going. I'm making sure he's got the plans with him, see? I drew up these plans to show just how I want the rigging to be. So he drives over to the rigger's—they're over in Charlestown, right next to the can over in Charlestown. I follow him over, but I don't go in. Those are good, reliable fellas in there, but you don't want them knowing everyone who's

---

*This was solely a Pino observation. Tony insisted that when, the previous winter, he first saw the vault door it was a dark color with the date of construction painted on it. Costa, Richardson, Geagan and Maffie have no clear memory of what color the vault door was in either 1948 or 1949. By the winter of 1949, the vault door was definitely off-white. FBI records do not indicate whether it had recently been painted. Boston Police Department and Brink's Incorporated information on this point was not made available to the author.

around. They know Barney from the smuggling days. They rigged a helluva lotta trucks for him.

"Now Barney comes out of there, and he's got the plates with him. I drive him back to Egleston Square, and then I go take the plates back to Abe—let myself into Abe's office and put the plates back."

The light in the fifth window went out the earliest on Monday night, usually between 6:45 and 6:55 P.M. This could be expected since the loading schedule on the clipboard in the office showed that only $1,500,000 to $2,000,000 was usually in the vault on Monday nights.

On Tuesday nights the light in the fifth window generally went off between 7 and 7:15, and the vault usually contained, according to the crew's interpretation of clipboard figures, between $2,500,000 to $3,000,000.

The fifth window was less predictable on Wednesday evenings. On some occasions the light had gone out as early as 7:15. On one occasion it hadn't gone out until 7:55. The clipboard reflected a variance of money on Wednesday. Figures as low as $2,500,000 to $3,000,000 had been computed. On one occasion it had been $5,500,000. Usually, the totals ran between $3,500,000 to $4,500,000.

The single most unpredictable night for fifth-window darkness was Thursday. This could be expected since Friday was the traditional payday for a majority of Boston area businesses. The light had often remained on past 8:30. The clipboard for Thursday night, as could have been expected, showed the greatest of vault holdings. The norm seemed to be $5,000,000 to $6,000,000. To the crew's delight $7,000,000 and $7,500,000 had also been noted.

Friday night was the next least predictable evening for the fifth window. The vault holding ranged from $4,500,000 to $5,500,000, but figures as high as $6,500,000 had been computed. The light was observed going out at 7:45, 8, 8:10, 8:15, 8:25 and once as late as 8:40.

Not only was the fifth window the most erratic on the heaviest payload nights of Thursday, Friday and Wednesday, respectively, but so were the lights in the fourth, third, second and first windows. Thursday and Friday were far more difficult than Wednesday. On these two evenings people had often been seen working in the counting room almost to the time when the vault door was closed. Sometimes they left early, turned the switches off for the lights in the first, second and third windows a full hour before or even an hour and a half before the vault was closed.

Try as he might, Pino couldn't establish a clear-cut operational pattern of when the counting room worked late and when it didn't. Checking the quitting time against a heavy delivery schedule the next day wasn't helpful. The counting room often remained operative the longest on nights when the Thursday or Friday or even Wednesday vault contents were the smallest. The robbers absolutely would not attempt to enter the premises while employees were in the counting room.

The fourth window in the line, the payroll wrapping room window, usually went off the same approximate time the three windows in front of the counting room went off—but not always. Seldom had anyone been seen working in the payroll wrapping room at night, yet the knowledge that this light might be left on after the counting room went dark made it all the riskier for the armed robbers, who had to cross through on their way to the vault room.

There were almost no problems with the counting or payroll wrapping rooms being illuminated on Monday or Tuesday nights. Those windows were usually dark by 6 P.M. at the latest. On these two nights the vault door closed pretty much on schedule—6:40 to 6:55 P.M. on Monday and 7 to 7:15 P.M. on Tuesday. These two nights, however, were when the least amount of money was in the vault.

"We ruled against Monday altogether," states Mike Geagan. "It wasn't worth our time. Tuesday we kept in. Tuesday sometimes went up to three million. What we were after was Thursday and then Friday. The big millions. After Thursday and Friday, Wednesday. That's the way we set it up. Thursday was uppermost in our minds."

The gang had penetrated and wandered through the Brink's premises about seventy-five times by count. They had studied files and re-created for themselves what they considered internal company security, but they had never learned that on Thursday evening an armed guard was often stationed in the glass-fronted booth equipped with a pull-down alarm in the general office looking out into the front hall—the hall they intended to enter on their way to the vault.

Barney Banfield picked up the stolen green Ford truck from the Charlestown canvas shop well after sunset. He affixed a pair of license plates he had stolen off a far larger truck in Concord and drove to Franklin Field. Barney got out, and Costa got in. Jimmy wheeled around Franklin Field, turned into Blue Hill Avenue, kept going on Blue Hill until he reached Number 780, entered the long driveway, switched off his headlights as he passed the barn, pulled in before the garage, left the motor idling as he jumped down, went to the door and knocked.

Pino lifted the newly installed crossbar and pushed the door open. Costa pulled the truck in and again stopped. Tony closed and rebarred the door, then ran forward, ducked behind the fake brick wall painted on the movie silver screen and tugged the guy line. The wall rose. Jimmy drove under and stopped. The canvas brick wall fell back in place in the darkness. Jimmy turned on the headlights. Tony ran over and flicked on the wall switch, revealing the secret sanctum whose brick wall had been whitewashed and whose windows had been painted black and covered with aluminum foil. Jimmy turned off the headlights and got out.

Pino began his inspection of the green Ford, now a canvas-backed pickup truck.

"I took one look at it and knew them fellows from Charlestown had done a beautiful job," Tony related. "They rigged her up like you wouldn't even know she was a pickup truck at all.

"Now let me explain what they done. The first thing was to make wooden bows, know what I mean? This pickup truck in its original state doesn't have a roof. All it's got is that flatbed behind her with metal sideboards [racks] going around her maybe three feet high. Them removable side panels [racks]. That's where you put the wooden bows, in them metal holders that hold the side panels in place. These bows hook into each side of the truck and look like them wire things you hit wooden balls under [croquet wickets]. Once you got all them bows up in place, you make your canvas and put it over. The canvas is built to go right over them bows and over the side panels, too. They fasten this canvas down with buttons. Snap the canvas into the buttons. So now what was a flatbed, an open panel truck, looks like a covered truck, because it's covered in back under a canvas roof and sides.

"So there it is, looking like a regular truck with a canvas back. This canvas has got a regular door you go in and out of in the back, but on the left side [left as you face the rear of the cab] is a trick door. Just looking, you don't know that door is there. It just looks like a regular canvas wall from the outside, but from the inside you just unbutton a couple of them metal snaps and pull it open. There you got your door for all the sugar to come through, see what I mean? Prince Street's one-way, so when the truck's parked in front of Brink's this canvas door will open up facing Brink's door [165 Prince Street].

"The rigged truck's got secret peepholes, too. We got lots of 'em put in so you can see from all directions.

"So now we got this lovely-looking canvas truck, and them rotten bastards tried to rob us, tried to charge fifty or a hundred more than they said they would. They were six days late in delivering, too, and the excuse they give is needing to send away for the metal buttons. They didn't have the right kind of buttons to snap her down, so they send away and try to charge us extra. Whoever heard of a hundred bucks for buttons? But there's nothing I can do about it because Barney already paid them cash on the line."

Tony Pino screwing up his face and flashing his ticlike grin and hopping up and down in place as if he had to take a leak and couldn't get his fly open—that was the description Jazz Maffie gave to show how very much Tony Pino wanted the suits and at the same time didn't want any outsiders to know where his new plant was. Tony Pino meeting the two outsiders on a side road late at night and making them get out of their truck and first tying bandannas over their eyes and then putting brown paper bags—without eyeholes—over their heads and making them lie in the back of their own truck so they wouldn't see where Tony Pino and Jimmy Costa were driving them—these were the nutty lengths Jazz Maffie related that nutty Tony Pino went to to get

hold of the suits and make sure that the outsiders wouldn't learn
the whereabouts of his plant. Tony Pino driving the truck right
under some nutty secret wall he was always talking about and
letting the two outsiders take off their double masks and unloading the 200 suits and putting them on racks and then, before re-
blindfolding the two outsiders, taking them over to the manhole
in the back and taking off the sewer cover and warning them
about the bottomless pit and dropping a couple of stones down
the pit to illustrate how long it took to hit bottom and then warning the two dazed outsiders that that's where they'd wind up,
down there in the bottomless pit, if they ever told anyone about
the plant—that was the finish of Jazz Maffie's story to show just
how paranoid Tony Pino was about keeping his joint a secret.

"A plant was becoming a big problem," Sandy Richardson relates. "We had everything set to go on the score, but we ourselves had nowhere to go. We had no plant. We couldn't make
plans about a count or even know where to pick up the guys if
we didn't have a plant.

"Skinhead had a plant. As a matter of fact, he had several
plants and he offered them. But listen to this: Skinhead refused
to let anyone in those plants; Skinhead had the balls to suggest
all the money be turned over to him after the score and that he
would count it by himself and tell us how much there was.

"I'll tell you something that is hardly easy to believe—Anthony was all for that idea.

"I told Anthony that for myself I'd call off the score rather
than let Skinhead get his hands on one extra cent that wasn't his.
I believe everyone else felt this way. The count would be made
with all of us there. All of us would go through the load and get
rid of the bad stuff [new bills that had consecutive and therefore
possibly traceable serial numbers]. All of us would divvy up the
good money. If Skinhead wanted to hold the money for some of
the guys, like he was supposed to, he could, *after it was counted.*

"What this meant was that Anthony would have to use Blue
Hill [*i.e.*, plant/garage]. I think at that time only Costa and myself had been inside. Maybe Mike had, too, but no more than
four of us.

"But Anthony didn't want to use it. A piece of work this size
would mean you had to ditch your plant after the count. You

wanted nothing that was traceable. You get rid of everything. Anthony, plain and simple, didn't want to give up Blue Hill, so we had no place to go.''

The man in the black DeSoto with New Jersey license plates drove past the gray Dodge standing in the Mount Hope Cemetery parking lot twice before pulling in and stopping some thirty yards away. He left the key in his car, walked in the darkness to the empty Dodge, got in and lit a cigarette. He heard his DeSoto start up and speed away.

Costa drove the DeSoto to the adjoining Calvary Cemetery and parked in a dim service driveway. Pino got into the back, hoisted the two suitcases on the floor to the seat, opened them, snapped on his penlight and stared down at an array of brand-new pistols and revolvers. After considerable examination, he removed six .38 caliber revolvers, four .32 caliber revolvers and two .45 automatics. The suitcases were snapped shut and put back down on the floor, but not before Pino had deposited $250 in one of them.

Costa drove the DeSoto back to the Mount Hope Cemetery parking lot, stopped, snapped the lights off and on twice before extinguishing them for good, left the engine idling, got out of the car and hurried into the bushes. He watched the dark figure of the man leave the Dodge, walk to the DeSoto, get in and drive away.

Costa abandoned the stolen Dodge on an isolated street in Quincy, strode around the corner to his own car and headed home.

"Joe McGinnis coming in for a full share? Oh, that was a real beauty. You could have knocked me down," states Jimmy Costa. "For chrissakes, Tony had been screwing guys out of their shares all his life, and along comes Joe McGinnis, and Tony screws him into money.

"When Tony brought in Barney and McGinnis, they were only supposed to have one share between the two of them. Tony said he wanted Joe in because Joe was helping with his deportation, but he would have wanted him anyways. That was the deal Tony made with Mike and Sandy to let Joe in, Joe only getting a half a share. The trouble was, no one outside of them and me knew it.

"When Mike and Sandy and Jimma didn't want to show up at all those crazy meets in Tony's house where nothing happened, Tony acted pissed off, but it was okay with him because Joe's share was riding. Tony let a lot of things ride on purpose. If you let something ride too long, you forget about it. That's what happened with Joe's share. By the time we got around to working out all the things Joe was supposed to do it was too late to bring up him only getting a half share. Sandy and Mike are the kind of guys who aren't going to screw up the works when it's going good. They won't screw it up if it's going bad either. So they kept quiet and swallowed Tony weaseling Joe in for an extra half share. But I don't think Mike ever forgave Tony for it."

Joe McGinnis' assignments were indeed numerous and important, as Pino outlined:

"Okay, we all agreed Joe don't count no money by himself. But we can't have all the other guys at the same place counting too. Right after the haul lots of people have to get back in circulation. So we decided some other fellas will stay with the sugar and count up maybe two or three million. We don't want all the sugar in the same place overnight. So that's Joe's first responsibility—taking the first couple of million when it's been counted by somebody else.

"Okay, the real count comes the next day. At noontime. Whichever fellas wanna be there can. It's always up to the fellas if they wanna be at a count or not. With Joe around I figure every one who can humanly be there will.

"Okay, now we have the second count. We divvy some of the money there. Then Joe takes what's left. That's another responsibility. We know what we got in good money and bad money. Joe gets rid of all the bad stuff. If we got big bills—thousanders—he burns them, too. Now lots of the guys don't wanna have their share on 'em after a big score like this. So Joe will hold it for them. He takes all the good money and puts it someplace safe. He's the keep. When the fellas want some of their share, Joe delivers it to them. He ain't only the keep, he's the delivery boy too. He's gotta get rid of everything else, too. He's gotta get rid of all the sacks we lug the money out in. We been watching

Brink's for a year, and that money of theirs is packed in bags or wrapped in paper. Sometimes that stack of thousands has paper bands around them. He's gotta get rid of all that, too. So that's what he's gotta do when it comes to money.

"Now he's got other things to do. He's responsible for ditching that rigged truck. He takes the truck away from the piece of work and scrubs her clean. Gets rid of the prints. Then he strips off the ribbing and burns it.

"And all the little white laundry sacks, they stay on the truck, too. And the rope and tape they stay on the truck. Everything that stays on the truck after the score, that's what Joe's gotta get rid of.

"No one touches the pistols," Tony pointed out. "The pistols don't stay on the truck. They come off the truck after the job, and I take care of them. The pistols are my responsibility."

Disposal of the costumes was Jimmy Costa's postrobbery assignment.

A meet was made in Tony's living room and the weapons brought out. Jazz selected the .45 caliber automatic. Mike opted for a .38 caliber revolver. Sandy favored a .32 caliber revolver. Jimma, Gus, Specs and Henry were recalled picking either .38s or .32s.

At another meet, Tony watched intently as Gus and Henry, both in their regular topcoats and soft hats, emptied their trousers pockets, walked up to two tape marks on the floor, closed their eyes, walked forward with one hand outstretched, stopped when Tony touched that hand, seated themselves cross-legged, took the bulging white laundry bag Tony gave them and waited for further instructions with their eyes closed.

"We practiced putting on the costumes," Geagan relates. "We marked out the back of the truck on Tony's floor. We knew it was going to be dead black in the truck. We couldn't let any lights go on in the back of the truck, and we weren't letting anyone say a word back there when we went in. We don't want any cars on the road driving past and seeing a cigarette being lit in a truck they were supposed to think was empty. We don't want a car pulling up next to us at a stoplight and hearing voices inside a truck they're supposed to think is empty. We don't want any kind of noise back there. And we don't want any noise when they're sneaking up to the vault. That was why we had the men empty their pockets. We don't want change rattling. When the men get on the truck, all they will carry in their pockets is a dollar bill or two to get home on or their car keys. We'll take that from them, too.

"We practiced everything they had to do on the truck in Tony's living room. And we practiced everything we would have to do in the joint there, too. Then I took all the men into Brink's, and we practiced right there in Brink's. We practiced a half dozen times in Brink's."

The light in the fifth window went out. Pino, Richardson and Geagan waited on the highest terrace of the playground stairway until the Pontiac they knew two Brink's employees would be driving off in passed overhead on Hull Street. They entered the common garage on Hull Street and made their way around and into the Brink's offices.

Doors were the main concern, particularly the locks in the doors beyond the three nearest the Prince Street main entrance for which they had keys.

"We were considering making even more keys," states Sandy Richardson, "but no doors beyond the first three were ever locked. From that corridor [*i.e.*, the corridor just beyond the No. 3 door which opened into the front hallway] there were three more doors before you got to the screen in front of the vault [*i.e.*, No. 4 door from the corridor in the counting room, No. 5 door, Dutch doors from the counting room into the payroll wrapping room, No. 6 door from payroll wrapping into the front of the vault room].

"There was some concern over the gate going into the vault [room]. It was a slide gate that latched from the other side. A pickup latch. As I remember, that was our biggest problem. We would be standing with our pistols pointing through the screen and telling the workers inside to come and lift that latch. We knew how it worked fairly well by now since we'd been opening it for almost a full year. If those workers balked and made a move for a gun, one of our guns might go off, and we didn't want that to happen.

"None of us are killers. We did all this work and planning to make sure no one got hurt—including ourselves. Even if no one got hit, guns going off would blow the job, so this gate was vital. That was why it was vital that two of the guys got into the back of that room [the vault room via the door from the check-in room] when we got up to the screen. The workers wouldn't feel inclined to try something if they were caught in the middle. All we wanted was to make sure they threw down their guns. If they didn't feel inclined to open the latch, one of our guys from the back could do it or Jazz could climb over the top. That screen wall was about eight feet high, and Jazz had climbed over it in nothing flat once or twice."

The two men heading around back would have to pass the door in the money cage, crawl through the metal box opening which had no door and enter the vault room through the door from the check-in room. Neither of these two doors had ever been found locked.

"I believe this is when we decided Henry would lead the guys in," states Sandy. "Henry was our best pickman. If any of those doors inside were locked—and that would have been the first time that ever happened to us—Henry could open them in a wink. Therefore, there was no need to make any more keys. I doubt if we would have had time if we had wanted to. We were just about to go. All that was needed was a plant."

Jazz Maffie responded to the call from Stretch, left Jimmy O'Keefe's restaurant, drove to the Harbor Motor Terminal, pulled in beside the gas pump and rolled down his window.

"How much you want, Mister?" Pino, decked out in greasy overalls, asked.

"Who's paying?" Jazz replied.

"You're paying, this is honest goddamn gas."

"Clean my window and give me a road map, okay?"

"I can't talk to you doing that. I gotta talk to you filling your tank with gas."

"Fill my tires with air."

"The air pump's busted. Tell you what—I'll only charge ya twelve cents a gallon."

"The guy who split the other half of the gas truck you grabbed only charges me six cents."

"Why do you always have to bust my back?"

Jazz shrugged, smiled, got out of the car and watched Pino fit the nozzle into his tank.

"I been thinking," Tony began. "Why don't we take the sugar to your father's house?"

"Oh, that's nice of you, but my father's got diabetes. He never uses sugar."

"Not that kinda sugar. The real sugar. The haul."

"Oh, that sugar."

"Look, we gotta arch it south, right? We can't be going over no goddamn bridges. We gotta go down around where most of the fellas are getting on or off."

"Where are we getting on and off?"

"I'm working on that. But it's gonna be south. Your father's house is south, see?"

"So's your house."

"My house is a goddamn apartment. You can't take seven million bucks into your own apartment and count it."

"Oh, you wanna take it to my father's house and count it, too?"

"Yeah, do the count."

"With my father and mother and my sister there?"

"We'll treat 'em to a movie."

"What's playing?"

"Whaddaya mean what's playing?"

"At the movies."

"How the hell should I know what's playing? I don't even know when we're going to hit the joint, so how can I know what'll be playing when we do?"

"Oh, well, when you find out, let me know."

"Fuck the goddamn movies. What about using your father's house?"

"How can I get him outta the house until I know what's at the movies?"

"What the goddamn shit ass movies got to do with anything?"

"Unless we know what's playing, we won't be able to get him

out of the house. He don't like movies, so it's gotta be something good."

"Whaddaya mean he don't like movies?"

"He doesn't speak English too well."

"My father doesn't speak English any better than your father, and he loves movies."

"Oh, well, let's send your father to the movies, and we'll take the money to his house. He lives farther south than anybody."

"We can't do that!"

"Why not?"

"My father would goddamn kill me if I pulled a trick like that."

"A trick like what?"

"Bring eleven fucking thieves and a hot haul into his house. He'd go through the floor."

"Well, I don't know if my father would go through the floor or kill anybody. All he'd do would be call up the cops and get us all thrown in the can!"

Sandy wouldn't hear of taking the haul to his home, and anyway he had plans for the house after the haul. Costa was even more adamant when it came to displacing his wife and children. Henry Baker turned almost as gray as his hair on his graying head when he was solicited. Tony had better sense than to suggest such an idea to Mike Geagan. Gus and Specs lived in hotel rooms when they were in Boston, and no one even considered driving as far out as Stoughton, where Specy's wife and adopted son lived and Gus' people had a farm.

Pino used these rejections and impossibilities to reurge the gang to accept Joe McGinnis' offer. The gang was agreeable—if Joe would let them all come to his plant for the count. Joe still wouldn't hear of it and suggested they use Tony's plant at Blue Hill. Tony still wouldn't hear of it.

Maybe Joe McGinnis had stolen more than $109,000 on a single armed robbery in the past, but none of the other crewmen had. Not that the $109,000 haul from Sturtevant was all that paltry. It had set a new record for the Greater Boston Area. It held up pretty well against what journalists commonly considered the largest armed theft in U.S. history—$427,000 taken from the Ruble Ice Company in Brooklyn, New York in 1932. There were larger thefts on the books—more than $1,000,000 taken off a train in Illinois and close to $2,000,000 coming from a bank in Nebraska—but these were the distant past, and the hauls included stocks and bonds as well as cash, and newspaper statisticians tended to stick solely to currency taken, so as far as most were concerned, Ruble was king and Sturtevant was a member of the court.

Needless to say, the $109,000 from Sturtevant was many a wide rung above what the men who were in on it—Pino, Geagan, Richardson, Maffie and Costa—usually grabbed. The bread-and-butter score for Tony and his regulars ranged from $5,000 to $15,000. Not that $10,000 or $15,000 was all that bad—not in the age when the FBI itself considered $25,000 a major haul.

The problem, if a problem existed, was that Tony Pino was going about planning a possible $6,000,000 to $7,000,000 job on a $15,000 mentality. Nowhere was this more in evidence than with alibis. The conspirators discussed their postrobbery movements to some extent during a series of meets in Tony's living room, but usually in general terms. As had always been true of Pino jobs in the past, one robber had little or no idea what the other intended to do subsequent to a few requisite post-haul activities. What had been applicable in the past for a $10,000 job was now applied to a potential $6,000,000 or $7,000,000 stickup: Each man was solely responsible for where he went, what he did and what he said following the score; each man would stay away from the next man unless otherwise instructed by Tony; each man would return to his usual way of life following the haul.

One previous rule was stressed: No one was to spend one cent of loot money in an ostentatious way.

"That's the coppers' best way of finding you," states Mike Geagan. "They wait for the man who goes around spending big. Throwing the dough away. Our men were told not to do that. Our men were told not to have one dollar more than they usually had in their pocket."

On the threat of death they were told.

"It was a '49 black Chevy four-door," Costa recalls. "Barney and me went up to Brockton to get it. Barney said he spotted it when he was going to knock over a house up there. The people were away on vacation. Barney left the silver alone and came back and got me. We went and grabbed the car. That was the car I was going to follow the truck in. I put it over at Savin Hill.''

Susceptibility to arrest and the ultimate availability of men for the immediate postrobbery chores were discussed at several meets in Tony's living room. Geagan was still on parole and had been questioned recently concerning several large stickups. It was imperative that he be home as soon as possible after the score. It was decided that whatever else, he would be let off the getaway truck first. Jimma Faherty had recently had his parole revoked, effective September 30, 1949, and was awaiting word whether it would be reinstated or he would be sent back to prison, so his time subsequent to the robbery was at best limited. O'Keefe and Baker were also on parole, but didn't seem concerned, said they could help out for a while. Pino, always a prime SP candidate in any Boston area robbery of note, insisted he would have to get off the truck as soon as possible and establish his alibi. Sandy and Gus had time. Jazz, not known to the police as anything other than a bookmaker, could be counted on as well. Costa, Banfield and McGinnis already had their postrobbery activities stipulated.

A plan evolved which called for all the men who would go to the robbery site, save for Pino and Geagan, to return to wherever the plant would be. Faherty would assist Costa in gathering up the costumes and the gun satchel and taking them away. Costa would subsequently drop Jimma off. Sandy, Henry, Jazz, Gus and Specs would unload the money itself. Barney would drive the truck away to whatever hiding place he and McGinnis chose, wipe it clean of fingerprints and then go out and establish his alibi. Jazz, Gus and Specs would also leave following the unloading. Sandy and Henry would stay behind and count as much of the $2,000,000 or $3,000,000 as they could before Jazz came back to relieve them. Jazz would continue counting until Barney showed up to take the tabulated amount away for safe overnight keeping. Just who would stay with the balance of the loot overnight wasn't resolved. It certainly wasn't going to be McGinnis.

Joe himself had made it clear he wasn't going anywhere near the loot until noon the next day, when the official count took place.

Banfield and Costa, each in his own car, began practicing the run into Brink's.

Pino did relent a degree in regards to the garage on Blue Hill Avenue. The premises could be used—but only as the starting point for the haul. The truck was moved in, and so were the costumes and rope and tape and sisal bags and laundry bags. The leather gun satchel remained at the Savin Hill plant, along with the hot Chevrolet from Brockton.

The meets in Tony's living room went on. More than were really needed. Someone or other suggested that they hit the joint on Halloween because they would be wearing Halloween masks. That was turned down because of what the police and newspapers still referred to as the Halloween Robberies—Sturtevant and American Sugar. Even the police might be able to put two and two together. Someone else suggested they go in around Thanksgiving. Pino gave a categorical no to that. Someone wondered aloud what the seven armed robbers on the premises should do if the Brink's guards balked at their command. And someone else said maybe they should bring in bigger guns, and Mike Geagan grew incensed at that and shouted, "Sure, why don't you bring in goddamn machine guns—try putting machine guns under those pea coats." And Specs O'Keefe, who was already starting to complain about all the delays and starting to blame Pino for the delays, got it in his mind that Pino had suggested taking in machine guns. And Joe McGinnis was getting pissed off at all the delays and blaming Pino. And Gus and Mike and Sandy and Costa were all going out and burglarizing other scores with Pino, and most of these scores had been found by Tony while he followed armored trucks belonging to companies other than Brink's. And Jimma Faherty was drinking too much to care about delays or anything else, and Jazz Maffie was in no hurry. And Jimmy Costa and Barney Banfield kept making practice runs from the Blue Hill garage into Brink's in their own cars and got it down pretty well. And assignments were given as to where each robber would get on the truck, and nobody knew where the hell they were going after the score because Tony Pino hadn't come up with a joint, and nobody but Tony Pino and Jimmy Costa and Mike Geagan and Sandy Richardson and Joe McGinnis knew this. And one of the guys who didn't know this was Specs O'Keefe, so he started bellyaching all the more to Gus, or at least that's what Gus told Jazz, and Gus told Sandy he thought they should hold off Brink's until they hit that civilian car that belonged to the armored truck service that Pino had followed and that picked up receipts from the racetrack that Sandy estimated ran to about $2,000,000 in cash. And Tony himself preferred ripping off the Brink's truck that always parked on the main street in Danvers. And Halloween passed while all this was going on and Thanksgiving passed and Jimmy Costa was running his butt between the lottery and Harbor Motor Terminal and driving for the out-of-town scores the regular crew and Gus were hitting and practicing with the cars for the Big Haul and every free night climbing onto the roof at 109 Prince Street and watching the employees in the vault room close up—and he didn't like the setup at all on Thursday or Friday night. On Thursday and Friday nights the lights were all wrong; the counting room had people in it on Thursday and Friday nights, people who often stayed until after the vault was closed.

Pino and Geagan kept sneaking into Brink's late at night and reading the clipboard, and as Thanksgiving neared, they saw the tally for Thursday and Friday nights go up to $9,000,000 and $8,000,000 respectively, and when Thanksgiving passed, the totals for Wednesday night started to go up.

"So I was stuck, see what I mean?" said Pino. "We had to get going. We had to hit her between Thanksgiving and Christmas when all them holiday receipts was in. We already seen nine million for Thursday, and we figure all it can do before Christmas is get healthier.

"So I said okay, you can use the goddamn plant. It damn near broke my heart. Blue Hill was the best goddamn plant I ever had in my life, but we had to get going. Thursday was our night to be the richest millionaires in the world.

"The last thing I think I done," Tony recalled, "was notch

them keys. I filed notches on the head so Henry could feel which was which with his gloves in in the dark. The downstairs door [the main door at 165 Prince] got one notch, and the metal door [the door from the staircase into the outer lobby] got two, and the one to the left [the door in the lobby opening into the corridor] got three.

"Oh, yeah, another thing. I give the fellas a code word. 'Paul Revere is off.' When they heard that, they know we were off and running for Brink's—'Paul Revere is off.' "

CHAPTER TWENTY-ONE

Lights and Window

Richardson jerked back the flap in the rear of the rigged truck. Maffie scrambled on. Pino slapped the back of the cab. Barney accelerated. Sandy rebuttoned the flap. Maffie felt his way through the darkness, touched Tony's hand, took the laundry sack given him and sat down. His eyes adjusted quickly. He began shedding his hat, topcoat and jacket. The truck stopped for Jimma and Henry to board, then drove on to where Gus and Specs were waiting. Sandy kept his eye to the rear peephole. The Chevrolet driven by Costa was about thirty feet behind. Pino moved through the darkness, checking each man's costume, made sure each had his gun. The wood beams creaked more than anticipated. Tony moved forward, slapped the top of the cab twice. Twice meant to slow down. The sisal bags and rope and tape were distributed. Pino again checked the men. Everything was fine. He took the large round ring bearing three notched keys out of his pocket and handed it to Henry Baker. Then he went to the front peephole.

South Station could be seen ahead. Pino whispered something to Sandy. The truck slowed to a stop. Sandy pulled open the flap. Mike Geagan jumped on. Barney accelerated too rapidly. Mike was almost thrown to the floor. Costumed robbers already seated fell back on one another. The cab roof was pounded twice.

Sandy checked out Mike's costume and gave him his sisal bag while Tony stayed at the front peephole. Wide Atlantic Avenue lay ahead. The police station came into view to the right. The flat ground to the left began to rise. The reinforced front of Copps Hill could be seen ahead to the left. Atlantic began to turn, continued to turn around the base of the hill. Atlantic became Commercial, and Commercial continued to turn, then finally straightened out. Tony could see the North Terminal building ahead to the left. He hurried back to the rear of the truck, grabbed onto the rigging, warned the others to brace themselves.

The truck slowed, turned sharply to the left, straightened out, seemed to continue on even more slowly. Pino kept his eye tight against the rear right peephole. Costa's car turned onto Prince. The vehicle and people doors of the garage building were seen. Moments later the door at 165 was visible. The truck decelerated to almost a crawl. Tony watched the edge of the building pass. He squinted up. Barney slowed to barely a crawl. He grumbled something that no one understood. The truck inched forward. His angle still wasn't right to see the windows over the playground. A few more feet of road were traveled, and then the truck completely stopped. Pino could see the windows—all were dark. He hurried forward and pounded hard on the cab—pounded four times. The truck lurched ahead and immediately took a sharp right turn.

The following Thursday night Costa started out twenty minutes earlier. The truck was already parked and waiting when he reached Atherton and Copley just behind Egleston Square in Roxbury. Jimmy raised and dimmed his lights. The canvasbacked truck started off. He followed behind about thirty to forty feet, fell back farther when the red taillights ahead glowed on. The Thursday before, he had been too close when gang members boarded. Maffie had been caught in his headlight beam. Tonight he didn't let that happen. All he could see ahead was a dark form climbing onto the truck. Jimma and Henry were dark forms to him, as were Gus and Specs when they got on some five minutes later. Geagan, unfortunately, was standing near a streetlight.

Jimmy let the back of the truck get some fifty feet ahead of him as he drove along Atlantic Avenue. The canvas-rigged Ford pickup maintained a steady forty-mile-an-hour pace. Jimmy sped up and narrowed the gap by ten feet when he saw Copps Hill begin to loom to the left. He momentarily lost sight of the rear red lights as they traveled around the Commercial Street circle at the hill base. He accelerated on the straightaway, was only twenty-five feet behind when the humped canvas-back truck slowed and turned left into Prince Street. As the truck crawled past the door at 165, he was no more than ten feet to the rear.

The truck slowed to a near stop just past the end of the building, suddenly shot forward, took a sharp right turn and sped into Lafayette. Jimmy pulled beyond the end of the building and gazed up. The lights were on in the first, second, third, fourth and fifth windows.

Jimmy accelerated gently, wheeled a hard right onto Lafayette, took another right onto Endicott at about five miles an hour. He drove somewhat faster up Endicott and around right onto Commercial, slowed again as he pulled back into Prince and parked opposite the garage and people door. He got out and started walking.

When he reached the playground, he knew he had moved too slowly. The top of the canvas rigging could be seen passing up on Hull Street. He increased his stride, entered the door at 109 Prince, took the steps he had so often taken in the past two at a time, reached the roof and glanced to his right. The truck was parked up in the shadows on the Snowhill side of the intersection.

Jimmy stared across the playground. The first five windows were still illuminated. The vault was clearly visible behind the fifth window. The vault was open. Jimmy raised his binoculars. Two men were handing canvas bags to another man inside the vault. The binoculars swung across the fourth window and stopped at the third. Two men were standing at one of the desks in the counting room talking. The binoculars moved to the second window. Two more men were seated at counting room desks, doing some type of paperwork.

The glasses swung ninety degrees to the right. Someone was coming forward from the truck. The glasses moved back to the fifth window. Grayish white canvas sacks were still going into the vault. Again the glasses moved, and then again. People remained in the counting room. The men standing atop Hull Street seemed to be staring at him. More sacks were going into the vault. Two of the men in the counting room left through the corridor door. Another left. More sacks went into the vault. The last man in the counting room, the one seated at a desk, rose, turned out all the lights and walked into the vault room.

Costa got ready to give a go-ahead signal. And as he did, the vault door closed. He flashed a different code instruction off to the right. The men standing on Hull Street scrambled back into the truck. The humped-back canvas Ford pulled away—headed for home.

"We went in there later in the night," Mike Geagan relates. "We read the chart. They had ten million six hundred thousand in there. That's what we missed. Ten million six hundred thousand dollars. It was right near Christmas. That's why we came right back the next night. Friday always held close to what Thursday had. This was Christmas time."

It was drizzling. Costa's binocular lenses were moist, but even so he could see that the vault was open and being loaded. All the other windows on the line were dark. He gave the go-ahead signal.

The truck was parked at a different angle from the night before. He could barely see even the top of the humped canvas-covered back, didn't observe any activity at all. Then, one by one, figures came into view at the head of the terraced staircase—two, three, four, then after a brief interval, five, six and seven semisilhouetted figures all with the look of Brink's armored car crewmen about them: peaked caps, square-shouldered jackets. One by one they descended to the second-level terrace, angled away back across and reached the steps leading down to the third and final far broader terrace.

The binoculars rose, swung to the left, stopped at the only illuminated window—the fifth window. The man kneeling before the open vault handed up bags. The man inside took them, placed them on a shelf in the rear. Another man came forward from the far end of the vault room, from the control room. The man kneeling before the vault stood up, went to talk with the man from the rear—from the control room.

Three, four, five capped coated figures reached the third terrace and started across the third terrace.

The man inside the vault stepped out and joined the conversation between the man who had been kneeling and the man from the control room. Two more men entered the vault room from the check-in room. One carried a Coke. One wore a uniform Brink's jacket. Everyone else, the other four, was in shirt sleeves. Three of the four in shirt sleeves wore gun holsters.

The sixth and seventh capped and coated figures stepped onto the third terrace and hurried to catch up to the line which was nearing the final staircase.

The man carrying a Coke gazed down at the yellow sheet the man from the control booth was displaying. The man with the Coke shook his head, raised the Coke bottle in the diection of the vault. The man in the uniform jacket and the man who had been kneeling walked over to the vault and pulled close the heavy door.

Jimmy Costa flashed a signal. The capped and coated figures turned around and started back up the terraced staircase.

"Let me tell you how much was in it that night," Pino says. "Mike and me came back and read the chart that night. We missed nine goddamn million dollars."

The glowing white ball atop the three-sided namesake building at the south tip of Times Square began its descent. Tony Pino listened to the event over a stolen radio console, heard that the blanket of watching faces below the tower numbered no more or less than on New Year's Eves gone by.

If the crowd was not as jubilant as usual, which was reported, perhaps there was cause. Not only was 1949 drawing to a close and a decade drawing to a close, but so was the first half of what Winston Churchill had already called "the horrible twentieth century." It hadn't started out that horrible, not for a young, energetic United States rich in natural and human resources. Allan Nevins summed up the first fifty years of the 1900's in a syndrome he called Audacious America; lauded Mark Twain whose "get rich schemes display a high deference to America's spirit of trial and error." Chicago, back in the early thirties, celebrated the period with a world's fair entitled Century of Progress.

For the better part of the last twenty-one years it hadn't been particularly unhorrible in the United States. America had reeled under a great depression and been attacked at Pearl Harbor and fought an arduous war it came close to losing, and now suddenly it seemed to have lost the peace—or at least seen the consolation of victory dissipated.

Many of the people gathered at Times Square and other places around the country this December 31 were relieved to see out the old year. The economy wasn't all that bad, consumer's goods were plentiful, the newest gimmick on the market was television, and the hottest book by far was the Kinsey Report. But a chill had benumbed the nation—that of a very cold war. China had fallen to someone called Mao and *Life* magazine in its current editorial stated the nation's number one priority was to resist the Communist threat, reminded readers of what Churchill had warned some time before: that America was going to inherit the naked threat of Soviet power. Russian might never loomed greater. Russia now had the A-bomb.

Harry Truman's red herring had come a cropper, and by New Year's Eve, 1949, a healthy percentage of Americans were truly frightened of all that the media was cranking out on the peril. Ever since Vassar graduate Elizabeth Bentley—whose efforts to turn herself in were ignored by the FBI for six and a half years— had managed to confess to the bureau the fact of her being a Communist and had implicated some thirty former government employees, "spy" had become a household word and a near national mania. A loyalty oath was in effect. The FBI had increased its manpower—and funding—and was checking to see which federal employee was linked to what un-American organization. Ex officio loyalty boards had sprung up. *Red Channels* was the unofficial official blacklist for the allegedly deceitful. Congressional committees were looking into subversive activities. The most publicized incident of the moment, the Hiss-Chambers affair, was latched onto by an obscure congressman from California by the name of Richard Milhous Nixon.

The worst was yet to come. North Korea was about to invade South Korea. The defection of Igor Gouzenko, a Soviet cipher clerk, had led the FBI to England's Scotland Yard and a scientist named Klaus Fuchs. Bureau men would soon be embarking on one of the largest manhunts in their history—tracking down Fuchs' American contact, Harold, who had helped steal the secret of the atomic bomb.

Nor had the pinnacle been reached in public hearings. Whittaker Chambers and Alger Hiss were scheduled for a face-to-face confrontation in the early part of January, 1950.

No one had openly accused top administration officials of being traitors—only because a near alcoholic, giggling, surly, pathological lying hack politician from Harry Houdini's hometown in Wisconsin hadn't stumbled on communism yet. But he was poking around to find some way to win an election most experts predicted he would lose. After all, you can't fart and belch and sip booze from a bottle in a paper bag on your side of the aisle and show up at your desk unshaved more often than not and be publicly selected as the worst of all United States senators serving on Capitol Hill and still expect the electorate to return you to office. You're pretty well sunk—unless, of course, you come up with a gimmick.

As the glowing white ball atop the Times building touched down and the year 1950 officially began, Americans had had just about as much reality as they could tolerate. If ever the nation needed a brief respite, was ripe for a diversion—any kind of diversion—now was the time.

In Boston four obscure thieves who were just as Irish and drank just as much as and probably more than Joseph M. McCarthy and seven equally obscure confederates—ten of whom were not even known to the FBI and seldom credited with more than ten to fifteen grand heists by the local cops—were inadvertently attempting to provide just that. They went back to Brink's for a fourth and fifth time in early January but again found the lights in the windows unsuitable. They argued among themselves about when to try again. Then the fat little one broke his own strict rule and took three or four of the others and robbed a joint he promised the majority he would keep away from. He used the Chevrolet his brother-in-law had swiped for the Big Haul for this job, so the brother-in-law had to go out and grab another car. Then the little fat one took the same boys out again, and they pulled another job and used the second car his brother-in-law had stolen. So now he told both his brother-in-law and one of the others in on the grab, told them at different times, to go out and grab another car. The brother-in-law stole another Chevrolet. The other went and got his lisping buddy, and they grabbed a Ford. And when on Monday morning, January 16, 1950 he and his buddy put on masks and went into the Statler Hotel and stuck up the cashier for $47,627, they didn't bother telling the others on the Big Haul team where they'd been or what they did. But the other nine knew something had gone on.

The cops turned up the heat.

CHAPTER TWENTY-TWO

Tuesday, January 17, 1950

6:15 A.M.

The house was chilly, the kitchen outright cold. Frost lay thick on the window. Sandy Richardson stood in his undershirt and heavy charcoal gray iceman's pants inspecting two sandwiches. One was liverwurst, lettuce and Swiss cheese, the other roast beef and lettuce. He took out the bread box, went to the refrigerator, retrieved two jars and a covered dish and made himself a butter, peanut butter and jelly sandwich. He poured a cup of coffee into the sink, rinsed out the cup and set it upside down in the rack.

"Getting a late start this morning, huh?" Richardson's son, Young Tom, commented on entering.

"Seem to have overslept. Can't understand why."

"Maybe you had a bigger bag on than you thought," Young Tom dispassionately suggested, reaching for the electric percolator.

"That's enough of that," Richardson counseled. "No coffee. You'll drink coffee after you're eighteen." He watched the youth shrug and start for the refrigerator. "And what may I ask are you doing up at workingman's hours?"

"Have to cram for a test."

"If you were in at night studying like you should be, you wouldn't have to worry about that."

"Pop, I'm not five years—"

"Don't 'Pop' me, young man. I think it's time you show some respect for your mother and the rules of this house. I don't want you carousing around when you're supposed to be home. And I want you home for dinner. Dinner with the rest of the family—not when you feel like coming in. Home for dinner with the rest of us starting tonight. Is that understood?"

"Sure thing, Pop," the youth said, bending into the refrigerator. "Who used all the butter?"

Richardson walked from the room leaving the roast beef sandwich behind on the counter. He stuffed the tails of the blue denim work shirt into his trousers, pulled on a gray wool sweater and lifted his heavy brown parka from the hall chair. Before stepping outside, he slid a knit seaman's cap down over his ears.

Sandy searched the dark overcast sky, then walked to the garage and got in his Pontiac. He shifted into neutral, pulled the emergency brake, switched on the ignition and coaxed the sluggish engine to a roar. He removed a wool glove and held his fist to the windshield, then under the dashboard. The defroster and heater both emitted a semblance of warm air. He opened the glove compartment. The two pints of whiskey were there. So were his black leather robbery gloves.

Sandy snapped on the radio as he pulled from his house, WHDM's *Herald-Traveler* newscast was in progress with a report on the $47,627 Statler Hotel stickup of the previous morning along with what sounded like a review of police efficiency by none other than the commissioner of the Boston Police Department, Thomas F. Sullivan. "Colonel Tom" assured that the massive dragnet mounted the day before would continue but strongly hinted that the unknown perpetrators would have already been in custody if all of Boston's bridges had been barricaded in the few minutes immediately following the heist. Barricading the bridges would have made Boston into a virtual island, thereby trapping the gunmen. "Not if they were heading due south," Sandy told himself.

Richardson wasn't much concerned that the heat was on. Heat of this specific nature had worked to the gang's advantage several times before. They pulled Sturtevant within twenty-four hours of the American Sugar caper. And Tony took a near diabolical pleasure coming in on the tail of a Ben Tilly job, seemed to know every big score Ben had lined up and would often pull one of his own as soon after as he could. Sandy wasn't much concerned with the newscast revelation that not only had Boston Garden—three short blocks from Brink's—reached its 14,000-person capacity the previous evening for Billy Graham's farewell revival meeting, but 5,000 additional believers had been turned away. He didn't doubt that Hull Street and Prince Street and Endicott Street and Commercial Street were swamped with believers parking their cars or looking for spaces at about the same time the vault in Brink's was being closed—the crew had never gone over to the joint on Mondays. They had tried every other night of the week so far, had tried Thursday twice as a matter of fact, but had never bothered on Monday—never would.

Something was concerning Sandy this morning, or at least making him uneasy, and he wasn't sure what. By the time he outran the overhead high voltage wires a musical commercial was playing.

He kept his hand on the dial, skipped between two other newscasts. The Police Department was quoted as saying its men had done a beautiful job in the Statler heist and the bridges were barricaded and the two suspects were in custody and the getaway car was either a dark late-model Oldsmobile sedan or Chevrolet sedan and other police officials felt the robbery might have been an inside job and the mayor of Boston felt the gunmen might have come from out of town.

On the weather front—and Sandy turned up the volume—a violent storm had swept across middle America from Texas to the Great Lakes, paralyzing the northern plains states with devastating blizzards, ice storms and sub-zero temperatures. New England could expect a fair and cold day with temperatures remaining in the low thirties and occasional snow flurries—barring trouble from the Appalachians.

Sandy was concerned over the effect continued delays would have on the crew. Specs was bellyaching about Tony and

McGinnis and Costa and Banfield's getting a full share and not taking any risk—not physically going into the joint. McGinnis had started calling O'Keefe the Rope Man—a derogatory aspersion to the fact that Specky's main contribution to the score, as far as Joe could see, was swiping some rope, helping cut it into strands and knotting the ends to ensure easier and better binding of holdup prisoners. Richardson had never been alarmed by the McGinnis/O'Keefe mutual complaint society, but now some of the others were griping. Gus had taken to blaming Tony for the delays. Even Jimma had been dropping remarks about either taking Brink's or forgetting Brink's. Then there was Tony himself. More and more Tony was suggesting they hold off on Prince Street so they could go hit a few more joints to which Brink's delivered money—or, better yet, hit a company armored car. Tony was becoming obsessed by the Brink's truck that parked on the main drag in Danvers.

No, as far as Sandy could see, they had to try tonight—weather permitting. And if it didn't work tonight, they'd go back tomorrow night and the night after that. Tuesday, Wednesday, Thursday or Friday and then the following Tuesday, Wednesday, Thursday and Friday. This was the plan Sandy himself and Mike Geagan had forced Pino to accept. Keep going over every night of the week except Monday until the lights in the windows were right. Sandy suspected, but would never admit, that the light in the fifth window might never be right.

He bypassed the road leading to South Boston and the waterfront.

Geagan paid the breakfast bill while Jimma picked up a morning paper that had been discarded. They walked out of the luncheonette and started down the street.

"Well, look at that," Jimma announced once he had turned to the front page.

"Somebody got robbed?" Geagan suggested.

"Always. But look down here. Down here they talk about us."

Geagan gazed over as they walked. "I don't see anything about us."

"It says right here than in the last nine months Boston has been plagued by eight major hijacking, safecracking and warehouse robberies. That's two-thirds us."

"Don't exaggerate," Geagan counseled, leading the way into a saloon. "We didn't hit more than fifty percent of them."

Phone calls were placed. Neither Tony nor Jimmy could be reached. Mike joined Jimma at the bar and ordered a whiskey.

"Not going to work today?" Faherty asked.

"No one will miss me."

"What if they do?"

"What if your wife tells somebody you got up this early?"

"I snuck out of the house."

"I'm always sneaking out of the house."

It had been embarrassing. And when Crowley's partner, Conaty, dropped by to see Tony, Tony let him know it had been embarrassing as hell. Hadn't he, Tony Pino, always been friends and cooperative with the cops? Hadn't he broken his back trying to figure out who was doing all the robbing in town and on those few occasions he did have a hunch, didn't he let Conaty and Crowley know? What good was it being cooperative if a couple of cops he never saw SP'd him on the street like he was a common criminal? Why should he give his professional opinion on who pulled the Statler heist if he was going to be treated like that—*taken down to headquarters and made to strip!* That's right, officer, made to *strip down to the skivvies in front of strange people!* Not even given the decent chance to go home and *put on new skivvies.* Made to strip down wearing *old skivvies that had holes in them!* No, no, don't try apologizing. You get Crowley over here so I can tell him what I think about you and him! Oh, Crowley's over seeing Joe McGinnis right now, is he?

"Not working today?" Henry said, leading Richardson to the rear of his vending machine storehouse.

"Mike's signing me in."

"Here it is," Baker announced, rolling out a shopping cart.

"It's too big for my car," Sandy said.

"Just take the basket," Baker suggested, removing the wire basket from the frame.

Sandy nodded and gazed around. "What are those?"

"Peach baskets."

"For smash?"

Henry nodded. "Want a couple?"

Sandy nodded.

Henry selected four paper-lined bushel baskets and gave them to Richardson, asking, "When will we know it's on?"

Sandy shrugged.

"If we go, don't forget the pinch bar," Henry reminded.

"I already told Tony."

8:45 A.M.

"Terminal," Costa said on picking up the office shack phone.

"Good weather?" Gusciora's voice asked.

"Not so good," Jimmy replied. "Maybe snow. Maybe worse."

"I heard good weather."

"Listen again. The Midwest is screwing up."

"When will we know?"

"Call back in an hour."

"Whatever you want."

McGinnis joined Pino in Tony's living room, didn't mention that Lieutenant Crowley had been by to see him concerning the Statler robbery, but did say not to worry, that he'd found out none of the crew had been picked up in the Statler Hotel dragnet. Tony didn't mention that Crowley's partner had been by to see him about the Statler job and had told him that Crowley was talking to McGinnis about the Statler job, but Pino did say to Joe that he already knew all but one of the fellows hadn't been grabbed because they called in like they were supposed to. The problem as Pino saw it was strictly weather. The problem as McGinnis saw it was weather and why one crewman had not been heard from.

*   *   *

Jazz Maffie rolled back and forth on the bed. He finally opened his eyes.

"Oh, hi," he said to his wife, who was rocking him by the arm.

"That man is calling," she told him.

"What man?"

"The one who always keeps trying to change his voice."

"Oh, that man."

Maffie flopped over on his stomach, brought a hand out from under the covers and picked up the receiver from the bedstand.

"Hello," he said.

"Why haven't I heard from you?" Pino asked confidently.

"Nobody hears from me when I'm sleeping."

"Well, we might not be off," Tony imparted.

"Oh. What does that mean?"

"What does that mean?"

"I'm never sure if off is on or on is off."

"Off is the opposite of what it sounds like."

"What's on?"

"The opposite of that, goddammit."

"Which are we?"

"I just mentioned."

"You just mentioned both things—on and off."

"We may not be off and running."

"Then we're on."

"We ain't anything until we know. We ain't going to know for a while."

"Then why the hell did you wake me up?"

Richardson parked near the corner of Wales and Harvard streets, Dorchester. Banfield drove up in a station wagon. The metal basket and peach bushel were transferred to Banfield's vehicle. Sandy locked his Pontiac and got in beside Barney.

Joe McGinnis called the weather bureau from his package liquor store. Pino, Richardson and Banfield stood at the counter listening to the brief conversation. McGinnis hung up and told the trio two things could happen. Boston might be hit with 3 to 5 inches of snow or the temperature could rise, causing rain.

"So I ask Barney, 'What can you handle?' " Pino stated.

" 'An inch of snow's okay,' he told me. 'Two or three inches of snow could be trouble going up and down them hills.' "

Jimmy Costa looked out the Harbor Motor Terminal office shack window and saw a snowflake. He grabbed up the phone and called McGinnis' store.

"Gimme Tony," he said when Banfield answered. Pino got on the line. "Hey, Tony, it's snowing."

"Whaddaya mean it's snowing?"

"I'm telling you I'm looking out the window and I seen snow coming down. Coming down from dark clouds."

"We got dark clouds over here, too. Only they're drizzling on us."

"Well, what the hell we supposed to do?"

After a pause, Pino reached a decision. "Keep watching the clouds till they make up their mind."

11 A.M.

Jazz Maffie showered, ate, and walked out on his porch. A telephone call brought him back to the living room.

"We still ain't sure," Pino said.

"Oh, sure. Sure of what?"

"Whether we're off or on."

"Off and running?"

"Yeah, we ain't sure."

"Why not?"

"Because we don't know if it's gonna drizzle or snow."

"Well, it ain't gonna snow."

"Sez who?"

"I said it's not going to snow."

"It's doing both right now. And some places it ain't doing either."

"Oh, don't worry about it. It's not going to keep on snowing."

"How the hell do you know what the weather bureau don't know?"

"Oh, somebody gave me a present."

"What did you say? Did you say 'present'?"

"Yeah, I got a present. For my birthday."

"A birthday present?"

"Yeah, that's when I got it."

"What the goddamn hell has all that got to do with snowing, for Jesus goddamn Christ?"

"Well, this present is one of them barometers. And I just looked at it. And I just went out on the porch and looked at my thermometer, too. My thermometer says thirty-four degrees, and my barometer says it's gonna stay pretty much like that. How the hell much snow you think you can get when it ain't freezing out?"

Pino walked into the Harbor Motor Terminal office and found an unexpected visitor.

"Morning, Ben," he told Tilly, "how's the pickpocketing coming?"

"About as good as your plans over in the North End, Tony."

"Been over eating spaghetti in the North End, have you, Ben?"

"Yes, sir. And every time I do I keep bumping into that kid of yours."

"Which kid is that, Ben?"

"Your fair-haired Polack one."

"Oh, yeah, I know that kid. He loves good food, so I been recommending him restaurants."

"If you want to do business with the Polack and the creep pal of his, go ahead. Only the next time you rat up to Crowley, don't mention my name."

"The next time you talk to Conaty, don't mention mine!" Pino suggested.

Ben shook his head. "Those two bums of yours talk with their mouths full. Everyone in town knows you sent them over to the Statler."

"If I did that, Ben, they sure hell beat me outta the receipts."

"Tony, I had cops on my butt all night and all morning. I got the same thing after your work in Hyde Park, and I'm sick and tired of it. When I have something substantial going, I give you the courtesy of not being caught by surprise. I expect the same back."

"You never gimme nothing. I always know what you're gonna do before you do it and act accordingly. If it makes you feel better, I'll give you a piece of advice. Keep on your toes for the next month. I feel my energy rising."

"About when?"

"Starting from the minute you walk outta here and stop pestering me about nothing. See you, Ben."

"See you around North End, Tony."

Banfield and Richardson arrived at the Harbor Motor Terminal some fifteen minutes after Tilly departed, about 12:30 P.M. A long-standing debate regarding transportation was continued with Pino and Costa. Several innovations had been tried during their last five trips into Brink's, and the four men in the terminal office were content with pickup locations for crewmen. But Barney hadn't been happy with the return arrangements—particularly having to make a stop at South Station so soon after they left the joint. And what if they ran into trouble and had to shift their getaway route and bypass South Station altogether? What would that do to Geagan's plans? Mike had to be out first and at South Station or his alibi wouldn't work. Jimmy Costa had suggested that should they go into the joint, Mike ride back with him in the follow car. Tony had said if you could work out the costume change, that was fine with him. Costa and Mike had worked out how the shedding of the costume and change back into civilian clothes could be effected in the car, so that was set. Now, as the four conspirators talked in the terminal office, Faherty's request also to leave in the follow car was examined. Barney was for it. The fewer stops he had to make, the better. Tony couldn't see any benefit, but Costa could. Simply assigning Faherty to him—that would kill two birds with one stone. Faherty, whose postrobbery time was limited, could help Jimmy with his chores and then be dropped off by Jimmy when they were completed. That would get both Costa and Jimma out of there faster. The same logistics applied to Geagan could apply to Faherty in regard to costume change after the haul. Sandy thought it was a good idea. Tony agreed.

Starting time was a far more relevant problem. The crew had made a run at Brink's once before on a Tuesday night, had reached the joint at approximately seven-ten—just as the light in the fifth window was going off. Should they go tonight, they not only had to allow for an earlier arrival, but had to make allowances for possible bad weather. Heavy rain or light snow could not only cut down their travel time, but also delay the normal rush traffic and lead to a jam-up or so. Tony suggested leaving at six and then adjusting forward wasn't too bad an idea. Barney felt a six-fifteen jump-off would get them there in good time.

McGinnis called in at approximately twelve-forty with the latest from the weather bureau. Barometric conditions indicated the chance for snow was remote. The Boston area could, however, expect an afternoon and early evening of overcast, intermittent drizzle or rain, and possibly patches of fog. In short, perfect crooking weather.

Jimmy Costa got on the phone and began alerting crewmen that as of 6:10 P.M. Paul Revere would be off and running.

CHAPTER TWENTY-THREE

Tuesday, January 17, 1950

12:45 P.M.

Pino and Richardson drove away from the Harbor Motor Terminal not having been inside Brink's for a full week, but aware that Tuesday was different from all other evenings in one major respect—the portable metal box containing the General Electric payroll was made up and waiting on the premises; perhaps the very same metal box Tony had seen back in 1944 and which was solely responsible for him and the regular crew making a near career out of robbing the armored car concern.

"The box had a metal swing top that was held down by a padlock," Sandy relates. "We therefore assigned our best lockman to open it—Henry. Henry was also responsible for going in the joint first and opening the three doors. He was the man with the three keys, and if the keys didn't work or the locks had been changed, he was the best we had for getting them open anyway.

"But on Tuesday night he had to carry the bar to open the box. Holding the bar under his jacket was trouble enough, so on Tuesday Specky was given the doors. He'd go in first with the keys and open up for the others."

On the previous Tuesday's run into Brink's Henry had been provided with a pry bar. After the aborted attempt he strongly urged Pino that the lock be snipped off with a pinch bar rather than the lid forced up by a pry, should they ever return on a Tuesday. Early this same day he reminded Richardson of this. Now, as Tony and Sandy went over the detailed check list driving across South Boston, a pinch bar was given high priority. No one, however, was assigned to obtaining one.

1 P.M.

William Paul Piveronas arrived at the Harbor Motor Terminal to begin his nine-and-a-half-hour shift as gas station attendant. Costa was free to leave, and he did.

1:20 P.M.

Barney entered the garage at Blue Hill Avenue, carrying two five-gallon cans of gasoline. The three-quarter ton canvas-backed green Ford pickup truck required only two and a half gallons before its tank was filled. Barney started the engine, opened the hood and was in the process of a tune-up when Tony and Sandy entered. The pair climbed into the back of the truck, took out the flashlights and beamed them down. Seven bulging white laundry bags stood aligned in the middle of the floor. Tony went to the first and, under Sandy's beam, began examining the contents. The pea coat was on top as it was supposed to be, a .32 caliber revolver in the pocket. A rubber pull-down mask, a replica of Captain Marvel's, was under the coat. Under the mask was the chauffeur's cap. Under the cap was a pair of rubbers. Pino moved on to the next sack.

1:40 P.M.

Costa took the pry bar, canvas gun satchel and key ring out of the cabinet in the Savin Hill garage and loaded them in his own car.

2 P.M.

Jazz Maffie arrived at Jimmy O'Keefe's restaurant near Massachusetts Avenue to begin his day of socializing and bet taking. Jimma Faherty was belting them down fifteen blocks away.

3:30 P.M.

The seven bulging white laundry bags were all checked out and aligned in the middle of the truck floor. The gun satchel was resting just behind the cab. Beside the satchel were extra large bags and the envelope-sized bags. The ten large sisal coffee sacks were double folded and lying in two stacks near the front right-hand corner of the truck. Also laid out on the floor were about forty strands of window sashing knotted at the ends and several rolls of adhesive tape. A utility box held several extra pairs of gloves should any of the robbers forget his own.

"Now the last thing I put on there was my Coca-Cola box," said Pino. "The box I'm gonna sit on. And I put the pry bar right next to that. I sent Jimmy out for some towels, and when he gets back, I put them on, too. That's for the fellas' faces 'cause we got drizzle outside.

"Okay, now let me tell you about the rest of the plant. We got a plywood table set up over by the wall. And we got four or five folding chairs next to that. That's where they'll do the count. Over on the floor there, we put a General Electric radio Barney boosted. That's so the fellas can have music while they count their millions.

"So now we got all that done, and we go over everything we gotta do after. Barney, Sandy, Costa and me is there. When they come back in here, Costa and Jimmy will strip off all the software. They take the bags and costumes. They take the gun satchel, too. Sandy and his fellas take off the four million. Now I wanna make sure Barney got it straight 'cause he's been drinking pretty good all day. Barney ain't to do nothing till the back of that truck is clean as a whistle. Then he takes off. Ditches her where he's supposed to. The other fellas unload the money and take off, too. Only Sandy and Henry stay and fast count a couple of million. Barney comes back and takes the millions over to Joe. Jazz comes over, too. Now if he gets there before Barney does, Sandy and Henry'll tell him how much they counted and get out and set their stories. Jazz is supposed to wait for Barney, and then he can go. Depending on the heat, I'll figure out who stays there overnight.

"So all of this takes time, see. We're probably over there two, three hours doing this. I don't want all the fellas going outta there till it's dark out."

4:39 P.M.

The sun set just as the almanac and Boston *Herald* had predicted. As the weather bureau had predicted to Joe McGinnis, drizzle was coming down and patches of fog were drifting along the harbor shoreline.

4:50 P.M.

Jimmy Costa checked out the black '49 Chevrolet in the Savin Hill garage, put two laundry bags under the front seat, drove home in his own car, bathed, put on dark trousers, a dark turtleneck sweater and went down to have dinner with his wife and children.

5 P.M.

Jazz Maffie called his wife from Jimmy O'Keefe's, learned that her brother-in-law had arrived and suggested they both meet him here at the restaurant at 7 P.M. sharp. Sandy Richardson dropped Tony Pino off at Egleston Square and went to have a drink. Jimma Faherty, who had been seen drinking heavily all afternoon, had barhopped himself back to the Uphams Corner area where he lived. Barney Banfield was nipping away pretty good in the rear of Joe McGinnis' package liquor store.

5:30 P.M.

Brink's cashier, Joseph L. Heinmeyer, completed his day's duties putting up payrolls in the money room cage and proceeded to make a premises' inspection. Five men were busily working in the vault room. Nobody was in the payroll room. Heinmeyer turned off the payroll room lights. No one was working in the counting room. The counting room light went off.

Heinmeyer started from the back of the offices overlooking Prince Street. Lights were shut off in the girls' locker room, girls' washroom, sales office, supervisor's office, manager's office and general office. Lights went off in the front hall. Heinmeyer locked the metal door leading into the offices, descended the front steps and turned off the stairwell. He stepped outside into the street, locked the metal door bearing the Brink's shield and numbered "165" and started for home.

5:30–5:40 P.M.

"Maybe in about an hour," Jimmy Costa—wearing a dark leather jacket and seaman's cap—said into the phone as a response to a call from Tony's cousin and one of the four partners in the Harbor Motor Terminal about when he could be expected over at the office. "I gotta take care of a few things first," Jimmy revealed and then left home. Sandy Richardson again found a parking spot near the corner of Wales and Harvard streets in Dorchester, locked his wristwatch, wallet and change into the glove compartment, got out, locked the Pontiac door, walked over to the plant, where Barney was already waiting with a fifth of rye. Sandy took a long, hard swig from the bottle. Tony finished dinner and, while Mary was still in the kitchen, moved the living-room clock back forty minutes, shouted he was going over to Joe's for a few minutes, left the apartment building by the back door which brought him over to Imbescheid's Package Liquor Store in less than a few minutes and agreed to call McGinnis as soon as he returned from the run.

5:45–5:50 P.M.

Costa parked his Buick on Rockmere Avenue, placed his wallet in the glove compartment, took out another wallet containing false identification and counterfeit driver's license, walked two blocks to the Savin Hill garage, unlocked the door, went to the cabinets, took out two flashlights, checked to make sure the beams in both were strong, put them both in his pocket, took out the binoculars Pino had purchased at the Lloyd Company, got into the black 1949 Chevrolet, checked to make sure a .45 automatic was in the glove compartment, drove the car out, stopped, locked the garage and headed for Egleston Square. Jazz Maffie told the hatcheck girl at Jimmy O'Keefe's to show his wife to the table he'd reserved when she showed up at 7 P.M. Then, as he'd been doing all afternoon, he slipped out of the restaurant without being noticed and without his overcoat and hat. Richardson let the trick brick wall fall back in place, hurried around and opened the garage door, waited for Barney to drive the humped-back Ford pickup truck through, locked the door, scrambled onto the canvas-rigged rear, moved forward and slapped the top of the cab. He held onto the overhead beams, anticipating Barney would start up too quickly—and Barney did—knelt down, found the first of the seven laundry bags and began changing into his robbery costume. Faherty staggered out of the barroom near Uphams Corner, immediately sobered up when he hit the street, strode down the block and got into the car Henry Baker was driving.

5:50–6:15 P.M.

Fire engines pulled out onto the street and stopped. Firemen piled off and raced for the curb. Costa reversed gears and tried to back out of the line of standing cars. A police cruiser pulled up beside him. The officer at the near window cocked a finger at Jimmy and shook his head. Pino stood in the darkness at the corner of Atherton and Amory Streets, Dorchester, with the collar of his coat jacket turned up, wiping the drizzle from his face with a soaked-through handkerchief. By the time headlights were seen on Atherton he was sneezing. The truck pulled to a stop several yards beyond him. He made a run for the canvas door being pulled open in the back, jumped up, twisted around in midair, missed the floor edge and plopped splashingly onto the wet pavement. He bounded up again, and with Sandy's help, scrambled under the canvas rigging. He simultaneously bitched about the truck being late and praised God for perfect crooking weather, then threw a minor fit when told Costa hadn't yet appeared.

Jazz Maffie parked on Bickford Street, took out his gray suede work gloves from the glove compartment, put his wallet, money and change in and locked the compartment door. Instead of getting out on the street per instruction, he kept the motor idling, turned on the radio, lit a cigar and kept watching his rearview mirror.

Costa shot across Columbus Avenue, barely missing an oncoming car, skidded, accelerated and lurched into Atherton Street. He sped past the Arcadia and Copley streets intersection. He slowed as he neared Amory. The truck wasn't there. He wheeled right onto Amory, raced along it for three short and one very long blocks, took a hard left across the viaduct and kept going until he turned right into Bickford. The truck was standing in the darkness and drizzle with its tail lights burning bright and somebody hoisting themselves into the back.

6:15 and on

They had all gone through it before, five times before, worked it out to a point of perfection and, they hoped, monotony. But anticipation hadn't allowed for much monotony in the past. This particular Tuesday night was colder and wetter and more uncomfortable in the truck than on any other evening, but that didn't lessen the anticipation, merely made it colder and wetter and more uncomfortable.

Pino slapped the back of the cab, held onto the side as the truck started up, moved through the darkness and helped open the thin pencil-sized bag. Jazz dropped in his car keys, managed to strip off his coat jacket and fold it while standing, sat down and braced himself up against a truck panel, opened the laundry bag Pino had shoved up between his legs, struggled into the pea coat, checked to make sure the .45 was in the pocket, pulled the rubber Captain Marvel mask all the way down over his face, then rolled it back up in the prescribed manner until it rode tightly on the crown of his head, placed the beaked chauffeur's cap atop it, pulled the rubbers over his shoes, reached back in the pocket of the suit jacket, took out and put on his gloves, slid the suit jacket into the now-empty costume bag, pushed the bag to Pino, stood up so Pino could check out the costume, took the two folded sisal sacks Pino handed him and tucked them in his belt under the pea coat, took several strands of the knotted-end rope Pino gave him and tucked them in his belt as well, waited until Pino again checked him out to make sure neither the rope nor the bags were showing, then sat back down.

Pino sat on his Coca-Cola box. Sandy stood with an eye at the front peephole over the cab and, when Calumet Street came into view opposite the Parker Hill playground, tapped Tony on the shoulder and managed to get to the rear of the truck without holding onto the overhead bows or stumbling. Pino was too short to reach the bows, almost fell before reaching the door, braced himself for the truck stopping. Barney braked to an abrupt stop. Tony tore open the canvas door. Sandy reached through, helped pull Henry Baker aboard, then Jimma Faherty. Tony buttoned the door back into place. Maffie extended a leg and kicked the back of the cab. The truck started up. Jimma had nothing to drop into the pencil bag and, since he put the pea jacket on over his suit coat, would have nothing to put in the empty laundry bag later except his soft hat. Henry had car keys and some change for the small bag; when he was costumed, he put an overcoat, soft hat and suit jacket into the bag. Jimma was given two folded sisal sacks. Henry was only given the bar—and loudly protested that it was the wrong kind of bar—a pry, not a pinch bar. Tony didn't know how that could be and whispered as much. Sandy swore under his breath.

As had been the case before, only Tony was at the front peep-hole when Gus and Specs came into view near City Hospital. Gus and Specs changed into their costumes. Gus was handed a good deal of rope and a sisal bag to put under his jacket. Specs got a bag and the ring containing the keys. Tony suddenly remembered to give Gus and Henry each a roll of adhesive tape and to give Sandy his two sisal bags. But he forgot to check Gus and Specs's costumes, Specs wasn't wearing rubber over his soft soled shoes,

In the past the six costumed conspirators had talked, even kidded around on the last half of the ride. In the past Tony had jumped up and almost shouted trying to keep them quiet. To-night he remained on his Coca-Cola box with nothing to do. There was no talking or whispering. What noise there was came from the flapping of a loose and undetected canvas end, an occa-sional tattoo of rain, an occasional passing vehicle and mostly the incessant creaking of the wooden rigging.

Costa was concerned by the lack of traffic. He kept about thirty feet behind as the truck reached the end of Albany Street, turned right onto Kneeland Street and followed Kneeland the several short blocks to another left and the beginning of Atlantic Avenue. The last two times Barney had driven this particular route there had been traffic all along the way and particularly by the time they reached Atlantic. Now hardly a headlight could be seen in the opposite drizzle-swept lane, just as few headlights had been seen until here. Nothing was coming up from behind. They had been alone all the way—had maintained an even forty- to forty-two-mile-an-hour pace; an uninterrupted pace—and ac-cording to Costa's rough calculations, they were far ahead of schedule. They were now less than two miles away from the joint and, as Jimmy calculated roughly, would be reaching Brink's at 6:35 or 6:40. No signal had been arranged whereby he could warn Barney to slow down. There was nothing perilous about arriving ten to fifteen minutes early. If all the lights in all the windows were on, the truck could go up and wait where it had waited when this happened in the past. They had waited twice before only to have all the lights go out simultaneously in one instance and the vault room light go out before the others in another instance. What concerned Costa the most was that in the nearly full year they'd been casing Brink's they'd never been over to Prince Street this early on a Tuesday night.

Patrolman William Savage had left Station Precinct House One and begun his rounds. Station One was in easy walking dis-tance of Brink's. Savage, a twenty-five-year veteran in the North End, knew that there was usually a parking problem in the Copps Hill area on the nights when basketball games were played at Boston Garden.

Pino heard Barney rap, rose from the Coca-Cola box and gazed out the front peephole. South Station was approaching to the right; a man was standing on a street corner to the left. Sandy whispered he'd take care of it alone, when the truck stopped, opened the flap and helped Geagan on. The truck started on its final leg of the journey.

Mike was costumed and inspected. Pino reached down, expecting to find three sisal bags still on the floor. He felt only two, didn't have time to search further or ask which robber had an extra bag. He tried to go over interior procedures with Geagan, made a big point about Baker and Maffie's going under through the money box half door and sneaking up on the vault room from behind. This was news to Mike—he always thought he and Baker were supposed to come in that way. A short but heavy burst of rain had been falling during this whispered conversation. Maffie didn't hear any instructions about his going in through the half door. All Baker knew was to follow Geagan once in the joint.

Patrolman Savage rounded the corner from Commercial Street into Prince Street and was surprised to find so very few cars standing along the curb. The veteran officer deferred going down Prince and checking the door of the North Terminal Garage building, including the metal one numbered 165 until after he wandered over to the Boston Garden three blocks away and determined why there was no traffic snarl.

The tandem of a humped canvas-backed Ford pickup truck and trailing Chevrolet sedan circled the drizzle and mist-licked northern crown of Copps Hill at an even forty miles an hour. Pino jumped from his Coca-Cola box, meaning to give the seven costumed gun-carrying men one final checkout.

Commercial Street was straightening out. Up ahead the North Terminal Garage building came into view. Hull Street passed to the left. Tony warned the others to brace themselves, himself held on as the truck slowed, then, amid creaking and groaning wooden bows, took a sharp left turn.

Pino moved back to the front peephole. A dim, inclement Prince Street lay ahead. One car was parked to the right under a streetlight. Up ahead, at the far corner of Lafayette Street, light from the candy store window spilled out on the wet sidewalk. Beyond, the panorama was dark and moist and cavernous.

Tony inched over to the side peephole. The truck had slowed

to a near crawl. Metal window gratings inched past. Then came the metal door bearing the shield and numbered 165. The end of the building was reached. The playground began.

Pino squinted up.

All was dark save for one window—the fifth window on the second level.

CHAPTER TWENTY-FOUR

The Biggest Haul of All

The canvas-backed dark-green Ford pickup truck swung wide, swung into and then away from the playground side of wet Prince Street, swung directly toward the lit windows in the tiny corner candy shop called Peppy's, swung farther and rocked into alley-wide, alley-dark Lafayette Street, splashed forward and climbed the curb in Lafayette, skimmed past a parked car and made a tight and easy right turn into Endicott, sped up and reached the corner at Commercial Street and had to stop because of traffic. And six to eight feet behind the truck—all the way—was the black Chevrolet follow car.

And walking across Prince Street and going into the corner candy store called Peppy's to buy a pack of cigarettes was a seventeen-year-old girl named Margaret.

The rigged truck pulled right into Commercial Street, shifted into a higher gear and drove along at slightly over twenty miles an hour. The black Chevrolet sedan stayed on its tail. The truck passed Prince Street. The follow car pulled into Prince and parked some ten feet from the corner along the right-hand curb. The truck slowed slightly as it passed the ground-level doors of the North Terminal Garage building. Jimmy Costa was out of the follow car, walking down Prince Street with a flashlight in one pocket, his .45 caliber automatic in the other and the binoculars under his jacket. The truck made a wide turn into Hull Street and shifted into a lower gear, and Jimmy Costa lowered his head and turned it slightly away as he strode opposite the candy store on the playground side of the sidewalk. And the rigged truck climbed slowly up Copps Hill on Hull Street and drew near the second-level garage doors. Jimmy Costa hurried his pace along the playground. The truck passed the second-level garage doors and drew near the garage door on the third level. Costa entered the front door of the apartment building at 109 Prince Street. The truck pulled past the third-level door and past the end of the garage building, leveled when Hull Street leveled near the Snowhill Street intersection, turned right into the intersection and pulled in and stopped on the right-hand side of Snowhill Street just beyond Hull Street. It stood motionless in the dark beside the burying ground.

Nineteen-year-old Edwin L. Coffin left his stepfather's apartment at 99½ Prince Street and started up Prince Street—in the direction of Brink's.

The rear door in the gray canvas covering the truck was pulled open. The first costumed robber jumped off, then a second, then a third.

Forty-five-year-old Thomas B. Lloyd, head cashier, as well as the man whom Pino had observed before and referred to as a "slow crapper," had left the vault room and was using the facilities of the men's washroom in the second-floor garage. Charles Grell was left in the vault room, and so was Herman Pfaff, and so was Sherman Smith, and so was James Allen, and all four of them wore glasses, and one of them must have gone out of the Vault Room, probably Smith, who probably went into the control room.

Costa ducked under the clothesline and kept low as he hurried over the roof atop 109 Prince Street. He stopped a foot from the edge, dropped to one knee, unzipped his jacket, took out the binoculars and trained them on the building wall about a hundred yards away and focused in on the only illuminated window—the fifth window.

The vault door stood open. Wide open. Three men were in the room. All wore glasses. All were jacketless. One had a shoulder holster.

Costa knew there were supposed to be a minimum of four employees in the vault room at closing time Tuesday. Often there had been five. He glanced over at Hull Street and didn't believe what he saw. Seven men, all capped and coated like Brink's armored truck personnel, were descending the steps between the top and middle terraces above the playground. As far as he knew, no one was supposed to get off the truck until he gave the signal.

Costa noticed, but wasn't much concerned with, the man on Prince Street walking in the direction of the candy store.

He raised the binoculars again. A shirt-sleeved, spectacled man was standing at the table to the right of the open vault door. Two more shirt-sleeved, spectacled workers—one wearing a shoulder holster—stood farther back in the room talking to each other. Just in focus to the rear of this pair was the top of the metal GE money box. Directly in front of the open vault door was a sled of some sort. On the sled was a small mound of gray canvas packages bearing pink paper slips.

Costa felt they had time before the vault was closed—but not much time. He knew he couldn't give the go-ahead signal until he was certain how many people were working upstairs—until the crew had a good chance at catching them all in the vault room together.

Nineteen-year-old Edwin Coffin ordered a pack of cigarettes from the part-time clerk at Peppy's candy store and wasted no time in striking up a conversation with seventeen-year-old Margaret.

O'Keefe led the line of seven pea-coated and chauffeur-capped robbers across the second terrace and down the staircase toward the third. Geagan was behind him. Behind Geagan was Baker. Behind Baker, Richardson and then Faherty. The two surest gunmen brought up the rear: Maffie and Gusciora.

Pino stood perspiring in the rear of the truck, his eyes pressed hard against the back peephole. Costa was perspiring on the rooftop, his eyes pressed hard against the binoculars his left hand was holding, the thumb of his right hand fidgeting with the switch on the flashlight which that hand was holding. Nothing had changed inside the vault room; no additional workers had appeared.

The column of costumed thieves stepped across the third and lowest terrace and out onto the double staircase, chose the flight to the right, headed directly toward the rear of the garage building, descended onto the wet asphalt of the playground, kept close to the building wall, reached a point almost directly under the fifth and illuminated window, slowed, waiting for a signal. No signal came. They stopped.

"What the fuck is going on?" Barney yelled back into the rear of the truck, and Pino, now taken to hopping from one foot to the other as if he had to leak badly, snarled back, "How the fuck should I know?" but there wasn't any signal, and there should have been by now. Costa up on the roof was damn near talking to himself because now there were only two spectacled workers in the vault room, and he wasn't giving any signal, not knowing how many were up there and where they were up there, and two of the seven capped and pea-coated robbers left the stilled column below the fifth window and were starting to straggle back toward the double staircases leading to the first terrace.

The third shirt-sleeved worker returned to the vault room; then a fourth, also wearing glasses and without a jacket, stepped back in; then came a fifth who didn't have glasses and didn't have on a jacket either and who was sipping from a bottle that looked to Costa like a Coca-Cola bottle.

Costa flashed the go-ahead signal.

The seven costumed robbers fell back into line under the fifth window and started across the playground for Prince Street.

Costa turned to his right and flashed in the direction of the Hull Street/Snowhill Street intersection on the crest of Copps Hill.

And Tony saw this signal intended for him and all but let out a shout. He ran to the front of the truck and pounded on the cab and shouted, "Mother of God, we're off," and Barney took off down the harbor side of Snowhill like such a shot out of hell that Tony was sent reeling backward over some laundry bags.

One by one the robbers came out onto Prince Street. Pino was shouting at Barney to slow down, slow down, and Barney took a left into Charter Street so hard and so fast that Pino was sent flying and Barney immediately took the left into Commercial so hard and so fast that Pino went atumbling.

O'Keefe came up to the metal door bearing the Brink's shield at 165 Prince and inserted the key with one notch on its head and opened the lock with no trouble at all and pulled open the door and stepped inside and one by one the others in the column began to enter.

And Barney came barreling down Commercial Street. The last of the robbers closed the door at 165 Prince and hurried up the first half flight of steps and reached the other six, who had stopped aligned on the second half flight. Seven hard-beaked chauffeur caps were raised by gloved hands in the nearly total darkness. Seven full-faced rubber masks were pulled down. Eyeholes were adjusted; caps reset and tugged at. Seven gloved hands reached into seven pockets for seven revolvers or automatics.

And Barney came barreling into Prince Street like a bat out of hell.

And nineteen-year-old Edwin Coffin suggested to seventeen-year-old Margaret that they leave Peppy's together and go over to the playground together and have a smoke together, and Margaret thought this a very fine idea indeed.

Barney overshot his preassigned parking spot opposite the door at 165 Prince Street. While Pino was holding on for dear life in the back, Barney backed up like a bat out of hell, hit the curb, shifted, shot ahead—shot right at Margaret and Edwin Coffin and Margaret would have been hit if Edwin hadn't pulled her out of the way and Barney slammed on his brakes and reversed and again shot back and slammed on his brakes and still wasn't in the right position and, because Edwin Coffin was walking up to the cab, didn't go forward again. He sat in the darkness, looking straight ahead and not moving a muscle, as Coffin came within a foot or two of the front left fender and said something and then turned and walked back to Margaret and with Margaret walked across the street and entered the playground. When Barney saw them disappear, he started forward again.

The key with two notches on its head opened the metal door at the top of the second-landing staircase. One by one, seven costumed and masked armed robbers entered and passed the dark unmanned guard booth in the outer lobby, then paused. The key with three notches fitted into the lock of the wooden door to the right in the lobby. The lock clicked. Mike Geagan, who was second in line, pushed past the man with the key, pulled open the door and, with a .38 caliber revolver firmly in his gloved hand, led the way down the pitch-black corridor and through the open door to the right. He slowed and signaled for the six behind him to slow. Cautiously and silently he crossed the unlit counting room, reached the grate-fronted window overlooking the playground.

Costa watched through his binoculars as the man with the Coke and without glasses pointed to something and one of the men with glasses nodded and headed for the rear of the vault room. And one of the other men with glasses went to the counter to the right of the open vault door. He saw yet another man in glasses come up and stop in front of the vault door—stop as if he might be getting ready to close the vault.

Then Costa saw the dark outline of a square-shouldered figure standing in the shadow of the first large window nearest Prince Street.

Then he saw the two people seating themselves on the steps of the staircase leading up to the first terrace in the playground.

Then he saw the man who had stopped in front of the open vault door step right into the vault itself. Then he saw the man with the Coke put the Coke down, kneel beside the sled, lift a package, call something out and hand the package up to the man standing inside the vault.

The flashlight beamed on and off. It beamed on and off a second time—completed a signal which meant that the vault was still open, that the armed theft should proceed.

Costa glanced down and noticed the truck was still backing up and pulling forward on Prince Street. And for the first time he noticed that the drizzle had stopped. He trained his binoculars on the dark window, saw what he thought were moving shadows at the second large window.

Six pairs of rubbers and one pair of soft-soled shoes stole single file past the double lines of desks in the counting room. Seven bulky figures—ranging in height from five seven to six one—each with a gun in one gloved hand and with his bulbous rubber-covered head held cautiously upright so as not to disrupt vision or upset the cap and make noise, trailed gingerly on behind the third and final window of the counting room.

Geagan led the column, heard voices coming from beyond the partially opened Dutch doors ahead, voices calling out numbers. He raised his gun hand in the dark without looking back, assumed that the six behind him would slow, reached out cautiously with his other hand. Chamois-covered fingers coaxed the top partition of the open Dutch door farther open, lowered, eased the bottom section wider open. The bottom section creaked, not loud, but audibly. The voices beyond stopped. The gloved hand raised in a warning of caution.

Costa peered hard through the binoculars, saw the cluster of shadows at a standstill behind the third window. Nothing was noted in the fourth and unlit window. The light remained on in the fifth window. The vault remained open, but now no one was inside. The man with the shoulder holster stood to the right of the door, stretching. The man beside him was looking down at a piece of paper or book. Another man was coming over to join them. The man without glasses was standing on the left side of the room, standing just behind the grillwork wall, standing next to the small table which held a telephone, standing right beside a pull-down alarm.

The head of the man without glasses was bowed and turned slightly to the side as if he were thinking about something or listening to something. Then he looked up, stared through the grillwork and on out the window over the playground, gazed off in the direction of the roof from which Costa was watching him. The man without glasses seemed to be saying something. He looked down at his wrist. The man with the shoulder holster turned and knelt before the open vault door . The two men to his right turned away from the window and looked down at a table. The man without glasses turned and walked from the grillwork, then stopped.

Costa saw the shadows behind the third window begin moving into the semidarkness behind the fourth window. He saw the fifth man in the vault room walk toward the rear and disappear to the left. That was all right. He was probably going into the control room, and Costa was confident that two of the gunmen were

already moving around back through the check-in room to inter-
cept him should he not return or return at the wrong moment.

A gloved hand raised in the semidarkness of the payroll wrapping room. A rubber face turned, saw other rubber faces backing up behind it. A gloved finger came down and pressed against
the thick immobile mouth, then rose again. The rubber head
turned back to the door leading out of the payroll wrapping
room. The gloved hand fell.

A pea-coated, masked and chauffeur-capped figure in dark
trousers strode silently out of the darkness, angled left and
stopped at the far end of the slanting, eight-foot-high grille barrier fronting the vault room, poked the barrel of a .38 through the
wide-gauge wire. A second costumed and masked robber appeared from the darkness and fell in to the left of the first, he
also pushed a gun nozzle through the grille. A third came forward, stepped in to the left of the second. A fourth moved up to
up to the left of the third. A fifth moved up. Then a sixth. Then a
seventh.

There were not supposed to be seven of them there!

There were supposed to be only five of them there! Two were
supposed to be around behind and coming into the rear of the
vault room from the check-in room. Jazz and Sandy realized this
almost immediately. So did Mike. But there was nothing anyone
could do.

And all four jacketless Brink's employees in plain view less
than five feet away didn't see one of them. All four employees
either had their backs to the grille or were looking away. All four
went right on doing what it was they were doing—tearing slips
off money pouches or calling out figures or writing in a ledger.

And all seven costumed and masked robbers went on standing there is silence with their pistols pointed at the four workers.
Jazz was breathing through his mouth and perspiring under his
mask, keeping his .45 trained on the employee kneeling in front
of the vault and wearing a shoulder holster, shifting his eyes up
as high as he could get them on the grille wall, thinking that if all
else failed, he could climb over the wall in nothing flat. Sandy
was perspiring, hoping he wouldn't have to fire, and keeping his
.32 caliber on someone standing over to the left and glancing
beyond at what seemed to be some dozen carts or sleds piled

high with tagged packages, maybe more than a dozen, maybe more than twenty or twenty-five—the floor was covered with them. Mike never did perspire easily and never did think about a gun he was pointing, and he was watching the man standing to the left, mentally measuring how far this man was from the stomp alarm in the floor, when he suddenly realized that no one on the crew had ever been designated to do anything at this particular point. He was just about to say something when one of the other robbers spoke up.

"Okay, boys, put them in the air."

All four of the employees looked around, saw the line of bizarre rubber faces topped by chauffeur caps stretched along the grille, saw the guns being held on them. All four employees gawked. One or two paled. One gasped. One said, "Oh, my God." One of the employees threw his hands high above his head. Two raised theirs more somnambulistically. The fourth man, the one kneeling directly in front of the open vault, the man wearing the shoulder holster, seemed incapable of motion.

A gun barrel twisted around and wagged at him. "Come on, come on. Get 'em up."

The kneeling man raised his hands.

A fifth employee emerged from the control room in the rear looking as if he were about to say something, gasped instead at the line of gunmen beyond the grille.

"That's right, it's a stickup," another robber said. "Put them in the air and do what you're told and no one will get hurt."

The fifth employee raised his hands.

"Get over here and open this gate!"

Not one of the Brink's men moved.

A pistol barrel again twisted around in its wide-gauge wire hole and pointed at the man still on one knee in front of the vault. "You, get over here and open up."

"Open up, Charlie," the only employee without glasses said from the corner of his mouth. "Open it up."

Spectacled Charles Grell rose slowly, his arms raised and wide apart and far from his shoulder holster. Then one of his hands seemed to falter, seemed to lower.

"I wouldn't do that, Charlie," cautioned a voice behind a pair of motionless lips, a voice that sounded to Jazz like Gusciora's.

Grell's arms rose higher. He walked hesitantly forward toward the row of guns and expressionless faces.

"Okay, Charlie," a voice that was Jazz's said softly. "Just take down one arm. Take it down slow."

Grell's hand came down, started for the doors and again seemed to falter.

"Lift it up and push her back, Charlie."

Grell did as he was told.

Costa saw the grille door slide open, saw the armed robbers bound through, then turned and hurried back across the roof.

Mike Geagan bolted to the rear of the vault room and began piling empty baskets up on a counter so that no one passing in front of the garage side of the control room window could see in, while another robber moved up and straddled the stomp alarm button in the floor and still another positioned himself in front of the pull-down alarm next to the phone. Another took Grell's gun from its holster and, with yet another, herded all five employees to the corner in front of the vault and forced them to lie down— lie facedown with their arms behind their backs. Knotted end rope strands came out from under pea coats and began lashing employees' wrists together. A roll of tape came out, and strips were torn off and slapped over the mouths of employees. Gloved hands removed the glasses from employees. Sisal bags were already out from under pea coats. Sandy left his lying open on the floor of the vault while he ripped white sheets off of brown paper packages on a lower shelf, tore the corners of the packages away to see if there was paper money or checks inside. The first three packages held checks and were pushed away. The next four contained paper currency and were stuffed into the sack. The robber above him and to the rear wasn't as choosy, he reached across an upper shelf and swept a full armload of tagged packages into a sisal bag. Jazz was kneeling beside a cart just outside the check-in room door, ripping pink sheets off canvas money bags before jamming them into his sack. The masked robber squatting at the next cart was tearing everything off; he tore the receipt sheets and brown paper wrappers and paper Federal Reserve money bands off crisp new bills and stuffed crisp new bills by the gloveful into a sisal bag. The robber at another nearby cart didn't bother removing anything; he tossed receipt-tagged package after receipt-tagged package into his bag as quickly as possible.

Costa gazed off to the right and saw two cigarettes glowing on the flight of steps closest to the back of the building across the playground. He lowered his head, picked up his stride and angled across the street. As he passed the cab of the Ford pickup truck, he nodded. The man in the dark beyond the window seemed not to notice; he remained motionless and staring dead ahead. Jimmy slapped on the canvas while making for the rear of the truck. When he stepped around behind the rigging, a white laundry bag was passed out. He bunched the bag under his jacket, walked on up to the black 1949 Chevrolet sedan, got in, pushed the bag under the seat, turned on the ignition, let the motor idle, didn't turn on the car lights, slid the binoculars and flashlights under the seat, opened the glove compartment door, set the .45 inside and left the compartment door open.

Geagan knelt and checked out the five employees lying facedown in the corner of the vault room floor. Their wrists were lashed tightly together behind their backs—perhaps too tightly. Their legs were securely bound together at the ankles. Mike nodded his approval. The two masked robbers standing over him hurried off. One pulled a sisal bag out from under his pea coat. The other removed a pry bar and made directly for the portable metal GE money box standing farther back in the room. Jazz threw the last of the packages on his cart into the bag, moved for the next cart, was beaten to it by another masked robber, headed for the money baskets on the counter, collided with yet another robber who had the same idea, retreated, hoisted up his bag and stepped around in front of the vault as another robber was backing out the vault door, pulling a bulging and filled sack after him. Once in the vault he found another robber busy at work in the rear and a high front shelf crammed full of packages.

The light in the sixth window went on—the window to the right of the vault room.

No one was on the roof at 109 Prince Street to see the light go on. No one on the premises was checking the corner guard booth off the front office to see if anybody was entering the garage—as Pino had ordered. No one in the vault room had talked or was talking and therefore could not give or receive any order, with the exception of Geagan, who every now and then saw something he wanted done and motioned to have it done. No one in the vault room was sure which of the rubber-faced robbers was which with the possible exception of the man trying to pry open the GE box—that was probably Baker. No one in the vault room seemed to be bothering with checking the contents of paper packages anymore. Some tore off yellow or pink or white receipt sheets, some did not. Many were not ignoring bags of smash as they knew they should even without Pino ordering it. Several were dropping bag after heavy bag of coins into their sisal sacks. Almost everyone was perspiring. Everyone was hurrying. No one seemed to know where to leave their big sisal bags once they were filled. Several were left near the open grille door. Several had been dragged as far as the counting room.

Pino was perspiring under the bows in the darkness of the canvas-covered rear of the truck; he hadn't stopped perspiring or pacing since Barney had finally come to a stop. He was beginning to mutter to himself while pressing an eye to the side peep hole and watching the door at 165, waiting for it to move just a fraction. That was the signal—the door opening just a fraction. "Come on, come on," he said under his breath. He moved away and paced a little and even hopped up and down a little and went back to the peekhole. "Come on, come on. Get a move on. Get a move on. Pick it up, pick it up."

Gloved and sweating hands stuffed canvas money bags into sisal sacks as fast as they could, dumped tray after tray after tray of small payroll envelopes into sisal sacks, tossed in brown paper packages and white paper packages and unwrapped packages of exposed currency and thick brown manila envelopes and thick white manila envelopes and thin envelopes and small cloth pouches, and sometimes white or pink or yellow sheets were torn from packages and tossed away and money baskets were often tossed away and carts were often kicked over, and the floor became so littered that one of the robbers almost tripped over a covered coaster edge and another slipped on a piece of discarded paper. One robber ran out and wedged certain doors with wastepaper baskets. Mike Geagan gave a signal or said something, and Sandy Richardson grabbed a bulging sisal bag and, running backwards, dragged it out of the vault room and through the payroll wrapping room and through the counting room and long corridor and through the front hall and down the first half flight of stairs and down the second half flight and left it inside the metal door opening onto Prince Street and numbered 165. And when he started running back upstairs, he had to get out of the way because two more robbers were running down the stairs, each dragging a sisal bag after him—sisal bags whose wide mouths were left open as they were pulled.

Activity in the vault room accelerated: More and more payroll envelopes were found and dumped; sacks came off the vault shelf; the robber with the pry bar worked more feverously than ever trying to open the top of the metal GE money box everyone knew held $1,000,000, more open-mouthed filled sisal bags were sped across the office and down the steps on the fleeting heels of backward-running robbers; sweat poured out from under masks, soaked through gloves and socks, made trousers stick to legs; robbers began working in pairs, one holding open a sack while another turned over and dumped out the contents of an entire basket; a second man joined the first, trying to wedge open the top of the GE box and its million-dollar load. .

And the breathing of many of the robbers became pronouncedly heavy and the last full cartload of packages was cleaned off and the last full money basket emptied and the last tray of payroll envelopes dumped out and yet another robber took hold of the bar and tried prying up the lid or breaking the padlock of the metal box and other gray knees dropped to the floor and gloved hands searched through the litter on the floor trying to find packages that might have fallen off early and more filled bags were scooted out the grille door behind a bounding dragger and someone went back inside the looted vault and grabbed a few of the remaining money coin sacks that had intentionally been left behind and someone on his hands and knees pulled away some discarded money baskets and shoved back an upended cart and let out a whistle and pointed to three whole baskets that had been obscured beneath the counter and another robber shook his masked head and whispered, "Government checks," and the discovering robber shook his head back and said something like "Like hell, not all of them," and he began piling packages into his sisal bag and Mike Geagan took the pry bar and tried his luck at opening the metal box he knew held $1,000,000 and couldn't open it and tried again and looked around and saw the last of the filled sisal bags being dragged out and looked around further and saw that only two other robbers were in the room with him and felt that the room was effectively sacked and told whoever it was off to his right to go gather up all the unused rope and tape and sisal bags and then turned to the robber to his left and tapped the top of the money box and said, "Let's roll her out of here," and the robber wanted to know how they would get her down the steps out front and Mike said, "We'll carry her down," and the robber thought she'd be too heavy to carry and that the noise made bouncing her down the steps would be too loud for safety's sake and Mike insisted she could be lifted and motioned to the other robber and they both bent down to see if they could lift the box and its million-dollar load. . . .

And then the buzzer sounded.

Every robber in the joint heard the buzzer. Every robber stopped what he was doing. Not one of them remembered seeing a buzzer that could be pressed anywhere.

The robber standing with Mike walked over the bound and gagged employees and knelt down beside one and said, "What does that mean?"

There was a muddled reply.

The robber realized the trouble, jerked the tape strip off the victim's mouth and repeated the question.

"It means somebody wants to get in," head cashier Thomas B. Lloyd told him.

"Well, how do we let him in?"

"You go down to the end of the dispatch room and you press a button."

Jazz Maffie heard this as he came back into the vault room, motioned to the robber standing over the employee to follow and dashed out across the payroll wrapping room and out into the counting room.

The buzzer sounded again.

Maffie and the other robber legged it down the corridor and out through the door to the right, hurried across the unlit general office, cautiously open the door just inside the rear hall to the right, eased into the corner guard booth and gazed out the side window into the garage. They noticed what no one else had noticed. Lights were burning in the garage. Not much light because the bulbs were of a low wattage, but enough to see a man standing at the door just this side of the protruding control room windows, waiting before the door that opened into the guard room.

"Let's go get him," a voice Jazz immediately recognized as Gus's said.

Maffie's masked head shook. "Let's see what he does first."

The man turned from the door, raised a hand and scratched his head, tucked something under his other arm that looked like a small package or lunch pail, walked past the rotunda window for the corner.

Maffie nudged Gus with his elbow, gripped his .45 more tightly in one hand, pushed open the door in the front of the booth with his other and stepped out into the garage. The man went into a booth just before the corner. Jazz and Gus returned to the corner guard booth.

And newly appointed garageman William Manter crossed the supply room, entered the supervisor's office and seated himself at the desk and began eating his lunch.

And Tony Pino paced the floorboards under the canvas rigging, muttering to himself, put his eye to the side peephole and paced and muttered some more.

Geagan stood in the ransacked vault room, listening to Maffie and Gusciora, and learned that an unknown man was on the premises. He gazed longingly down at the GE box but decided not to take any chances. His gloved hand raised and pointed toward the door in the grille wall.

Four perspiration-soaked robbers walked from the vault room and into the darkness of the payroll wrapping room, leaving no one behind to guard the prisoners. Single file they crossed the counting room, and whoever it was who was supposed to take the wastepaper baskets away from the doors forgot in at least one instance—but not as badly as whoever it was who was supposed to take the rope and tape and extra sacks. They ran into two more robbers heading back to the vault room and motioned them to turn around. They bumped into a third robber heading back, one who ignored their signal to go on downstairs—one who muttered something about leaving something behind in the vault room. Geagan said, "Okay, go back, but when you come out make sure you close the doors." One by one they came out of the long dark corridor and across the shadowy front hall and down the first half flight of stairs. Sisal bags were piled up on the bottom steps of the second half flight, and several robbers stopped here. Several more squeezed through the sacks on the main-floor landing, got off to the right behind them. One or two ripped the rubber masks off their sweat-drenched faces and emitted audible sighs of relief. One or two left their masks on after Geagan took off his and signaled that all the others should do the same. Geagan pointed out assignments, deployed the men amid the crush of sacks as he thought best to create a human conveyer belt. He waited for the last man to return from upstairs. Then he gripped the doorknob, turned it carefully, felt the lock tongue depress. He pushed the door open several inches, then pulled it close, reopened it a crack and peered out.

Pino saw the signal, all but shouted as he slapped the top of the cab—and did shout when he realized Barney had let the idling motor die. The starter whined, the engine kicked over, and the truck lurched across the street, climbed the curb, overshot the door, backed up and stopped. Costa pulled the Chevrolet out into the middle of the street, let it stand idling.

The metal door at 165 Prince Street flew out and open. The secret canvas door in the canvas side of the truck flew in and open. Two costumed robbers bounded on beside Pino. Large, open-mouthed sisal bags flew out of the Brink's door and into the truck. Bag after bag flew out, and in less than twenty-five seconds the haul was loaded. Geagan and Faherty hurried up the street to where Costa was parked.

Richardson closed the door at 165 Prince Street.

"Where's the metal box?" Pino called out.

"We couldn't get it," Sandy whispered as he ran up.

"Whaddaya mean you couldn't get it? You gotta get it!"

"We couldn't get it. Now get out of the way and let me on."

"That box is what started it all. That box is got a million smackers in it. I been dreaming of that box for six years!"

"Let me on, for Gods sakes."

And Pino went bananas, absolutely ape. He kicked at Richardson, yelled at Richardson, ordered him back into Brink's and was about to jump off the truck and go in himself when Maffie bear-hugged him from behind and lifted him off the floorboards and clamped a hand over his mouth. He still struggled and even hit Jazz's gloved hand. Sandy jumped on board, and someone else banged on the cab roof and somebody began snapping the trick door in place.

And Barney took off like a bat out of hell. And Maffie fell back and let his grip on Pino go. And Pino scrambled to his feet and tried to run for the trick door. And Barney wheeled as hard a right as he had ever wheeled. And Pino went flying as he had never flown.

Costa, Faherty and Geagan looked ahead through the windshield of the follow car and watched the rigged truck jump the curb as it bounded into Lafayette Street, noticed the right canvas side mushroom out as if it were going to explode.

Nineteen year old Edwin Coffin glanced up from his nocturnal playground activities on the outside staircase in time to see a gray canvas-backed truck climb the curb and drive into Lafayette Street followed by a dark car.

CHAPTER TWENTY-FIVE

Disputed Time

The truck rocketed up Lafayette Street, skidded around the corner into Endicott Street, spun its wheels on the wet pavement, shot forward, reached the end of the block, slowed down and made an easy right turn onto Commercial and approached Prince Street at approximately twenty miles an hour. As the follow car emerged from Endicott and fell into the rear, it accelerated past the North Terminal Garage building and Hull Street, then, as the road began to circle Copps Hill, maintained a constant speed of forty miles an hour.

Geagan, sitting in the back seat of the Ford sedan, stripped off his mask and costume and rubbers, stuffed everything into an empty laundry bag, took his own hat and car keys and change and driver's license out of the other laundry bag Costa had handed him. Faherty sat panting in the front seat with his costume on his lap, waited for Geagan to hand forward the filled sack, then deposited the robbery gear.

Some of the men in the rear of the truck were standing amid the bulging sacks of loot, removing their costumes; others were sitting. Almost everyone was breathing hard and perspiring.

"If anyone was talking, I didn't hear them," states Richardson. "Anthony was moving around passing out the laundry sacks with our clothes and personal effects. Some of the guys didn't use the sacks when they were empty. They threw their costumes on the floor.

"I was thinking the faster we got out of there, the better for all of us. We just had gone through an ordeal. After it's over, the tension almost grinds you."

The tandem of truck and follow car continued along Atlantic Avenue. Once across the Summer Street intersection, Costa pulled to a stop. Geagan jumped out.

"I had my car parked down near Congress Street," states Mike. "The law would be coming to me first, so I had to go home. I would have liked to have been along with the men instead. There was a lot to do, but I drove for home. It was like a battlefield. After the attack the fear sets in."

The drizzle turned to rain. Costa sped up, flashed his highway lights, couldn't see anything on the avenue ahead. He increased his speed to nearly sixty miles an hour. Red taillights were spotted in the distance, then a familiar silhouette of square canvas.

"Tony Pino was sitting on a Coca-Cola box and keeping quiet, so I thought he was really pissed off," states Maffie. "Somebody said, 'I bet we grabbed four million dollars.' That's all I remember anyone saying. I wasn't thinking about that, and I wasn't worrying about getting pinched. I might have been thinking why Barney Banfield was taking his sweet time, but the first thing I know the truck started to slow down and Tony Pino got off his Coca-Cola box."

Richardson was waiting at the rear when the truck came to a stop, pulled open the canvas door for Pino.

"If you hadn't stolen more goddamn money than anybody in the world," Tony told Sandy, "I'd kill you with my bare hands for leaving the metal box behind." Then he jumped off and hurried home.

"Okay, so now I call my lawyer and tell him I'm coming over to see him as soon as I stop at my aunt's," Tony said. That was the plan, see. I'm planning to go over to Joe's liquor store and buy my aunt this bottle of brandy. So I tell Mary that's where I'm heading for. And going out the front door, I bump into this woman friend of Mary's and ask if she knows the time. She says it's seven fifteen. It's only seven five when I change the clock back, but what the hell.

"So I walk around the corner instead of using the alley. I want everyone else in the world to see me. I start up to Joe's package liquor store, and Mother of God, I couldn't believe it. There was Joe standing out in front big as life talking to Lieutenant Crowley. Okay, I stop and say hello to them and ask Joe if I can have credit for a couple of bottles of this Metaxis brand. You always wanna ask for something people is gonna remember. Nobody forgets a name like Metaxis. Joe says okay, okay. Then I give the signal, see, I ask Joe what time it is. If I ask the time, that meant the job come off. If I don't ask, it mean we busted again.

"So Joe says it's seven ten, and I could of killed him. Officer Crowley don't look at his watch, but now he's got seven ten psychologically stuck in his subconscious mind. That goddamn McGinnis coulda told six forty-five or six fifty just as easy.

"I go in and ask the clerk for this Metaxis, and I ask him the time, too. He looks at the clock and tells me it's seven ten. I get the two bottles, and I come out and start talking to Joe and the lieutenant. The lieutenant asks me what I know about a piece of work over at the Statler Hotel—the stickup the day before. He tells me he's getting a lot of heat about it. I tell him I don't know a thing about the Statler, and I start wondering what the hell's gonna break loose any minute now."

Barney Banfield pulled to a hard stop. The Chevrolet pulled to a stop beside it. Richardson and Gusciora were the first to jump off the truck. Costa and Faherty hurried from the car and headed for the truck.

"You never saw people working faster in your life," asserts Jazz Maffie. "That stuff was flying off the truck. It was like one of them movie-picture comics, them cartoons where everything's speeded up. Some of those big wastepaper sacks flew off the truck all at once. Jimmy Costa and Jimma Faherty took their lives in their hands trying to get onto the truck.

Costa and Faherty jumped on and began collecting the laundry sacks.

"I grabbed Tony's gun satchel and tossed in the loose guns. Some guns were laying loose on the floor, and they weren't supposed to be. A lot of the costumes were laying around loose, too. It was a madhouse in the truck for a couple of seconds, and then the guys got the money sacks off. Jimma ran around picking up everything that was left. I jumped off and started carrying armloads of junk over and dumping them in the trunk of the car. Jimma got off, too, with an armload. And then that goddamn Barney takes off. He's supposed to wait until we got everything off the truck, but he takes off before. There's still some empty bags on the truck and Tony's gun satchel is still on the truck."

A few more people joined the sidewalk conference in front of the Imbescheids' package liquor store.

"So now Crowley changes the conversation," Pino related. "I stick around for a few minutes but tell them I gotta go see my sick aunt."

Pino started for this corner and waved to Boston Police Officer John J. Tierney, Division 13, who would recall the time as being approximately 7:30 P.M.

"We dragged the big wastepaper sacks over and lined them against the wall," Sandy Richardson relates. "What was supposed to happen at this time was everyone leaving except Henry and myself. What *did* happen was Costa and Jimma left and Jazz and Gus and Specs stayed around. One of them lugged over one of the sacks and dumped it on the table. The stuff all fell out and covered most of the table. We tore open some of the packages and spread some of the money out. One of the guys threw some of the loose money up in the air. To be truthful, I may have thrown some money up myself. Anthony would have had a heart attack if he saw us.

"That went on for about five minutes, and then they left. Gus and Jazz and Specs. Henry and I stayed and started cleaning up. Henry turned on the radio. We expected some kind of report somewhere. Henry kept changing the station, but we couldn't find anything about Brink's."

Costa and Faherty were driving in the Chevrolet sedan along Columbia Road with their radio on.

"There was nothing about Brink's coming in," Costa relates. "I took a right at Columbia Square and passed a joint that has a clock in the window. It ain't even seven thirty yet. Christ, it ain't even seven twenty-five. I can't figure what those guys over in

Brink's are doing. Then for a minute I get a chill. I thought maybe something bad happened in the joint they didn't tell me about. But Jimma said hell, no. He said all that happened was the Brink's guys got tied up good and tight.''

Brink's cashier Thomas Lloyd lay back to back with Brink's armored truck driver Charles Grell on the vault room floor and tugged and strained and twisted and finally ripped his hands free. He jumped up, tore the tape from his mouth and, ankles still bound, began hopping toward the phone table. Another holdup victim, James Allen, managed to shed his bindings just as Lloyd pulled the ADT alarm.

"Call headquarters," Allen shouted.

"Christ, I don't know the number," Lloyd yelled back.

"Devonshire 1212!"

At 7:27 P.M. the tape alarm machine at American District Telegraph sounded. A minute after that the Boston Police Department was notified there was 'trouble at Brink's.'' Four minutes after that the first patrol car responded to the North End radio alert and pulled up in front of the Chamber of Commerce building. While the armed officers dashed across the Federal Street sidewalk to the glass doors, a second prowl car arrived. A minute or so after that, Jazz Maffie moseyed into Jimmy O'Keefe's restaurant and lost himself at the crowded men's bar, while reporter Tom Sullivan, along with photographer Meyer Ostroff, used the side steps from the ground floor of the North Terminal Garage, where their newspaper, the Boston *Record,* parked its truck, took them two at a time and came out into the second level of Brink's garage, expecting that an armored car had been robbed, never suspecting there was a money room on the premises. He found Police Captain John Ahern at sea in the middle of the floor, asking, "How the hell do we get into this place?''

At 7:35 P.M. Jimmy Costa and Jimma Faherty were inside the Savin Hill plant, unloading costumes and bags. Costa, who knew there were six pistols on the rigged truck Barney had prematurely driven away, now found another eight weapons—which meant the gang had come from Brink's with four more handguns than they had taken in. Tom Sullivan and Meyer Ostroff followed Captain Ahern and a plainclothes detective into the vault room, which looked as if "a bomb had exploded inside it," and got one of the dazed hold-up victims to help them move a table which shouldn't have been moved. Ostroff climbed on top and began taking pictures, while Ahern questioned the other four employees—and from the beginning all five eyewitnesses never could agree on how many men had stuck them up.

Tony Pino poured Aunt Elizabeth a glass of Metaxis brand, then left to join his lawyer. Boston police headquarters received confirmation from the scene that an armed theft had been perpetrated at Brink's and perhaps as much as $100,000 stolen. Costa drove his Buick toward Uphams Corner, glanced down and noticed Jimma Faherty was wearing the rubbers he should have taken off on the getaway ride from Brink's, so Jimma took off the rubbers and, to Costa's amazement and despair, tossed them out the car window.

By 7:45 P.M. the Brink's premises were being inundated by policemen and reporters, and despite repeated shortwave radio corrections, prowl cars continued to arrive at the Chamber of Commerce building. Mike Geagan was in the basement of his home washing his infant daughter's clothes; Jimma Faherty was drinking like a fish with friends at Gusti's Restaurant at Uphams Corner; Jazz Maffie was ordering dinner with his wife in the dining room at Jimmy O'Keefe's restaurant; Specs O'Keefe and Stanley Gusciora were at a downtown bar having drinks with two girlfriends; Barney Banfield was in Joe McGinnis' secret plant at Jamaica Plain, swigging whiskey with one hand and wiping fingerprints from the rigged truck with the other hand. Sandy Richardson and Henry Baker were seated at a table, listening to the radio and inspecting stolen packages and tossing crisp new bills whose serial numbers ran in sequence into a sisal sack designated for "bad money" and fast counting the old or used bills and dumping them in a sisal sack being utilized for "good money."

By 8 P.M. the bridges leading out of Boston were sealed off by the Boston Police Department, officers were at the railroad and bus terminals, and every last man of the Massachusetts State Police was on alert. Other troopers were delaying airplane takeoffs at Logan Field, checking passengers, and commercial radio programs were being interrupted by bulletins of the robbery. Jimmy Costa arrived at the Harbor Motor Terminal and joined Tony Pino and the lawyer for a discussion of lease adjustment on the property.

At 8:30 P.M. the assistant special agent in charge of the FBI's Boston field office, Billy West, learned of the robbery at home—while listening to a commercial radio program—and called the night duty agent at his office, who didn't know a thing about Brink's. Fifteen minutes after that a tipsy Barney Banfield drove across the Wellington Bridge between Somerville and Medford. He reached into Pino's leather gun satchel, which never should have been left on the rigged truck, and, without disassembling them, tossed the weapons out the window, handguns as well as Tony's rifles and shotguns, and hurled the satchel into the water as well. A minute or so later he discovered two more weapons on the seat and pulled off the bridge and into Somerville and stopped along the banks of the Mystic River, not more than a block from where Geagan's mother-in-law lived, and hurled the pair of handguns into the water—at low tide. Not too long after that, Jimma Faherty, who intended to use arrest for drunkenness as his alibi, drunkenly broke a couple of windows and managed to get arrested—for suspicion of robbing a drugstore some months before.

At approximately 9:30 P.M. the first two FBI agents, Jack Kehoe and Leonard Frisoli, arrived at Brink's and found the premises swarming with people and "totally chaotic," saw that the robbery area had not been "preserved"—that the crowd inside was disturbing vital evidence, trampling money sacks to the point where cash lay exposed. Kehoe got an early indication the theft might fall under federal jurisdiction: He retrieved a paper money band from the Federal Reserve Bank.

By 10 P.M. the entire eastern seaboard down to the Virginias had been alerted, and almost every primary and secondary highway in Massachusetts had been blocked. Cars, buses and trucks were being stopped, and "numbers" of license plates belonging to parolees and ex-convicts were being flashed. The increasing snowfall had all but shut down Logan Airport, but public and private airfields throughout the state were being checked, as were abandoned roadhouses and boarded-up summer camps. The Boston Harbor Patrol was cruising through heavy seas in order to frustrate an ocean getaway. And around Copps Hill police and feds worked independently, knocked on residents' doors, trying to locate eyewitnesses to any part of the heist. Over at police headquarters the largest assemblage of brass since the tragic Cocoanut Grove fire was told by BPD Superintendent Edward W. Fallon that as much as $1,000,000 might have been stolen and that one eyewitness to the getaway had been located. He further stated something he absolutely could not have known at this early juncture—that *seven* costumed and masked armed robbers had perpetrated the crime.

At 10:30 P.M., with commercial radio news bulletins announcing the first million-dollar cash stickup in American history, Jimmy Costa dropped in on Richardson and Baker and was told the tally to date was slightly over $1,000,000 in good usable bills with five and a half sisal sacks of loot still to be counted. Costa took $20,000 and left. Jazz Maffie showed up shortly after that, as per plan. Then, not according to plan, Gusciora and O'Keefe wandered in. None of the three wanted money. Banfield, who was expected, showed up with Joe McGinnis, who was unexpected. McGinnis announced the heat was so intense and so many cops had come to question him regarding Brink's that he didn't dare take the counted money for overnight safekeeping as was previously agreed. Rather than argue, Henry Baker said he knew a person who could "hold" part of the haul. A wire shopping basket containing $380,000 in counted bills was taken from the room. Before leaving with Baker and the basket, Richardson helped himself to $10,000. McGinnis eyed the sack containing some $60,000 in "bad money," took Maffie aside and suggested maybe the bad money should not be destroyed as planned, perhaps it should be "laundered"—chemically processed to look old and used. Maffie responded sharply and negatively. Joe tried the idea on Gusciora and O'Keefe, was again rebuffed. Banfield and McGinnis departed. A few minutes after that, Maffie, Gusciora and O'Keefe turned off the light and left the loot—which they were certain exceeded $2,000,000 in usable money—alone.

Jimmy Costa stopped by Pino's apartment, gave his brother-in-law $10,000 in stolen money, departed immediately for home. Sandy Richardson dropped his $10,000 off at a friend's house, got back in his car, opened the glove compartment, took out the bottle of whiskey and, as he drove, began drinking with a vengeance.

By 11 P.M. the headquarters meeting was over and the BPD's manhunt shifted into high gear. Word went down to SP every known criminal in the area. Word also went down not to bother with Pino and McGinnis. Lieutenant James V. Crowley had talked to both of them shortly after 7 P.M.—while the robbery was believed to be in progress. High on the Boston police list of parolees and ex-cons to be questioned were Mike Geagan, Henry Baker, Specs O'Keefe and Stanley Gusciora. Gusciora and Banfield were also on the "numbers" list of license plates being radioed by the state police.

Sandy Richardson took a long swig from the bottle, poured the remaining whiskey on his jacket and shirt, walked from the car into his living room, stripped to an undershirt, plopped down in an armchair. When his wife returned from visiting her sister, he pretended to have passed out. He heard her mutter a few unsympathetic words and stride off to the bedroom. He heard his son entering the house. Sandy lit a cigarette, His son dawdled in the kitchen. Sandy puffed harder. He heard the youth starting for the living room. Sandy closed his eyes, lay back as far as he could, let the cigarette drop on his chest. The boy entered to see the cigarette burning through his father's undershirt, burning the skin, and let out a shout. Wife and son poured water on the smoldering flesh, but still couldn't wake Sandy, who they assumed was dead drunk, assumed had been dead drunk and sitting in the chair all evening.

At 11:15 P.M. Jazz Maffie slipped unnoticed into Jimmy O'Keefe's busy restaurant for a second time since the robbery, glanced into the dining room and saw his wife still chatting to the off-duty waitress she had been chatting with when he had excused himself fifty minutes earlier, headed into the bar. Jimmy Costa opened the basement closet, which had held Tony's tools and tumblers at 3 Fuller Street, reached up on a top shelf, opened a Monopoly set, placed his $10,000 of stolen money in with the printed bills of the game. Specs O'Keefe discovered the lobby of the Copley Square Hotel was teaming with cops, walked over to the house phone, called upstairs to his room, heard someone pick up, heard a muffled male voice in the background saying, "Answer," heard his girl say hello, hung up and left undetected.

Edward Souci, special agent in charge of the FBI's Boston field office, arrived home from a speaking engagement in Pittsfield, Massachusetts, answered the ringing phone and was told by his old chum, commissioner of the Boston Police Department, Thomas A. "Colonel Tom" Sullivan, "There's been a big loot at Brink's." Souci showered and got to Brink's shortly before midnight, found the premises as jammed and disorderly as when his subordinates had entered more than two and a half hours before. From the moment he walked in, Souci wanted the case for the FBI but wasn't certain what if any federal statue had been broken. He ordered his operatives to continue doing what they had been doing—investigate to see if the bureau had a legal right to investigate. Souci didn't have to mention that the special agents should keep out of the police's way. There had been bad blood between the FBI and BPD for quite some time. Souci's friendship with Commissioner Sullivan didn't help. Rank-and-file cops disliked Colonel Tom almost as much as they disliked the bureau.

Tony Pino waited until he was certain Mary was asleep, got out of bed and went into the bathroom to check the ten grand Costa had given him. He saw that $1,600 was in "new bills" with consecutive serial numbers and almost tearfully flushed all $1,600 down the toilet, not realizing the money was absolutely good, wasn't recorded anywhere.

It was past midnight and snowing heavily when Stanley Gusciora, who was being sought for questioning by both the BPD and state troopers, slammed on his brakes and skidded into the rear of a car already at a red light. A Boston police cruiser pulled up, assessed the damage as light, checked the licenses and registrations of both drivers, sent Gusciora on his way with a warning to be more cautious.

Specs O'Keefe sneaked up to his hotel room. Maffie and his wife left Jimmy O'Keefe's restaurant and drove home. By two o'clock all robbers and abettors were asleep in beds of their own choosing—including Jimma Faherty, who was snoring away in a jail cell.

During a 2:15 A.M. news conference at Brink's, BPD Superin-

tendent Fallon stated that the robbers had made off with
$1,000,000 in cash and $500,000 in securities and went on to
itemize the money left behind: $50,000 in coins, an $880,000 payroll for General Electric and $120,000 in receipts from Filene's
department store—$1,050,000 in all. Fallon had no doubt it was
an inside job and probably "planned for weeks with blueprints
and rehearsals." The thieves obviously had had keys to the
premises, inasmuch as the company reported no keys missing,
and must have had copies made.

According to Fallon, the heist was so perfectly conceived
"they could have marched fifty men in there and cleaned out the
whole place, including the one million dollars left behind because they couldn't carry it."

Like the press, Fallon became accusatory of Brink's, wanted
to know why no burglar alarm had sounded, why there was so
little premises security, why the company never asked for police
protection.

Fallon pledged the greatest manhunt in Boston's history but
admitted "his department had little or nothing to work on. Witnesses don't agree on the description of the men, and the only
voice they heard was that of the leader which was mumbled and
muffled through the mask he wore.

"No one knows how the men drove up to the place or where
they parked. We have witnesses who believe that one man was
left in each of two cars and a third served as lookout."

A 3:30 A.M. Division 1 BPD journal entry—the official sum-
mary of the crime and police knowledge—set the time of perpetration at 7:10 P.M., stated that seven armed men—all between
twenty-five to thirty-five years of age and standing five seven or
five eight and weighing 160 to 170 pounds—entered the premises
with keys, approached the "checking cage," held up the five
employees, then filled two large bags with packages of money.
Also stolen were four handguns belonging to Brink's. Left behind as evidence were six pieces of adhesive tape, a quantity of
awning rope and a chauffeur's cap. The robbers left "by the
front of the building." All seven of the holdup men wore pea-
coats, dark trousers and hooded masks. Six had worn rubbers,
and one had on brown shoes. Six had on chauffeur's caps, a seventh a tweed cap. An eighth man had remained outside in a large

black sedan during the robbery. He was described as being fifty years of age, five feet eight inches tall, weighing 180 pounds and wearing a dark overcoat with a light-brown soft hat.

By the morning of January 18, 1950, Boston papers and those around the world were bannering the "biggest" robbery in U.S. history, were extolling the thieves with such phrases as the "cream of the crime world." In the days and years to come Brink's would become the most publicized holdup in modern times, would be lauded by the FBI itself as the "crime of the century" and the "perfect crime" and "fabulous robbery."

By the morning of January 18 America from coast to coast was witnessing the largest manhunt in history. In the days and years to come the Brink's investigation would grow far larger, would become the most widespread and expensive criminal search ever launched in America (approximately $29,000,000).

By the morning of January 18 nowhere was the heat more intense than in Boston. Nowhere was the behind-the-scene politicking more intense as well. The anti-FBI, anti-Commissioner Sullivan members of BPD, who were the overwhelming majority, wanted the investigation for themselves, felt the bureau had no legal ground on which to enter the case. The boss of the Massachusetts state troopers intended to go along with them, in sympathy at least. Ed Souci and the special agents of the Boston field office did want the case, but many feared the police were right, that they didn't have legal jurisdiction, that no federal law had been broken. What mattered was that J. Edgar Hoover had made up his mind the robbery was a matter for the bureau. In those days J. Edgar was a monumental power. In those days "Mr. Director" got what he wanted.

At approximately 7:30 A.M., January 18, Tony Pino sat in his kitchen, munching a bowl of cornflakes, listening to a radio news account of the manhunt. He heard what many of the newspapers had already printed—that the modus operandi of the crooks who pulled Brink's was similar, if not identical, to that employed in the Sturtevant robbery of 1947. Tony deduced he could not avoid being SP'd and possibly forced to strip. He rushed into the bedroom, could not find a presentable pair of underdrawers, drove across a city that was enduring the most massive dragnet

ever, reached Filene's Department Store, waited on the sidewalk for the door to be opened, entered with the first wave of
early-bird shoppers and boosted two pair of jockey shorts. He
noticed that black socks were on sale, so he snitched a dozen of
them for good measure.

AFTERMATH

The United States Attorney granted the FBI final jurisdiction to investigate the armed robbery at Brink's under a federal statute relating to the theft of government property, which stipulated that a minimum of $100 in cash be taken, on the specific assumption that checks belonging to the Veterans Administration had been stolen from the vault room and that among the checks were at least $100 in cash. The thieves, who went through the sacks of veterans' checks, say there was no currency whatever inside. The bureau synthesized its file title for the case to Robink—Robbery-Brink's. Rather than code it 47, the designated number for theft of government property, all material received a 91 prefix—federal bank robbery. Robink 91-5535, the five thousand and thirty-fifth crime to be investigated since the Federal Bank Act of 1934 had been legislated.

The statute of limitations for federal investigations ran only three years at that time. Every FBI field office in the country participated in Robink 91-5535. The crux of activity was in Boston. The bureau's top troubleshooter went to the city and headed the investigation. Extra agents and equipment were sent in. Extra office space and secretaries were added. From the beginning cooperation with the Boston Police Department was one-sided; the FBI took what it needed from the BPD and gave little in return. During the short period that the investigation concentrated on specialized felons such as bank robbers and jewel thieves, not all that much was needed. As the search expanded to include most every criminal in Boston, police assistance was vital. The FBI, throughout the country, had had few dealings with workaday crooks, common street crooks. From the beginning, the bureau ran afoul of many influential people and institutions in Boston and Massachusetts. The FBI rebuffed attempts by the state's attorney general to grant amnesty to any of the actual robbers who would come forth and identify his confederates. This would come back to plague them.

The bureau's "no comment" policy unless Washington approved received a generally hostile reaction from the news media, and the news media would give more space to Brink's than had ever been given a nonpolitical crime. This was ironic. One of the reasons J. Edgar Hoover wanted the case was the publicity the robbery received. When the FBI did release statements, they were matter-of-fact, bland, often bore an ominous reminder of how imperiled the nation was with the perpetrators still at large. This was counterproductive to bureau image, often exposed the FBI to ridicule. The robbers hadn't harmed any of the holdup victims. The public and media found a great deal of humor and ingenuity in seven men, who, wearing full-faced funny rubber masks, walked big as life into Brink's vault room and for the first time in memory took more money than had ever been taken before and disappeared without a trace, befuddling law enforcement officers and seeming to get away with it.

Ed Sullivan trotted a team of masked and peacoated and chauffeur-capped gun-carrying men out before his television cameras and introduced them as the Brink's robbers—to hearty applause and laugher and one or two cheers. Fred Allen's Oriental Dick Tracy, One Long Pan, sipped a cup of ten-cent coffee and over America's airwaves spit up and announced, "Biggest robbery since Brink's." When, on posting a $100,000 reward, the president of Brink's said he'd rather the crooks be brought in dead than alive, local papers got a rash of letters and calls wishing the robbers well and damning the victimized company.

None of the rubber masks or rubbers or laundry bags would ever be found. With the exception of the one chauffeur's cap left behind in the vault room, none of the costumes would be found. Jimmy Costa burned them to ashes in the furnace at 3 Fuller Street a week after the holdup. None of the guns Costa had disassembled and tossed into the Charles River or the weapons Banfield had thrown from the bridge would ever be recovered. One of the two revolvers Barney had hurled into the Mystic River from the Somerville shoreline was discovered and identified as being taken from a Brink's vault room employee the night of the robbery—which caused Geagan, whose mother-in-law lived a block from the recovery site, to blow up at Joe McGinnis. Edwin Coffin did point out for special agents a truck similar to the one that he had seen on Prince Street, and it was learned that a truck of this description had been stolen from Lalime and Partridge, but this didn't bring the FBI any closer to identifying the masked crooks or knowing where they had gone once they were beyond narrow Lafayette Street. Other neighbors who had seen men in the area of Brink's at the time were found, but they didn't add anything of relevance. And none of the physical evidence—the gun found in Somerville or the GE box and strands of rope and chauffeur's cap and pieces of tape and samplings of vault room receipt forms—bore latent fingerprints or other identifying marks indicating who the masked robbers were.

The five employees who had been held up by the masked gunmen were investigated and repeatedly reinterviewed by special agents, as was the garage attendant who had rung the buzzer while the robbery was in progress. All would be forced by Brink's officials to take lie detector tests. All would remain under suspicion of complicity in various newspapers and among certain law officials. Five of the six would have nervous breakdowns.

Every past and present Boston Brink's employee and customer was checked, as well as everyone who had used or had access to the garage building. Anyone who as much as had replaced a spark plug or pumped a gallon of gas into a Brink's truck was checked. Every place pea coats and rubbers and chauffeur's caps and rope and tape could be had was checked. Most every garage and parking lot in Boston was checked to see if the getaway truck or follow car had been there. Sewers and warehouses in the area were checked to see if loot had been stashed, and to this purpose, a grave in Copps Hill burying ground was opened. And from it all, nothing was found or learned.

The whereabouts of most every known and suspected crook in Boston on the night of the robbery was checked, and nothing was developed. The whereabouts of every notorious criminal in the country on that night was checked, and nothing was developed. Deals in exchange for information were offered to convicts serving time and criminals about to be convicted and big-time racketeers who needed favors, and nothing was developed. The routine Boston underworld informers were paid or coddled or coerced, and many names were repeated over and over again, including McGinnis and Pino and Geagan and Richardson and O'Keefe and Gusciora and Baker. Ben Tilly was mentioned most of all, and from what the FBI knew and had observed they deducted that Tilly possessed the capacity for planning and perpetrating the crime. Tilly became the prime Boston area suspect. The Sturtevant robbery was mentioned often as being a prototype of Brink's, and the bureau, which had looked into but not investigated that 1947 holdup, believed Sam Granito was the boss of the operation, didn't feel Tony Pino possessed the capacity to run Sturtevant, let alone Brink's—and never would. Even so, ten of the actual robbers, including Tony, were placed under day and night surveillance, along with Tilly and about twenty other Boston criminals.

It was eventually stated that $2,775,395.12, of which $1,218,211.29 was currency, had been stolen from the vault room. Of the currency, serial numbers were known for 24,050 individual bills totaling $98,900. The public circulation of these serial numbers created a gigantic treasure hunt across the United States—and brought not one result. The day and night "hot surveillance" placed on prime Boston suspects saw not a single marked bill being passed; nothing else indicating any had participated in the robbery was noted.

In truth, neither the bureau nor Brink's ever knew exactly how much was taken from the vault room. Among the missing loot were "sealed packages"—sums of money which had not yet been counted by the owner, such as the telephone company's monthly service receipts from customers. The crooks themselves never knew how much they had stolen. The heat was so intense the day after the robbery, the day of the scheduled "long count," that they rushed their tally and came up with $98,000 in bad or "new bills," and $1,100,000 in good or usable bills. In addition to this and because of the heat, they had allowed Joe McGinnis to do something they had always feared: take away two and a half sisal sacks full of uncounted packages. Joe also took $98,000 in bad bills and $800,000 in good or usable money and was later given the $380,000 "good" money Baker had protected on January 17. Before leaving the count, Maffie, Gusciora and O'Keefe each took $100,000. Mafffie later discovered his $100,000 was only $81,000. All crew members expected the two and a half uncounted bags to yield no less than another half million in good money. Some expected it to be far more. Whatever, each crook expected his share of loot to be at least $140,000. The crew's misgivings of McGinnis proved true. Joe proceeded to rob his fellow robbers, claiming that the good money he took away from the count only came to $400,000—even though the others had counted it at an $800,000. He also claimed that the two and a half untabulated sacks had yielded not one cent in good or usable money, and that Baker returned only $100,000. He not only said this, but demanded money back from Maffie. He couldn't demand it back from O'Keefe and Gusciora because the two had left town. McGinnis might well have been abetted in this theft among thieves by Pino. Joe McGinnis did strip down the getaway truck per instruction, but he didn't ditch it on a street corner as he was supposed to. This would always confuse the FBI, as well as many gang members. Joe kept the truck and tried to sell it back to Tony Pino. Pino never dared tell other crewmen of this additional double cross. He was afraid they were already planning to kill McGinnis. If the heat hadn't been so intense, if most of the robbers weren't under twenty-four-hour-a-day surveillance or being spot-checked when they least expected, if perpetrating a homicide would not have pointed a finger at them, they might well have done damage to Joe.

When the FBI, acting on a tip, moved in on a garage where the truck was stashed, McGinnis and Banfield cut the vehicle apart with blowtorches, stuffed the smaller parts into the sisal bags Joe had tried to sell Tony, piled everything onto a truck, avoided what they thought were pursuing bureau cars and in the dead of night tossed the lot—large disassembled sections and filled sacks—into a Stoughton, Massachusetts, commercial dump which was not far from both the Gusciora family farm and the home of O'Keefe's estranged wife and adopted son. Specs and Gus were outraged and rightly so. The bureau began looking harder in their direction. The bureau began tracing the sisal bags as far as South America, with no results. The bureau's Washington lab was unable to find any relevant fingerprints or marks on the disassembled truck sections or the bags.

It was the local police and Boston police who found the truck parts in the dump. FBI special agents came right in under the nose of Jim Crowley, loaded every last scrap and bag onto a rented truck, outraced and lost tailing reporters. The trucknappers could not use their primary hiding place to stash the parts because it was already occupied; other agents had stolen Ben Tilly's car for a few hours and were, without court sanction, installing an electronic listening device.

Ben Tilly was still local bureau men's first choice as the possible mastermind and organizer of Brink's. Next came Joe McGinnis. J. Edgar Hoover favored Willy Sutton, who had escaped from prison and was at large.

Six months after the robbery the Boston agents, through what at best was coercion and at worst blackmail, turned a well-connected area man into what they considered their first truly reliable informant. He named nine of the actual robbers—everyone but Maffie and Faherty. According to the source, McGinnis was the brains and boss and Tony Pino the second-in-command. It was a ranking the bureau would never dispel. Ben Tilly was also believed to have some high-level involvement. Emphasis shifted to the McGinnis-Pino crowd, but about twenty Boston crooks were still afforded "hot" surveillance.

Informant information had also indicated O'Keefe and Gusciora were to embark on an auto trip into the Midwest. The FBI's cross-country stakeout lost Gus and Specs as the pair left Chicago, heading back east. Alerts to notify the bureau and not interfere with the two suspects' journey if their car was spotted backfired when the sheriff of the county jail at Towanda, Pennsylvania, apprehended them. Gus and O'Keefe had robbed two stores during their Pennsylvania trek. Stolen guns and clothing

were found in their automobile. Gusciora pleaded guilty to a robbery charge and was sent to Pennsylvania Western State Penitentiary near Pittsburgh, where he would remain for the better
part of five and a half years. O'Keefe pleaded not guilty on June
12, 1950, and was sentenced to ninety days in the Bradford
County Jail at Towanda for loitering with known criminals—to
wit, Gus. After that time had been served, he received another
three years at Bradford for violation of the Uniform Firearms
Act. Following that, he would have to stand trial in McKean
County, Pennsylvania, on the same offense for which Gusciora
received a five to twenty year sentence at Western State. Despite all this, O'Keefe was on parole for several Massachusetts
convictions.

Whether the FBI was involved in these harsh sentences re-
mains moot. But new types of heat were being exerted on
O'Keefe. He had a reputation for not doing time well. His legal
fees for fighting the convictions would be costly.

The FBI would later avow that sheer deduction had put them
on the trail of the actual crooks, that each suspect interviewed
had a tendency voluntarily to repeat, without being asked
specifically, the time "seven o'clock" and state exactly where
he was and what he was doing at that specific hour on the night
of January 17, 1950. If not 7 P.M. exactly, certainly 7:10 P.M.
was a stumbling block for bureau investigators. It had become
the official time the robbers were believed to have entered
Brink's. Indications are, the thieves were leaving the premises
or en route home by 7:00. The majority of alibis given by the
gang were corroborated by people who honestly remembered
seeing them at places other than Brink's at the alleged time of
perpetration. Nowhere were alibis more authoritatively verified
than with McGinnis and Pino. When special agents interviewed
James V. Crowley on August 24, 1950, the BPD lieutenant
confirmed having been with Tony and Joe at the time they
claimed—around 7:10 P.M. In subsequent interviews he would
stretch the period between 7 and 7:25 P.M.

Delving into the robbers' actual financial history garnered little for the bureau. Everyone seemed to live on exactly what he
earned at a legitimate job or quasi-legitimate job and, in some instances, observably stole. Pino was seen boosting a five-cent

plastic cup from a dime store. Nothing he purchased in a year couldn't have been had on his declared income of between $4,000 and $5,000. Special agents were aware of Joe McGinnis' running an illicit whiskey still somewhere in New England, but he more than got by on what his package liquor store alone netted him. The FBI wasn't above trying to apply economic heat by interfering with livelihoods, even illicit livelihoods in hopes of, among other things, forcing one of the suspects to crack or go to stolen Brink's money—marked money. Nothing of consequence resulted from pressure placed on the union-controlled docks where Richardson and Geagan worked, but special agents were adept at having tête-à-têtes with Pino and Costa's lottery salesmen and scared most of them off. Boston bureau men made no bones about whom they suspected. Many a special agent told Tony and Costa and Baker and Geagan they knew they were in on Brink's. Overt or "open" surveillance, letting the crooks know they were being watched, was a bureau policy. Bumper-to-bumper automobile surveillance often became a game, particularly between FBI man Ed McNamara and Pino. When a suspect was paying for something in a store, it was not uncommon for a bureau agent to walk up, pluck the bill from the crook and either check its serial numbers then and there or replace it with currency of his own.

Congenial relationships developed among certain of the pursuers and pursued. One Thanksgiving Costa's wife brought out dinner to a pair of special agents sitting in a car surveilling her house. The agents eventually parked around the corner and out of sight of neighbors so as not to embarrass Costa's children. But the overt surveillance was embarrassing, a stigma for the suspects' families. This was also a part of bureau strategy. Still, not one marked dollar was retrieved from the crooks. Nothing else was found that implicated them. No amount of heat indicated anyone was ready to confess. No one, however, was putting all the eggs in one basket. Twenty Boston area crooks continued receiving the hot surveillance treatment.

Special agents' confidence that they were on the right track was buttressed when intercepted messages O'Keefe was smuggling out of Bradford County Jail to Pino and McGinnis left no doubt that Specs was dunning them for money, was threatening them. Specs' legal expenses had bankrupted him and were draining his sister, brother-in-law and brother. Henry Baker and a McGinnis cohort by the name of John "Fats" Buccelli were observed visiting O'Keefe in jail. More threatening notes were sent by O'Keefe. Special agents went to interview Specky, got nowhere. According to Geagan and Richardson, the crew had raised a fund of $50,000 and sent it along to Specs' contact.

Willy Sutton was captured and said he had nothing to do with Brink's. Nevertheless, J. Edgar Hoover wasn't convinced his Boston field office was on the right track. Eighteen months after the robbery the FBI had major investigations in progress on 5,000 criminals throughout the United States, was able, under the guise of Robink 91-5535, to establish nationwide files in a category its specialization of the past had ignored—general crime.

With the three-year federal statute of limitations running out and no break in sight, the bureau, determined to keep the case under its jurisdiction, decided to go along with the Irish Gang, played a desperate gambit that it hoped might induce the actual robbers to "find their tongues": They instituted a federal grand jury hearing in the United States District Court of Massachusetts. O'Keefe and Gusciora were brought back from Pennsylvania imprisonment for *the United States* v. *John Doe,* otherwise known as the Brink's robbery. During the twenty-five secret sessions, sixty-five witnesses, including every one of the actual crooks, except Faherty, were called before the panel. Many witnesses refused to say anything and were charged and convicted of contempt, including Jazz Maffie, who received a one-year jail sentence. Relatives of O'Keefe suffered the same treatment. James V. Crowley swore that he had seen Pino and McGinnis in front of the liquor store at 7:10 P.M.* the night of the crime. The jurors refused to pass down indictments "mainly due to three conditions": (1) the participants in the crime were effectively disguised; (2) the lack of eyewitnesses to the crime itself; (3) the refusal of certain witnesses to give testimony and the inability of the grand jury to compel them to do so. Regardless of the guarantee of secrecy, a bureau request for court per-

---

*This time is based on the remembrance of three former FBI agents.

mission to conduct wiretaps on two relatives of Specs found its way to the press. O'Keefe and Gusciora were named in headlines as Brink's robbers.

Despite the federal statute of limitations' having run out, the FBI continued its investigation. It was now in a footrace with two other organizations to whom jurisdiction had legally passed—the office of the Massachusetts state's attorney and the Boston Police Department. The commonwealth's statute of limitations on armed robbery ran for six years, which meant there were thirty-six months remaining in which to crack the case or see the perpetrators freed of prosecution for all time. And no one wanted to crack it more than Lieutenant James V. Crowley, who visited O'Keefe at the Bradford County Jail and applied increasing pressure on McGinnis and Pino. The number of Boston bureau agents exclusively assigned to Robink 91-5535 diminished dramatically; by the end of 1954 it would be down to four full-time investigators, the year after that, two.

Another strategy for keeping the heat on suspects in hopes of garnering a confession evolved among local, state and federal authorities. It was the first exclusively legalistic method to date, and in many instances the FBI's massive Robink file provided the data for action. Jazz Maffie, who had successfully beaten the contempt conviction for his refusal to answer federal grand jury questions regarding Brink's, spent nine months in federal prison on an income tax filing violation. Mike Geagan served two months in the house of correction for leaving the scene of an auto accident. Sandy Richardson, who had not been arrested in seven years, and then only for drunkenness, was arrested three times in seven months—for drunkenness. Jimmy Costa, who only once in his entire life was pinched for speeding, was pinched twice in eight months for speeding. Jimma Faherty, the off-again, on-again, off-again suspect, had his parole revoked owing to "Unsatisfactory Conduct, Drunkenness, Refusal to Seek Employment and Association with Known Criminals" and was sent back to state prison for seven months. Barney Banfield could have been arrested a dozen times for drunkenness, but he was being afforded immunity by federal agents hoping that he and Joe McGinnis would lead them to the illicit distillery McGinnis was running in New Hampshire—and eventually Barney did.

Tony Pino's golf ball theft in 1948 was cited as a felony, used by the U.S. Immigrations to reinstitute deportation proceedings under a new statute which made two-felony arrests the criterion for such action.

Tony was placed in detention as Specs O'Keefe, out on bail, returned to Boston after having served nearly three years and eight months at the Bradford County Jail on offenses which, under ordinary circumstances, would have required no more than eighteen months of incarceration.

O'Keefe's legal prospects were bleaker than ever. He faced probation defaults at Boston's Central Court dating back to several 1945 convictions and was due to return to Smithport, Pennsylvania, and answer to the burglary offense which had sent Gusciora to Western State Penitentiary. He was desperate for funds with which to fight those actions. He also hadn't learned that Joe McGinnis had clipped the gang on their robbery shares. He visited Maffie and demanded some $80,000 in Brink's loot he claimed he left with Jazz. Maffie said it had never been $80,000, only about $30,000 and that, per Specky's own instruction, he had given every cent of it to O'Keefe's brother and sister.

The day Universal Pictures set up its cameras in front of Old North Church and began filming *Six Bridges to Cross,* based on Boston *Globe* reporter Joe Dineen's fictitious account of the Brink's robbery, fifteen blocks away O'Keefe and an ex-con pal, John Carlson, kidnapped Jimmy Costa off a street corner. The next day Tony Pino was released from federal detention, pending a U.S. Supreme Court decision on his deportation action, and met with O'Keefe. Tony secured Costa's release with half of the $7,500 demanded as ransom. As FBI agents followed up on the rumored kidnapping and went to interview Costa and Carlson, O'Keefe was almost killed in a hail of bullets from the machine gun of fugitive assassin Elmer "Trigger" Burke. O'Keefe, unaware of his assailant's identity, went to Pino's house, accused Tony of the assault and failed in his attempt to get the final $3,500 in ransom he felt was owed him. With Carlson, O'Keefe marched into the family-owned vending machine offices of Henry Baker and at gunpoint ordered Henry's brother to write him out a $3,500 check. He was told there was no money in the bank to cover such a withdrawal. O'Keefe said he'd be back the next morning to collect cash, was good to his word and had an inept shoot-out with Henry Baker on the sidewalk. Trigger Burke tried a second time, machine-gunned at O'Keefe in a parking lot late at night, nicked Specky in the wrist. O'Keefe went into hiding. Word spread in the underworld of the assassination attempt, of the possibility Specs was dead, of who had shot him. The BPD, via New York detectives, learned the identity of the gunman. Burke was apprehended on a Boston sidewalk. His room was searched, and a machine gun found. Possession of such a weapon was a mandatory life sentence in Massachusetts. During questioning Burke spoke in the third person, refused to answer who had hired him, but made no bones about coming to Boston to do "some rubbing out" of the O'Keefe creep. Boston evening and morning papers of June 18 and 19, 1954, blazed with news of Trigger's arrest and an admission of having wounded O'Keefe. Once more, Spec's name made headlines.

Suffolk County District Attorney Garrick Byrne was intent on prosecuting Burke for either homicide or attempted murder, as well as possession of a machine gun. While questioning John Carlson, he learned that O'Keefe was alive. Byrne got Carlson's signed statement of meeting the wounded Specky after the shooting incident, plus a promise to contact the fugitive and try to convince O'Keefe to come in and have a talk with the DA. Carlson's secret statement found its way to the press. Again, Specky was in the headlines. When he didn't turn himself in to Byrne, O'Keefe went on the city's ten-most-wanted list. When he failed to appear at a scheduled hearing in Boston's municipal court, Judge Arlow found him in default of probation and issued three warrants for Specs on counts dating back to July 5, 1945— negligently operating a car; carrying a weapon on his person in a car; obliterating serial numbers on a firearm; receiving firearms with the knowledge of serial numbers having been removed. O'Keefe was also slated to answer a charge of "Lewd and Lascivious Cohabitation" growing out of his girlfriend's admission that she and the fugitive had an out-of-wedlock living arrangement. Judge Arlow swore out a fourth warrant for his arrest that same day. When still on this same day O'Keefe failed to appear in Dorchester district court on a traffic violation, a fifth warrant went out for his arrest. The following day, July 1, 1954, a Pennsylvania court of appeal rejected O'Keefe's lawyer's 'bid to overrule a March 29, 1954, conviction for the Smithport County robbery in June, 1950. All in all, Specs owed Pennsylvania three to twelve years of penal time and Suffolk County, Massachusetts, twenty-seven months.

O'Keefe was apprehended on August 1, 1954, by a Worcester, Massachusetts, policeman. He was returned to Boston, where Garrick Byrne pressed him for a shooting accusation against Elmer Burke. O'Keefe intimated the matter went far beyond Burke. Byrne, who had had no part in the Brink's robbery investigation and only minimal dealings with the FBI on other matters, felt O'Keefe was insinuating that the matter had something to do with Brink's. The DA told Specs to be explicit, warned the prisoner to give out with facts or face Byrne's personal wrath. O'Keefe opted for silence. Byrne marched right into a municipal courtroom and, without mentioning Brink's, demanded O'Keefe's immediate incarceration on the twenty-seven months of time owed the county. While the matter was being considered, Specs was sent over to the Charles Street Jail and was suddenly transferred when it was realized Elmer Burke was an inmate. The following day John Carlson left his home to buy some cigarettes and was never heard from again. Two days after that, on August 5, extra guards were called to a jailhouse and may have scared off potential gunmen intent on killing O'Keefe while he was being driven to court. On Saturday, August 7, 1954, O'Keefe arrived at the Hampden County Jail at Springfield, Massachusetts, to serve twenty-seven months. Twenty days later Elmer Burke made a spectacular escape from the Charles Street Jail.

The day after Burke's escape the BPD located the abandoned getaway car in a hospital parking lot and staked out the area. Five hours after that, a late-model Oldsmobile drove past the parking lot, circled the block twice more slowing down in front of the lot on each occasion, then drove off. The Oldsmobile was found to be registered to Pino's sixty-eight-year-old Aunt Elizabeth. Tony—who had both conceived and participated in the Burke jailbreak—couldn't be found. An eleven-state alarm went out for his apprehension. On August 8 Pino showed up at police headquarters and explained he was certainly circling around the parking lot, looking for a parking space because his wife's daughter was across the way in the hospital having a baby. And indeed, she was having a baby. Three days later Pino was before a grand jury explaining his whereabouts on the day of Burke's escape. A day after that he was preinterviewed for yet another crime commission probe. A month later he was seized by immigration officials and incarcerated as a "Threat to Public Safety and the Security of the Community." At a hearing the immigration attorney guffawed, linked Pino to Burke, was forced by the defendant's lawyer, Paul Smith, to make a public apology to Tony—which wound up in the headlines.

Smith, as the hearing continued, was able to get into the record that the deportation action was a harassment technique being employed against Pino by the FBI. Nevertheless, Pino remained incarcerated until December 10. On advice from legal counsel, eighteen days later, Jimmy Costa and his son-in-law refused to tell a state crime commissioner whether Tony Pino had used stolen Brink's money to finance the lottery in which he and Jimmy were partners.

On January 28, 1955, Joseph Sylvester "Barney" Banfield died of what was listed as "natural causes.' Most of the gang assumed the real cause was alcoholism. He was forty-five years old. No one knew for certain, but his fellow crew members were of the opinion Joe McGinnis had kept the majority, if not all, of Barney's Brink's loot.

On Wednesday, March 23, 1955, a court in Canterbury, New Hampshire, found Joe McGinnis guilty of unlawful possession of a distillery and violation of Internal Revenue laws. The conviction, with its thirty days' imprisonment and $1,000 fine, was overruled by a higher court on the grounds that the search and seizure of the still were illegal. On April 11, 1955, the United States Supreme Court ruled that Pino's 1948 larceny of a dozen golf balls had not "attained such finality as to support an order of deportation."

Tony and all the other crooks in Boston had stood the heat, had only nine months to go before the statute of limitations ran out and they were, for all time, beyond the law.

For the FBI and Jim Crowley and the Massachusetts attorney

general this left only two possible candidates for turning state's evidence—Gusciora and O'Keefe.

Gus had spent five full years in Western State Penitentiary, had endured—according to his lawyer—unmerciful beatings, showed no indications of being "cooperative" toward the law.

O'Keefe, like Gusciora, had served nearly five years behind bars and been publicly named a Brink's robber. But Specs had endured a great deal more. It was his brother and sister and brother-in-law who had been cited for contempt of the federal grand jury and sentenced to jail and had their names on the front pages of newspapers along with his estranged wife. In the course of assisting O'Keefe and their own legal battles, his relatives had been bankrupted. His brother-in-law lost the saloon he operated and was deeply in debt and driving a truck. O'Keefe's sister was working at a hospital at a menial job. His estranged wife and adopted son were destitute. His girlfriend had been arraigned and humiliated when the "Lewd and Lascivious Cohabitation" charge hit the papers. He, and possibly other gang members, had been robbed of their rightful share of the Brink's loot. His best friend was missing, undoubtedly had been murdered by or on instruction from gang members. Two attempts had been made on his life. Once out of Hampden County Jail he faced a long term in a Pennsylvania prison. Regardless of all this, O'Keefe blamed the bulk of his woes on the FBI, couldn't conceive of cooperating with them, had refused to talk to special agents. He had chatted with BPD Lieutenant James V. Crowley on several occasions and even listened to what a member from the Massachusetts attorney's office had to say. But "ratting" was anathema to him. He was of and from the street. Law was the enemy.

Whatever was technically due him from the Brink's robbery was of no consequence to O'Keefe. He needed money for his wife and stepson and sister and brother-in-law. After the state statute of limitations ran out, he would have no leverage with the other robbers. Correctly assuming that all his smuggled communications would be read by the Law, O'Keefe sent carefully worded messages—ones he felt couldn't incriminate him in a courtroom—to McGinnis and Pino. The meaning was unmistakable and threatening: Come up with the money or else. He got no response.

A second batch of messages went out—more strongly worded. When he still didn't hear, he got word through to Pino and
McGinnis' lawyer. The attorney visited Specs, was told to tell
McGinnis that O'Keefe wanted an answer. Other friends who
came to see Specky were given similar messages.

McGinnis appeared at Hampden County Jail, was refused ad-
mittance. Edward A. "Wimpy" Bennett, a McGinnis emissary,
arrived, was granted a meeting, told Specs the gang would give
his wife $5,000 and "take care of him later." According to
O'Keefe, he accepted the offer. According to gang members,
Bennett said O'Keefe turned down the proposal, demanded
$50,000 or nothing.

Many of the robbers were broke. Many felt that the funds
they had given O'Keefe were enough. Some suggested having
O'Keefe committed to a mental institution. Majority consensus
was that O'Keefe was too potent a crook to rat. Consensus was
that even if he did rat, it wouldn't hold up in court. The prosecution would need a corroborating witness for anything O'Keefe
said on the stand.

Bennett returned to Hampden County Jail and not only told
O'Keefe there was no money at all coming, but confided the
gang was planning to have Specky declared insane.

With less than a month left before the statute of limitations
lapsed, O'Keefe told a few close friends who visited him to
spread word he was definitely considering talking to the law, to
let the news travel around town fast so the gang would hear. It
traveled fast. No one from the gang showed up. But Jim Crowley showed up—and the FBI knew it. The FBI also learned from
one of its informants the time was right to visit Specs.

Jack Kehoe, one of the first two special agents to reach
Brink's the night of January 17, and John Larkin, who had been
assigned to the case the next morning, set out for Hampden
County Jail. They were the last two bureau men assigned to Robrink 91-5535 on a full-time basis and had no idea whether Specs
would see them or not. No agents had talked to O'Keefe in more
than a year. Specs did see them but made the pair stand out in
the corridor and talk to him through the call door. O'Keefe continued to blame the FBI for his troubles, was both negative and
evasive in whatever else he said, steered a thousand miles clear
of Brink's. The special agents were sympathetic to his troubles,

dwelled on how badly other gang members had treated him, how well and "high" other gang members were living while he remained in jail, brought up Elmer "Trigger" Burke. They hinted that once he did get out of prison the others might very well try to kill him again. The date was December 27, 1955, and Kehoe and Larkin reminded O'Keefe that in twenty days they would be helpless to take any action against the gang, would no longer be able to do anything in O'Keefe's behalf. No deal was offered. No guarantees were made. The interview lasted more than three hours, and at one point O'Keefe stared down at the floor and, after shaking his head for several moments, said, "There are just too many involved. I don't see any possible way it can be worked out. I'll have to think it over." O'Keefe said that if he went on talking to the FBI, he wanted to talk to "brass"—a person in authority.

Hurried calls to Washington received minimal enthusiasm from a senior headquarters official who had long had his fill of the Pino Crowd theory. If there was to be brass, Boston was told, make it local brass.

Edward J. Powers was the sixth SAC to head the Boston field office since the robbery. When he received the assignment, he felt he was being sent to "Siberia," sent into "exile." He had been warned by associates to beware of the Irish Gang of agents, had been briefed in Washington by a Hoover aide and told that when it came to Brink's, "stay off the Pino Crowd" and come up with some new approach to cracking Robink 91. When he arrived at Boston in September, 1957, he did try new approaches, found the Irish Gang patient and courteous and cooperative and ultimately was convinced the Pino Crowd had to be the perpetrators.

Powers was the brass who accompanied John Larkin to Hampden County Jail on December 29, 1955. He wasn't sure if O'Keefe would see them. He wanted the case for the FBI and had uneasy feelings that if O'Keefe finally did decide to confess, he might bypass the bureau and get to either James Crowley or the state's attorney. O'Keefe saw them. From the very first he took to Ed Powers and talked more freely. The session ended at 3:50 P.M. with O'Keefe remaining noncommittal, but at least saying he wanted "more time to think it over," suggesting Powers "stop by again within the next couple of weeks." Powers reminded O'Keefe that "time was running out" and that if he "intended to do anything, he should not delay any longer." O'Keefe nodded.

At 2:15 P.M., January 6, 1956—with eleven days remaining before the statute of limitations ran out—Powers and Larkin sat down with O'Keefe at Hampden County Jail. O'Keefe showed them a copy of the 1955 issue of *Coronet* magazine containing an article by J. Edgar Hoover entitled "What Makes an FBI Agent?" O'Keefe was particularly concerned with a section of the story which explained that the bureau was a fact-reporting investigation agency—not the law itself, not the court. O'Keefe, speaking obliquely, voiced a distrust of the Boston court system, but he did seem to like DA Garrick Byrne. Powers intimated that the case could end with Byrne prosecuting and, in response to a question, said the bureau might even try to get a reduction in O'Keefe's pending Pennsylvania prison term. Powers offered to protect O'Keefe's relatives if a trial should take place. O'Keefe, talking hypothetically, asked if Gusciora had to be involved. He was told there was no way Gusciora could be overlooked. O'Keefe seemed to cool on the idea of "cooperating." Powers and Larkin stressed all he'd been through, all that his family had suffered, how badly the gang had treated him— that they might try to kill him again. O'Keefe shifted the conversation to other things.

Somewhere in the middle of a reply to some question or other on some unimportant subject, Specs O'Keefe bowed his head, took a long drag on his cigarette and remained silent. Then he looked up at Powers.

"All right," the inmate said. "What do you want to know?"

Garrick Byrne agreed to try the case and had no objection to the FBI's arresting the suspects on federal warrants. On January 11 the U.S. Attorney at Boston authorized special agents to file complaints charging eleven crimnals with various counts of theft of government property, bank robbery, as well as assault on Brink's employees during the taking of money and conspiracy to receive and conceal stolen money. Fear that a local reporter might leak the story prematurely, thereby cracking the news blackout and alerting the robbers, prompted a premature arrest raid, which Sandy Richardson and Jimma Faherty were able to elude. Pino, McGinnis, Maffie, Costa, Geagan and Baker were seized.

On May 16, 1956, after being on the national ten most wanted list for four months, Richardson and Faherty were apprehended in a Dorchester apartment. The FBI, which led the raid, had learned of their whereabouts via an informer. Informer information, not Police Department deduction as publicly stated, led to the June 3 pickup in Baltimore of a man carrying currency identified as being stolen in the Brink's robbery—bills every one of the gang members had been led to believe Joe McGinnis had destroyed, as per agreement. On June 4 special agents and police entered the basement office of a construction company on Tremont Street, Boston, tore away a wall partition, removed a "picnic-type cooler" and from the cooler recovered more than $56,000, including $51,906 which were identified as having been stolen from Brink's—more of the consecutive serial-numbered bills McGinnis was supposed to destroy. The owners of the construction company were arrested—Wimpy Bennett, who had visited Specs O'Keefe at Hampden County Jail in Springfield, Massachusetts, and Fats Buccelli, who had visited O'Keefe at the county jail at Towanda.

At 6:10 P.M., Stanley Gusciora, thirty-six, died at the Norfolk State Prison Colony Hospital. The coroner reported the indicted Brink's robber had died of natural causes—to wit, "tumor of the brain—acute cerebral edema." The gang believed he died as a result of the constant beating he had taken at Western State Penitentiary. Gus had received $98,000 in stolen Brink's money. No one is certain what he did with these funds.

FBI fears that O'Keefe might have changed his mind and not testify against his former crooks because of his close friendship with Gusciora ended. Apprehension that a jury might not accept his uncorroborated testimony remained.

The trial of the eight men accused of robbing Brink's began on August 6, 1956, under the strictest security regulations ever seen in Boston, amid some of the greatest press coverage ever remembered. In the following two weeks, 1,200 prospective jurors were eliminated as the defense counsel invoked 262 peremptory charges. After another week and 500 more interviews, a fourteen-member jury was assembled.

Passes for the trial were scalped for as high as $100 a pair. A glass window was built into the wall between the court chamber and an adjacent room so the overflow press corps could be accommodated. Armed guards lined the street between the court building and the jail whenever the defendants were transported back and forth. Armed guards patrolled the courtroom building inside and out. Armed guards stood at the door watching spectators enter the court chamber and searched anyone who struck them as suspicious. Armed guards stood in the courtroom.

Pino, Geagan, Richardson, Maffie, Costa, Baker and McGinnis had "stood mute" at the original arraignment, had refused to utter a single word, had had the court enter pleas of not guilty for each of them. At the trial they refused to testify in their own defense. Specs O'Keefe testified for the prosecution, was billed as the "star witness," proved to be just that. The prosecutor highlighted the fact that O'Keefe had removed lock tumblers from the premises and helped obtain the rope and tape used during the heist, avoided the fact that beyond those achievements the witness had done little else and knew little else concerning where and how the remainder of the gang's equipment was had—astutely leaving an impression that Specky was a vital cog in the organization, preparation and perpetration of the crime. Defense attorneys could not trip O'Keefe up. O'Keefe reaffirmed Garrick Byrne's opening description of McGinnis as the boss and brains—and Pino as the aide-de-camp.

It may have taken two votes; it may have taken three. At the earliest it was over by 12:15 A.M. on Saturday, October 6. At the latest, 12:45 A.M. The jury found the defendants guilty of all the charges of the indictments—every last count of every indictment. Then, according to one juror, feeling it "might not look good" if they returned to the courtroom so soon, they sent out for sandwiches.

On October 9, 1956, Judge Felix Forte passed the sentences. Pino, Costa, Maffie, Geagan, Faherty, Richardson and Baker received life sentences for robbery, two-year sentences for conspiracy to steal, eight to ten years for breaking and entering at night. McGinnis was charged with being an accessory before the fact, was given eight life sentences, plus sentences of two years, two and one-half to three years and eight to ten years.

All eight robbers were removed to the state prison at Walpole,

Massachusetts. On July 1, 1959, the State Supreme Court turned down appeals by the eight convicted felons. On November 16 the United States Supreme Court refused to review the conviction.

John J. O'Keefe, according to court records, but commonly known as Joseph James O'Keefe or Specs, received concurrent sentences of three to four years on three counts of armed robbery, three to four years for breaking and entering a building to commit a felony at night, and three to four years on three counts of violation of general laws, Chapter 265. He was sent to the Middlesex County Jail, in Cambridge, Massachusetts—across the river from Boston—where heavy security was afforded him.

It had taken six years and eleven men to steal a reputed $2,700,000. It had taken another six years and an estimated $29,000,000 to catch them. Now, officially, the incident was over.

Jury members of the Brink's trial held an annual reunion for thirteen years—on each January 17.

The eight convicted robbers became celebrities at Walpole Prison. None of the crew, except Pino, would have much to do with Joe McGinnis. Mike Geagan wouldn't talk to Tony. Costa discovered an assistant warden having a homosexual encounter with an inmate and used the incident to get cooperation for smuggling washing machines into the institution so that he and Tony could open a private laundry. The prison printing press was used to make up laundry tickets and flyers which announced clothes could be washed at a nominal fee. Inmates who continued using the prison's free laundry often found the buttons missing from their cleaned uniforms and often had their entire load of wash stolen. Pino also ran a private kitchen.

Felix Forte received considerable praise and notoriety for being the "Brink's judge," gave at least one paid lecture on his experiences at the trial, retired from the bench and taught law in Boston, where he was also active in Italian-American community affairs. He died in 1975.

Wimpy Bennett and John Buccelli, along with Jordon Perry, Jr., the man arrested in Baltimore, were convicted of charges involving their possession of $56,521 in stolen Brink's money.

This is the only robbery currency ever recovered. Bennett and Jordon were each sentenced to one year's imprisonment. Buccelli received a two-year sentence. On June 19, 1958, Buccelli was found shot to death in an automobile which had crashed into a truck along a Boston street. Bennett disappeared years later, is believed to have been the victim of underworld assassination. Neither death is attributed to Brink's. Pino claimed no direct information on what stolen bills which were supposed to be destroyed were doing sealed in a wall of an office he and McGinnis were known to have visited, "theorized" that Joe McGinnis had sold the entire cache of some $90,000 in "bad money" to Bennett and Buccelli for fifteen cents on the dollar.

Elmer "Trigger" Burke was arrested by FBI agents at Folly Beach, South Carolina, on August 27, 1955. Burke was returned to New York City, placed on trial, lectured the court on justice, and was found guilty of murdering his pal Poochy Walsh in 1952. On January 9, 1958, Burke died in the electric chair at Sing Sing prison.

Lieutenant James V. Crowley retired from the Boston Police Department, died in the early 1970s before the author began this story. Pino swore that Crowley's appearance at Joe McGinnis' package liquor store the night of January 17, 1950, was strictly luck, that the time was definitely 7:10 P.M. The FBI was fully prepared to attempt to discredit Crowley in the courtroom should he have maintained the time he quoted to the federal grand jury, had alerted a New Hampshire police official who could cite Crowley as being Pino's alibi in an early 1930 robbery. Crowley was aware of this plan. Called to the witness stand by Paul Smith, Crowley, under oath, stated that he reached the package liquor store at "about 7:30," that Tony Pino arrived "between five minutes of eight and eight."

In 1960 Specs O'Keefe was released from jail. The prison time owed Pennsylvania had been dropped. He was a free man and a marked man. O'Keefe went into hiding, eventually took the assumed name of Paul Williams—Paul coming from the brother-in-law he liked so well, Paul Hooley, and Williams as in Ted Williams, the great Boston Red Sox star. Ed Powers, the FBI agent to whom O'Keefe confessed, arranged for Bob Considine to write a book about O'Keefe and the robbery. The motive was strictly monetary. The FBI had made financial guarantees to O'Keefe. The book was published by Random House in 1960 under the title *The Men Who Robbed Brink's*. McGinnis was again portrayed as the boss and mastermind. Specs was elevated to a co-planner.

In 1960 the FBI published a twenty-six-page information sheet on Brink's in which the heist was described as the "crime of the century," the "fabulous robbery," "the perfect crime." The bureau still considers its investigation and breaking of the case among its foremost achievements and has on display in the Washington headquarters a Brink's exhibition, including a model of the Prince Street office, currency found in the wall and part of the cut-up getaway truck. Photographs of all the perpetrators are also shown, with O'Keefe's picture definitely having been retouched. If pressed, the bureau will say that it believes O'Keefe underwent plastic surgery. He did not. The FBI had held up O'Keefe as an example to other would-be criminal confessors, had pointed out how well it took care of Specs after he cooperated. The extent of bureau assistance was in finally giving O'Keefe $5,000. The bureau provided no protection after his release, no assistance in obtaining work—nothing. It didn't even help him to secure false credentials.

In February, 1961, Henry Baker died in the Norfolk Prison Hospital of natural causes. He was fifty-four years old and the only one of the "regular" crew of robbers to receive a full first share of Brink's loot—$100,000. None of the surviving gang members know what he did with the money.

On October 5, 1966, Joe McGinnis died while kneeling at prayer in his Walpole Prison cell. He was sixty-three years old. Joe, during his internment, had become a "religious nut." He also crafted leather goods, wallets and purses. None of the surviving robbers, with the exception of Pino, have any idea how much Brink's loot McGinnis had dealt himself. Tony, while saying he had no direct information on the subject, estimated Joe's take could have been as high as $200,000. Nothing is known about what became of McGinnis' robbery share or the other "millions" he was supposed to have.

On January 6, 1971—fifteen years to the day O'Keefe had said to FBI agents, "All right. What do you want to know?"—Jimma

Faherty, who was out of prison on parole, died. He was fifty-nine years old. Faherty received the smallest share of robbery loot, approximately $78,000, spent the majority of this buying into bars around Boston, most of which went broke. The balance of money is believed to have been spent on drinking.

Mike Geagan was released on parole in December, 1967. He was fifty-nine years old and had served ten years and ten months in prison for his part in the robbery. He calculates his share of loot coming to just below $100,000. Of this $60,000 was invested in a suburban Boston dance hall which failed. The balance of stolen money "just petered out." Geagan returned to his wife and resumed working as a longshoreman. Several years later he and his wife separated.

Jazz Maffie was released on parole in January, 1969. He had served thirteen years and nine months for Brink's and was fifty-seven years old. Maffie returned to Boston and his wife and children somewhat of a local celebrity. He resumed playing golf and visiting his favorite restaurants. He took a job as an automobile salesman, which he still manages to hold. He still manages to sleep late. Maffie received $89,000 in Brink's loot, blew almost all of it gambling, the major share bet away at the racetrack.

Jimmy Costa was fifty-three years old when he was paroled in September, 1969. He had served nearly fourteen years in prison for Brink's. A goodly share of his $89,000 in Brink's loot had been lost trying to maintain the lottery and other enterprises the FBI managed to force out of business. At least three thousand had been donated to the fund for Specs O'Keefe. The balance had been eaten up by legal expenses. Costa returned to his wife and children, a prison trained watch repairman, found employment with a watchmaker, moonlighted in real estate and various business promotions. In 1975 his parole was revoked by his implication in more than $1,000,000 in counterfeit $20 bills, and he was sent back to Walpole, where he is as of this writing.

Sandy Richardson left prison on parole in August, 1970, after serving nearly fourteen years and three months of a life sentence. He was sixty-four years old. Richardson's wife and children were waiting for him. He returned to his old job as a longshoreman, socially spent time with Maffie, occasionally with Geagan and Pino. He wasn't particularly comfortable with the local fame being a Brink's robber brought. Sandy received $83,000 in loot, spent a good deal of it on drinking and gambling, paid out a lot of it into the fund raised for O'Keefe, spent the balance on his legal expenses in connection with the Brink's trial.

In July, 1971, after serving fourteen years and nine months for the crime he conceived, organized, planned and oversaw, Tony Pino was out on bail. He was sixty-three years old and, just before leaving Walpole, sold the "private laundry business" for $1,000, which he didn't share with Costa, who, in fact, had founded the laundry. As had happened back in September, 1944, Mary was waiting for him, along with Jimmy Costa. Tony joined Mary in the Mattapan home he purchased while still under FBI surveillance—a house close to the one his father had built, close to the cemetery. One of his first orders of business was to straighten out the contract he had placed back in Walpole on O'Keefe's life. A dispute had arisen over price. Pino was interested in a cut-rate rubout, kept changing the money he was willing to pay. Tony swore to having received only $89,000 in Brink's loot, part of which was lost in businesses he claims the FBI forced to fail and others which failed while he was in prison. None of the other survivors believe that is where his money went or that he only received $89,000. Pino offered no other explanation on his financial position. He met parole requirements by working as a handyman-janitor in a liquor store.

In October, 1972, Pino, Costa, Maffie and Richardson, all who had publicly denied complicity in the Brink's robbery, sat down with the author and began "confessing." One thousand hours of taping resulted.

Edmund L. McNamara, the FBI agent who played bumper tag with Tony Pino in the early years of the manhunt and who became commissioner of the Boston Police Department, is currently the head of Ogden Security Inc., an organization providing physical security for industrial establishments. Ronald "Buck" Weaffer—the Boston bureau agent who was in charge of the operation which actually broke the case for the FBI informants—is currently assistant court clerk at the Middlesex County Courthouse. Leonard Frisoli, one of the first two agents to arrive at Brink's the night of January 17 and one of the last four to be assigned to Robrink 91 on a full-time basis, is currently president of Special Agents Consultants, Inc., at Newton, Massachusetts. John F. Kehoe, Jr., the special agent who arrived at Brink's with Frisoli and was among the last two assigned to the investigation on a full-time basis, is state public safety commissioner for the Commonwealth of Massachusetts—which means he heads the state police as well.

John P. Larkin, the other of the last two special agents assigned to Robrink 91 full time and who was present when Specs O'Keefe said, "All right. What do you want to know?" was assistant attorney general for Massachusetts in charge of the Organized Crime Division. He is now attached to the State Alcoholic Beverages office.

Edward J. Powers, special agent in charge of the Boston field office and the man whom O'Keefe credited for making him confess, is executive director of the New Hampshire Sweepstakes Commission. Beyond his brother, sister and brother-in-law, O'Keefe's single ally during and after his prison stint was Powers.

On release from jail in 1960, Specs O'Keefe drifted to the West Coast, signed on as an able-bodied seaman for a short time, worked in a liquor store, twice was employed to manage apartment buildings, did a stint as a cook and chauffeur to Cary Grant (who had no idea who Paul Williams was), wandered into the Midwest and became the chauffeur and deckhand for a wealthy Chicago attorney, came back to New England, but never to Boston. From August, 1973, to 1975, the period the author was interviewing the other gang members in Boston and working on the book, O'Keefe was in New Hampshire. He stayed with Powers and his wife for a time, then took an apartment in Manchester and worked as a custodian in a local high school. O'Keefe believed that the other gang members would have him killed if they could find him, but he didn't seem to care or be frightened. He wasn't particularly resentful that except for $5,000, the FBI had not, in any way, assisted him. He began to think that perhaps "ratting" had not been the wisest course of action. If nothing else, being an informer had deprived him of returning to Boston. And he dearly missed the city and his old friends there.

O'Keefe went back to California and on March 4, 1976, died of a heart attack under the assumed name of Paul Williams. He was six days short of being sixty-eight years old, had spent the last sixteen years of his life in exile, had spent all but a short period of the decade before that in jail.

Two years and five months earlier, on Thursday, October 4, 1973, one of the last things Tony Pino revealed to the author was that he intended to kill Specs O'Keefe.

Ten hours after that, at approximately 2 A.M. October 5—the exact day on which his father had died and the very day on which, eight years earlier, Joe McGinnis had died—Tony Pino went to his kitchen not feeling so good, looked for something to settle his stomach, sat down on a kitchen chair, suffered a heart attack and died.